The Great Financial Crisis in Finland and Sweden

The Great Financial Crisis in Finland and Sweden

The Nordic Experience of Financial Liberalization

Edited by

Lars Jonung

DG ECFIN, European Commission, Brussels, Belgium

Jaakko Kiander

Labour Institute for Economic Research, Helsinki, Finland

Pentti Vartia

Research Institute of the Finnish Economy, ETLA, Helsinki, Finland

Edward Elgar

Cheltenham, UK • Northampton, MA, USA

Published by
Edward Elgar Publishing Limited
The Lypiatts
15 Lansdown Road
Cheltenham
Glos GL50 2JA
UK

Edward Elgar Publishing, Inc.
William Pratt House
9 Dewey Court
Northampton
Massachusetts 01060
USA

A catalogue record for this book
is available from the British Library

Library of Congress Control Number: 2009930854

Mixed Sources
Product group from well-managed forests and other controlled sources
www.fsc.org Cert no. SA-COC-1565
© 1996 Forest Stewardship Council
FSC

ISBN 978 1 84844 305 1

Printed and bound by MPG Books Group, UK

Contents

Contributors

Peter Englund is a professor of banking at the Stockholm School of Economics, Stockholm, Sweden. Prior to joining the Stockholm School, he was a professor at Uppsala University. He also holds a part-time position as professor of real estate finance at the University of Amsterdam. He has published articles in major journals in the fields of public economics, banking, and housing and real estate. Currently his main research interests are in real estate economics. Englund is the secretary of the committee for the Sveriges Riksbank Prize in Economic Sciences in Memory of Alfred Nobel.

Klas Fregert is an associate professor at the Department of Economics at Lund University, Sweden, where he received his PhD in 1994. His research has mainly focused on macroeconomic history, in particular economic policy and the labour market. Currently he works on the interaction between fiscal institutions and fiscal policy in 18th-century Sweden. Together with Lars Jonung, he has co-authored a widely used textbook on macroeconomics in Swedish.

Thomas Hagberg is an economist, currently working as Audit Director at the Swedish National Audit Office (SNAO). Prior to joining SNAO, he worked at the Public Finance Analysis Unit of the Swedish National Institute of Economic Research (*Konjunkturinstitutet*) in Stockholm and before that at the Swedish National Financial Management Authority. His research is focused on Swedish economic crises. He holds an MSc in Business and Economics from the Stockholm School of Economics.

Lars Jonung is, since September 2000, a research adviser at the Directorate-General for Economic and Financial Affairs of the European Commission (DG ECFIN) in Brussels, dealing with macroeconomic issues. He was previously a professor of economics at the Stockholm School of Economics. His research is focused on monetary and fiscal policies, monetary unions, exchange rate arrangements and the history of economic thought. Jonung has published several books and articles in English and Swedish.

Jaakko Kiander is currently director of the Labour Institute for Economic Research in Helsinki. Previously he was scientific director of the Yrjö Jahnsson Foundation (1989–94), and research director at the Government Institute for Economic Research (1999–2006). In 1997–2001 he was the director of a multidisciplinary research programme on the Finnish economic crisis funded by the Academy of Finland. He has authored several books and articles in labour economics, public finance and economic policy. He obtained his PhD from the University of Helsinki.

Ari Kokko is professor at the Copenhagen Business School, Copenhagen, Denmark. His teaching, research and publications cover issues related to international trade and investment, economic development and technology transfer with a focus on Asia. Kokko is a member of the advisory board of the Swedish International Development Cooperation Agency, an adviser to the Vietnamese Minister of Agriculture and Rural Development, and the chairman of a Swedish government commission studying the development of Swedish market shares in world exports. Before joining EIJS, Ari Kokko held a chair in International Business at Åbo Akademi, University of Turku, Finland.

Jaakko Pehkonen is a professor of economics at the University of Jyväskylä, Finland. He has been the Dean of the School of Business and Economics since 1998. Previously he worked at the Helsinki School of Economics and the Academy of Finland. He holds a PhD from the University of Jyväskylä. He is a member of the Research Council for Culture and Society of the Academy of Finland and he has served at the European Association of Labour Economists as a member of the executive committee and at the Finnish Economic Association as the chairman of the board. He also holds several positions in private companies. He has published on labour and regional economics.

Ludger Schuknecht is a senior adviser in the Economics Directorate-General of the European Central Bank where he contributes to the preparation of monetary policy decision-making. He was previously head of the ECB's fiscal surveillance section, following assignments at the World Trade Organization and at the International Monetary Fund. His recent research focuses on public expenditure policies and reform and the analysis of economic boom–bust episodes. He authored *Public Spending in the 20th Century: A Global Perspective* together with Vito Tanzi.

Erling Steigum is a professor of economics and head of the Department of Economics at BI Norwegian School of Management in Oslo. He was previously a professor at the Norwegian School of Economics in Bergen. He is a fellow of CESifo and chairs the Investment Strategy Council for the Sovereign Wealth Fund of the Norwegian Government. His main research work is on monetary and fiscal policy and open economy macroeconomics.

Kenji Suzuki is an associate professor of political economy at the School of Global Japanese Studies at Meiji University in Tokyo, Japan. He was previously an associate professor at the European Institute of Japanese Studies at the Stockholm School of Economics in Sweden. His main research interest is concerned with the decision-making process and outcome of public and private organizations in Japan, Sweden and other developed countries.

Mika Tujula is a senior economist in the Monetary Policy Stance Division of the European Central Bank (ECB), primarily dealing with household financing and flow of funds related issues. He previously worked in the Fiscal Policies Division of the ECB and in the Economics Department of the Bank of Finland. His research has mainly focused on fiscal policy related topics. He studied economics at the Helsinki School of Economics, Helsinki, Finland.

Pentti Vartia was in 1983–2005 the Director of ETLA, the Research Institute of the Finnish Economy. He has been a member of several professional and scientific societies and foundations such as the Finnish Society for Economic Research (Chairman 1973), the Yrjö Jahnsson Foundation (on the Board since 1978, Chairman since 2008), the Finnish Economic Association (President 1979), the Finnish Cultural Foundation (Board member 1994–2002, Council member since 2003), the Finnish Academy of Technology since 1993, the *Association d'Instituts Européens de Conjoncture Economique* (AIECE) (President 1998–2004), and the International Institute for Applied Systems Analysis (IIASA) (Council member since 2002). He holds an MSc (in aeronautical engineering) from the Helsinki Institute of Technology and a PhD (in economics) from the University of Helsinki. He is the author of several books and articles.

Claus Vastrup is a professor of economics at the University of Aarhus since 1983. Before moving to Aarhus, he previously spent some years working with *Danmarks Nationalbank* and the University of Copenhagen. He has been a deputy chairman (1985–87) and later the chairman (1987–93) of the Danish Economic Council. Vastrup has been on the board of the Danish Institute of International Affairs (DUPI) (1995–2002). He is one of the authors of the report on the economic aspects of 'Denmark and the EMU' published in 2000.

Vesa Vihriälä is, since February 2004, State Under-Secretary for Economic Affairs in the Prime Minister's Office and the Secretary General of the Economic Council of Finland. He was previously the managing director of the Pellervo Economic Research Institute. He worked in the Bank of Finland for over a decade, including a three-year period as head of the financial market department during the financial crisis of the early 1990s. He studied at the University of Helsinki and MIT. Vihriälä has also worked at the OECD in Paris. His doctoral dissertation examined the role of banks in the Finnish boom–bust cycle in 1986–95.

Preface

This book studies the deep crisis that hit Finland and Sweden in the early 1990s, a crisis with devastating effects. The Finnish and Swedish experience of boom, bust and crisis is compared across time and across countries. The first part of the volume contrasts the experience of Finland and Sweden. The second part brings in an international perspective. The third part presents the lessons from the crisis of the 1990s.

This volume is the outcome of a joint Finnish–Swedish project, 'Crises, macroeconomic performance and economic policies in Finland and Sweden in the 1990s: a comparative approach', headed by Lars Jonung on the Swedish side and by Pentti Vartia on the Finnish side. The project was one of many within a wide-ranging Finnish–Swedish research program entitled *Kahden puolen Pohjanlahtea* (in Finnish) and *Svenskt i Finland – Finskt i Sverige* (in Swedish) – translated officially as 'Interaction across the Gulf of Bothnia'.

Three Finnish foundations, *Finlands Akademi, Svenska litteratursällskapet i Finland* and *Stiftelsen för Åbo Akademi,* and two Swedish foundations, *Vetenskapsrådet* and *Riksbankens jubileumsfond*, sponsored this unique cross-country research venture that ran in the period 2000–03, involving about 120 scholars from a wide array of specialties in 17 different projects. The program aimed at studying the contacts between Finland and Sweden, their long joint history of strong economic, social, political and cultural ties. Before 1809 they were one country. Today, they are economic partners, but also competitors on world markets; similar, but also different in many aspects.

This immense project was reported in four volumes, in Finnish as well as in Swedish, published in 2005–07. We contributed four chapters in the third volume with the Swedish title *Från olika till jämlika*, edited by Juhana Aunesluoma and Susanna Fellman, published by *Svenska litteratursällskapet i Finland*, Helsinki, 2006. Those four chapters correspond to Chapters 2, 4, 5 and 9 in this volume.

At an early stage we wanted to present our work in English and extend it with comparisons with other countries that have faced financial crises, in particular Denmark and Norway, the Nordic neighbours of Finland and Sweden. We were pleased that Claus Vastrup agreed to cover the Danish case and Erling Steigum to deal with the boom and bust cycle in Norway.

Similarly, we managed to involve Ludger Schuknecht and Mika Tujula from the ECB in a study of the Finnish–Swedish boom–bust cycle seen in an international perspective. Our extension in scope and in coverage has been time-consuming. After a very long gestation period, we have finally brought our work to fruition.

Several seminars were organized during our project, not only in Finland and Sweden but also, perhaps most memorably, in Villa Lante, Rome. In these seminars, the contributions finally selected for this volume, as well as other studies, were discussed. Many of them have in one form or another been published elsewhere.

We are deeply indebted to all involved in the time-consuming work behind this volume. We would like to thank Franklin Allen, Michael Bergman, Michael D. Bordo, Eric Clapham, Thomas Hagberg, Michael Hutchison, Ari Hyytinen, Jarmo Kontulainen, Mika Maliranta, Anne-Marie Pålsson, Michael Rafferty, Kari Takala, Hans Sjögren, Hans Tson Söderström and Lars-Erik Öller. We owe a special thanks to Thomas Hagberg for his excellent involvement in our project. We apologize to those not mentioned by name above. We appreciate the support given by our home institutions: ETLA in Helsinki, the Stockholm School of Economics and DG ECFIN, European Commission, Brussels.

Helsinki and Brussels, November 2008

Lars Jonung, Jaakko Kiander and Pentti Vartia

1. Introduction

Lars Jonung, Jaakko Kiander and Pentti Vartia

'It' – that is, a deep depression – cannot happen here. This was the general attitude among economists, policy-makers and the public in Finland and Sweden prior to the early 1990s. Why should a depression take place in an advanced Nordic welfare state with a long tradition of full employment policies and strong labour union influence on the design of economic and social policies? Indeed, the macroeconomic record of Finland and Sweden during the post-World War II period was characterized by stable growth and low unemployment. Moreover, these two countries and their Nordic neighbours, Norway and Denmark, seemed to be able to combine an egalitarian society with strong economic performance.

But 'it' happened – to the great surprise of many.[1] The picture of the successful Nordic economies was shattered at the beginning of the 1990s when Finland and Sweden faced a severe crisis, falling real income, soaring unemployment and exploding public deficits. Previously, few understood that the macroeconomic policy regimes and thus the macroeconomic stability that had evolved in Finland and Sweden after World War II rested on far-reaching external and internal financial regulations. The system of capital account (foreign exchange) controls isolated the two countries financially from the rest of the world, in this way allowing domestic credit market regulations, setting interest rates and determining the allocation of capital according to political priorities.

In the early 1980s, the financial systems of the two countries underwent major deregulation. In several steps the Nordic economies became financially integrated with world capital markets. This process gave the impulse to a boom–bust cycle with devastating consequences. Finland and Sweden went into the deepest depression of the post-World War II period in the early 1990s.

The contributions in this volume examine the macroeconomic and financial developments in Finland and Sweden before, during and after the deep crisis of the 1990s, and compare them across time and across countries. The unique feature of this book is the comparative approach adopted. Chapters 2–5, the first part of the volume, focus on Finland and Sweden. Chapters 6–9, which form the second part, bring in an international perspective. Here the record of boom–bust cycles and financial crises of other countries is considered and contrasted with the case of Finland and Sweden. Finally, Chapter 10 condenses the lessons from the Nordic crises of the 1990s. Chapters 2–10 are summarized below to give an overview of the contents of the volume.

1.1 PART I: THE CRISIS OF THE 1990S IN FINLAND AND SWEDEN

In Chapter 2, 'The great financial crisis in Finland and Sweden: the dynamics of boom, bust and recovery 1985–2000', Lars Jonung, Jaakko Kiander and Pentti Vartia explore the anatomy of the boom, the deep depression and the recovery in the Finnish and Swedish economies in the period 1985–2000. They divide these 15 years into three phases: the boom and the overheating of 1985–90, the outbreak and spread of the crisis to all sectors of the economy in 1990–92, and the recovery process 1993–2000. The comparative perspective of Chapter 2 reveals that Finland and Sweden followed a strikingly similar pattern of economic policies, macroeconomic performance and institutional changes. The two countries behaved as if they were 'economic twins'.

The authors, inspired by the debt deflation theory of Irving Fisher, focus on the interaction between financial market developments and general economic activity in Finland and Sweden. When their story starts, the monetary policy of both countries rests on a pegged (fixed) exchange rate. This 'initial condition' turns out to be a crucial feature in the drama that follows.

For the boom phase, Jonung, Kiander and Vartia demonstrate how financial deregulation started off a process of credit expansion, asset price inflation, rapid growth in consumption and investment, an inflow of foreign capital, loss of foreign competitiveness, and speculation against the pegged exchange rates in both countries. For the bust phase, they describe a vicious circle of rising real rates of interest, falling asset prices (asset price deflation), financial fragility, exploding budget deficits and rising unemployment. Finally, the process came to an end when the central banks were forced to abandon the pegged exchange rate regime and allow the *markka* and *krona* to float in the fall of 1992. The authors stress the role of monetary and fiscal policies first in creating and then in alleviating the crisis. Finally, they examine the recovery phase.

How could the Finnish and Swedish economies end up in such deep and long-lasting stagnation? Why did policy-makers allow this to occur? Jonung, Kiander and Vartia answer by identifying the forces, domestic and international, behind the exceptional depth of the crisis in the two countries. In short, policy-makers did not understand the forces that they set in motion by financial deregulation. There was a lack of accurate forecasts and analyses of the effects of financial liberalization. Attempts by governments to reduce budget deficits through tax increases and expenditure cuts reduced private demand and made the crisis still deeper. The deregulation was in itself a desirable and long-delayed step to reform the Finnish and Swedish economies. However, in order to avoid starting a boom–bust cycle, it should have been carried out in combination with measures that counteracted the credit boom that emerged.

The lack of financial knowledge leading to disastrous policy mistakes is fairly easy to explain. Pre-crisis thinking in Finland and Sweden on macroeconomic issues was strongly dominated by the experience from the post-war growth period and by the Keynesian approach with its stress on flow concepts and neglect of financial variables. The fact that the role of portfolio imbalances was disregarded was largely due to the system of strong regulation of the financial system in Finland and Sweden in place during the post-World War II period up to the financial deregulation in the late 1980s. As financial markets were held dormant, knowledge of the effects of financial forces became meagre.

A new economic order emerged in both countries after the depression of the early 1990s based on the free flow of capital across borders, stronger central bank independence, and convergence to the EU institutional framework. Both countries adopted an inflation target for monetary policy shortly after their currencies were floated. In January 1999 Finland joined the euro area. Sweden has chosen to remain outside with an inflation-targeting central bank. The inflation rate has been kept at low levels in both Finland and Sweden, significantly lower than the rates of the 1970s and 1980s. It remains to be seen whether Finland and Sweden – after Sweden's decision in September 2003 to remain outside the euro area – will evolve along significantly different macroeconomic paths. Will the two economically identical twins now separate, after following the same stabilization policy road throughout the post-war period? Jonung, Kiander and Vartia leave this question to the future to be answered.

In Chapter 3, 'Financial crisis in Finland and Sweden: similar but not quite the same', Peter Englund and Vesa Vihriälä focus on the financial and banking aspects of the crisis of the 1990s. They trace in detail the process of deregulation of banking and financial markets that occurred in both countries in the 1980s. As a result of financial liberalization, instead of being forced to invest in government and housing bonds, banks became free to lend where return prospects were best. They were no longer affected by lending guidelines. For the first time in decades, banks and other financial institutions, like any retail business, were able to compete freely for borrowers. The financial deregulation took place in economies with a suppressed demand for credit, largely due to the combination of high inflation and low or negative real after-tax interest rates.

As expected, the deregulation triggered lending booms in both countries. But it was not the lending booms *per se* that led to the subsequent crises, according to Englund and Vihrälä. Rather, the crises were due to the combination of several extraordinary shocks and serious policy mistakes, both concerning macro policies and regulatory policies.

The years around 1990 were unusually turbulent with a series of negative international macro shocks. First, the increase in European interest rates had particularly negative effects in countries with high government debt, like Sweden. Second, external demand declined in response to the higher interest rates and the crisis in the Persian Gulf. Third, the ERM crisis set off turmoil in exchange markets with a strong impact on small countries like Finland and Sweden, trying to defend pegged exchange parities increasingly removed from their fundamental values. Finally, the collapse of the Soviet export market hit Finland.

The pegged exchange rate regime followed by both countries was a crucial factor in the crisis scenario. When financial liberalization unleashed suppressed demand and stimulated growth, attempts to tighten monetary policy were largely futile. The exceptionally strong political commitment to the pegged exchange rate failed to maintain confidence in the exchange rate regime. When the financial positions turned more vulnerable, attacks on the peg of the *markka* and the *krona* became more frequent.

In the end, the pegged exchange rate regime had to be abandoned. The Finnish devaluation in 1991 helped export recovery to start earlier. But the decision to devalue rather than float left the pegged exchange rate still subject to speculation, thereby contributing to high interest rates. This, combined with windfall losses from loans denominated in foreign currencies, weakened the financial position of the domestic sector in Finland. From the point of view of the domestic sector, including the banking sector, the Finnish approach to floating was less successful than the Swedish one, with just a brief period of very high interest rates before floating in November 1992. Obviously, both countries would have benefited from an earlier floating, according to Englund and Vihriälä.

The recession that started in both countries around 1990 hit a banking system with low solidity, high-risk loan portfolios and highly leveraged borrowers. This triggered dynamic responses that banks and regulators were unaccustomed to. The interaction between falling asset prices, declining collateral values and rising credit losses was a phenomenon that hardly any of the actors had previously experienced. The crisis in the financial system became deep. Englund and Vihriälä stress that crisis management and resolution policies were fast and strong-handed in Finland and Sweden. The financial sectors were substantially restructured. They recovered from the crisis relatively quickly. After the crisis, they emerged as highly efficient.

In Chapter 4, 'The crisis of the 1990s and unemployment in Finland and Sweden', Klas Fregert and Jaakko Pehkonen investigate the character, causes and aftermath of the huge unemployment of the 1990s in Finland and Sweden. They ask whether the current high unemployment is a legacy of the crises of the 1990s. Any attempt to evaluate the cost of the crises must take into account this possibility.

The crises in Finland and Sweden are alike in their initial timing, both starting in 1991 and ending in 1994. Finland's crisis was deeper in both absolute and relative terms on all the unemployment measures they use. The non-employment rate, which takes into account both changes in the open unemployment rate and the outflow from the labour force, gives an upper limit of the increase in total unemployment. It rose in Sweden by 10 percentage points whereas in Finland it increased by 15 percentage points. By this measure, the Finnish crisis was 50 per cent worse than the Swedish one. A likely explanation is the corresponding steep decrease in job creation in Finland, which did not occur in Sweden.

Sweden had a quick recovery until 1994–95, after which unemployment remained constant until 1998, whereas Finland was in a recovery process for the rest of the 1990s. After 1998, when unemployment began to decrease in Sweden, the two countries also differ in that the inflow into unemployment and the duration of the average spell of unemployment continued to decrease in Finland, whereas the recovery from 1998 in Sweden was due solely to a sharp decrease in duration. One legacy of the crisis shows up in the share of temporary employment, which rose substantially in both countries in the 1990s.

The authors estimate Okun and Beveridge relations with structural breaks, which imply that the structural unemployment rate doubled in both countries in the early 1990s. These findings corroborate those of previous studies, which suggest, on average, a rise of about 4–6 percentage points for Finland and 2–4 percentage points for Sweden in structural unemployment. The authors also attempt to measure the contributions of possible causes to the changes in the structural unemployment rate, by using previously estimated models. These are based on panels of OECD countries, which link unemployment to institutional factors and the business cycle.

Fregert and Pehkonen suggest that the rise in unemployment and its persistence at a high level was mainly due to a combination of aggregate demand shocks and several small effects stemming from changes in institutions, aggravated by lagged adjustment. Since there is no one major factor that could be singled out, Finland and Sweden are prime candidates for the hypothesis that a negative demand shock together with rigid institutions leads to long-lasting effects.

The estimates by Fregert and Pehkonen demonstrate that structural unemployment remained constant in both Finland and Sweden over the late 1990s. For the early 2000s, the evidence suggests a modest decrease in structural unemployment, mainly due to lower rates of taxation, a lower replacement rate in the pension schemes and lower union density in both countries. Thus, most of the decline in open unemployment in the late 1990s and early 2000s was due to positive demand shocks. The authors stress that these findings should be treated as preliminary since they doubt the ability of existing models to fully explain the observed decrease in unemployment in Finland and Sweden.

In Chapter 5, 'How costly was the crisis of the 1990s in Finland and Sweden?', Thomas Hagberg and Lars Jonung set the crisis of the 1990s in a historical perspective by comparing the cost of the crisis of the 1990s with the costs of other major depressions in Finland and Sweden. Their analysis is based on a crisis chronology for Finland and Sweden from which they calculate the cost of major crises since the 1870s.

Finland and Sweden were spared severe economic depressions in the post-World War II period prior to the 1990s. In order to find crises on the scale of the 1990s, Hagberg and Jonung have to go back to the inter-war years and the classical gold standard period before World War I. Their survey of the literature on crises identifies three crisis episodes for Finland and six for Sweden worthy of comparison with the disaster of the 1990s. In addition, the two countries were deeply affected by World Wars I and II – Finland more so than Sweden due to its direct involvement in the hostilities. For this reason they include the war periods in their estimates of the costs of depressions.

A crisis brings costs to many groups in society – to banks, to the public sector, to those who become unemployed, to holders of equity and so on. Hagberg and Jonung focus on the costs to society at large in terms of output, employment and industrial production foregone during the years of crisis. They cover these three time series in order to get a comprehensive picture.

Judging from their calculations, the crisis of the 1990s was very costly compared with all major crises since the 1870s. In Finland, the loss in real income in the 1990s was the largest of any peacetime crisis. In Sweden, only the depression of the 1930s caused a larger loss in real income. The loss of industrial output remained moderate in both countries compared with other major crises. Employment in the two countries, however, was hard hit during the 1990s. The cumulative employment loss is the greatest on record, considerably higher than during the depression of the 1930s.

The impacts of the oil crises of the 1970s (OPEC I) and early 1980s (OPEC II) were dissimilar. OPEC I stands out as a crisis in both countries, though deeper in Finland than in Sweden. OPEC II, on the other hand, did not create a crisis in Finland and caused only minor losses in Sweden. Policy-makers apparently learned from OPEC I how to handle OPEC II. The two world wars emerge as the most costly of all the depression episodes examined.

The numerical results in Chapter 5 demonstrate the severity of the crisis of the 1990s. It was unusually deep and prolonged. It occurred after a long period of peacetime prosperity and growth, so long that policy-makers and the public probably thought that a deep depression could not happen again. Closing their chapter, Hagberg and Jonung guess that one reason why the crisis of the 1990s turned out so costly was that it came as such a surprise.

1.2 PART II: THE INTERNATIONAL CONTEXT

In Chapter 6, 'The boom and bust cycle in Finland and Sweden in an international perspective', Lars Jonung, Ludger Schuknecht and Mika Tujula compare the boom–bust cycle in Finland and Sweden 1984–1995 with the average boom–bust pattern in industrialized countries as calculated from an international sample for the period 1970–2002. They start by adopting a technique to separate boom–bust episodes from standard business cycle phases for a large number of countries. In this way, they obtain a dating of boom–bust episodes to use when calculating the average behaviour of the variables they want to study in a comparative perspective.

Next, Jonung, Schuknecht and Tujula identify the driving forces behind the boom–bust pattern in Finland and Sweden, starting from a brief summary of the cyclical experience of the two Nordic countries based on Chapters 2 and 3 in this volume. This account helps them to identify key variables, such as domestic credit, asset prices, real interest rates, exchange rates, the current account, real growth, output gaps, consumption, investment, exports, employment, real labour costs, fiscal balances and public debt, to be examined more closely in the cross-country comparisons.

Two clear conclusions emerge from their comparisons between the Finnish–Swedish boom–bust pattern and that of other OECD countries as displayed in a large number of figures. First, the Finnish–Swedish pattern is much more volatile than the average. The boom as well as the bust is bigger in the two Nordic countries. This holds for practically every time series compared. Second, the bust and the recovery in the two Nordic countries differ far more from the international average than the boom phase does. The bust is much deeper and the recovery comes earlier and is more rapid than in the other countries of the sample.

Jonung, Schuknecht and Tujula explain the more volatile character of the Finnish and Swedish boom–bust as being due to the design of economic policies in the 1980s and 1990s. The boom–bust cycle in Finland and Sweden 1984–95 was driven by financial liberalization and procyclical monetary and fiscal policies, causing large and unexpected swings in the real rate of interest transmitted via the financial sector into the real sector and then into the public finances. Several factors contributed to the highly procyclical policy, most prominently the defence of the pegged exchange rate. The authors conclude that the Finnish and Swedish crisis of the early 1990s should be viewed as part of a full-fledged boom–bust cycle.

In Chapter 7, 'The boom and bust cycle in Norway', Erling Steigum presents roughly – but not exactly – the same story of boom and bust for Norway as told in Chapters 2 and 3 for Finland and Sweden. In all three countries, the initial impulse originated from measures to deregulate the financial system while maintaining a pegged exchange rate. The financial deregulation set off a lending boom, partly financed by capital inflows, driving up asset prices, reducing savings and causing high inflation, low unemployment and loss of foreign competitiveness, eventually turning into a bust, a recession and a systemic currency and banking crisis. In the end, Norway, just like Finland and Sweden, was forced to abandon the pegged rate of the Norwegian *krone*.

Steigum describes first the initial conditions. Prevailing institutions and views of policy-makers in Norway were roughly the same as in Finland and Sweden in the early 1980s. The monetary regime was based on a pegged exchange rate. Economic policies were selective and interventionist, a tradition going back to the 1940s. The deregulation of the Norwegian credit market took place in 1984–85, after many decades with caps on interest rates, quantitative regulations on the lending of commercial banks, and credit rationing.

The financial liberalization triggered a strong lending boom in 1985–87, financed by huge capital inflows. Norwegian banks were not prepared for this change in the financial environment. During the lending boom, 'bad banking' behaviour was widespread, such as giving strong incentives to inexperienced and newly recruited staff to 'sell' new loans without giving appropriate considerations to the risk of future loan losses. Generous tax deduction rules for nominal interest payments kept the after-tax real rates of interest close to zero, creating powerful incentives for households and firms to borrow and spend. The household saving rate turned negative for four years (1985–88). Real estate prices and stock prices increased rapidly. High growth of private consumption and investment generated a strong business cycle boom. In 1987, the rate of unemployment was only 1.5 per cent, triggering double-digit wage inflation.

The fall in the oil price in the winter of 1985–86 had strong and negative effects on the current account and on the government's fiscal position. The new Labour government in 1986 carried out a devaluation of the *krone* by 10 per cent and a policy of fiscal tightening. The government told *Norges Bank*, the central bank of Norway, to use the interest rate instrument to bolster the credibility of the pegged exchange rate of the *krone*.

The boom ended abruptly with a surprisingly deep recession in 1988–89, followed by stagnation and low growth, disinflation and increasing unemployment during the period 1989–2003. The bust was fuelled by disinflation, less generous tax rules and rising German rates of interest. The relative price (to the consumer price index) of non-residential real estate in Oslo peaked as early as 1986, and then fell by 56 per cent from 1986 to 1992. During the same period, the average after-tax real interest rate increased from about 1 per cent to more than 7 per cent. During the bust, bank loan losses reached levels not seen since the inter-war period. Still, it was three years from the onset of the recession in 1988 before a systemic banking crisis hit Norway in 1991.

Steigum demonstrates that the boom–bust cycle in Norway was not as severe as it was in Finland and Sweden, where it occurred a few years *after* the Norwegian boom–bust. The Norwegian boom was also shorter, probably due to the oil price shock in 1986 hitting Norway as an oil exporter. In addition, the Norwegian crisis was not as deep. Speculative attacks against the pegged exchange rate were more pervasive in Finland and Sweden, where the currencies were clearly overvalued prior to the attacks. In Norway, a speculative attack took place in December 1992 after – and probably inspired by – those in Finland and Sweden in the fall. At that time, the government had already salvaged the banking industry. When *Norges Bank* let the *krone* float, it fell by only 4 per cent. Later it recovered. This initial fall was much smaller than the depreciation registered in Finland and Sweden.

Norwegian monetary policy was procyclical during both the boom and the subsequent stagnation period due to the pegged exchange rate policy, as was the case in Finland and Sweden. The fiscal policy tightening from 1986 on was crucial in curbing the boom. The government waited too long, however, before giving fiscal stimulus after the recession. The changes in the tax rules regarding tax deductions for interest payments had a procyclical effect.

The rapid rise in interest rates stemming from Germany after its reunification had devastating effects. At that time the Norwegian banking industry was weak due to many years of losses and low profitability. Although the bank losses as a percentage of outstanding loans in Norway were not as huge as those in Finland and Sweden, the Norwegian banking crisis was just as systemic and dramatic. In 1991–92, the government rescued the three largest commercial banks (*Christiania Bank*, *Den norske Bank* and *Fokus Bank*), as well as a number of savings banks and medium-sized commercial banks. At this stage, Norwegian banks, particularly commercial banks, were poorly capitalized compared with those in Finland and Sweden. The aggregate bank loan losses were similar in size in Denmark and Norway, but the Danish banks had a much stricter capital requirement at the outset. In Denmark, there were no major bank failures, let alone any systemic banking crisis.[2]

The Norwegian method of rescuing the banking system was different from the Finnish and Swedish approach applied shortly afterwards. In Norway, the government took over the ownership of the large commercial banks by writing down the equity capital of the former private owners to zero before injecting new capital. The Norwegian government did not set up a separate entity to manage and recover non-performing loans (a 'bad bank'). Moreover, no blanket guarantee for banks' liabilities was issued in Norway as it was in Sweden.

Steigum notes that Norway was a Nordic pioneer in the sense that the boom–bust cycle in Norway occurred a few years before the boom–bust in Finland and Sweden. It may seem surprising that Finland and Sweden, being close neighbours to Norway, did not learn any policy lessons from the Norwegian process as it unfolded. One reason is that events followed each other very closely in the three countries, so there was not much time for policy-learning. Another reason may be that, once the process of financial liberalization had started, it was too late to take action. The ride in the roller-coaster was already on its way towards financial disaster. In addition, the experience of Norway was probably viewed as exceptional due to Norway's large reliance on revenues from its oil and gas sector.

In Chapter 8, 'How did Denmark avoid a banking crisis?', Claus Vastrup explains how Denmark became a Nordic exception by staying on a monetary regime based on a pegged exchange rate and not being pulled into a systemic currency and banking crisis like Finland, Norway and Sweden. According to him, a combination of microeconomic and macroeconomic developments contributed to Denmark being spared the Nordic boom–bust pattern, although substantial problems emerged in the Danish banking sector as well as in the Danish economy in the 1980s and early 1990s.

Financial liberalization was carried out at an earlier stage in Denmark than in the other Nordic countries, several years prior to the deregulation in Finland, Norway and Sweden. The Danish deregulation was undertaken in the midst of a recession, and thus had no major impact on the stability of the banking sector at the time of liberalization. However, the financial position of commercial banks in Denmark deteriorated in the late 1980s. The problems peaked in 1991–93 when the total losses and loss provisions reached more than 5 per cent of GDP. As Vastrup demonstrates, the Danish banking system was able to absorb these losses and loss provisions because Danish banks were well capitalized – better than the banks of the other Nordic countries. The Danish banking system benefited also from more stable macroeconomic conditions in Denmark at the end of the 1980s and in the early 1990s than in the other Nordic countries.

The Danish economy was in a precarious situation in the early 1980s. Unemployment was high, deficits on the current account were large, and both inflation and interest rates were on the rise. In addition, policymakers faced a credibility problem as the Danish currency had been devalued several times and public sector deficits were large. At this juncture, Denmark decided to adopt a stability-oriented approach based on a pegged exchange rate.

The new policy approach was eventually successful. The firm commitment to the pegged exchange rate removed the inflation and devaluation bias of the past. A tight fiscal policy gradually eliminated the deficit on the current account by 1990, turning it into a surplus of 3 per cent of GDP in 1993. However, in the long process of turning the current account around in the 1980s, Denmark's competitive position did not improve and economic growth was low, although positive and stable. Unemployment increased steadily from 1987 and reached more than 9 per cent when the international economic conditions deteriorated in 1992–93.

Fiscal policy turned expansionary in 1993 and particularly in 1994, ending a period of distress in the banking sector. Due to the surplus on the current account, the pegged rate remained credible. Following gradual reforms of the labour market and cautious demand management in the second part of the 1990s, unemployment fell to a level below that of most other European countries.

The European currency crisis in 1992–93 and the short-term Danish deviation from the pegged exchange rate regime did not undermine the stability of either the Danish economy or its banking sector. Denmark avoided the devastating crisis that hit Finland, Norway and Sweden at this time. Instead, according to Vastrup, the most important macroeconomic threat to the stability of the banking system was the low rate of economic growth and the deflation of property prices in the late 1980s and early 1990s.

The case of Denmark demonstrates that financial deregulation may be carried out without causing a major financial crisis, contrary to the experience of the other Nordic countries. Danish monetary and fiscal policy maintained macroeconomic stability, the process of liberalization followed a proper sequencing, and commercial banks were well capitalized.

In Chapter 9, 'The Nordic and Asian crises: common causes, different outcomes', Ari Kokko and Kenji Suzuki provide a comparison of the Nordic and Asian financial crises. Their main message is that the causes of the two crises were largely similar, but that the patterns of reform and recovery differed between the Nordic and the Asian case.

First, Kokko and Suzuki trace the causes of the crises to simultaneous increases in the demand for and supply of credit due to financial liberalization. Both regions experienced export booms and rising demand for credit during the 1980s. In the Swedish case, the export boom was triggered by a series of currency devaluations in the early 1980s. In large parts of Southeast Asia, there was a shift from import substitution to an export-oriented growth strategy supported by devaluations. The increase in credit demand, originating in the expanding export sectors, gradually spread to other parts of the economies, including consumer credit.

Normally, the increase in credit demand would have been dampened by rising interest rates, but this did not happen because of developments on the supply side. The domestic credit markets in both regions were deregulated, international capital flows were liberalized, and banks began to compete for customers and market shares. Thanks to the resulting increase in credit supply, real interest rates remained low, and asset prices began to increase. Very soon, other prices were also rising.

In countries with pegged exchange rates (like Finland, Sweden and Thailand), the high rate of domestic inflation soon led to a reduction in international competitiveness. The export boom was replaced by a current account deficit financed by foreign borrowing. This deficit – which reflected a low domestic savings rate and a credit boom – could be sustained as long as foreign lenders were willing to provide the necessary funding. The crisis broke out when they started doubting the sustainability of the deficits and the pegged exchange rate, and refused to roll over maturing loans.

Countries with floating exchange rates (like South Korea) experienced a similar process with an appreciation of the real exchange rate: high domestic interest rates initially attracted so much foreign capital that the current account deficit did not cause any depreciation of the Korean currency.

Once the crisis was under way, it spread rapidly through the economy. The stock market and property bubbles began to deflate. Banks and other financial institutions were forced to reduce their lending, and a downturn in production and employment followed. The fall in asset prices, eventually coupled with a reduction in the inflow of foreign capital, led to banking and currency crises. In the Nordic countries, there was also a crisis in public finances: the reduction in employment activated automatic stabilizers that pushed up huge public budget deficits.

The recovery from the crisis was very rapid in Finland and Sweden. The weakest banks and financial institutions were liquidated. Public funds were used to transfer problem credits to special asset management corporations. Within only a few years, the banking system had recovered and was breaking even. Substantial structural changes were undertaken in the industrial sector. Even the public budget deficits were eliminated a few years later.

In most of East Asia, by contrast, it took much longer to resolve the crisis. Kokko and Suzuki argue that it was not until 2004–05 that East Asia shook off the crisis. They propose several reasons why crisis resolution in Finland and Sweden was more efficient. First, they assert that the crisis in East Asia was deeper than the Nordic crisis, and therefore harder to resolve. This was partly due to weak supervisory institutions and unclear accounting rules, which allowed enterprises and financial institutions to take on excessive risk, and partly the result of a development strategy that promoted risk-taking. The links between political and economic interests throughout Asia made managers, investors and lenders act as if the state guaranteed some of the business risks.

Second, the recovery in Finland and Sweden was facilitated by their accession to the European Union. On the one hand, the EU pressured them to reduce their public deficits to sustainable levels, which gave the governments an important argument in the domestic debate with various interest groups that demanded compensation for losses incurred during the crisis. On the other hand, membership of the EU promoted trade as well as an inflow of foreign direct investments, generating growth and employment.

Third, the Nordic countries benefited from a favourable phase in the international business cycle, with the emergence of the 'new economy'. In Asia, the recovery process included both the downturn in the IT sector in 2000 and the aftermath of the terrorist attacks in the US in 2001.

Finally, Finland and Sweden displayed a higher degree of 'organizational learning capacity' in policy-making than most Asian countries, according to Kokko and Suzuki. As a result, decisions were made in extensive consultation with different groups in society, the resulting policies were transparent, and they were implemented with relatively little interference from interest groups. In large parts of Asia, by contrast, decision-making systems were hierarchical and compartmentalized, with fewer sources of information, fewer challenges to established interpretations of information, and more discretionary decision-making and interference from interest groups. Thus, on the basis of their comparison, Kokko and Suzuki suggest that the most remarkable feature of the Nordic crisis was the rapid recovery.

1.3 PART III: LESSONS FROM THE NORDIC CRISES

In Chapter 10, ‘Twelve lessons from the Nordic experience of financial liberalization’, Lars Jonung summarizes the main findings in the previous chapters of this volume with the aim of turning them into policy recommendations. Thus, he tries to identify common elements in the Nordic experience. They are easy to find as the boom–bust stories of Finland, Norway and Sweden are largely identical.

Before presenting his message, Jonung emphasizes that lesson-drawing is not an exact science; it is strongly influenced by subjective judgements. Given this caveat, he suggests 12 policy lessons from the Nordic experience, organized under three headings: first, how to liberalize without causing a boom–bust cycle; second, how to deal with a financial crisis; and, third, the long-run effects of financial integration.

Jonung stresses that several of his lessons are closely related and that some of them are more important than others. Most of them stem from one source: the lack of knowledge of the dynamics created by financial liberalization. According to him, financial ignorance among policy-makers, forecasters, bankers, economists and the public turned out to be the key to the Nordic boom–bust cycle.

Under the first heading of how to liberalize without creating a crisis, Jonung proposes eight lessons, most of them expressed as warnings against policy mistakes. In his first lesson, he makes a plea for knowledge about the forces unleashed by financial liberalization to become widespread. A thorough understanding of the workings of financial markets is crucial to make financial liberalization and financial integration successful.

His second lesson concerns the dangers of backward-looking policy learning. The Nordic policy-makers made themselves prisoners of the past by regarding the crisis of the 1990s as identical to the devaluation crises of the 1970s and 1980s. For this reason they decided to defend the pegged rate to avoid repeating the failed policy of devaluations, thus making the financial crisis of the 1990s deeper than it would otherwise have been.

The third lesson states that large, rapid and unexpected swings in the real rate should be avoided. A more gradual approach, smoothing movements in the after-tax real rate, should restrain or even prevent boom–bust episodes from occurring during financial deregulation. The fourth and fifth lessons are warnings against the types of procyclical stabilization policies and procyclical sequencing of financial reforms that destabilized the Nordic economies in the 1980s and 1990s.

After these warnings, Jonung concludes that a systemic financial crisis of the Nordic type cannot be prevented by financial micro-based supervision, the effectiveness of which is limited. Next, he argues that financial repression should be avoided – a simple lesson but not always an easy one to follow. He has a positive message as well when pointing to the case of Denmark to demonstrate an important lesson: financial liberalization can be crisis-free if it is combined with proper countermeasures.

The second set of lessons from the Nordic experience covers the proper policy response to dampen the impact of a crisis, once it has broken out. The most important one concerns the benefits of rapid crisis management. Quick, transparent and determined government actions to maintain public confidence in the banking system reduce the impact of a financial crisis and allow for a rapid recovery of the financial system.

Jonung argues that the Nordic crisis reveals that the lender-of-last-resort function of central banks is inadequate to support ailing banks. The policy lesson is that in a solvency crisis the government, not the central bank, should serve as the supporter of last resort of failing financial institutions. Turning to the policy advice of the IMF during the Nordic crises, Jonung makes a case that the IMF failed to understand the economy-wide impact of the process of financial deregulation that started in the mid-1980s. The policy lesson for a country in a crisis is to rely on advice and guidance from many sources, not only from the IMF.

The third set of lessons concerns the long-run effects of financial integration on the design of stabilization policies, on efficiency and growth and on the distribution of income and wealth in the Nordic economies. Here financial liberalization contributed to major changes, some of which transformed the Nordics into fast-growing economies during the long recovery phase. The lesson is that once financial markets are internationally integrated, pressure emerges to adjust domestic regulations and institutions to international patterns. In Jonung's opinion, these effects are far-reaching, although they have so far not been given the attention they deserve.

Are these 12 lessons applicable outside the Nordics? Jonung replies in the affirmative. He argues that the Nordic experience of financial liberalization has much in common with that of other countries opening their financial system to the rest of the world. As a common pattern exists across most crisis-hit countries, he concludes that the Nordic lessons are of a general, not specific, nature.

In his summary, which may also serve as a summary of this introductory chapter, Jonung states that the Nordic record of financial integration and of the financial crises of the 1980s and 1990s adds to our understanding of the causes and consequences of financial crises. The financial opening-up of Finland, Norway and Sweden started a sequence of events that brought these economies into deep depression. At this stage, in retrospect, the Nordic crises generate policy recommendations of a general nature that deserve close attention.

NOTES

1. The 'it' metaphor for the Great Depression of the 1930s in the United States is found in Chapter 1 in Minsky (1982).
2. See Chapter 8 on the Danish record.

REFERENCE

Minsky, H.P. (1982), *Can 'It' Happen Again? Essays on Instability and Finance*, New York and London: M.E. Sharpe.

PART I

The crisis of the 1990s in Finland and Sweden

2. The great financial crisis in Finland and Sweden: the dynamics of boom, bust and recovery, 1985–2000

Lars Jonung, Jaakko Kiander and Pentti Vartia

INTRODUCTION[1]

The beginning of the 1990s witnessed a severe recession in Western Europe. The climax was the European currency crisis in the autumn of 1992 and summer of 1993. The recession turned most severe in Finland and Sweden, the northern periphery of the continent. The timing and the nature of the deep crises in the two countries were astonishingly similar – it was the crisis of the twins. To policy-makers and economists the power of the crisis came as a major surprise. The general view had been that such a depression could not happen in advanced welfare states like Finland or Sweden with a long tradition of full employment policies and strong labour union influence on the design of economic and social policies.

Figure 2.1 demonstrates that the annual percentage growth of GDP was negative over the period 1991–93 in both countries. Unemployment mirrored the depression, shooting up in both countries in the early 1990s. The rate of unemployment rose from a level of around 3 per cent in Finland during 1989–91 to around 18 per cent at the beginning of 1994. Unemployment in Sweden followed the same pattern, starting from around 2 per cent in 1990 and rising to a level of 10 per cent during the period 1993–97.[2] The co-variation between economic developments in Finland and Sweden was high, although the depression was deeper in Finland than in Sweden. A comparison across industrialized countries for the period 1970–2000 reveals that the boom–bust cycle in Finland and Sweden 1984–95 was more volatile than the average boom–bust pattern.[3]

The severity of the crisis of the 1990s is brought out when all the major crises that have hit the Finnish and Swedish economies in the last 130 years are compared.[4] Measured by the output loss, the depression of the 1990s was the most severe peacetime crisis during the 20th century in Finland, more severe than the Great Depression of the 1930s. Even unemployment

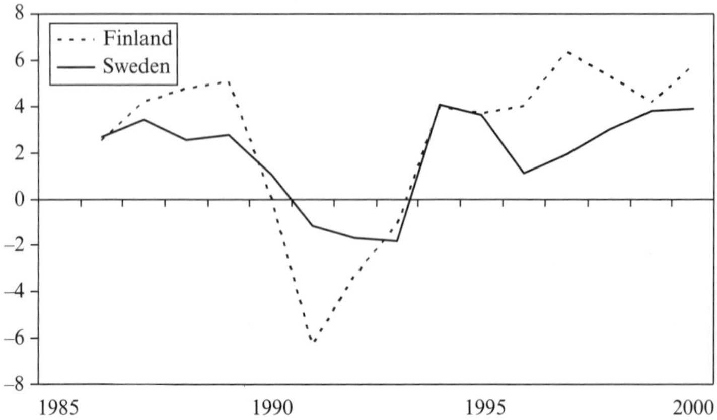

Figure 2.1 GDP growth in Finland and Sweden, 1986–2000 (yearly percentage change)

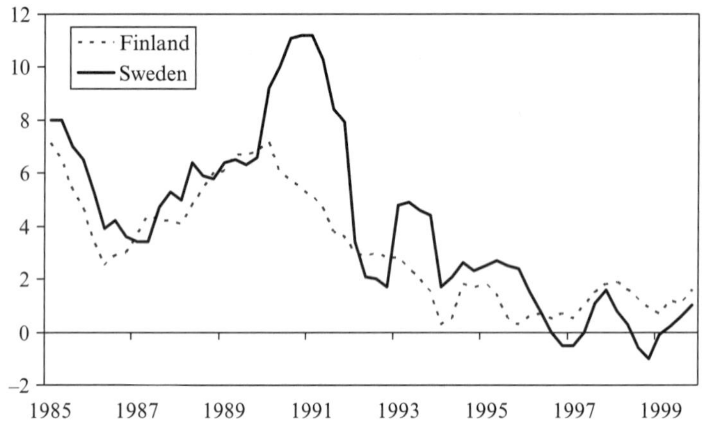

Figure 2.2 Inflation in Finland and Sweden, 1985–2000 (per cent)

rose to a higher level than during the 1930s. In Sweden, the crisis of the 1990s was the second worst during international peacetime. Only the depression of the 1930s exhibited a larger output loss.

The depression brought down the rate of inflation significantly. From the end of the 1980s to the end of the 1990s Finland and Sweden experienced disinflation (Figure 2.2); during a few months in the 1990s the price level actually fell – inflation turned into deflation. The crisis of the 1990s marks the transition from an accommodative stabilization policy regime characterized by high inflation to a stability-oriented one with low inflation.

The aim of this chapter is to examine and explain financial and macroeconomic developments in Finland and Sweden before, during and after the crisis of the 1990s, using a comparative perspective. By now there are several studies focused on either the Finnish or the Swedish crisis experience.[5] Here we cover both countries at the same time in a search for similarities and differences. First, we present the analytical framework, inspired by the work of Irving Fisher on debt deflation. Next we describe the initial conditions in place before the beginning of the process that culminated in the crisis. Then we examine the record of the period 1985–2000, split into three phases: first, the run-up in 1985–90 to the crisis, the boom; second, the outbreak, spread and effects of the 1990–93 crisis, the bust; and, third, the ensuing recovery in 1993–2000. Finally, we address two major questions raised by the crisis record: first, why was the pegged exchange rate defended so stubbornly, and second, what policy lessons emerged from the crisis?

2.1 THE CONCEPTUAL FRAMEWORK

How could the Finnish and Swedish economies end up in such a deep depression? How could policy-makers committed to full employment allow widespread unemployment? To answer these questions we first have to identify the forces, domestic and international, responsible for the exceptional depth of the crisis and then find a suitable framework to account for them. We also have to explore the mindset of policy-makers and economists during this period to understand their actions and advice.

We find it fruitful to start from the conventional view of the causes and consequences of the many financial crises that occurred in the 1990s.[6] In our opinion, the crisis in the two countries was closely related to the financial liberalization of the mid-1980s. The Finnish and Swedish crisis during the early 1990s should thus be viewed as a predecessor of the crises in Asia and Latin America later in that decade.[7]

A growing body of comparative research has identified central elements of the boom–bust cycles during the 1990s.[8] The starting point in Figure 2.3 is a small open economy with a pegged exchange rate and extensive financial regulation of domestic and international credit and capital flows as well as of the domestic interest rate, which is generally kept below the level that would be determined by a ‘free’ market outcome.

The boom–bust process starts with a deregulation of financial markets, inducing a lending boom and an inflow of capital to finance domestic

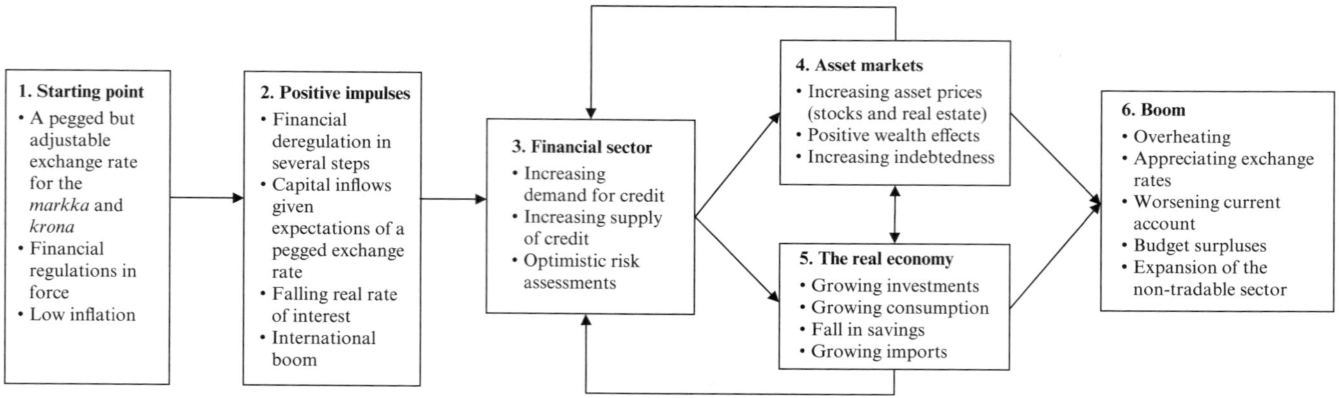

Figure 2.3 The boom phase in Finland and Sweden, 1985–90: a stylized picture

investment and consumption. The combination of financial deregulation and a pegged (fixed) exchange rate contributes to a speculative bubble, characterized by rising inflation rates and inflationary expectations, especially in asset markets such as the market for stocks and real estate. At this stage, the real rate of interest is low or even negative, which further spurs asset price inflation. This creates positive wealth effects, which in turn lead to a further strengthening of aggregate demand. During the expansion phase, the pegged exchange rate is perceived as irrevocably fixed by investors.

Eventually, unexpected negative impulses change the economic and financial outlook (Figure 2.4), and the credibility of the pegged exchange rate is put in question. The capital inflow is reversed into an outflow. The credit expansion comes to a halt, turning into a contraction. Domestic policy-makers try to stop the capital outflow and attract foreign capital by raising interest rates, which hurts indebted firms and households. The real rate of interest rises quickly, undermining balance sheets and thus the stability of the domestic financial system by creating credit losses. The harder the central bank tries to defend the pegged exchange rate with high interest rates, the deeper the crisis becomes. The financial bubble turns into a bust with a sharp increase in the number of bankruptcies and in the number of unemployed. Finally, the central bank is forced to abandon the peg and allow the currency to float. The decision to float is followed by a sharp fall in the foreign value of the currency. Domestic interest rates are lowered. The first step to recovery is taken.

The account above, summarized in Figures 2.3 and 2.4, fits nicely with the story of boom and bust for Finland and Sweden. Prior to the boom of the late 1980s, both Finland and Sweden maintained pegged exchange rates and strongly regulated financial markets. Both countries liberalized their financial markets in the mid-1980s in a way that induced rapid credit expansion, low real rates of interest, capital imports, growing trade deficits and asset bubbles during the latter half of the decade. During the boom, according to some estimates, the unemployment rates were below the natural rate in both countries. The sharp increase in asset prices increased household wealth.

When the real interest rate rose sharply, asset prices started to fall and finally collapsed. The borrowers and the financial system were put under severe pressure due to negative wealth effects.[9] Output and employment decreased and the budget deficits rose sharply, reflecting the workings of automatic stabilizers as well as government support given to the financial system. Speculative attacks eventually forced Finland and Sweden to abandon their pegs and allow their currencies to float during the fall of 1992. The depreciation that followed from the floating eased the depression and became the starting point for the recovery.

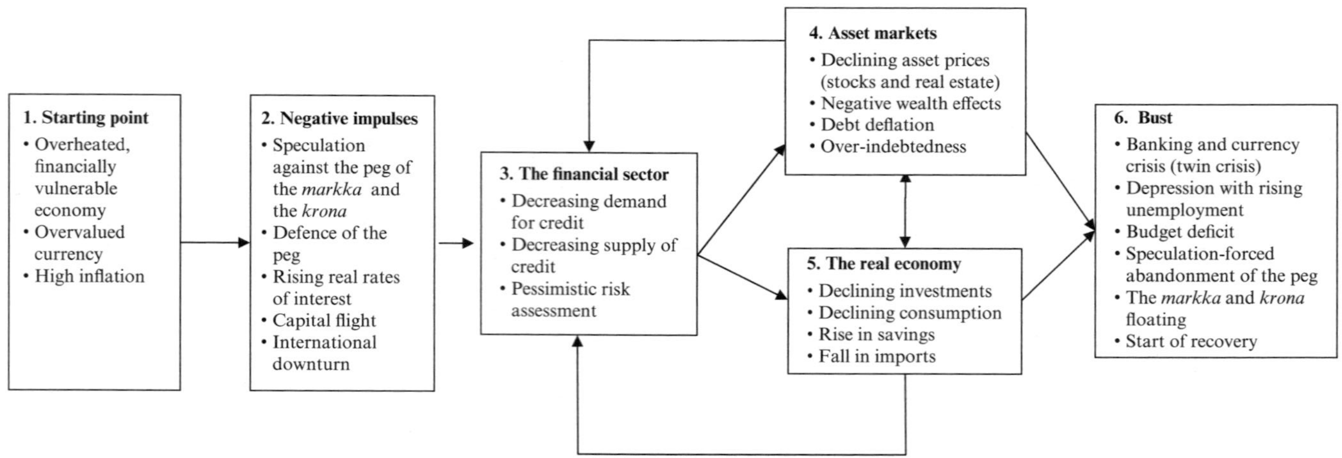

Figure 2.4 The bust phase in Finland and Sweden, 1990–93: a stylized picture

The way the crisis is summarized above has much in common with Irving Fisher's analysis of the Great Depression in the United States in the 1930s. Fisher stressed the effects of changes in the balance sheets of the private sector brought about by macroeconomic developments: 'In the great booms and depressions . . . [there have been] two dominant factors, namely over-indebtedness to start with and deflation following soon after'.[10] Fisher depicted debt deflation as a process where indebted economic agents become over-indebted, when actual income (earnings) and real interest rate developments do not meet previous expectations. Over-indebted economic agents, facing mounting liquidity problems, are suddenly forced to sell so much of their assets that asset prices start to fall. The fall in asset prices brings about a decline in their net wealth, as the nominal value of their debt to banks and other financial institutions remains unchanged. Falling asset prices undermine the value of the collateral used for taking loans, leading to additional forced sales.

The process becomes cumulative and self-enforcing: the stronger the fall in prices, the larger the volume of forced sales of assets pledged as collateral. Bankruptcies and credit losses are integral parts of the process of debt deflation, which finally threaten the liquidity and solvency of the whole financial system.

Fisher studied debt deflation in the United States in the 1930s, when consumer and wholesale prices as well as asset prices were falling at the same time. In addition to the collapse in asset prices, the general price level fell by about a third. However, Finland and Sweden's experience in the early 1990s demonstrates that a debt deflation process can occur when asset prices are falling, while the consumer price level remains fairly stable or is even rising. The rate of inflation was reduced during the crisis but it remained positive. Thus, disinflation, but no deflation of wages and prices, took place in both countries.[11]

The traditional Keynesian approach tends to ignore the balance sheet adjustments that were at work in the Finnish and Swedish financial systems in the 1990s. In the standard aggregate demand model, the attempt by economic agents to cut their spending as their incomes decline sets off, through various multipliers, a decline in production because the expenditures of one economic agent are the revenues of another. This leads to output losses because prices and wages are assumed to be inflexible or sticky.

Fisher's analysis is focused on the workings of financial markets. Here the existence of inflexible nominal debt contracts is a major feature behind the wealth effects driving the debt deflation process. When prices fall and real interest rates rise, the real value of nominal debt such as bank loans increases. The process brings about a rise in the sales of assets and a reduction in borrowing and consumption while savings increase. This vicious circle was a major feature in the crisis of the 1990s in Finland and Sweden. Indebted households and firms ended up in a situation described by Fisher as 'Then we have the great paradox which, I submit, is the chief secret of most, if not all, great depressions: the more the debtors pay, the more they owe.'[12]

The attempt by some households and firms to shore up their financial positions by refraining from spending and selling assets thus affects the wealth positions of others. In the depression of the 1990s, cutbacks in consumption and investment weakened the profitability of viable companies and lowered their stock prices, exacerbating problems of over-indebtedness. When prices of equities and housing fell, households and firms with 'healthy' balance sheets also increased their savings and reduced consumption and investment.

The forced sales of assets as part of the debt deflation process did not affect households in an even manner, even though there was a sharp fall in the value of all dwellings. Households that took loans to buy houses when high prices prevailed in the late 1980s were affected the most. According to Statistics Finland, in the early 1990s roughly half of Finnish households had debts while the other half were debtless. About 10 per cent of the indebted households had their debt restructured in 1992 and 1993, while 20 per cent did so in 1994.[13]

Our study will stress one element lacking in Fisher's original analysis. He examined the case of the United States, a fairly closed economy in the 1930s. However, Finland and Sweden in the 1990s were small, open economies with large tradable sectors. We thus examine debt deflation in an open economy. One of our major findings is that the deflation spiral was effectively stopped when Finland and Sweden abandoned their pegged exchange rates. When the two countries were forced to adopt a floating exchange rate in the fall of 1992, the deflationary forces were arrested. True, the depreciation of the domestic currencies that occurred when the currency peg was eliminated also created negative wealth effects when the real value of foreign nominal debt rose. However, these effects were countered by the rapid increase in exports after the crisis, driving the recovery. This chain of events illustrates an asymmetry between the tradable (open) and non-tradable (sheltered) sectors during the boom–bust cycle.[14]

The standard argument by economists against the use of devaluations is that they are ineffective in the long run. They improve export performance in the short run but eventually increase inflationary pressures, thus bringing about demands for new devaluations, in this way creating devaluation cycles. This argument was an important factor behind the Finnish and

Swedish 'hard' currency policy after the experience of the devaluations of the late 1970s and early 1980s.[15]

The financial crisis of the 1990s demonstrated, however, that the policy of the hard *markka* and the hard *krona* actually amplified the boom and deepened the economic downturn. When an economy has ended up in a debt deflation process with an overvalued currency, loss of competitiveness, rising current account deficit and mounting financial imbalances due to rising real rates of interest and falling asset prices, the policy-makers can and – as a normative proposition – should arrest the process by a change in the foreign value of the domestic currency. This was a major policy lesson that Finland and Sweden were forced to learn in the early 1990s. In short, devaluation was deemed a better alternative than deflation by policy-makers.

Following the insights of Irving Fisher, we may classify the crisis of the 1990s as a real interest rate crisis, since the significant rise in real rate of interest constituted a central feature of the boom–bust cycle.[16] We may also label it as a financial crisis as financial developments gave the impulse for the boom–bust. As stressed in this chapter, the 'twin' crisis in Finland and Sweden was very similar to the crises in other economies that deregulated their financial markets while maintaining pegged exchange rates.[17] Norway went through a similar boom–bust process to that of Finland and Sweden.[18] This similarity between Finland and Sweden and other nations provides firm support for analysing the crisis as a financial one. True, the crisis had many dimensions, involving imbalances within both the financial system (the banking crisis) and the foreign exchange market (the currency crisis). The latter crisis was manifested by the speculative attacks on the pegged exchange rate of the *markka* and the *krona*.[19] In this sense it was a twin crisis as the concept is used to describe financial crises in the world economy in recent decades.

2.2 THE POLICY FRAMEWORK PRIOR TO FINANCIAL LIBERALIZATION

An understanding of the institutions and economic policies that evolved in Finland and Sweden after World War II helps us to clarify the policy reactions during the years 1985–2000. Both Finland and Sweden became early members of the Bretton Woods system, pegging their exchange rates to the US dollar. Finland signed the articles of agreement in 1948 and paid up her share to the IMF in June 1951. The exchange rate was set at 231 *markkaa* to the dollar. Sweden joined in August the same year. The rate for the *krona* was set at 5.17 *kronor* per dollar, and was kept constant by the *Riksbank* for 20 years. Finland had the same objective but devalued the *markka* in 1957 and in 1967.

Capital account controls (foreign exchange regulations) served as a wall behind which the central banks determined the rate of interest as well as the distribution and size of credit flows. Monetary policy was used to subsidize those sectors of the economy that the government wanted to support with low interest rates and an ample supply of credit. Since interest rates were kept low and the tax system allowed large deductions for the cost of borrowing (deduction for the payment of interest rates on loans), private sector demand for credit was typically greater than the available supply. As international financial markets deepened, so did the possibility of speculating against pegged exchange rates. Financial market integration contributed to the downfall of the Bretton Woods system in the early 1970s. Still, after its demise, capital account controls remained in force in Finland and Sweden until the end of the 1980s.

In the 1970s, full employment was the main policy goal, one reason being the strong political position of labour unions. Both countries had, and still have, some of the largest shares of unionized workers in the OECD countries. Wage negotiations were based on centralized negotiations between confederations of employer associations and trade unions. The results were then applied first at the union level and then at the firm level. The goal of maintaining full employment contributed to expansionary fiscal and monetary policies. This led to low rates of unemployment, high rates of inflation and several devaluations during the period 1976–82. The discretionary exchange rate flexibility created the necessary adjustment of real wages required for maintaining full employment and external balance.[20]

The devaluation policy reached a climax during the second oil crisis. The Centre-Right government in Sweden devalued the *krona* by 10 per cent in September 1981. Immediately after the election in 1982, when the Social Democrats regained power, an 'offensive' 16 per cent devaluation (originally intended to be 20 per cent) was carried out. The idea was that Sweden would gain a competitive advantage for a few years. The devaluation option would then be closed forever, according to the political rhetoric. Finland followed the Swedish devaluation of 1982 in order to protect its competitive position vis-à-vis Sweden.

Prior to the crisis of the 1990s, both Finland and Sweden appeared to be small, rich welfare states immune to the high unemployment that had plagued most Western European countries since the 1970s. Labour market policies were used in both countries to reduce long-term unemployment.[21] The Finnish and Swedish economies were characterized by high taxes and large public sectors. To many, they appeared to be successful models for economic policy. Few understood that the macroeconomic policy regimes of the two countries rested on a system of strong capital account regulations which isolated the two countries from the rest of the world.

2.3 THE 1985–90 BOOM: FINANCIAL LIBERALIZATION AND OVERHEATING

We examine the boom of the late 1980s by looking first at the developments in Finland, then in Sweden, and finally summarizing the common features of the boom in the two countries. We adopt the same arrangement in the following sections on the 1990–93 crisis and the 1994–2000 recovery.

2.3.1 The Boom in Finland

Macroeconomic developments

The drawn-out process of financial deregulation started in the mid-1970s when a money market emerged. In the 1980s, the Bank of Finland allowed banks to handle foreign exchange affairs, a move that increased short-term capital flows. By the mid-1980s, the lending rates of banks were deregulated and companies were allowed to borrow abroad. When the Bank of Finland started with open market operations in 1987, a modern financial market was created. The pressure to deregulate increased as the liquidity in the corporate sector grew from foreign trade. A market for short-term lending outside the banking system emerged as well.

During the period of regulated financial markets, the Bank of Finland was able to control bank lending because, in the absence of free international capital movements, banks were typically indebted to the central bank. The Bank of Finland set the terms for central bank borrowing which the banks followed.[22] It was not always possible to get a loan at the prevailing interest rate even with sufficient collateral. Thus, the Bank of Finland was able to regulate the availability of credit for firms and households via the banks as well as via the rate of interest.

This system of financial governance changed significantly when capital movements were liberalized and the interest rate controls phased out in the mid-1980s. Households and companies, previously accustomed to living in a world of credit rationing, responded by increasing their debt significantly (Figure 2.5). As a result, bank lending to the non-bank public doubled during the latter half of the 1980s. Lending in foreign currency rose dramatically, too. The inflow of foreign capital increased liquidity and fuelled the domestic credit expansion.

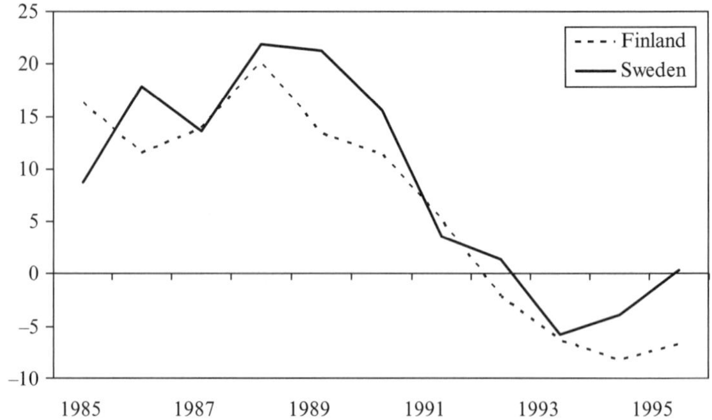

Figure 2.5 The volume of credit in Finland and Sweden, 1985–95 (yearly percentage change)

The growth of private consumption accelerated along with the easing of the availability of credit in the latter half of the 1980s. The demand for housing, real estate and stocks led to a rise in their prices. The rise in the value of assets and the ensuing rise of expectations of future increases in prices fuelled consumption through wealth effects. The increase in wealth enabled additional borrowing by increasing the value of collateral, without households feeling that they were becoming over-indebted. The rise in borrowing was partly driven by the fact that expenses for interest payments were deductible from income before taxation, causing low after-tax real rates of interest (Figure 2.6).

The real economy, especially the construction sector, grew strongly in the latter half of the 1980s. The Finnish economy was characterized by a rapid growth in GDP and a boom in the labour market. Widespread optimism and strong economic growth led to a shortage of labour and accelerating wage inflation due to wage drift. In 1989 the unemployment rate was 3 per cent and long-term unemployment was almost non-existent. At the same time, nominal wages rose by 10 per cent that year.

The rise in asset prices sparked optimism (Figure 2.7). The increase in share prices was seen as the result of the new financial integration between Finland and the rest of the world, which increased the price of previously undervalued Finnish shares. In the media, the yuppie culture and the new 'casino economy' was portrayed favourably. The business papers were filled with success stories from the stock market, contributing to a general sentiment of optimism and encouraging risky investments.[23]

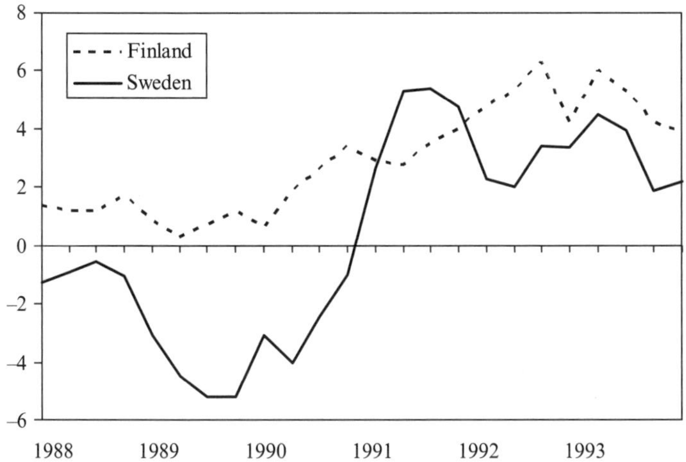

Note: The real rate of interest ex post after tax is calculated by the following: (1 – tax rate on capital) ∗ nominal interest rate – inflation rate.

Figure 2.6 Real rate of interest ex post in Finland and Sweden, 1988–93 (per cent)

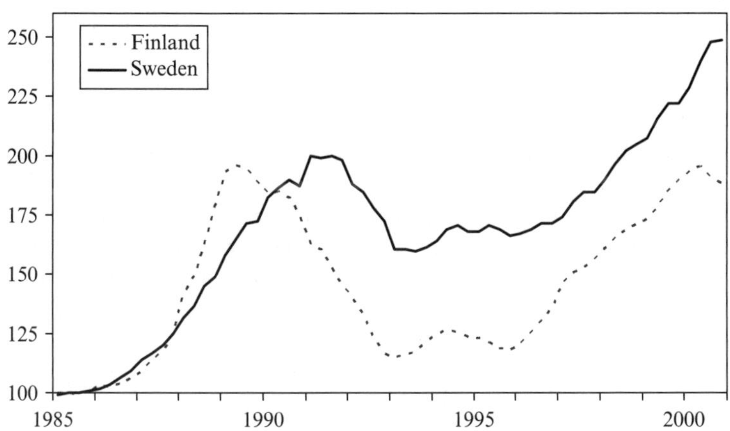

Figure 2.7 House prices in Finland and Sweden, 1985–2000 (1985=100)

Economic policies

In order to dampen the boom, the Bank of Finland made attempts to raise interest rates in 1987–89. The impact of its actions was at first negligible, however, because inflow of foreign capital offset the tightening of domestic

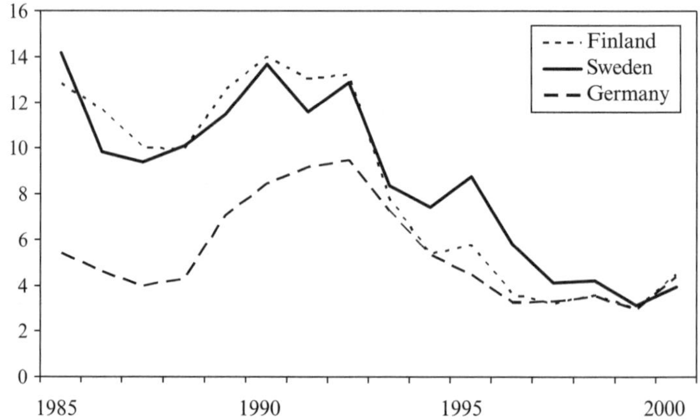

Figure 2.8 The three-month interest rate in Finland, Sweden and Germany, 1985–2000 (per cent)

monetary conditions. The situation changed in 1989, when foreign investors started to have doubts about the credibility of the pegged exchange rate. Still, companies that took on foreign credit did not fully understand that the large differential between domestic and foreign interest rates was a sign of exchange rate risk.[24] Figure 2.8 shows the differences between Finnish, Swedish and German interest rates.

Since monetary policy was committed to maintaining the pegged exchange rate for the *markka*, the responsibility for stabilizing the economy was de facto assigned increasingly to fiscal policy. Indeed, the central government ran a surplus for a few years, but this was attributable mainly to exceptionally strong economic growth, not to any fiscal tightening.

At the same time as financial markets were deregulated, a tax reform was carried out at the end of the 1980s, easing income taxation, even though it should have been tightened for cyclical reasons. The aim of the tax reform was to improve economic incentives and foster neutrality of taxation by widening tax bases and lowering tax rates. Attempts to scale back the tax deductibility of interest payments on loans for consumption and housing had little success. Since the interest rates on bank loans were deducted in taxation, real after-tax interest rates were barely positive, and the relatively high nominal interest rates were not high enough to dampen credit-fuelled demand.[25]

The Economic Council, a discussion forum led by the prime minister, addressed issues related to monetary and exchange rate policies several times. Officials from the Bank of Finland testifying before the Economic Council warned about the dangers of overheating and the rising current account deficit. In March 1989, the general secretary of the Economic Council, Seppo Leppänen, presented a report which later became famous as the *Current Account Problem in Finland.* The risks of indebtedness were depicted in a crisis scenario, where 'borrowing quickly becomes uncontrollable' and the 'Finnish economy may in the 1990s be driven into a period marked by permanently low growth, high unemployment, a low investment rate, a high government deficit, a current account deficit and instability in the labour markets'. The scenario was not taken seriously at the time, however.

The tightening of fiscal policy was also hampered in the late 1980s by constitutional obstacles to austerity measures, notably the fact that a simple parliamentarian majority was sufficient to increase spending while a two-thirds majority was needed for reductions in entitlement programs.[26] Prime minister Harri Holkeri together with the minister of finance, Erkki Liikanen, made attempts to tighten policy, but spending cuts were rejected by the opposition.[27]

The central goal of the Bank of Finland, namely to keep the *markka* exchange rate pegged (the policy of the stable *markka*), was temporarily relaxed when the central bank decided to revalue the *markka* by 4 per cent on 17 March 1989. The government and the Bank of Finland justified this action by asserting that it aimed at dampening inflation.[28] The revaluation led to higher domestic interest rates, which were intended to dampen the overheating which was still seen as a major problem at that time. In hindsight, the revaluation of the currency aimed at curbing the boom came too late. Export prices had been rising since 1987. This positive terms-of-trade shock had spilled over into the economy in the form of rising wages and rising raw timber prices. The revaluation tried to neutralize the positive terms-of-trade shock, but it was two years too late. Instead, it contributed to the overvaluation of the Finnish *markka*, and by making imports cheaper it also widened the current account deficit. It soon became clear that the revaluation deepened the coming current account crisis.

The revaluation of the *markka* also created a credibility problem for policy-makers as it was not consistent with the pegged exchange rate policy. A more proper response, given the pegged exchange rate, would have been to leave the exchange rate unaltered and conduct a more restrictive fiscal policy.[29] Devaluation expectations already existed prior to the revaluation and did not disappear afterwards. The low credibility of the exchange rate policy was apparent in the interest rate differential between Finland and Germany (Figure 2.8).

As the outlook for the Finnish economy grew bleaker, interest rates rose sharply. The situation worsened as a result of the simultaneous increase in international rates following the German reunification. The boom ended in 1990 as higher real rates of interest led to falling asset prices, falling profits and increasing savings. The Finnish economy started to slide into an exceptionally deep currency and banking crisis.

2.3.2 The Boom in Sweden

Macroeconomic developments

World War II unleashed a process of far-reaching regulation of the Swedish economy. At the start of the war, capital account controls (*valutaregleringen*) were introduced. They were complemented in the 1950s by a series of instruments that made it possible for the *Riksbank* to set the interest rate and steer credit flows according to political priorities. The objective of the regulation of the financial system was to facilitate a policy of low interest rates (*lågräntedoktrinen*), which aimed at keeping interest rates below the levels that would have prevailed in the absence of the regulatory system.[30]

Step by step, these regulations were abolished in the 1970s and 1980s. Just after the 1985 election, the governing board of the *Riksbank* abolished the quantitative controls on lending by commercial banks. This step, later dubbed the November revolution, had a significant – although unexpected – effect on macroeconomic developments over the next ten years.[31] It was regarded rather as a technical measure not expected to have any significant real economic consequences.[32] As it turned out, the 1985 financial deregulation was an important first step in the march towards the crisis of the 1990s.

The deregulation should be judged against the imbalances that had characterized private sector portfolios prior to the November 1985 decision. Companies and households had been restricted in their choice of portfolio compositions due to the extensive credit market regulations, high inflation and a tax system that favoured borrowing. The financial deregulation of 1985 fundamentally affected this incentive structure by creating strong incentives for companies and households to increase their borrowing at prevailing interest rates. It also changed the environment for banks, now facing more open competition for market shares. Banks adjusted to the new situation by expanding credit as borrowers stood in line to increase their debts.

The result of the new structure of incentives was that debt increased dramatically between 1986 and 1988 (Figure 2.5). A large part of the expanding volume of credit was channelled into the asset markets, that is, into the property and share markets. The private sector utilized the rising value of its assets as collateral for further borrowing.

The process was fuelled by a rising rate of inflation, which peaked in

1990 (Figure 2.2). The real after-tax interest rate was negative for many investors due to the combination of high inflation, high inflation expectations and the rules of the tax system. The low and often negative real interest rates made it tempting to raise loans – both within Sweden and from abroad – for investments and consumption (Figure 2.6). The final result was the creation of a financial bubble in the Swedish economy, built on excessive indebtedness within the private sector and a corresponding overlending within the financial system.

The credit boom was reflected within the real sector of the economy as well. Consumption became the driving force, while the savings ratio declined. During the most intensive boom period, households consumed more than their disposable income. Government finances improved rapidly during the overheating since the sharp growth in consumption resulted in growing tax income from value added taxes. The budget even showed a small surplus in the late 1980s, creating a significant decline in the debt-to-GDP ratio.

The labour market was driven by strong demand from the domestic (non-tradable) sector, in particular from the construction sector. New construction was favoured by the increases in the price of real assets. It was also heavily subsidized through the design of the housing policy of the government. Significant wage drift emerged. The labour market became overheated with unemployment of less than 2 per cent at the end of the 1980s.

As a consequence of the rapid domestic expansion, the export sector (the tradable sector) was squeezed. The growth in exports became negative while imports soared. The current account worsened towards the end of the 1980s after the recovery in the wake of the 1981–82 devaluations. Gradually, Sweden slid into a cost crisis, temporarily covered up by domestic expansion.

Other factors also fuelled the economic upturn. The fall in oil prices in 1985 gave the world economy a positive impulse. The expansionary American stabilization policy contributed to a long period of international economic upturn that commenced in 1982–83. It reached a peak in 1989–90, when all indicators pointed to an overheating of the Swedish economy. The overheating was characterized by a much faster rate of domestic inflation and lower domestic unemployment than in the rest of the world, and a worsening of Swedish competitiveness. This undermined the credibility of the pegged exchange rate for the *krona*.[33]

Economic policies

The expansionary impulse that the deregulation of 1985 created was not countered by any contractionary policy measures until 1989–91. The conduct of fiscal policy in combination with the financial deregulation thus became the prime reason for the overheating, the cost crisis and the financial imbalances that appeared in the form of over-indebtedness and over-lending during the latter part of the 1980s.

Monetary policy had, since 1982, been founded on the pegged exchange rate of the *krona*. The devaluation in 1982 was declared the last of its kind. The *Riksbank* did not counter the overheating by revaluing the *krona* as its Finnish counterpart did. The responsibility for the stabilization policies thus fell solely on the ministry of finance. In February 1990, the government proposed a freeze on all wages, prices and dividends for two years and a limitation of the right to strike. The freeze package triggered a government crisis.[34] The Social Democratic government resigned. Kjell-Olof Feldt, the minister of finance, left. The new minister of finance, Allan Larsson, took over an economy that was entering into a deep crisis.

In October 1990, as a consequence of a speculative attack on the *krona*, a new austerity package was introduced. At the same time, the government announced that Sweden would apply for EU membership, a measure that can be viewed as an attempt to shore up the credibility of the *krona*. In May 1991, the *Riksbank* attempted to strengthen the credibility of the *krona* by abandoning the currency basket and pegging the *krona* to the ECU. In September 1991, a major financial institution, the *Nyckeln*, collapsed – an event that is commonly regarded as the start of the bust phase.[35] The very same month, the Social Democratic government lost the election to parliament. A four-party coalition formed the new government with Carl Bildt from the Conservative party as prime minister. The new government inherited an economy in rapid decline.

2.3.3 The Common Pattern

Macroeconomic developments in Finland and Sweden during the 1980s were almost identical. The controls over capital flows and interest rates had given the central banks a significant degree of freedom to conduct monetary policy in spite of the pegged exchange rate regime. The financial liberalization of the 1980s affected the incentives of borrowers and lenders in a fundamental way. As a consequence, bank lending increased dramatically. It was channelled to the asset markets, mainly to the real estate and stock markets, raising asset prices and thus private wealth. A new feature appeared in the business cycle, namely asset prices increasing much faster than consumer prices.

The process of financial regulation was accompanied by rising inflation and inflation expectations. The real interest rate after tax fell below zero for many investors through a combination of high inflation, high inflation expectations and the rules of the tax system.[36] The low real interest rates made it tempting to borrow, both domestically and abroad, for consumption and investment. The result was a financial bubble built on over-indebtness and over-lending within the financial system.

Initially policy-makers were unwilling to change either monetary or fiscal policy in response to the boom. Monetary policy was confined to defending the pegged exchange rate. Finland made an unsuccessful attempt to revalue its currency. A forceful restrictive fiscal policy would have been necessary to control the expansion in the aggregate demand, but such a policy did not come about in either country.

Financial deregulation was the key to the start of the boom. However, the liberalization was pushed through without any serious public debate. It was not presented as part of a larger policy program, but rather as a series of technical changes. There was no common knowledge of the consequences of financial deregulation, though a few experts warned of the dangers. A critical discussion emerged only afterwards about the deregulation of the financial markets, in particular concerning the sequence of the deregulatory steps.

2.4 THE BUST 1990–93: OUTBREAK, SPREAD AND EFFECTS OF THE CRISIS

2.4.1 The Bust in Finland

Macroeconomic developments

Even if the employment outlook remained good, reasons for concern gradually emerged in the summer of 1989. Stock prices began to fall in April 1989 after the central bank's decision to further revalue the overvalued currency. An early sign of the brewing storm was the first bankruptcy of a highly leveraged listed investment company (*Mancon*) in the spring of 1989. Short-term interest rates rose in the autumn by 4 percentage points. At the same time, another listed company, the flagship of the Finnish shipbuilding industry, *Wärtsilä Marine*, filed for bankruptcy. At the end of 1989, the Finnish public was shocked by the news of the suicide of the CEO and president of the Finnish savings bank group's *SKOP-Bank,* Matti Ali-Melkkilä. The rise in interest rates and the fall in stock prices, with fateful consequences for *SKOP-Bank*'s investment strategy, were thought to be a factor contributing to his death. The situation in the banking sector was rapidly deteriorating. In the spring of 1989, the demand for housing slackened, the selling times grew longer and the rise in prices came to a halt. As the stock of unsold housing began to grow, prices gradually started to fall, a devastating process that was to last for four years.

Despite the increase in uncertainty, GDP growth was still 5.4 per cent in 1989, the same as in 1988. However, on a monthly level the output started to contract towards the end of 1989. Unemployment was still at a record low: about 3 per cent in the entire country and only 1 per cent in Helsinki. Throughout 1990, short-term interest rates remained at high levels and asset prices continued to decline. After good results in 1989, the profitability of companies and banks weakened sharply in 1990.

The Finnish economy also faced a series of negative external shocks in 1989–91. There was a clear slowdown in the international economy, and European interest rates rose in 1990. Finland was also affected by the collapse of the Soviet Union and the subsequent reduction in Finnish–Soviet trade in 1990–91. Export earnings decreased 10 per cent in 1991. Furthermore, the Finnish terms of trade deteriorated by more than 15 per cent. This adverse terms-of-trade shock would have required a swift reduction of labour costs or a devaluation/depreciation for Finland to maintain its international competitiveness.

Weak export performance together with sizeable current account deficits (about 5 per cent of GDP) caused growing uncertainty in the foreign exchange market and speculative attacks against the *markka*. The Bank of Finland raised interest rates in order to defend the pegged – and clearly overvalued – exchange rate. On average, short-term rates were 13 per cent in 1989–92. Disinflation was faster than anyone had expected and high real interest rates together with shrinking asset values depressed domestic demand. Private investment was reduced by 50 per cent and private consumption by 10 per cent in 1990–93. Disposable household income fell and the savings rate increased.

As a consequence, domestic demand collapsed and GDP fell by 13 per cent from mid-1990 to mid-1993. It was not until 1996 that the pre-crisis GDP level was reached. The negative demand shock affected employment and unemployment as well as public finances. The beginning of the 1990s thus witnessed a radical change from almost full employment to the longest mass unemployment in Finnish history. The demand for labour fell within three years (from 1990 to 1993) by almost 20 per cent and the rate of unemployment rose from 3.5 to 20 per cent. The fall in demand for labour was strongest in the private sector, but the public sector – mainly local government – contributed as well. For the first time in modern Finnish history, public employment decreased (by 10 per cent in 1992–94).

Both the central government and local governments took harsh measures to reduce public spending. Notwithstanding the increasingly restrictive fiscal measures, very large fiscal deficits appeared and the development of public debt turned explosive. In order to reduce fiscal deficits, the government increased income taxes, payroll taxes and consumption taxes in 1992–94. At the same time, taxes on profits and capital income were reduced.

The sharp fall in share prices and real estate weakened company balance sheets during 1989–92 and reduced the net wealth of households. The corporate sector responded to the crisis by cutting costs and selling off assets. This further sharpened the debt deflation spiral in the economy. As the numbers of sellers increased and buyers decreased, prices fell. The downturn in the economy was followed by a marked increase in the number of bankruptcies.[37] This led to a further fall in investment and consumption and thus forced the economy deeper into depression.

During the boom, households had increased their consumption in relation to disposable income and the savings rate turned negative. During the depression the opposite happened. Within three years the savings rate climbed from minus 2 per cent of disposable income to plus 10 per cent. High real interest rates in combination with weaker expectations led to falling investment, first in the construction sector.

Economic policies

After the parliamentary election in March 1991, the new Centre-Right government under prime minister Esko Aho was immediately faced with the worst crisis in the post-war period. The new government declared that it would stick to the policy of the pegged exchange rate, much to the surprise of its traditional supporters in the electorate and its economic advisers. The Bank of Finland supported this policy, and the government had to back it.

The Swedish decision to unilaterally peg the *krona* to the ECU in May 1991 complicated matters. After prolonged arm-wrestling, the Bank of Finland called upon the government to unilaterally peg the Finnish *markka* to the ECU as well. Many argued for a minor devaluation in conjunction with an ECU-peg, or at least for a rolling back of the 4 per cent revaluation of the *markka* two years earlier. Two members of the board of the Bank of Finland, Markku Puntila and (former prime minister) Kalevi Sorsa, were clearly opposed to any devaluation. Other directors, such as Ele Alenius, Esko Ollila and Bank governor Rolf Kullberg, would have supported such a move. Harri Holkeri, former prime minister, who had returned to his post as one of the executive directors at the central bank, was not present at the decisive meeting on 3 June 1991. According to Kullberg (1996), Holkeri was 'satisfied with the group's decision' to peg the *markka* to the ECU at an unchanged rate.[38]

Governor Kullberg did not like the idea that the board of the central bank would be split in its decisions. Since two influential members of the board made clear that they opposed any exchange rate realignment,

Kullberg was not willing to take a risk and have a vote. As a result, the majority of the board accepted the view of a strong *markka* as a vocal minority proposed that there would be no devaluation when the *markka* was tied to the ECU.

The government could have forced the central bank to accept devaluation. However, there was a clash within the government on this issue. Prime minister Aho – and probably also the majority of the members of the government – was in favour of a mini-devaluation. President Mauno Koivisto also backed the government's devaluation stance.[39] The minister of finance, Iiro Viinanen, was against any devaluation, while the minister of foreign affairs, Paavo Väyrynen, supported a bigger devaluation. However, when the government got the message that the central bank wished to keep the exchange rate unchanged, it decided to support this line of action. The ECU-peg was approved almost unanimously by the parliament.

The decision to peg the *markka* to the ECU was of no help to the Finnish economy. The exchange rate was still overvalued and interest rates remained high. GDP and employment continued to fall. As devaluation was ruled out for political reasons, the government tried to resort to new incomes policy measures. The discussions between the government, unions and employers started in August and continued until November 1991. The objective of this 'internal' devaluation was to render an external devaluation unnecessary.[40] The government wished to reduce nominal wages by 5 per cent. Prime minister Aho decided to put the former Social Democratic prime minister and then board member of the Bank of Finland, Kalevi Sorsa, in charge of the negotiations on 20 September 1991. The heads of the central trade union organizations approved an agreement which would have lowered nominal wages by 3 per cent and shifted 4 per cent of pension contributions from employers to employees, thus cutting the employers' labour cost by 5 per cent. The chairman of the Federation of Trade Unions (SAK), Lauri Ihalainen, described the birth of the Sorsa package as follows:

> It was an exceptionally difficult matter in principle. The idea was to make a wage-cutting deal in the hope that it would prevent devaluation and enable us to cope with the situation via so-called flexibility. I was personally involved in the talks and after a lot of deliberation we got a decision made in SAK, but it was an extremely painful process.[41]

However, the package was subsequently shelved after two weeks of intensive negotiations, because the powerful trade unions (paper and metal industry workers) within the export industry did not accept it. They understood that an 'internal' devaluation was not the best alternative for the export industry.

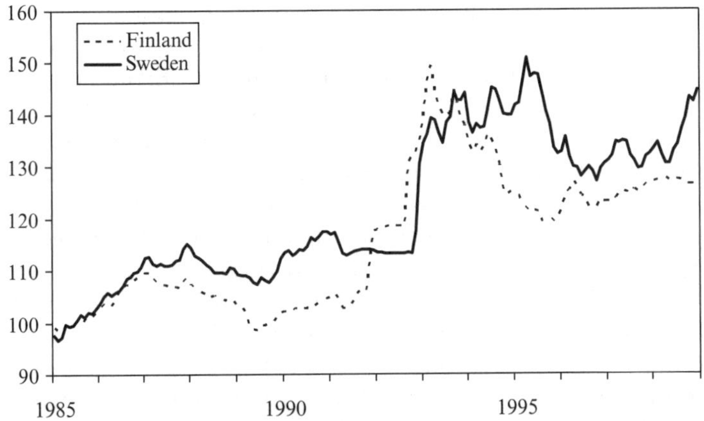

Figure 2.9 The Finnish and Swedish exchange rates against the ECU basket, 1985–99 (1985=100)

When it became apparent that there would be no reduction of nominal wages, the credibility of the pegged exchange rate collapsed. In the face of the currency outflow, the Bank of Finland tried to support the exchange rate by raising the overnight rate of interest to 50 per cent. It also pushed the one-month inter-bank market rate (Helibor) to 27 per cent. However, these interest rates were not high enough to stop the run on the Bank's reserves. These drastic measures only weakened the credibility of the pegged rate. Eventually, the Bank of Finland was forced to devalue the *markka* by 14 per cent on 15 November 1991 (Figure 2.9).

It is not very likely that the implementation of the Sorsa package would have improved economic growth during the crisis. A wage cut would certainly have improved competitiveness, slowed inflation, curbed purchasing power and therefore improved the current account as well as lowering interest rates – but probably only for a while. Another problem was that it would have strengthened deflationary developments, which would then have exacerbated debt problems and pushed the Finnish economy deeper into crisis.

A common view of the Finnish crisis is that it became deep because of idiosyncratic export problems caused by the Soviet collapse in 1990–91. This was certainly a severe exogenous shock as about 20 per cent of Finnish exports went to the Soviet Union in the 1980s. In hindsight, the collapse of the Soviet trade caused only a temporary export shock; total exports decreased by 10 per cent in 1991. Such a shock would not alone have been sufficient to cause a major recession. However, it is difficult to say what the effect of the 1991 export shock on investor confidence was.[42]

The collapse of the Soviet Union placed a burden on Finland also indirectly via world trade. The reunification of Germany – which can also be considered a consequence of the political weakening of the Soviet Union – boosted Germany's budget deficit and fuelled inflation. Due to the anti-inflation policy of the *Bundesbank*, European interest rates climbed in the ERM – within which Finland was committed to keep its exchange rate pegged. This in turn deepened the recession in Western Europe. Exports to Germany grew due to the reconstruction in East Germany, but export demand in other European countries as well as in North America fell in 1991.

During the European currency crisis in September 1992, the capital outflow from Finland increased and the Bank of Finland lost reserves. At this stage, there was no alternative but to leave the ECU-peg. Finland let the *markka* float on 8 September 1992. The *markka* rate fell by about 10 per cent that month and depreciated by a further 20 per cent in subsequent months (Figure 2.9).

2.4.2 The Bust in Sweden

Macroeconomic developments

As in Finland, the boom in Sweden ended in 1989–90. The main driving force behind the bust was the strong and unexpected upturn in the real rate of interest adjusted for taxes. The Swedish rate of inflation decreased markedly after having reached a peak of about 10 per cent in 1990 (Figure 2.2). Inflationary expectations, which followed actual inflation with a small time lag, started to decrease around 1991. A major tax reform, dubbed 'the tax reform of the century', carried out in 1990–91, worsened the conditions for loan-financed investments and favoured savings.

International factors forced Swedish real interest rates upwards, in particular the German reunification, which induced the *Bundesbank* to raise German and thus European interest rates. The *krona* was subject to several speculative attacks due to the falling credibility of the pegged *krona* rate policy. The *Riksbank* had to defend the *krona* rate by raising the Swedish short-term interest rates to a level unseen in the rest of Europe.

When the real rate of interest rose, the price of assets declined in a downward spiral. The fall in asset prices reduced fortunes, since they had been financed by loans of which the nominal value remained unchanged. The downturn became cumulative through expectations that asset prices would continue to fall.[43] The number of bankruptcies increased dramatically.[44] Söderström (1996, pp. 174–9) estimated that the value of tangible assets in Sweden declined by about 30 per cent, from SEK 3500 billion to SEK 2500 billion. He also assumed that the private sector tried to counteract the wealth loss by increasing its financial savings by amortizing its loans and thereby trying to rebuild its equity.[45] Households also increased savings by cutting down on consumption, primarily of durable consumer goods. The savings ratio increased from a negative level at the end of the 1980s to about 8 per cent in 1993. This change in private savings was a significant feature of the crisis.

At this point, it became apparent that the many years of regulated low interest rates had resulted in considerable over-investment. The rise in the real rate of interest revealed excessive holdings of assets, mainly in the form of housing, at the beginning of the 1990s. The revaluation of property and other assets brought with it an abrupt freeze on investment within the housing sector – a sector that had previously been considered a major engine of the Swedish economy. In addition, the last parts of the capital account controls were abolished in 1989, inducing an outflow of capital from Sweden.

As in Finland, the real interest rate shock created a sharp fall in aggregate demand. Unemployment increased from a level of around 2 per cent to a level close to the OECD average of over 8 per cent. Employment fell sharply. The number of bankruptcies skyrocketed just as in Finland. In 1990 inflation was 10 per cent per annum; in the mid-1990s it was down to 2 per cent. Available indices for asset prices show deep deflation during the years 1990–93 (Figure 2.7).

The rapid increase in real interest rates undermined the financial system, creating a banking crisis. The government intervened to prevent a major financial collapse. A bank support authority was set up and two banks, *Nordbanken* and *Gotabanken*, ended up as government-owned.

As a consequence of the decline in economic activity, the rise in unemployment and government support to the financial sector, the budget deficit increased alarmingly. The national debt in relation to GDP reached the highest figure registered since World War II, considerably higher than during OPEC II. The expansion of the national debt occurred more or less automatically; it was the result not of discretionary decisions but rather of the workings of automatic stabilizers.

Economic policies

The Centre-Right government that came to power after the election in 1991 was firmly set to continue the pegged *krona* rate policy. From the start it chose to focus on supply-side policies, that is, on structural reforms of the Swedish economy to increase its growth potential. However, the new government soon faced the same catastrophic developments as in Finland.

Domestic developments – a growing financial crisis, a fall in industrial output and rising unemployment – undermined the credibility of the pegged *krona* rate. Stabilization policy was trapped in a situation where external conditions (the currency crisis) required contractionary measures, while domestic considerations (the banking crisis) demanded expansionary policy. The more the *Riksbank* tried to defend the pegged *krona* rate by raising interest rates, the deeper the domestic crisis became.

With the European currency markets facing unrest in September 1992, the *Riksbank* defended the *krona* by significantly raising its overnight rates. For a very short period, the marginal interest rate, the overnight rate, amounted to 500 per cent. The government and the opposition party, the Social Democrats, agreed to back up jointly two austerity packages in September to avoid a devaluation of the *krona*. Bengt Dennis, governor of the *Riksbank*, played a highly active role in this process.[46] However, the defence of the *krona* broke down in November 1992 when the *krona* came under massive speculative attack. A floating exchange rate was introduced on 19 November 1992, amounting to a substantial depreciation of the Swedish currency – close to 30 per cent (Figure 2.9).

The downturn was halted by the depreciation of the *krona* and the Swedish economy turned upward during 1993. As had been the case after the devaluations in the 1970s and early 1980s, exports and thus industrial output increased. But the crisis left a lasting legacy in the form of high national debt and high unemployment during the rest of the 1990s.

2.4.3 The Common Pattern

The recessions in Finland and Sweden started with an increase in the real rate of interest and, after a while, a debt deflation process set in. In this regard, it is proper to classify the crisis as a real interest rate crisis that spread to all parts of society via the balance sheets of companies and households. The value of assets fell as the real interest rate rose, while the nominal value of debts remained unchanged. The losses of wealth became enormous, forcing an adjustment of portfolios, leading to lower consumption and investments and an increase in savings. The harder households and companies tried to improve their wealth position by selling assets, the deeper the crisis became.

In parallel with the domestic banking crisis, Finland and Sweden were hurt by their overvalued currencies and the weakened credibility of their pegged exchange rates. The central banks were forced to raise domestic interest rates to defend the pegged rates against speculative attacks, which worsened the domestic situation. The process continued until Finland and Sweden were forced to let their currencies float and depreciate during the fall of 1992. Afterwards, as interest rates were reduced, the crisis was checked and the recovery eventually started.

The process demonstrates the difficulties inherent in a policy of pegged exchange rates in a world of free capital markets during a debt deflation process. Falling asset prices, financial instability, widespread bankruptcies and banking crises cannot be countered successfully as long as the defence of the pegged exchange rate requires high domestic interest rates.[47]

2.5 THE RECOVERY 1993–2000

2.5.1 The Case of Finland

Macroeconomic developments

The floating of the *markka* in September 1992 allowed the Bank of Finland to cut short-term interest rates by 10 percentage points within a couple of months. If we believe that excessive monetary tightening was the main cause of the recession, then it is proper to conclude that the biggest macroeconomic change contributing to the recovery was the loosening of monetary policy, including the currency depreciation in the aftermath of the 1992 EMS crisis. The lowering of interest rates helped to first stabilize and then reflate asset prices, ending the deflationary process. Savings rates started to fall and private consumption and investment began to grow again in 1994. The Finnish economy started to recover by the end of 1993. After that the Finnish GDP grew on average about 4.5 per cent annually during the rest of the 1990s (Figure 2.1).

Net exports were the first component of GDP to recover, improving already at the darkest moment of the recession in 1991 (not because of increasing exports but due to declining imports). In 1993, exports clearly exceeded the pre-crisis level. The average rate of growth of Finnish exports in 1992–2000 was high, about 10 per cent per annum. As a result, the volume in 2000 was more than double the pre-crisis level.[48] Such growth went beyond all expectations. Three major factors explain it: the depreciation of the exchange rate, wage moderation and strong productivity growth.

The Finnish currency depreciated in 1991–93, first by the devaluation in November 1991 and then by the floating after September 1992. The cumulative depreciation of the external value of the *markka* was more than 30 per cent. It rapidly led to a significant improvement in the competitiveness of exports. The persistent competitiveness problem, which constrained Finnish exports in 1989–91, was thus solved when the Finnish *markka* was allowed to float with many other EMS currencies in the autumn of 1992.

Export growth was clearly faster than the development of domestic demand, which remained subdued and did not exceed the 1990 level in real terms until 1999. In this respect, Finland differed from other European countries, where the growth contributions of external and internal sources were much more balanced. Rapid export growth together with depressed domestic demand caused an unexpectedly strong improvement in the current account, which went quickly from a deficit of 5 per cent of GDP to a surplus of 7 per cent of GDP in a few years.

The effect of the depreciation turned out to be surprisingly long-lasting. According to the standard view of macroeconomic textbooks, a nominal change in the exchange rate has only a temporary effect on production. In the long run, prices, not volumes, are affected. This pattern is not supported by the Finnish post-crisis experience: the effects of depreciation at the beginning of the 1990s were maintained well into the first years of the 21st century.

Although domestic demand and investment remained depressed throughout the 1990s, the growth of GDP in the post-crisis years was impressive. In 1994–2000, the annual growth rate averaged 4.5 per cent. As a result, the rate of unemployment was reduced from 17 per cent in 1994 to 10 per cent in 2000 and to 6 per cent in 2008. Total employment rose by 25 per cent at the same time, and the employment rate increased by 11 percentage points. In 2007, the aggregate employment exceeded the pre-crisis level. Employment could have increased more quickly if economic growth had been stronger in labour-intensive sectors such as services and construction. However, until 2000 the main contributors to Finnish economic growth were exports and industrial production, which helped to improve average labour productivity while making economic growth less labour-intensive.

Although the improvement in competitiveness was initially achieved through the depreciation of the *markka*, the depreciation was not permanent. Part of it was clearly due to temporary overshooting. The Finnish currency appreciated again in 1995–96 before it was irreversibly linked to the euro (Figure 2.9). More lasting factors contributed positively to competitiveness, most importantly wage moderation and productivity growth. From 1995, wage moderation was achieved through economy-wide agreements between the government and the labour market parties. Wage moderation was supported by tax reductions – average income tax rate was reduced by 8 percentage points in 1996–2007.

The recovery period was characterized by rapid productivity growth. Finland made a qualitative leap from an economic structure dominated by mostly resource-based heavy industries to one with knowledge-based, mostly ICT, industries as a leading sector. It is rare for a new industry to become dominant so quickly, and the growth of the electronics (ICT) industry in the post-recession years was truly spectacular. Its output multiplied more than sixfold and its relative share grew from 8 per cent to over

27 per cent of total industrial production – while total production almost doubled. In 1992, the metal, paper and pulp, food and chemical industries were all bigger than the electronics sector, but by 2000 it had overtaken them to become the single largest sector. In 2000, Finland's *Nokia* Group was the world's biggest manufacturer of mobile phones.

The great depression and subsequent recovery during the 1990s led to a fundamental 'Schumpeterian' restructuring of the Finnish economy.[49] Many inefficient establishments were closed and more efficient ones opened within existing firms and industries. In many cases, full exit or entry was not observed but labour was shifted from less productive to more productive plants. There were thus microeconomic forces behind the Finnish recovery, involving structural changes and creative destruction. Productivity improved due to investment in machinery and equipment, private and public investment in R&D, training and education.

The average labour productivity in Finland moved closer to the productivity frontier of the United States and surpassed that of EU15 during the second half of the 1990s. The growth of industrial production in 1992–2000 was higher than ever before, an average of 7 per cent per annum. The annual rate of labour productivity growth in manufacturing was also exceptionally high.

The role of the 'new economy' was decisive in the Finnish productivity miracle. The rise of wireless communication technology, often described as the *Nokia* cluster after *Nokia*, the leading firm in this field in the 1990s, manifested these structural changes. The spectacular ICT sector growth contributed significantly to the growth of Finnish GDP, exports and productivity. The share of business sector value-added produced by the ICT sector rose by almost 10 percentage points in the 1990s. Industrial R&D spending grew faster than in any other OECD country throughout the 1980s and 1990s.

The depreciation put more strain on firms in the closed (non-tradable) sector, which had acquired large foreign currency debt. The real value of their debt rose sharply through the devaluation and the depreciation that occurred with the floating of the *markka*. Closed sector companies did not have offsetting growth in exports to rely on. On the contrary, the revenues of these firms were hurt by the contraction of domestic purchasing power triggered by the devaluation and the depreciation of the *markka*. The closed sector was thus squeezed from two directions: first, by a rising real debt burden and, second, by falling domestic demand.

Economic policies

Prior to the floating of the *markka*, a common view was that it would be disastrous, and there would not be any easy way to achieve lower interest rates, except through a painful process of structural adjustments. However, to the surprise of politicians and the public alike it was suddenly possible to reduce interest rates by almost 10 percentage points in a short time. Finland adopted an inflation target in 1993, and three years later, in 1996, decided to fully join the euro area. In 1999 the *markka* was irrevocably pegged to the euro.

As the economic crisis with its mass unemployment and tight fiscal policy made Esko Aho's Centre-Right coalition unpopular, the Social Democrats regained power in the parliamentary election of 1995. A new 'rainbow coalition' led by the Social Democratic Party leader Paavo Lipponen, consisting of Social Democrats, Conservatives, the Green Party and even the Left Alliance (the former Communist Party), stayed in power until 2003.

The first years of the recovery phase, 1994–97, were characterized by tight fiscal policy aimed at consolidating public finances. Within seven years, 1994–2000, the total public sector financial balance moved from a deficit of 6 per cent of GDP to a surplus of 7 per cent of GDP.

It may be tempting to suspect that the impressive economic performance of post-recession Finland – high growth, rising productivity and employment – was caused by a wave of structural reforms. However, there were few major institutional reforms – apart from the aforementioned public support to R&D and higher education – which could have improved productive potential and work incentives. Nevertheless, gradual change took place when many income support schemes lagged behind wage increases and labour taxes were reduced.

At the end of the 1990s, the level of social spending (excluding unemployment-related expenditures) was about 10 per cent lower than at the beginning of the decade although the number of pensioners had increased. The volume of public consumption, that is public services, was reduced by 10 per cent in the midst of the recession. At the same time, other public expenditures increased, mostly owing to increased social spending caused by high unemployment. Later on, when unemployment declined, spending on transfers started to decrease. The budgetary cuts were initially justified as necessary savings, and later as a method to improve the work incentives of the unemployed. Most voters accepted them reluctantly as they were presented as the only way to save the basic structure of the Finnish welfare state.

All European countries went through reforms and adjustments during the 1990s. Yet all of them have ultimately remained examples of the European social model with strongly regulated labour markets. Perhaps the biggest change in the 1990s in Finland was the adoption and wide acceptance of a policy of long-term wage moderation. This was an expected response, even in unionized labour markets, owing to high unemployment. For the unions, this represented a positive alternative to being marginalized or excluded from decision-making. The Centre-Right government in power in 1991–95 expressed its intentions to reduce the role of trade unions and to abolish the old corporatist wage-bargaining system dominated by central organizations of trade unions and of employers. These initiatives were successfully opposed by the trade unions, which twice threatened to call a general strike.

In the 1990s, fiscal policy was thus more or less procyclical in Finland. In the first half of the 1990s, fiscal policy was tightened by discretionary tax increases and spending cuts. These policies aimed at fiscal consolidation and fulfilment of the EMU convergence criteria. The large deficit was not much helped by the spending cuts made in the same years; higher taxes and reduced public spending squeezed domestic demand and increased unemployment, which led to higher than expected social spending and lower than expected tax revenue.

In the latter half of the 1990s, lower interest rates and the previous budgetary cuts created new leeway for policy-makers, who used the higher than expected tax revenues to finance tax cuts and increase public spending. In the environment of falling real interest rates, improved competitiveness and growing employment, expansionary fiscal policy was no threat to fiscal stability. The spectacular improvement in fiscal balances achieved in 1995–2000 was caused not by fiscal tightening but by strong growth, lower interest payments and declining unemployment-related expenditures. After six years of rapid growth and falling unemployment, Finland had a record high (7 per cent of GDP) fiscal surplus in 2000.

2.5.2 The Case of Sweden

Macroeconomic developments

The depreciation of the *krona* in November 1992 marked the culmination of the crisis and the beginning of the recovery in Sweden. As the *krona* was floating, interest rates were gradually lowered. The turnaround and the recovery started in 1993. Economic growth turned positive in 1993 and remained strong throughout the rest of the 1990s, with the exception of a short downturn in 1996–97 (Figure 2.1).

As in Finland, exports were the major driving force behind the Swedish recovery, growing strongly and increasing as a share of GDP. In 1992 exports amounted to 28 per cent of GDP. By the end of the decade the number was over 45 per cent – a remarkable development within less than a decade.[50] There is no similar case in Swedish economic history.

Several factors contributed to this sharp expansion in exports. First, the large and persistent depreciation of the *krona* after November 1992 increased Swedish competitiveness. Actually, the Swedish depreciation remained stronger than the Finnish in the mid-1990s. As in Finland, wage moderation and improvements in productivity facilitated the growth of exports. *Ericsson* held a position in Sweden similar to that of *Nokia* in Finland.[51] Exports were also favourably affected by Sweden's entry into the EU in 1995, which promoted trade directly and indirectly by promoting foreign direct investment, not least in the rapidly growing ICT sector.[52]

The rise in domestic demand during the recovery phase was markedly lower. Both private and public consumption grew more slowly than GDP during the years following the crisis. At the same time, the household savings rate remained at a higher level than before the crisis, indicating a continued improvement in the balance sheets of the private sector.

The effects of the crisis on employment were more prolonged. The low unemployment rate that prevailed during the 1980s was never reached again in the 1990s. Open unemployment started to decline from the high level of around 8–10 per cent by the end of 1997. The high and persistent rate of unemployment contributed to wage moderation in the 1990s and well into the new century.[53]

The move from the pegged exchange rate regime to inflation targeting in 1992–93 had a profound impact on the behaviour of the labour market participants. The new regime of low inflation contributed to non-indexed two-year collective wage agreements in 1993 and to three-year contracts from 1995 until 2008. Judging from the emergence of three-year collective wage agreements, confidence in the new regime of inflation targeting developed quickly. In this sense, it stands out as a successful regime, at least so far. Of course, there is no guarantee that the inflation-targeting regime will remain associated with long-term contracts in the future.[54]

Economic policies

The fall of the *krona* in November 1992 allowed the *Riksbank* to move to lower interest rates. Policy-makers were not ready to go back to a fixed *krona* rate again. The *Riksbank* announced unilaterally a policy of inflation targeting in January 1993. The target rate of inflation was set at a 2 per cent yearly increase within a range of plus/minus 1 per cent.[55] The *Riksbank* declared that the new target range was to be binding from January 1995. The parliament backed the inflation target officially in the spring of 1993. The rate of inflation and inflationary expectation declined surprisingly quickly towards the level set by the *Riksbank*, suggesting that the new monetary policy regime gained credibility.

As in Finland, the government lost the election in the fall of 1994 immediately after the crisis, yielding power to the Social Democratic opposition. There was initially some uncertainty about the economic policies of the new government – was it going to contract or expand fiscal policy? However, uncertainty was dissolved when the new government launched a program of fiscal austerity. As the crisis had caused enormous budget deficits, large cuts in government expenditures and tax increases were deemed necessary by Göran Persson, the new minister of finance.[56]

As the economy was recovering after the floating of the *krona*, the deficit as a share of GDP decreased quickly and government debt in relation to GDP was brought down significantly during the latter part of the 1990s.[57]After a period of tight fiscal policy, Göran Persson moved to the post of prime minister, which he held from 1997 to 2006.

As a consequence of the crisis, the procedure of fiscal policy-making was reformed. Expenditure ceilings were introduced and a surplus target of 2 per cent of GDP over the business cycle was established. The crisis thus brought about a new framework for monetary as well as fiscal policy-making. Since Sweden decided by referendum in September 2003 not to join the euro, it is likely that the inflation-targeting regime will remain in place for the foreseeable future.

2.5.3 The Common Pattern

Finland and Sweden experienced the same path of recovery during the years 1993–2000, shortly after the trough of the crisis. The long recovery was facilitated by sharp depreciation of their currencies and the rapid fall in the short- and long-term interest rates. Monetary policies in both countries turned expansionary after the decision to float in the fall of 1992. The main force behind the recovery was the depreciation of the *markka* and the *krona* that followed the decision to let the two currencies float. The competitive advantage created by the depreciation was surprisingly long-lasting. Exports grew strongly and the surplus on the current account increased, making it possible to reduce the volume of foreign debt held by the public and private sectors.

As the economies started to grow during the recovery, budget deficits were reduced through the workings of automatic stabilizers. During the recovery, tight fiscal policies were directed at bringing about budget surpluses and reducing government debt. The welfare state – that is, the large public sector – in both Finland and Sweden remained basically unchanged during the 1990s although the replacement ratios of many benefits decreased. The recovery did not bring about any major scaling down of public services.

High unemployment explains why the recovery was able to take place without large nominal wage increases. Unemployment fell slowly during the latter half of the 1990s, but employment did not return before the turn of the century to the high levels recorded during the boom years prior to the crisis.

The crisis caused a major restructuring of Finnish and Swedish industries, making them more dynamic and competitive. The rise in information and communication technology (ICT)-related industries, notably *Nokia* in Finland and *Ericsson* in Sweden, constituted a remarkable part of the recovery. Productivity improved significantly during the recovery phase; productivity growth became high and persistent in both countries, above the EU average.

In both countries, financial liberalization contributed to changes in the stabilization regime, causing the end of the pegged exchange rate regime. Both countries adopted initially a floating rate and inflation targeting. Eventually, Finland became a member of the euro area, while Sweden remained outside after the euro referendum in 2003.

2.6 WHY WAS THE PEGGED RATE DEFENDED SO STUBBORNLY?

As seen from the account above, policy-makers in Finland and Sweden defended the pegged exchange rate stubbornly – and at a high cost in terms of output and employment lost. The whole political establishment, as well as the economics profession, supported the hard currency policy right up to the bitter end. Economists often argue that politicians are inclined to adopt short-term expansionary policies that turn out to be inflationary in the long run. However, in Finland and Sweden the opposite pattern was registered in the early 1990s. Policy-makers carried out a contractionary policy in order to avoid inflation in the long run – while bringing about a deep crisis.

This pattern must be explained as the outcome of a learning process of policy-makers and economists alike. In short, the experience of the devaluations (or soft currency policies) and the high rate of inflation in the 1970s and early 1980s accounts for the hard currency policy of the late 1980s.

2.6.1 The Case of Finland

During the immediate post-war decades, Finnish macroeconomic developments were characterized by rapid but unstable growth and chronic balance-of-payments problems. As inflation was faster than in competitor countries, this caused competitiveness problems, which were ultimately solved by devaluations. Major devaluations in 1957, 1967, 1977 and 1982 inspired the development of a theory of devaluation cycles, where a devaluation boosts competitiveness, profitability, investment and growth in the short run but in the long run causes faster domestic inflation than in the rest of the world.

In fact, the Finnish experience of high inflation and repeated devaluations did not differ from that of some other industrialized countries. During the post-war years, the Finnish *markka* tracked the value of the currencies of France, Britain and other Nordic countries relatively closely. However, it weakened appreciably compared with the 'hard' currencies of Germany, Switzerland and Japan. After the collapse of the Bretton Woods system in the early 1970s, Finland tried to continue with a pegged exchange rate policy to keep the average value of the *markka* stable. The average exchange rate was defined by weighting selected currencies according to their shares in Finland's foreign trade.

Devaluations remained a main instrument of Finnish macroeconomic stabilization policies up to the 1980s. Deliberate currency depreciation was used with apparent success during the international recessions of the 1970s and the early 1980s to boost Finnish exports. However, the soft currency policy faced increasing criticism – not only from the central bank but also from economists. In fact, there had been an almost constant debate among economists and central bankers about the desirability and usefulness of devaluation policies since the 1950s.

Eventually, a critical view of the policy of repeated devaluations emerged – first among economists. Now, it was argued that such a policy would gradually shape the expectations and behaviour of economic agents in a way that eventually would reduce the benefits of a devaluation policy.[58] Seen in the long run, the devaluation cycle would create higher inflation than in other countries, without any lasting gains in economic growth.[59]

The policy of discretionary devaluations was relatively easy to conduct in the environment of regulated capital movements in the 1960s and 1970s and even at the beginning of the 1980s. It was possible to decide about devaluations in the spirit of consensus when all parties – especially trade unions – were taking part. Policy-makers were able to conduct such operations without the fear of adverse financial market reactions because international capital movements were regulated and foreign currency speculation was thus limited.

The growing integration of international financial markets in the early 1980s highlighted the need to break away from the Finnish devaluation cycle. After the 1982 devaluation, strong support emerged among Finnish economists and politicians for the stable *markka* policy. The anti-devaluation policy gained considerable credibility when the Bank of Finland succeeded in defending the *markka* in August 1986 against a small-scale speculative attack. At that time the Bank of Finland quickly ended exchange rate speculations by temporarily raising the call rate to 40 per cent.

The stable *markka* policy was also supported by developments in economic theory, stressing the role of credibility and norms, and downplaying traditional Keynesian demand management. This change was related to the rational expectations revolution and to growing support for monetarism. The new theories essentially suggested that monetary policy-makers should concentrate on fighting inflation and fostering stability and credibility. Leading politicians adopted the new view as well. After the devaluations at the beginning of the 1980s, there was a strong wish – openly declared – to keep the devaluation window closed. The pegged rate was to act as an anchor for economic policy and as an insurance against inflation.

The currency crisis in 1991–92 was viewed as the ultimate test of the pegged exchange rate policy. The problems in the foreign exchange market were regarded as an opportunity to prove the will to stick to the pegged *markka* policy, to prove that the old way of devaluations was finally abandoned. Politicians were given a unique opportunity to gain credibility for what they had been saying for about a decade. If this battle could be won, the expectations of future devaluations would become weaker.

A freely floating *markka* and a price stabilization target did not appear on the agenda, either within the economics profession or among policy-makers, until after the defence of the *markka* had broken down. At the beginning of the 1990s, pegged exchange rates were the norm in Western Europe as well as in Finland. Policy-makers thus had to choose between fighting to maintain the peg and gain credibility for such a policy or giving up and returning to a devaluation strategy that they had condemned. Politicians also wished to prepare the Finnish economy for future membership of the EU, and it was believed that abandoning the currency peg would harm that goal.[60] The political incentives were clearly in favour of a stubborn defence.

2.6.2 The Case of Sweden

The Swedish defence of the pegged *krona* rate, with an interest rate of 500 per cent for a very brief period and a broad political backing for the 'crisis packages' in September 1992, attracted international attention. Hardly any other country showed such determination to keep its exchange rate pegged. Many currencies with a pegged rate were victims of speculative attacks during September 1992 when Great Britain, Italy and Finland adopted a floating exchange rate. Sweden was forced by speculation to let the *krona* float two months later, however, on 19 November 1992.

Why was the pegged exchange rate of the *krona* so forcefully protected in the fall of 1992? The answer is found in the lessons economists and politicians drew from the devaluations of the 1970s and 1980s. The pegged exchange rate was an instrument to achieve low and constant inflation and at the same time function as an intermediate target for the *Riksbank*. The main lesson was that Sweden ought to avoid a 'soft peg' and adopt a hard currency policy.

This lesson emerged gradually in the 1980s. This view, in which inflation stabilization is seen as the all-embracing norm for economic policy and a pegged exchange rate is regarded as the primary tool for achieving a stable price level, was first advocated by the SNS Economic Policy Group in its reports from 1985 to 1992. The Social Democratic government's January 1991 budget proposal was firmly in favour of a low-inflation policy, giving higher priority to low inflation than to full employment. The ECU-peg in May 1991 was a part of this policy.

The non-socialist parties in opposition also embraced the new rule-based philosophy. In the run-up to the 1991 election, the Conservative Party and the Liberal Party prepared an economic policy program, *Ny start för Sverige* (A new start for Sweden), much inspired by rule-based thinking and supply-side economics. The opposition parties arranged a series of five joint seminars with economists from February to April 1991. These seminars revealed how deeply rooted rule-based thinking was with leading economists. One economist, Ulf Jakobsson, described the economists' perception of fiscal, monetary and tax policy as follows:[61]

> There is now consensus that the possibilities of stabilizing the economy through fiscal policy are strongly limited . . . In the future, the role of fiscal policy will be severely restricted. After all, we have chosen to pursue a pegged exchange rate policy. . . . We have to invest in credibility and use the economic downturn to bring down the rate of inflation. . . . Fiscal policy can only cause harm, whereas structural policy is of the utmost importance. An internal devaluation cannot be recommended.

The outcome was that *Ny start för Sverige* emphasized growth and supply policies such as deregulation, privatization and structural reforms. The program was founded on a pegged exchange rate for the *krona*. It also proposed a more independent role for the *Riksbank*, as well as promoting economic growth as the means to 'pull Sweden through the crisis'. The crisis itself was described as having been caused by the Social Democratic choice of 'the third way'. Anne Wibble (1996, p. 213), who became minister of finance 1991–94, noted that the economists present at the spring 1991 seminars all conveyed the same message, that of 'pursuing a hard currency policy'. Anne Wibble (1994, p. 18) described the planning of the non-socialist government before the transfer of power:

> The program, which we had worked out together with the Conservative Party during a series of seminars in the winter and spring of 1991, shows good insight into the requirements of structural policy, but – for explicable reasons – not the acute crisis that we faced during our first autumn in power. Needless to say, neither did we have insight into the currency crisis we had to take care of in the autumn of 1992.

The new government that took over after the 1991 election was determined not to use changes in the exchange rate, that is, devaluations, as an economic policy measure. Anne Wibble referred to her own experience of earlier devaluations, which 'had not solved any problems'. She partly attributed the attitude of the government to her own experience (Wibble, 1994, p. 23):

> From the very start, the government had appointed the pegged exchange rate as the anchor of economic policy. From my days as a political officer working for previous non-socialist governments, I had learned that reoccurring devaluations did not solve anything. After the 1982 super-devaluation, the Social Democrat government had made it clear that the devaluation was the last of its kind. New devaluations would impair the credibility of Sweden. In addition, the Governing Board of the Riksbank had decided to tie the Swedish krona to the ECU index on 17 May 1991, i.e. to the European Community currency basket that was formed to further support fixed exchange rates. In this, we were fully intent on continuing the policy of the previous government.

As the newly appointed minister of finance, she considered it her prime target to counteract the acute crisis by strengthening the credibility of the pegged exchange rate by limiting the budget deficit through raising taxes and reducing expenditures. So, during its first year in power, the non-socialist government stood firmly by the pegged exchange rate policy.

Strengthening the budget became the lodestar of the agreements reached between the non-socialist government and the Social Democratic opposition in September 1992 when the *krona* was under speculative attack. The threat of a new devaluation gave rise to a unique political unity rallying around the pegged exchange rate. At the end of September, the government and the opposition tried to carry through an internal devaluation by reducing employer contributions, a step that the minister of finance considered to be a first attempt at dissolving the rule-based policy. The ministry of finance planned for further internal devaluations, but these plans were abandoned when the *krona* was allowed to float in November 1992.

The official forecasts from the *Konjunkturinstitutet* (the National Institute of Economic Research), the *Riksbank* and the ministry of finance turned out to be severely wrong. They were based on macroeconomic models made for regulated financial markets, which did not include the financial processes that created the crisis of the 1990s. They were not able to handle a process driven by an increase in the real rate of interest, the fall of asset prices, international currency crises and currency speculation. The forecast errors thus became greater as the crisis deepened. Likewise, the commercial banks, in whose own interest it should have been to forecast the financial crisis, were not able to publish any warnings of the gathering storm.

The macroeconomic development surprised not only forecasters but also policy-makers responsible for stabilization policy. They were dumbfounded by both the strength of the boom phase and the economic recession. Kjell-Olof Feldt (1994, p. 67), minister of finance 1982–90, described the lack of understanding in the early 1990s as follows: 'Today, it is clear that neither the Social Democratic government during its last years in power, nor the non-socialist coalition that came into power in 1991, were aware of the extent of the economic abyss that spread out before them.' Bengt Dennis, governor of the *Riksbank* 1982–93, arrived at a similar assessment of the crisis:

> The Riksbank predicted to the same meagre degree as the Swedish Financial Supervisory Authority and the Ministry of Finance the actual extent and depth of the banking crisis. We did detect increasing problems in the financial sector at an early stage, but we expected the course of events to calmly fizzle out thanks to the reconstruction we knew we would have to undertake.[62]

The financial markets in Sweden had been regulated since World War II – so long that economists, forecasters, policy-makers, bankers and the public lacked knowledge about the role open and freely functioning financial markets can play. This knowledge was lost behind the thick walls of capital account controls. There was initially hardly any understanding of how the prerequisites for the stabilization policy had changed as Sweden had become more integrated with international financial markets.

2.6.3 The Common Pattern

In Finland as well as in Sweden the pegged exchange rate was strongly defended during the first phase of the crisis. The main reason for this determined policy response was the lessons drawn from the devaluation policy during the 1970s and early 1980s in both countries. The major lesson emerging from this backward-looking process of learning was to avoid a 'soft currency' policy.[63] The common opinion among both economists and policy-makers was that the devaluations had not solved the economic problems in the long run, only masked them in the short run.

A pegged exchange rate policy was viewed as a more promising strategy – as a way of breaking away from the devaluation cycle. The idea was that the pegged rate should act as the anchor for monetary policy and serve as the tool to achieve low inflation and thus create a proper climate for growth and employment. Both countries also chose to move closer to the EEC, by pegging their exchange rates to the ECU.

An additional reason why the pegged exchange rate was defended so energetically was a general lack of knowledge of the workings of financial markets, the role of portfolio imbalances, of boom–bust patterns and of speculative capital flows in a world of pegged exchange rates and free capital flows across borders. Policy-makers and economists in Finland and Sweden did not understand that the financial deregulation of the 1980s had fundamentally changed the prerequisites for the pegged exchange rate policy. There existed hardly any knowledge of financial and banking crises. The crisis thus came as a surprise to policy-makers, economists and the public in both countries.

2.7 POLICY LESSONS FROM THE CRISIS

Depressions usually start a process of re-thinking economic policies. Indeed, the crisis of the early 1990s in Finland and Sweden set off a lively debate among economists and policy-makers about the proper strategy and institutions for stabilization policy-making. This process led eventually to the adoption of a new macroeconomic policy regime in both countries. Although, the preceding boom-and-bust patterns in Finland and Sweden were almost identical, Finland eventually adopted a permanently fixed exchange rate by joining the euro, while Sweden decided to remain outside the euro area with a floating rate.

2.7.1 The Case of Finland

There are reasons to expect that the severity of the Finnish depression would have led to calls for major policy reforms. However, this was not the case. On the contrary, it was widely thought, at least among policy-makers, that there was nothing wrong with the basic design of monetary and fiscal policies. Even after the collapse of the pegged rate in November

1991, the prevailing view was that the old model of economic policies based on a pegged exchange rate for the *markka* should be continued. Many policy-makers believed that the crisis was caused by the irrational or nearsighted behaviour of banks, investors, consumers and trade unions – thus not by faulty policies. Although the Finnish currency was allowed to float for four years, 1992–96, together with many other European currencies, the long-term goal of exchange rate stability was not abandoned. As soon as it was possible, Finland joined the ERM in 1996 and the EMU fully in January 1999 by becoming a member of the euro area when it was founded.

An important lesson from the crisis was that indebtedness and financial risks within the private sector ought to be more closely supervised. Bank supervision was reformed and a new agency with more powers was established to replace the old Bank Supervision Agency.

The recession caused growing budget deficits and a rising public debt in 1991–93. The fiscal balance deteriorated as a result of the crisis by almost 15 per cent of GDP in 1989–93. This was a shock to politicians and bureaucrats, accustomed in the past to almost permanent surpluses in public finances. Fiscal policy was tightened already in 1992 in order to restore a public sector surplus. This target was achieved in 1999, after seven years of deficits and various austerity measures. Tight fiscal policies were continued after the recession, and the maintenance of 'sound' fiscal balance became a cornerstone of post-crisis economic policies. Most of the post-recession budgetary savings were made in different income transfer programs, while public consumption and investment were allowed to grow in order to maintain and improve employment.

During the crisis, labour taxes were increased heavily. However, the post-crisis fiscal adjustment was not carried out by raising taxes but by restricting the growth of public expenditures. In fact, it was the aim of the post-recession governments (led by the Social Democrats) to reduce taxes on labour and improve work incentives through benefit reforms. A new flat tax of 25 per cent for profits and capital income was introduced in Finland in 1993, replacing the old system with high nominal marginal tax rates and relatively low effective tax rates. Raising other taxes initially compensated for this change. As a result, labour incomes and private consumption were more heavily taxed by the end of the 1990s than before.

National incomes policies in the form of social pacts and highly coordinated collective bargaining have played a central role in Finnish macroeconomic development for a long time. After unsuccessful attempts by the Centre-Right government in 1991–95 to decentralize the wage-setting system, the broad coalition governments of 1995–2003 returned to the old regime of centralized incomes policies, supporting wage moderation through centralized wage agreements, and by tax reductions and by giving a voice to the social partners in questions related to social policy and industrial relations. In 2007, however, under the new Centre-Right government, largely because of initiatives by the employers, a less centralized model was adopted with more flexibility to individual industrial sectors and to individual companies in wage setting.

2.7.2 The Case of Sweden

The conventional view regarding the proper design of stabilization policies changed fundamentally due to the financial crisis and the move to a floating exchange rate for the *krona*. The basic lesson was that Sweden should not return to a pegged but adjustable exchange rate for its currency. Financial deregulation and the internalization of capital markets meant that any pegged rate was threatened by strong speculative pressure whenever inconsistencies between the pegged rate and domestic developments appeared.

In January 1993, the *Riksbank* announced an inflation target for its policy to be effective as of January 1995. The target was set at a 2 per cent rate of inflation per annum within an interval of plus/minus 1 percentage point. With this step, the *Riksbank* officially replaced the pegged exchange rate with an inflation norm. The *Riksbank* took this decision at its own discretion, without the declared support of the *Riksdag* or the government.

The crisis in the early 1990s affected the institutional environment for economic policy-making to a larger extent than any other event in Sweden during the 20th century.[64] The lessons were primarily learned after the failed defence of the *krona* in 1992, but were based to a large extent on experience and research prior to the fall of the *krona*. As long as the *krona* rate remained pegged, verbal support for the hard currency approach was more or less unwavering. But the floating paved the way for a new debate, new investigations and new views.[65] Soon the lessons of the crisis were transformed into new legislation concerning the institutional framework for monetary and fiscal policy.

One major lesson of the crises is that the *Riksbank* should have a clearly defined and legislated price stability target or inflation target for its activities. From this follows that the *Riksbank* should have an independent position which reduces the possibility for the government or other parties to influence monetary policy. By the end of the 1990s, these lessons had been incorporated into new legislation concerning the role of the *Riksbank*. In November 1998, the *Riksdag* passed a new *Riksbank* Act, which entered into force on 1 January 1999.

The Act is based on two principles. First, the target of price stability is written into its fourth paragraph: 'The objective of the *Riksbank* is to maintain a stable monetary value.' The target is not given as an exact number but should be interpreted as equalling price stability or a low rate of inflation. The task of more clearly defining a stable monetary value is delegated to the *Riksbank*.

Second, it gives the *Riksbank* a more independent position: 'The *Riksbank* is responsible for monetary policy. No authority can decide on how the *Riksbank* should deal with monetary policy issues' (*Riksbank* Act §12). The bank is protected from direct political influence through provisions preventing members of the Executive Board, whose job it is to formulate monetary policy, from being a member of parliament, a minister, a government employee or a member of a political party. The lessons for monetary policy and for the institutional changes that followed rested implicitly on the idea that the Swedish financial system will in the future be open towards the rest of the world.

The crisis of the 1990s also provided lessons for fiscal policy that were eventually put into new legislation. The significant budget deficits and the rapid rise in the public debt in 1991–94 were considered by many to be the sign of a lax budget process. Had the budget process been more stringent, the problems would have been less obvious, according to this view. These lessons resulted in a number of institutional reforms carried out during the period 1994–96 with the aim of improving budget discipline in the *Riksdag*. The parliamentary term of office was prolonged from three to four years, which can be seen as way of creating scope for long-term fiscal thinking.[66] A limit was set on public expenditures by the *Riksdag* in the spring of 1995, effective from the spring of 1996. Today, the budget is dealt with by the *Riksdag* with the help of a general budget ceiling approach aimed at restricting the forces that increase public expenditures.

The financial crisis brought about changes concerning deposit insurance and financial supervision. The pre-crisis implicit safeguarding of deposits was transformed into a scheme of explicit deposit insurance after the crisis. The *Riksbank* took it upon itself to systematically monitor the financial system with the aim of 'detecting possible signs of potential financial problems and systemic risks'.[67] The surveillance is reported in the Financial Stability Report (formerly known as the Financial Market Report), of which the first issue was published in November 1997. This report is now published twice a year. The financial crisis also confirmed a division of responsibility between the government and the *Riksbank*. The government, or to be more precise the ministry of finance, should be responsible for solvency issues, while the *Riksbank* should be responsible for the supply of liquidity.[68]

2.7.3 The Common Pattern

The crises in both countries affected the thinking about and thus the design of the institutions for stabilization policy-making. The central bank was given a more independent position. Both countries became members of the European Union in 1995 and thus adopted the convergence criteria of the Maastricht Treaty. Finland eventually moved to full membership in the euro area. Sweden maintained its national currency. Initially, Finland returned to the traditional mode of centralized wage bargaining. Sweden took no such steps. Instead, wage bargaining became less centralized.

The crisis had similar political consequences. In the years of the deep recession, 1991–94, both countries had Centre-Right governments. This was exceptional. A coalition government led by Social Democrats has been the rule in Finland, while a Social Democratic government has been the standard arrangement in Sweden in the post-World War II period. The crisis had a clear impact on election outcomes. In Finland, the Social Democrats returned to power via a coalition government in 1995. In Sweden, the Centre-Right government formed in the fall of 1991 became the victim of the crisis. The Social Democratic party returned to power in the fall of 1994 as the incumbent government was blamed for the crisis. The unique power of the Social Democratic party was re-enforced in the elections of 1998 and 2002,[69] while in Finland the Social Democrats lost control in the election of 2003 but stayed in the government with the Centre party. A Centre-Right government was established in Sweden after the election of 2006 and in Finland after the election of 2007.

As stated above, Finland and Sweden adopted different exchange rate policies around the turn of the century, even though the crises were very similar in both countries. In Sweden, the foundations for a new institutional framework for the monetary and fiscal policies were laid, based on an independent central bank and inflation targeting. Finland, on the other hand, abolished its national currency by adopting the euro. Here the economic twins parted from each other – Finland opted for membership in a monetary union, Sweden for a freely floating exchange rate.

2.8 CONCLUSIONS

Finland and Sweden were economic twins in the sense that they followed the same economic path during the last quarter of the 20th century. They were hit simultaneously by a crisis that was the most severe of the post-World War II period. The anatomy of the crisis was identical in the two countries. The financial deregulation of the mid-1980s, while both countries were on pegged exchange rate regimes, was the starting point for the boom–bust cycle. First, it contributed to low real rates of interest and rapid growth in the volume of credit, thus creating a boom at the end of the 1980s. Next, the credit expansion was stopped and both the Finnish and Swedish economies ended up in a deep crisis. The domestic crisis in combination with the unrest on the European currency markets spelled the end of the pegged exchange rate policy in the fall of 1992.

The financial liberalization eventually undermined the pegged rate regimes in Finland and Sweden. This is a clear illustration of the view that a pegged exchange rate, international capital mobility and monetary policy sovereignty do not mix, commonly described as the macroeconomic policy trilemma for an open economy.

The crisis was a balance sheet crisis as changes in the real interest rates, in asset prices and in wealth played a central role in the process of boom and bust. Irving Fisher's theory of debt deflation provides a fruitful approach for analysing the sequence of events leading to the crisis. The crisis was triggered by an increase in the real rate of interest through a rise in the international interest rate level, tighter domestic fiscal and monetary policies, changes in the taxation of interest payments and falling inflation rates. High after-tax real interest rates undermined the value of the assets of households and corporations, creating a process of falling asset prices. This, in turn, led to severe problems in the financial system and large budget deficits as the governments were forced to socialize the losses caused by the debt deflation process.

Why was the crisis allowed to become so deep? One contributing factor was the lack of accurate forecasts and analyses of the effects of financial deregulation in an open economy. The macroeconomic consequences of falling asset prices were not understood by policy-makers. They were unaware of the chain of events they had unleashed. In hindsight, the severe underestimation of the impact of disinflation on portfolio balances and on asset behaviour, aggregate demand, investment and savings and the consequent fall in production was a major error by forecasters, policy-makers and economists before and during the crisis.

This lack of knowledge is easy to explain. Pre-crisis macroeconomic thinking in Finland and Sweden was strongly dominated by the Keynesian approach with its stress on flow concepts and its disregard of financial variables and balance sheet developments. An analysis of balance sheet imbalances moves the focus from aggregate flows to financial stocks such as the assets and liabilities of households and firms. The disregard of the role of portfolio imbalances was largely due to the system of heavy regulation of the financial system in Finland and Sweden that was in place during the post-World War II period up to the financial deregulation in the mid-1980s. As financial markets were held dormant, knowledge of the effects of financial forces became weak.

A strong reason for stressing the importance of the financial system in the type of crisis that hit Finland and Sweden in the early 1990s is the striking similarities between the Finnish–Swedish crisis and other crises that later in the 1990s hit economies that deregulated their financial systems while trying to maintain pegged exchange rates.

The defence of the pegged exchange rate was initially strong and stubborn. The broad political consensus on defending the peg was a reaction to the devaluation policies of the 1970s and 1980s. The goal of the hard currency policy was to prevent a new devaluation cycle with high inflation rates. Eventually, both countries had to give in and let their currencies float. The recovery was then driven by falling interest rates and a strong rise in exports due to the depreciation caused by the floating. Unemployment remained high for more than a decade after the crisis.

As a result of the experiences from the crisis, both countries reformed their institutional systems for pursuing stabilization policies and introduced more independent central banks. In January 1999 Finland joined the euro area. Sweden has so far chosen to maintain a currency of its own. The inflation rate has been kept at low levels in both Finland and Sweden, significantly lower than the inflation rates of the 1970s and 1980s.

It remains to be seen whether Finland and Sweden – after Sweden's decision in September 2003 to remain outside the euro area – will evolve along significantly different macroeconomic paths. Have the two economically identical twins separated, after having followed the same stabilization policy road during the post-World War II period? The future will tell.

NOTES

1. We would like to thank Thomas Hagberg for excellent research assistance. Klas Fregert, Peter Jennergren, Jarmo Kontulainen, Göran Lind, Juha Tarkka and Max Watson have given us constructive comments. We have benefited from the comments from seminar participants at the Bank of England and at the ECB. Sophie Bland has given us linguistic guidance. This chapter is an abridged version of Jonung et al. (2008).
2. See Chapter 4 in this volume for a comprehensive study of the high unemployment in Finland and Sweden in the 1990s.
3. See Chapter 6 in this volume.
4. See Chapter 5 in this volume.
5. The literature on the crisis of the 1990s in Finland and Sweden is substantial. For earlier studies on the Finnish crisis, see among others Bordes et al. (1993), Åkerholm (1995), Kiander and Vartia (1996a), Kiander and Vartia (1996b), Honkapohja et al. (1996), Honkapohja and Koskela (1999), Ahtiala (2006) and Honkapohja et al. (2009). For studies of the Swedish crisis, see Jonung and Stymne (1997), Söderström (1995, 1996)

and Jonung (1999, Chapter 9). Jonung et al. (1996) cover both the Finnish and Swedish records of boom and bust. See also Chapters 3–6 in this volume adopting a comparative perspective.

6. See, for example, Krugman (2000) and Rose (2001).
7. This is the view propagated in Chapter 9 in this volume.
8. By now the literature on financial crises in the 1990s is immense. For surveys see, for example, Bordo (1998), Eichengreen (2003) and Hunter et al. (2003).
9. For an in-depth study of financial developments during the financial crisis in Finland and Sweden, see Chapter 3 in this volume.
10. Fisher (1933). Fisher's approach has much in common with the theory of balance sheet crisis. See for example Allen et al. (2002).
11. The applicability of the debt deflation theory to a situation where the general price level does not fall has been addressed by Tobin (1980), Minsky (1982), King (1994) and Wolfson (1996).
12. Fisher (1933). See also Fackler and Parker (2005).
13. The most common way to alleviate debt problems was to modify the repayment schedule or change the interest rate paid on loans. In 1994 there were about 17000 Finnish households that got their banks to agree to lower the rate of interest charged on their loans. About 8000 people arranged for debt restructuring in 1994 in a court of law, while 11–12000 did so in 1995 and 1996.
14. This sectoral asymmetry during boom–bust cycles is examined by Tornell and Westermann (2005).
15. See Jakobsson (2003) for a discussion of devaluation cycles in Finland and Sweden.
16. This interpretation can be found in Bäckström (1998), Jonung and Stymne (1997) and Söderström (1996) among others. See also the assessments of the crisis in Drees and Pazarbasioglu (1998), an IMF report dealing with the Swedish crisis. There were, of course, more traditional factors driving the crisis, but they played a less prominent role than financial factors.
17. See Chapter 9 in this volume on the Asian crises in the late 1990s.
18. See Chapter 7 in this volume.
19. The connection between the banking crisis and the currency crisis is emphasized by Bengt Dennis (1998, pp. 213–36), who was heading the *Riksbank* 1982–93.
20. See, for example, Santamäki-Vuori and Parviainen (1996).
21. Santamäki-Vuori and Parviainen (1996).
22. Descriptions of the 'old' system can be found in Pekkarinen and Vartiainen (2002) and Kullberg (1996). See also Lassila (1993) and Honkapohja and Koskela (1999).
23. Pentti Kouri, venture capitalist in cooperation with George Soros, became famous and highly controversial due to the 'Kouri deals' on the Helsinki stock exchange during the boom. See Kouri (1996).
24. The interest rate differential was so large that many economists thought that over the long run it was worthwhile to take foreign currency loans. For example, Juhani Huttunen of the Federation of Finnish Industries stated in the *Helsingin Sanomat* on 14 December 1989: 'Foreign currency loans are now six percentage points cheaper than *markka*-denominated loans. If a company must invest or for other reasons take a long-term loan, it is worth borrowing in foreign currency. The interest rate differential can bear considerable exchange rate risk in long-term loans.' Unfortunately, some companies applied this idea to short-term loans as well.
25. Newspaper reactions to proposals to constrain the credit expansion by tax measures were hostile. See Hautala and Pohjola (1988).
26. This was pointed out by Harri Holkeri, the prime minister. Requests for austerity measures were also made by Mauno Koivisto, Matti Korhonen and Sixten Korkman, leading policy-makers at this time, according to interviews made by researchers of SITRA in 1995. SITRA, a semi-public think tank, carried out extensive interviews of about 70 decision-makers involved in the economic crisis. The interviews are lengthy and classified but researchers have got permission to use quotes from them. Mauno

Koivisto was president 1982–94, prime minister 1968–70 and 1979–82, central bank governor 1970–79, social democrat, and strong defender of the hard currency policy. Matti Korhonen was chief of staff at the office of prime minister Harri Holkeri in 1987–91. He held several positions in the employers' organizations before and after. He was one of the architects of the hard currency policy. Sixten Korkman was chief economist at the ministry of finance 1988–95, before that economist at the Bank of Finland, later director general for economic and social affairs of the general secretariat of the Council of the EU. During the economic crisis, Korkman proposed that monetary policy should focus on price stability and fiscal policy on budgetary balance, and labour market organizations should decide upon wages and employment.

27. Legislation was later (in 1992) reformed by the Centre-Right government of prime minister Esko Aho so that budgetary changes could be decided by simple majority. This reform was accepted by the opposition party as well.
28. Rolf Kullberg in an interview by Kiander and Vartia (1997).
29. This was stressed by, among others, Sixten Korkman, in an interview by SITRA in 1995.
30. See Jonung (1993) on the rationale behind the low interest rate policy and for an account of the rise and fall of the credit market controls.
31. When Kjell-Olof Feldt, minister of finance, approached Olof Palme, the prime minister, to discuss the coming decision of the *Riksbank* to deregulate, he realized that this step was a milestone:

   > The political meaning was crystal clear: it meant that social democracy, after decades of resistance, abandoned one of its most symbolic bastions for managing the Swedish economy to the market powers. Although the management during recent years had been just that, i.e. symbolic, it was still a major concession to the neo-liberal ideology which we as Social Democrats had spent so many years fighting. (Feldt, 1991, p. 260)

   It proved difficult for the minister of finance to gain the prime minister's approval. Olof Palme's thoughts were elsewhere, but he finally answered: 'Do as you please, I don't understand much of it anyway.' With this reply the road was open for the *Riksbank* to abolish the ceiling on lending and take the decisive steps towards financial deregulation.
32. See Svensson (1996) for a detailed description of the decision process behind the November revolution in 1985.
33. Lindberg and Söderlind (1991) demonstrate that expectations regarding future devaluation were well developed in the financial markets throughout the 1980s – a sign that the pegged exchange rate for the *krona* was not credible.
34. A freeze on prices and restrictions on rents were introduced on 7 February 1990 as a result of the crisis. They were abolished on 12 April the same year.
35. The collapse of *Nyckeln* came as a complete surprise to the public. There was no publicly available information that signalled in advance the problems facing this company, according to Jennergren (2002).
36. See also Chapter 3 in this volume.
37. See Figure 3.3 in Chapter 3 in this volume.
38. For more details on these events, see Kullberg (1996, pp. 151–62).
39. Koivisto (1994, p. 364).
40. It was thought at first that the depression was a normal economic downturn due to weakening competitiveness and should thus be counteracted by a lowering of the Finnish cost level. The deflationary effects of such a step were not considered.
41. According to an interview conducted by SITRA in 1995. See note 26 on the SITRA interviews.
42. See Kiander and Vartia (1998) on the role of the collapse of the Soviet Union.
43. The real rate of interest determines the value of existing assets (capital stocks) as well

as the value of planned investments (flow of new capital). A doubling of the real rate of interest would halve the value of a 'perpetual' capital asset.

44. See Figure 3.3 in Chapter 3 of this volume.
45. The size of the real rate shock within the private sector can be estimated in various ways depending on the choice of period, the real rate of interest used (ex ante or ex post) and choice of taxable entity. Söderström (1996, p. 176) set the real rate shock as an increase from minus 3 per cent to plus 8 per cent, that is, a total increase of 11 percentage points. See also Figure 2.6.
46. Dennis (1998, pp. 57–96).
47. The Finnish and Swedish crisis record is an illustration of the famous macroeconomic policy trilemma for an open economy.
48. See Figure 10.1 in Chapter 10 in this volume.
49. See Maliranta (2003).
50. See Figure 10.1 in Chapter 10 in this volume.
51. The role of the ICT sector in raising labour productivity growth is examined by Edquist (2005).
52. See SOU 2008:90 for a broad study of the evolution of Swedish exports in the period 1995–2006.
53. See Chapter 4 in this volume.
54. On this point see Fregert and Jonung (2008) demonstrating that the inflation-targeting regime after 1993 is associated with less macroeconomic uncertainty than any other policy regime since 1908.
55. See the contributions in Jonung (2003) on the adoption and the evolution of the inflation target of the *Riksbank*.
56. It is an open question to what extent the policy of fiscal tightening contributed to or dampened the recovery. See Chapter 10 in this volume.
57. See also Chapter 9 in this volume.
58. See, for example, Eriksson et al. (1990) and the SITRA interviews in 1995 with Korhonen, Viinanen, Talonen and Niskanen.
59. The debate about the devaluation cycle was initiated by Jouko Paunio in the late 1960s.
60. See, for example, the SITRA interview in 1995 with Korhonen.
61. Bergström (1993, pp. 197–8).
62. Dennis (1998, p. 213).
63. See Jonung (1999) for a discussion of the backward-looking learning process among Swedish economists and policy-makers during the period 1970–95.
64. The interpretation of the depression in the 1930s did result in a new view concerning stabilization policies. The legal regulations concerning monetary and fiscal policy, however, remained more or less unchanged during the 1930s, in sharp contrast to events in the 1990s.
65. The pattern is familiar from previous episodes when the *krona* has deviated from a fixed exchange rate and been allowed to float. The debate on stabilization policy reached a peak after World War I – Sweden having abandoned the gold standard in 1914 with the outbreak of the war – and again after the decision of the *Riksbank* to abandon the gold standard of the inter-war period in September 1931.
66. After the fall of the *krona*, the Centre-Right government appointed a committee to present proposals concerning the future policies of Sweden. The committee, headed by Assar Lindbeck, suggested a large number of reforms. Some of them were implemented. See Lindbeck et al. (1993).
67. Bäckström (1998, p. 17).
68. Dennis (1998, p. 232) arrives at the conclusion that 'When the next banking crisis occurs, both the government and the Riksbank will have the same division of tasks as during the latest crisis.'
69. The Swedish pattern after the crisis in the 1990s is similar to the pattern of the 1930s. The Social Democrats gained political control in 1932 as a result of the depression and

remained in power until 1976. The crisis of the 1990s gave the Social Democrats a government position, though for a shorter time than the depression of the 1930s.

REFERENCES

Ahtiala, P. (2006), 'Lessons from Finland's depression of the 1990s: what went wrong in financial reform?', *Journal of Policy Reform*, **9**, 25–54.

Åkerholm, J. (1995), 'Financial deregulation and economic imbalances in the Scandinavian countries', in R. Dornbusch and R. Parks (eds), *Financial Opening. Policy Lessons for Korea*, Söul: Korea Institute of Finance.

Allen, M., C. Rosenberg, C. Keller, B. Setser and N. Roubini (2002), 'A balance sheet approach to financial crisis', IMF Working paper, WP/02/210.

Bergström, H. (1993), 'Flerpartisamarbete i regering och opposition' (Cooperation between many parties in the government and in opposition), in B. von Sydow (ed.) (1993), *Politikens väsen. Idéer och institutioner i den moderna staten*, Stockholm: Tidens förlag.

Bordes, C., D. Currie and H.T. Söderström (1993), *Three Assessments of the Finnish Economic Crisis and Economic Policy,* Helsingfors: Finlands bank.

Bordo, M.D. (1998), *Currency Crises (and Banking Crises) in Historical Perspective*, Stockholm School of Economic Research, report no. 10.

Bäckström, U. (1998), 'Finansiella kriser – svenska erfarenheter' (Financial crises – Swedish experience), *Ekonomisk Debatt*, **26**, 5–19.

Dennis, B. (1998), *500%*, Stockholm: DN.

Drees, B. and C. Pazarbasioglu (1998), 'The Nordic banking crisis. Pitfalls in financial liberalization', Occasional Paper 161, Washington, DC: IMF.

Edquist, H. (2005), 'The Swedish ICT miracle – myth or reality?', *Information Economics and Policy*, **17**, 275–301.

Eichengreen, B. (2003), *Capital Flows and Crises*, Cambridge and London: MIT Press.

Eriksson, T., A. Suvanto and P. Vartia (1990), 'Wage formation in Finland', in L. Calmfors (ed.), *Wage Formation and Macroeconomic Policy in the Nordic Countries*, Stockholm: SNS Förlag.

Fackler, J. and R. Parker (2005), 'Was debt deflation operative during the great depression?', *Economic Inquiry*, **43**, 67–78.

Feldt, K.O. (1991), *Alla dessa dagar – i regeringen 1982–1990 (All these days – in the government 1982–2000)*, Stockholm: Norstedt.

Feldt, K.O. (1994), *Rädda välfärdsstaten! (Save the welfare state!)*, Stockholm: Norstedts.

Fisher, I. (1933), 'The debt-deflation theory of great depressions', *Econometrica*, reprinted in M.D. Bordo (ed.) (1999), *Financial Crises*, vol. 1, Cheltenham, UK and Northampton, MA, USA: Edward Elgar Publishing.

Fregert, K. and L. Jonung (2008), 'Inflation targeting is a success, so far: 100 years of evidence from Swedish wage contracts', *Economics: The Open-Access, Open-Assessment E-Journal*, **2**, 2008-31, http://www.economics-ejournal.org/economics/journalarticles/2008-31.

Hautala, U. and I. Pohjola (1988), 'Hintatietoisuus ei ulotu kulutusluottoihin' (The consumers are not aware about consumption credits), *Helsingin Sanomat*, 8 November.

Honkapohja, S. and E. Koskela (1999), 'The economic crisis of the 1990s in Finland', *Economic Policy*, **14**, 399–436.

Honkapohja, S., E. Koskela and J. Paunio (1996), 'The depression of the 1990s in Finland: an analytic view', *Finnish Economic Papers*, **9**, 37–54.

Honkapohja, S., E. Koskela, W. Leibfritz and R. Uusitalo (2009), *Economic Prosperity Recaptured: The Finnish Path from Crisis to Fast Growth*, forthcoming, Cambridge, MA and London: MIT Press.

Hunter, W.C., G. Kaufman and M. Pomerleano (2003), *Asset Price Bubbles: The Implications for Monetary, Regulatory and International Policies*, Cambridge, MA and London: MIT Press.

Jakobsson, U. (2003), 'Devaluation cycles in Sweden and Finland', in K. Alho, J. Lassila and P. Ylä-Anttila (eds), *Economic Research and Decision Making – Essays on Structural Change, Growth and Economic Policy. Essays in Honour of Pentti Vartia on the Occasion of his 60th Birthday*, Helsinki: Taloustieto Oy.

Jennergren, P. (2002), 'The Swedish finance company crisis – could it have been anticipated?', *Scandinavian Economic History Review*, **2**, 7–30.

Jonung, L. (1993), 'The rise and fall of credit controls: the case of Sweden 1939–89', in M.D. Bordo and F. Capie (eds), *Monetary Regimes in Transition*, Cambridge: Cambridge University Press, Chapter 11.

Jonung, L. (1999), *Med backspegeln som kompass – om stabiliseringspolitiken som läroprocess*, Rapport till ESO, Ds 1999:9, Finansdepartementet, Stockholm.

Jonung, L. (ed.) (2003), *På jakt efter ett nytt ankare – från fast kronkurs till inflationsmål, (Searching for a new anchor – from a pegged exchange rate of the krona to an inflation target)*, Stockholm: SNS förlag.

Jonung, L. and J. Stymne (1997), 'The great regime shift: asset markets and economic activity in Sweden, 1985–93', in F. Capie and G. Wood (eds), *Asset Prices and the Real Economy*, London: Macmillan, Chapter 1.

Jonung, L, J. Kiander and P. Vartia (2008), 'The great financial crisis in Finland and Sweden. The dynamics of boom, bust and recovery, 1985–2000', European Economy, Economic Papers, no. 350, December, Brussels: European Commission.

Jonung, L., J. Stymne and H.T. Söderström (1996), 'Depression in the North. Boom and bust in Sweden and Finland, 1985–1993', *Finnish Economic Papers*, **9**, 55–71.

Kiander, J. and P. Vartia (1996a), 'The great depression of the 1990s in Finland', *Finnish Economic Papers*, **9**, 72–88.

Kiander, J. and P. Vartia (1996b), 'The crisis of the hard currency regime in Finland', in P. Nenonen (ed.), *Antti Tanskanen 50 vuotta – kirjoituksia kansantaloudesta (Antti Tanskanen 50 years – publications in economics)*, Department of Economics, University of Jyväskylä.

Kiander, J. and P. Vartia (1997), 'A governor defends his record', *Central Banking*, Autumn.

Kiander, J. and P. Vartia (1998), 'The depression of the 1990s in Finland: a Nordic financial crisis or a result of the collapse of the Soviet Union', in T. Myllyntaus (ed.), *Economic Crises and Restructuring in History: Experiences of Small Countries*, St. Katharinen: Scripta Mercaturae Verlag.

King, M. (1994), 'Debt deflation, theory and evidence', *European Economic Review,* **38**.

Koivisto, M. (1994), *Kaksi kautta I (Two periods. Memoirs of the president of the republic)*, Helsinki: Kirjayhtymä.

Kouri, P. (1996), *Suomen omistaja ja elämäni muut roolit (The owner of Finland and the other roles in my life)*, Helsinki: Otava.

Krugman, P. (2000), 'Introduction', in P. Krugman (ed.), *Currency Crises*, Chicago, IL and London: University of Chicago Press.

Kullberg, R. (1996), *. . .ja niin päättyi kulutusjuhla (. . .and then the consumption feast ended)*, Helsinki: WSOY.

Lassila, J. (1993), *Markka ja ääni (The markka and voice)*, Helsinki: Kirjayhtymä.

Lindbeck, A. et al. (1993), *Nya villkor för Sverige (New conditions for Sweden)*, SOU 1993:16, Stockholm. The main report was published in English as A. Lindbeck et al. (1994), *Turning Sweden Around*, Cambridge, MA and London: MIT Press.

Lindberg, H. and P. Söderlind (1991), 'Hur trovärdig var den fasta växelkurspolitiken 1982–1990?' (How credible was the pegged exchange rate 1982–1990?), in L. Jonung (ed.), *Devalveringen 1982 – rivstart eller snedtändning?*, Stockholm: SNS förlag.

Maliranta, M. (2003), *Micro Level Dynamics of Productivity Growth: An Empirical Analysis of the Great Leap in Finnish Manufacturing Productivity in 1975–2000*, ETLA A:38, Helsinki.

Minsky, H. (1982), *Inflation, Recession and Economic Policy*, Brighton: Wheatsheaf.

Pekkarinen, J. and J. Vartiainen (2002), *Finlands ekonomiska politik. Den långa linjen 1918–2000* (*Finland's economic policy. The long tradition 1918–2000*), Fackföreningrörelsens ekonomiska forskningsinstitut, Stockholm.

Rose, A. (2001), 'Discussion of Bordo, Michael, Eichengreen, Barry, Klingebiel, Daniela and Soledad Martinez-Peria, Maria (2001)', *Economic Policy*, **32**, 75–7.

Santamäki-Vuori, T. and S. Parviainen (1996), 'The labour market in Finland', Labour Institute for Economic Research, Studies 64, Helsinki.

Söderström, H. (1995), 'Realräntechock, skuldsanering och budgetunderskott. En balansräkningsanalys av den svenska depressionen' (Real interest rate shock, debt reconstruction and budget deficits), *Ekonomisk Debatt*, **23**, 189–202.

Söderström, H. (1996), *Normer och ekonomisk politik (Norms and economic policy)*, Kristianstad: SNS.

SOU 2008:90, *Svensk export och internationalisering* (Swedish exports and the process of internationalization), Stockholm.

Svensson, T. (1996), *Novemberrevolutionen. Om rationalitet och makt i beslutet att avreglera kreditmarknaden 1985 (The November revolution. On rationality and power in the decision to deregulate the credit market)*, ESO-rapport, Ds 1996:37, Finansdepartementet, Stockholm.

Tobin, J. (1980), *Asset Accumulation and Economic Activity – Reflections on Contemporary Macroeconomic Theory*, Oxford: Blackwell.

Tornell, A. and F. Westermann (2005), *Boom–bust Cycles and Financial Liberalization*, Cambridge, MA and London: MIT Press.

Wibble, A. (1994), *Två cigg och en kopp kaffe* (*Two cigarettes and a cup of coffee*), Kristianstad: Ekerlids.

Wibble, A. (1996), 'Ekonomerna och 90-talskrisen' (The economists and the crisis of the 1990s), in L. Jonung (ed.), *Ekonomerna i debatten – gör de någon nytta?*, Stockholm: Ekerlids, Chapter 11.

Wolfson, M. (1996), 'Irving Fisher's debt-deflation theory: its relevance to current conditions', *Cambridge Journal of Economics*, **20**, 315–33.

3. Financial crisis in Finland and Sweden: similar but not quite the same

Peter Englund and Vesa Vihriälä

INTRODUCTION[1]

In both Finland and Sweden, the general macroeconomic depression in the early 1990s was associated with a deep financial crisis, involving a currency crisis, a banking crisis, and widespread debt service difficulties in the non-financial sector. These episodes have much in common with the financial crises experienced in several developing countries in the recent past. In particular, they were preceded by financial liberalization and a credit boom. In the case of developing countries, inadequate institutions have often been blamed for what happened. 'Crony capitalism', corruption, bad statistics, and the expectation of international rescue operations have been cited as important factors leading to an unsustainable boom and a later collapse.

In the Nordic countries such institutional weaknesses are less likely explanations. These countries are among the most highly developed and least corrupt countries in the world. Nevertheless, the boom-and-bust experiences seem very similar to those of many developing countries, suggesting that other factors must have been important. Macroeconomic policies constitute one set of candidates; in particular, both Finland and Sweden unsuccessfully tried to stick to a pegged but adjustable exchange rate regime just as so many developing countries have done. Similarly, despite generally highly developed institutions, the financial and regulatory systems were ill-prepared to cope with the forces that were unleashed by financial liberalization.

Once the crises hit, the authorities intervened heavily. Failing banks were kept alive through massive public support, and far-reaching guarantees of bank liabilities were issued. In spite of this, there was some disruption of financial intermediation, which may have exacerbated the general economic depression. The direct impact of government intervention was to prevent the market mechanism from restructuring the distressed financial sectors, which, particularly in Finland, displayed a clear over-capacity before the crisis. The end result was a consolidation of the banking sector in both countries. The operational efficiency increased substantially, and Swedish and Finnish banks turned quite profitable, in contrast to those of Japan, another developed country that ended up in financial crisis in the early 1990s.

In this chapter, we first give a concise description of the crises, including their background, the evolution of the main events, and government policies. Second, we look at the consequences of the banking problems for the real economies. Finally, we try to isolate the key factors behind the emergence of the crises and the relatively speedy recoveries. We hope that the experiences of these two neighboring countries with many similarities, but also with several distinguishing features, can help in understanding the general phenomenon of financial crises.

3.1 THE FINANCIAL SYSTEMS IN THE EARLY 1980S

3.1.1 Bank-dominated Intermediation

In the early 1980s, the Swedish and Finnish financial systems were still comparatively undeveloped, particularly given the otherwise advanced nature of the two economies. The Finnish financial system was much smaller than those in continental Europe, not to mention the Anglo-Saxon countries, with a ratio of total financial assets to GDP of less than 60 per cent of that in Germany. The Swedish system was somewhat more developed, with roughly the same relative size as in Germany. In terms of structure, the financial systems were closer to the continental-European model, with intermediaries dominating the channeling of funds, than the Anglo-Saxon model, with the securities markets playing a major role. In both countries the ratio of assets held by financial intermediaries to total financial assets was comparable to that of Germany and markedly higher than in the United States.

Stock markets were poorly developed, particularly in Finland, and played a limited role in financing new investment. This was partly a result of deliberate policies. The tax systems favored financing investment through retained earnings due to the double taxation of dividends, and in Sweden also through subsidies available to firms that set aside profits to special funds rather than paying dividends. As a result, stock market capitalization remained under 10 per cent of GDP in Finland and under

30 per cent in Sweden in the first half of the 1980s, far below the level in many other countries. This was to change with soaring stock prices in the 1980s. When stock prices peaked in 1989 capitalization rates had doubled in both countries.

Among intermediaries, banks played a dominant role. In both countries, banks provided a wide variety of services following the universal bank tradition, and their economic importance tends to be underestimated by looking at asset shares. In Finland, the number of banks was as large as 632 in 1985. Almost all operated in just one or a few municipalities – 254 savings banks and 370 co-operative banks. Individual savings and co-operative banks were formally fully independent entities, but could be considered as two bank groups covering the country as a whole. First, the savings banks jointly owned a commercial bank – *Skopbank* – that acted as a central bank, providing liquidity and various specialized services to individual savings banks. Alone in the group, *Skopbank* had access to central bank and foreign financing. Second, credit risks were spread among all savings banks via a guarantee fund and a mutual insurance company for deposits of individual banks. Third, business strategies and marketing were often centrally designed. Similarly, the co-operative banks with their jointly owned commercial bank – *Okobank* – formed a separate banking group.

Apart from the two local bank groups, the Finnish bank market had three major actors: the two commercial banks *Kansallis-Osake-Pankki* (*KOP*) and *Suomen Yhdyspankki* (*SYP*), and the post office bank (*PSP*). The commercial banks were the most versatile and provided lending and other services to large corporations. *PSP* had some privileges in the management of government liquidity and was often 'the second bank' of large corporations. The savings banks focused on housing and real estate lending, while the co-operative banks specialized in agricultural and small enterprise lending. Yet, banks also competed actively, particularly in the household deposit and loan market. Housing loans were particularly important, as the role of separate mortgage institutions was small.

In Sweden, the most important intermediaries were banks and mortgage institutions. Some mortgage institutions were owned by major bank groups, whereas others were independent (for example, *Stadshypotekskassan*). Historically, banks accounted for the major fraction of lending to the public. After World War II, commercial banks provided around half of total bank lending. Several of the banks (in particular *Skandinaviska Banken*, *Svenska Handelsbanken* and *Stockholms Enskilda Bank*) had a major influence on corporate governance of Swedish corporations by acting as 'house banks', by being represented on boards of directors, and by direct ownership influence. In particular, the Wallenberg family exerted much of its influence through its dominance of *Stockholms Enskilda Bank*. The government-owned post office bank accounted for some 10 per cent of total lending, and played an important role for payments by operating a giro system. It was merged in 1974 with a government-owned commercial bank to form *PK-banken*. Just like Finland, Sweden also had two strong groups of savings banks (*sparbanker*) and co-operative banks (*förenings-banker*), with their main customer bases in the household, small business and agricultural sectors of the economy.

The bank dominance was gradually broken during the post-war period. In 1986, lending from housing mortgage institutions, with 37 per cent of the total, was almost as large as bank lending, with 39 per cent. The rapidly growing group of finance companies, which were to play an important role in the early phase of the Swedish banking crisis, had another 8 per cent of the market. Insurance companies and pension funds also provided substantial lending to the non-financial business sector by re-lending of employers' pension contributions. This was more or less automatic and did not entail any risk-taking for the lenders, as loans were guaranteed by third parties, often banks.

3.1.2 Pervasive Regulation Confined Business Opportunities

The activities of financial institutions were tightly regulated in both countries by various conduct rules. In Finland, banks were subject to a reserve requirement, used for monetary policy purposes. More importantly, their pricing policies were severely constrained by ceilings set by the central bank on each institution's average and top lending rates. In addition, all banks were required to offer the same interest rate linked to the central bank base rate in order for the interest income to be tax-exempt for depositors. Most deposit accounts adhered to this requirement. Lending was not explicitly regulated, but the central bank issued guidelines, according to which, for instance, business investment was to be given priority over loans for consumption.

In Sweden, banks, insurance companies and other institutions were subjected to *lending ceilings*, typically formulated as limits on the growth rate of the stock of loans to low-priority purposes (in practice household loans, except for the purchase of newly constructed homes). *Liquidity ratios* required banks to hold a minimum fraction of their assets (over 50 per cent around 1980) in bonds issued by the government and by mortgage institutions. *Placement requirements* put a similar restriction on the investments of insurance companies. The huge supply of bonds was the result of large budget deficits and an ambitious program for residential investment.

Liquidity ratios and placement requirements were adjusted to ensure that the desired residential construction could be financed at below-market interest. With more than 50 per cent of their assets in bonds, typically with long maturities and with interest rates being fixed for five years at below-market levels, Swedish banks and insurance companies had in effect been transformed into repositories for illiquid bonds, crippled in fulfilling their key function in screening and monitoring loans for consumption and investment.

Interest regulation put a cap on lending rates and limited the ability of banks to capture scarcity rents created by the lending ceilings. As a result lending was effectively rationed. Bank actions were also continuously scrutinized by the *Riksbank*, whose views on proper bank behavior were communicated in weekly meetings between the governor and representatives of the major banks.[2] The net of regulations imposed on banks benefited other financial institutions. In particular, finance companies, originally focusing on activities like factoring and leasing, expanded aggressively into regular lending.

In both countries, regulated interest rates were low relative to inflation, making real rates negative for long periods of time and creating constant excess demand with credit allocated by other means than prices. Despite low interest rates the absence of alternatives – particularly in Finland – kept depositors willing to deposit in banks. Stock and bond markets were small and illiquid and investments abroad were either prohibited or subject to special permits.

Further, the tax systems – with nominal interest payments deductible against marginal tax rates from 50 up to 80 per cent in Sweden – contributed to making the after-tax real interest rate even more strongly negative. Clearly this was not an equilibrium situation. It could only be sustained through regulations and rationing. Regulations had a major impact on bank balance sheets and cost structures and risk profiles. Banks held bonds and corporate and household loans, which, even though formally risky, entailed almost no credit risk for several reasons. First, the debt service burden never became too severe. Real lending rates were low and often negative, and economic downturns usually resulted in devaluations, which by increasing inflation created a real transfer from depositors to borrowers. Second, lending rate regulation allowed banks to use creditworthiness as the key rationing device. Third, ceilings on average lending rates allowed banks in Finland to transfer interest payments from customers in financial difficulties to healthy customers: lowering rates for the former could at least partially be compensated by increasing rates to the latter without violating the regulations and without fear of losing customers.

3.1.3 Bank Efficiency Generally Low

Interest rate regulation and the lack of competition protected bank interest margins. Yet bank profitability was relatively weak in both countries. One reason, particularly in Finland, was the high operating costs caused by large and expensive branch office networks. Local bank markets were largely oligopolistic, with a small number of banks offering a homogeneous set of services. In the absence of effective price competition, banks competed mainly on the quality and availability of services, mostly through setting up new offices to increase the convenience of deposit and loan customers. This structure was not stable, however, and the potential for cost savings by avoiding the duplication of bank offices triggered a wave of bank mergers in Sweden in the 1970s and 1980s. In Finland the bank structure remained essentially unchanged until the crisis years, although the number of both savings banks and co-operative banks declined through mergers.

Profitability varied a great deal among banks. In both countries the weakest banks were the savings banks. They were often inefficiently small, and they had a weak position in the profitable business of lending to corporations. In Sweden the average rate of return on equity within the savings banks group was consistently a couple of percentage points below that of other banks in the early 1980s.[3]

3.2 FINANCIAL LIBERALIZATION – THE INITIAL IMPACT

3.2.1 Gradual Deregulation

Many strains developed in the regulated financial systems over time. Circumvention of the regulatory constraints became more widely spread, increasing the dissatisfaction of those households and firms that did not want to bend the rules or could not easily do so. At the same time, technological developments and internationalization made many actors – particularly major corporations – less dependent on the inefficient domestic credit markets. As a result, the rationale of regulations was increasingly questioned, and a gradual liberalization process started in the early 1980s in both countries. Although both the starting positions and the end results were similar in the two countries, the sequence of events differed (Figure 3.1).

In Finland, the process got underway in 1980 when banks were allowed to cover their commercial forward positions with transactions in foreign

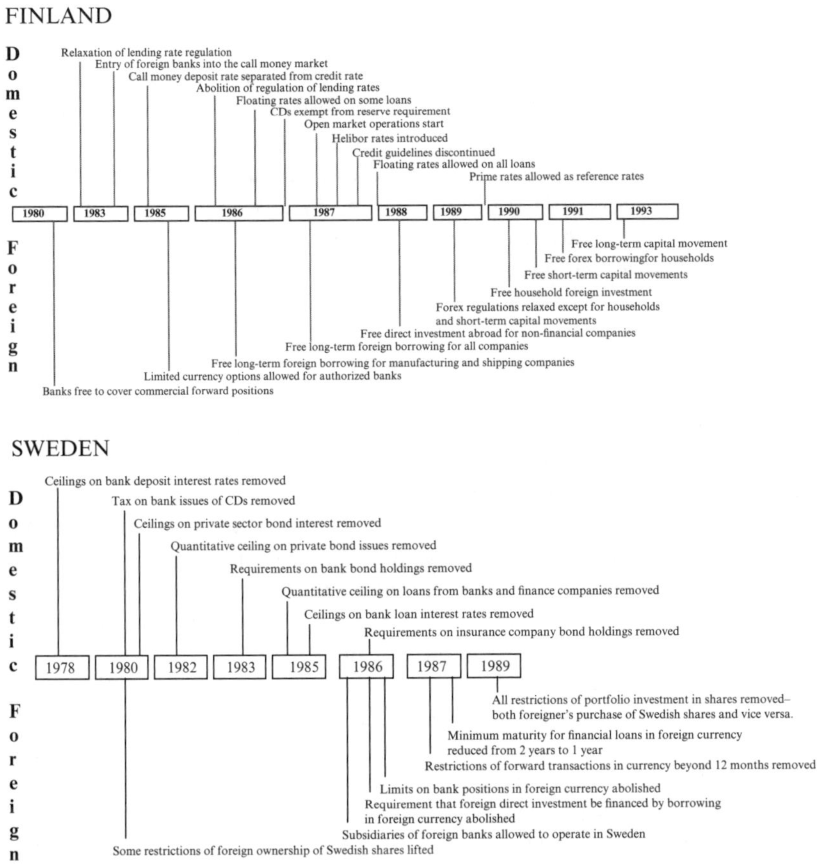

Figure 3.1 Deregulation of financial markets in Finland and Sweden, 1980–93

money markets. Domestic deregulation started in 1983 with some easing of the lending rate regulation. After several gradual liberalization measures, restrictions on lending rates were fully lifted by early 1986. Simultaneously, steps were taken to create a true domestic money market. Certificates of deposit (CDs) were exempted from cash reserve requirements at the beginning of 1987. As the central bank started market operations in CDs (its own and those of commercial banks) in 1987, volumes increased rapidly and the CD market became the core of the money market. The abolition of credit guidelines and the lifting of remaining restrictions on the use of floating rates in loan contracts completed the domestic liberalization by the beginning of 1988.

In Sweden, new legislation in January 1980 allowed banks to issue certificates of deposit, as an exception to the general prohibition on the issuing of bonds and similar instruments by banks. The CD market developed rapidly, demonstrating that it should be possible to conduct monetary policy through open-market operations in treasury bills or similar instruments, in Sweden just as in other countries. This set the stage for further deregulation of domestic transactions, which took place in a couple of swift steps. The key move was the removal of the lending ceilings for banks and the placement requirements for insurance companies in November 1985.

In both countries, there remained important elements of capital account regulations that were only gradually lifted between 1986 and 1989. Some regulations were abolished in 1986 and 1988, but Swedish banks remained restricted on the forward market, and foreigners remained restricted in their access to the Swedish money and bond markets. It was only with the final abolition of capital account controls in July 1989 that the *krona* money and bond markets came to be fully integrated with international markets. In Finland, inward long-term capital movements were fully freed by mid-1987. Outward capital movements were liberalized later, starting with direct foreign investment in 1988. The last restrictions on short-term capital movements were lifted at the end of 1990.

Liberalization expanded banks' choice set of assets and liabilities. Instead of being forced to invest in government and housing bonds, Swedish banks were now free to lend where return prospects were best. Similarly, Finnish banks were no longer affected by lending guidelines, although their importance had already diminished substantially before their final abolition. Perhaps even more important was the change in refinancing opportunities. Improved access to foreign sources of funds helped banks and other financial intermediaries to reduce their dependence on central bank funding, and the growth of the domestic money market gave individual banks much more freedom in refinancing and helped the banking sector to tap funding from the domestic non-financial sector.

Under the regime of financial regulation, obtaining a loan from the bank had been a sort of privilege. The abolition of lending controls now allowed and forced banks to compete much more freely for borrowers, as in any retail business. The new environment reduced the segmentation of financial intermediation. In Finland, savings and co-operative banks could expand lending to firms that previously had mainly relied on commercial banks. In Sweden those institutions that had been more loosely regulated – finance companies and to some extent insurance companies – had thrived as a result of regulatory arbitrage. Most finance companies had expanded from their original activities such as leasing, factoring and credit cards into direct lending, where regulation gave them greater freedom than banks had. Now that banks had entered into the markets previously in the domain of the finance companies, these were pushed into higher risk markets. Being unable to receive deposits or to issue bonds, finance companies were financed partly by direct borrowing in banks and partly by commercial paper (*marknadsbevis*), typically guaranteed by banks. As a result, Swedish banks became indirectly exposed to credit risk, a fact that became fully visible only when the banking crisis erupted.

3.2.2 Lax Regulatory Framework

Before the liberalization, prudential regulation played a relatively minor role in both countries. With limits both on the amount of lending and on interest rates, banks had little incentive to take on extra risk. Risk-taking was also severely constrained by rules that limited the types of business allowed to banks. In Finland, savings banks and co-operative banks, for instance, were prohibited from granting credit without 'secure collateral'. With conduct rules now being relaxed, banks were given new opportunities to expand and take on excessive risks. It was gradually recognized that prudential requirements became more important in the new situation. However, reforms were diluted and delayed for many reasons and the regulatory framework remained unchanged in most ways.

A central aspect of modern bank regulation is the system of capital requirements that obliges banks to hold a certain amount of capital, in proportion to a weighted sum of different classes of loans and other assets. Towards the end of the 1980s, capital requirements were modified in both Finland and Sweden as part of an international harmonization, following the recommendations by the G-10 group within the BIS in 1987. In Finland, prudential regulation was in general fragmented with different laws for different types of banks. Capital requirements were low: 4 per cent for commercial banks and 2 per cent for savings banks and co-operative banks. Furthermore, a large number of local banks were permitted to operate with less than the stipulated 2 per cent capital as a transitional arrangement. The rationale for applying a lower ratio for the local banks had been that their lending was less risky than that of the commercial banks. Smaller risks were thought to stem, for instance, from the aforementioned 'secure collateral' requirement. Although tightening of capital requirements was also widely recognized as necessary in Finland, the process was delayed, not least because of stiff resistance from the savings and co-operative banks. As a result, prudential regulation remained essentially unchanged until January 1991, when the new Deposit Bank Act took effect, by and large meeting international standards. The reform was too late to have an impact on bank behavior in the crucial years following the liberalization.

In Sweden, the structure and level of the capital requirements were broadly in line with the Basel recommendations already in the mid-1980s – with one important exception. Lending to housing and real estate was treated as relatively safe and collateralized real estate loans and mortgage-institution bonds were subjected to lower capital requirements than other forms of lending. Only in the midst of the banking and real estate crisis did Sweden adapt the international view on real estate lending, effectively sharpening capital requirements.[4]

3.2.3 Financial Supervision Slow to React

Financial supervisory responsibility was split between various government agencies in both countries. In Finland, banking supervision was handled by the Bank Inspectorate, which was directly responsible for the commercial banks. In the case of other bank groups it was assisted by the Savings Bank Inspectorate and the Co-operative Bank Inspectorate. These two supervisory bodies were subordinated to the Bank Inspectorate, but in practice they operated rather independently and in close collaboration with the key decision-makers in the two banking groups. Supervision of insurance companies was, in turn, in the hands of the Ministry for Social Affairs and Health. No major reform of financial supervision took place during the years of liberalization, although some technicalities were changed in connection with the new Deposit Bank Act in 1991. Only in 1993 was a new supervisory body, the Financial Supervision Authority, created. Even then, insurance supervision was kept separate.

In Sweden, prudential regulation was handled by two agencies, *Bankinspektionen* for banks (including savings banks) and *Försäkringsinspektionen* for insurance companies. In 1991 the two agencies were merged into a single Financial Supervisory Authority, *Finansinspektionen*. This merger was undoubtedly well motivated as a reflection of ongoing structural changes within the financial industry, making the dividing line between banking and insurance increasingly blurred. At this time, however, the reorganization may have contributed to diverting the attention of the supervisors away from the emerging systemic crisis to issues of internal organization.

The resources devoted to financial supervision were small by any standards in both countries. Perhaps because of this, but presumably also owing to tradition, the approach to supervision was rather legalistic. An in-depth study of the Finnish Bank Inspectorate by Halme (1999) suggests that banking supervision was rather passive and in fact allowed the bending of some key prudential rules. This contributed to highly vulnerable risk positions among the savings banks in particular. One such instance was the requirement for 'secure collateral', which was interpreted very loosely. Similarly, according to Halme, bank supervision permitted the savings banks to use value adjustments to bolster bank capital in a way that was in flagrant conflict with the Finnish Accountancy Act and sound accounting procedures.

In Sweden, *Bankinspektionen* played a somewhat active role when problems emerged in a couple of minor savings banks around 1990 by acting as a mediator and contributing to private reconstructions. When the crisis grew into more of a systemic crisis, however, its role became marginal. Much of the limited resources for supervision were spent on rather peripheral issues. Consumer protection was very much in the forefront of the political agenda in the late 1980s, and as a result there were fewer on-site inspections of banks after 1985 compared with earlier periods (Sjöberg, 1994).

3.3 THE LENDING BOOM

3.3.1 A General Lending Frenzy

Financial liberalization coupled with a favorable macroeconomic environment created conditions conducive to rapid credit growth. The devaluations of the early 1980s had improved external competitiveness in both countries, the world economy was growing rather robustly, and declining oil prices improved the terms of trade. Particularly in Sweden, fiscal policy remained expansive for several years.

Years of credit rationing had prevented many households and smaller firms from borrowing as much as desired at given interest rates. In Finland, households were less indebted than in many other countries, with a total debt of less than 60 per cent of the household disposable income. In Sweden, by contrast, aggregate indebtedness of the household sector was close to 100 per cent of disposable income, relatively high by international standards. This is largely explained by government-subsidized lending schemes for newly constructed housing and favorable student loans. Despite this there were pockets of unsatisfied credit demand.

In both countries, high inflation – combined with interest payments being tax-deductible at marginal tax rates of 50 per cent or more – made borrowing attractive despite high nominal short-term rates. The situation of negative after-tax real interest rates (measured ex post) prevailed in Sweden throughout the 1980s. In Finland, decelerating inflation increased real rates in 1986 and 1987, but faster inflation in 1988 and 1989 brought them back close to zero. Given the long history of negative real rates, the ex ante real rates may also have been very low in Finland throughout the second half of the 1980s. Under these conditions there was a large pool of customers willing to borrow when credit became freely available. The scene was set for a credit boom.

Lending evolved broadly in the same way in both countries, with Finland leading somewhat in timing. The initial acceleration of credit growth came in 1985 in Finland and in 1986 in Sweden. In Sweden, finance companies and other non-bank intermediaries were particularly active at this initial stage. In Finland, both banks and non-bank intermediaries expanded rapidly in 1985. After a temporary slowdown (in Finland in 1986 and in Sweden in 1987), credit growth accelerated again in 1988. At this stage banks played the predominant role. In both countries, bank lending grew by around 30 per cent in nominal terms. Although inflation accelerated, real lending growth was close to 25 per cent. The fact that the overall interest margin of banks, if anything, declined somewhat, suggests that an outward shift in bank credit supply was an essential element of the story. See Figures 3.2a and 3.2b.

In Finland, tightening of monetary policy and special measures to rein in bank lending (a special cash reserve requirement calculated on the basis of credit growth during 1989) slowed down bank credit expansion in 1989 and even more in 1990. In Sweden, real bank lending continued to expand at a rate of between 15 and 20 per cent in both 1989 and 1990. The break came only in the second half of 1990 in response to tightened monetary policy and a tax reform that cut the marginal tax rate on interest

Figure 3.2a Real growth of bank lending and the interest margin in Finland, 1985–95

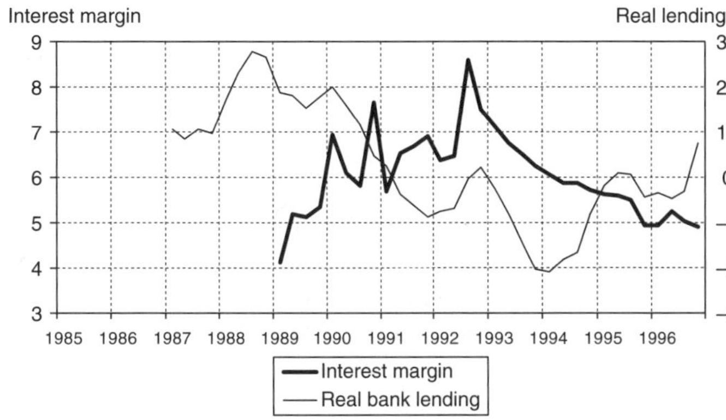

Figure 3.2b Real growth of bank lending and the interest margin in Sweden, 1985–96

deductions from 50 to 30 per cent. As a result, the after-tax real interest rate increased sharply, and finally became positive. Lending started to fall in real terms from the second quarter of 1991.

3.3.2 Asset Prices and Bank Profits Fuel Credit Growth

The loosening of credit constraints had its strongest effects on those sectors that had earlier been hardest hit. Consumption of durable goods and housing investment by households and investment of closed-sector firms were most strongly affected. Readily available finance also spurred merger and acquisition activity, which in Finland was further supported by a tax reform in 1988.

Additional demand inflated real estate and stock prices, in turn bolstering borrower balance sheets (see Figure 2.7 in Chapter 2 for housing prices). This supported further lending, which in turn fed back into asset prices. Even though household indebtedness increased substantially in relation to disposable income, it was matched by a parallel increase in asset values. The ratio of debt to total assets remained essentially unchanged at around 22 per cent in Finland and increased by less than 5 percentage points to close to 40 per cent in Sweden by the end of the decade; see Clapham et al. (2002). Presuming the higher asset prices to be sustainable, household borrowing did not appear excessive from the lenders' point of view.

Bank lending was also bolstered by higher bank profits and improved solidity. The rapid extension of new loans added to fee income, as did increased stock and money market activity. Good earnings growth also made bank cost-effectiveness (revenue/cost ratios) look better, in many cases masking weak underlying profitability. As subsequent developments demonstrated, the increased profitability was largely an illusion, since it did not account for the credit risks. Fees and interest income were recorded immediately whereas credit risks manifested themselves only later.

Ex post it is quite obvious that there was an asset price bubble, in the sense of higher prices than could easily be explained by fundamental factors. This emerged as a result of several mutually reinforcing factors. Highly over-optimistic – even irrational – expectations may have played a role, but such an outcome could also be explained by fully rational agency theoretical arguments; see, for example, Allen and Gale (2000).

3.3.3 Some Lenders More Aggressive

Financial deregulation affected competition both within the banking sector and between banks and other financial intermediaries. Generally, there was now scope for more intense competition, since banks and other actors faced fewer restrictions. The relative competitive positions of different actors were also affected, triggering shifts in market shares between banks and other lenders.

In Finland, the most aggressive player was the savings bank group. Between the end of 1986 and 1990 the combined lending by the savings banks and *Skopbank* grew by over 140 per cent, compared with a little over 90 per cent for the co-operative banking group and less than 80 per cent for the commercial banks. The rapid expansion of lending and entry into new business areas were deliberate strategic choices of *Skopbank* and the largest individual savings banks. The intention was to 'grow out' of profitability problems caused by high costs.[5] Another part of the strategy was to incorporate a major industrial conglomerate within the 'sphere of influence' of the group. In 1987, *Skopbank* became a majority shareholder in the metal industry company Tampella. It was also very active in 'cornering' companies by obtaining substantial stakes for later sale to strategic buyers.

In Sweden, competition between bank groups had already intensified before the deregulation. Banking legislation was made neutral across savings banks, co-operative banks and commercial banks in 1969. At that time, savings banks were gradually losing their traditional dominance in household deposits, and had to resort to increased borrowing from other financial institutions for funding. To handle this problem the savings banks tried to expand away from their almost exclusive dependence on the household sector. The share of lending to industry in total savings bank lending grew from 6 per cent in 1980 to 13 per cent in 1985 and 20 per cent in 1990.[6] At first, this was not associated with an increase in total lending. In fact, the lending market share of the savings banks fell during the first half of the 1980s, and it was only following the deregulation that they started to gain market shares again, with *Första Sparbanken* being particularly expansive.[7] Among the commercial banks, those banks with a weak position in corporate lending – in particular *Nordbanken* and *Gota Bank* – expanded most strongly, whereas other banks – primarily *Handelsbanken* – were more cautious.

In both countries the most aggressive actors were also the weakest in terms of capital and underlying profitability. This is in line with a 'gamble for resurrection' approach in response to liberalization: weak profitability, or low 'charter value', increases the willingness to take on risks. American evidence in support of such risk-shifting or asset substitution behavior has been provided by Keeley (1990). Vihriälä (1997, Chapter 3) provides analogous evidence for Finnish savings banks: the weaker bank profitability and capital position at the outset of the liberalization period, the stronger the subsequent credit growth. Differences in profitability and capital are sufficient to fully explain the difference in lending growth between savings banks and co-operative banks. Bad incentives seem to have been a key factor in explaining the degree of credit expansion and – as we shall see – the depth of the banking problems.

The deregulation also had an impact on competition between banks and other intermediaries. The Swedish finance companies provide a good example. These companies had earlier taken advantage of a loosely regulated position and expanded from activities such as leasing, factoring and credit cards into direct lending. Immediately after the deregulation the finance companies continued to expand at a faster rate than other financial institutions. However, after a couple of years the effect of the removed restrictions on banks became evident, when banks entered into the markets previously in the domain of the finance companies, which were now pushed into higher-risk markets. As a result, these companies lost market shares at a rapid pace from 1988. Banks were not only competing against the finance companies but also doing business with them in the form of short-term lending and by guaranteeing their commercial paper programs. In 1990, 5 per cent of all bank lending went to finance companies compared with 1 per cent in 1985. As we shall see, this now turned out to be risky business as the credit losses among the finance companies continued to grow.

3.3.4 The Result: Vulnerable Financial Positions in the Non-financial and Financial Sectors

Total credit expanded at an unprecedented rate in both countries in the second half of the 1980s. Firms and households alike became highly indebted relative to income flows. By the peak of the boom, household

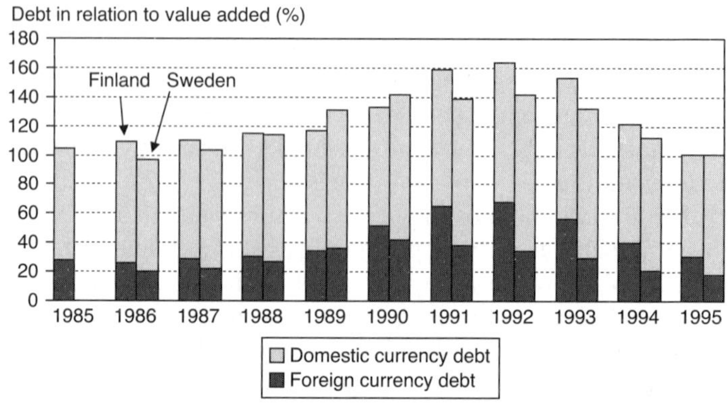

Figure 3.3 Corporate sector indebtedness in Finland and Sweden, 1985–95

debt as a fraction of disposable income had increased by some 20 percentage points to 80 per cent in Finland and by 30 percentage points to 130 per cent in Sweden. Corporate sector indebtedness increased in a similar fashion. The ratio of corporate debt to nominal GDP increased from 60 per cent to some 80 per cent in Finland and from about 70 per cent to more than 90 per cent in Sweden.[8] (Figure 3.3.)

Table 3.1 Comparison of selected credit booms

Crisis		Average real lending growth prior to crisis	Average domestic credit-to-GDP growth prior to crisis	Domestic credit to GDP (right scale)
1998	Philippines	0.21	0.15	0.70
1998	Thailand	0.19	0.14	1.34
1998	Indonesia	0.14	0.05	0.59
1998	Korea	0.13	0.05	0.78
1991	Finland	0.12	0.08	0.95
1988	Norway	0.10	0.09	0.70
1990	Sweden	0.10	0.06	0.87
1989	Japan	0.09	0.04	1.39
1992	Mexico	0.07	0.02	0.31

Source: IFS, WDI, authors' own calculations.

As a whole, credit growth was rather typical for countries that were to have banking crises. In fact, as seen from Table 3.1, the real growth of credit during the boom period was even higher in the more recent banking crisis countries in East Asia – Korea, Indonesia, Thailand and the Philippines – but the resulting ratios of domestic credit to GDP were as high in Sweden and Finland as, for example, in Indonesia, the Philippines or Mexico.

A particularly important feature was the large fraction of debt in foreign currency, even among firms with no foreign currency revenues that would have needed hedging. Both countries defended fixed exchange rates by high interest rates. As a result, substantial gains could be made by borrowing in foreign currencies and investing in *kronor* or *markkaa* – as long as there was no devaluation. Many borrowers, primarily large corporations, tried to take advantage of the large interest differences. In Sweden the fraction of bank lending to the non-bank public denominated in foreign currency increased from 24 per cent in 1986 to 44 per cent in 1990.[9] Finland witnessed a similar change: the share of foreign denominated debt in total corporate debt rose from 23 per cent in 1986 to 39 per cent in 1990. Since little of this was hedged by forward contracts, the corporate sector became vulnerable not only to income and interest rate shocks but also to exchange rate movements.

The balance sheets of the intermediaries changed in the process. The share of ordinary deposits as a source of finance decreased substantially. Instead, many banks became highly dependent on money market funding as well as foreign interbank and bond finance. This was especially true for *Skopbank* and the large savings banks in Finland.

3.4 THE MAIN EVENTS OF THE CRISIS

3.4.1 Tight Monetary Conditions Stop the Expansion

Early signs of over-extension and distress emerged in both countries in 1989. Stock prices and real estate prices peaked, some months earlier in Finland than in Sweden. Interest rates had already started to increase in 1988, primarily as market responses to imbalances in the economies. In addition, foreign interest rates increased, particularly in Germany. However, apart from occasional episodes of higher interest rates to defend the exchange rates, there were few signs so far in the financial markets of either country that signaled a crisis.

The attempts by the central banks to rein in credit expansion and overheating had been frustrated by the fixed exchange rate regime: interest rates could not be raised very much as long as confidence in the currency peg led to large short-term capital inflows. Capital flows not only prevented a major hike in the *krona* and *markka* rates but also financed an increasing share of bank lending denominated in foreign currency at relatively low interest rates.

Given the impotence of monetary policy, repeated calls were made in both countries for tighter fiscal policies. But for a long time they went unanswered. In Sweden, there had been broad recognition since 1987 that the economy was overheated. The open unemployment rate reached an all-time low of 1.4 per cent in 1989, and prices continued to rise faster than in other countries. However, there was little parliamentary support for a restrictive fiscal policy, and public consumption continued to increase, by about 5 per cent in real terms in both 1988 and 1989. In Finland taxes were cut, new transfer programs were enacted and old ones expanded. Macroeconomic policies were still supporting growth rather than restraining it.

In Finland, this impasse led the monetary authorities to try two special measures to slow down credit expansion in the spring of 1989. First, the exchange rate band was widened and shifted so as to allow an immediate revaluation of the *markka*. This induced expectations of depreciation, which increased money market rates and made borrowing in foreign currency more expensive. Second, banks were subjected to a special cash reserve requirement, the size of which increased with the rate of credit expansion. Initially, the effects appeared to be modest. Credit stocks and nominal GDP both continued to display two-digit growth rates in 1989, in Finland just as in Sweden.

However, towards the end of 1989 (in Finland) and in early 1990 (in Sweden) there was a significant tightening of monetary conditions, mainly led by market impulses. Foreign interest rates rose substantially and strong expectations emerged about depreciation of the currencies, driving the domestic interest rates up even further (see Figure 2.8 in Chapter 2). In Finland the special cash reserve requirement also started to contribute, and the lending growth of most banks decelerated rapidly.[10]

Higher interest rates and falling asset prices were soon followed by weakened domestic demand. In 1990, private investment started to decline and consumption stagnated in Finland. In Sweden, consumption was declining but investment still continued to grow in 1990. Weakening demand and increasing interest expenses led to a dramatic reduction in corporate earnings. Some firms started to have problems in servicing their debts. High interest rates and weaker cash flows exerted further downward pressure on asset prices. Lower collateral values in turn increased banks' exposure in the case of default. Credit losses still remained small, but the financial sectors started to feel the pressure in both countries.

While the Finnish banking sector as a whole was still making profits, the most aggressive bank – *Skopbank* – displayed a substantial loss in 1990, as earlier capital gains turned into losses and fee income was sharply cut by reduced trading activity. The bank – which had come under special surveillance by the authorities in late 1989 – was required to design a restructuring program aimed at reducing its risk exposure. As a part of the program, the controlling owners – the savings banks – had to make a FIM 1.3 billion capital injection to boost *Skopbank* capital.

3.4.2 Further Shocks Increase Pressures in the Financial Markets

Weak economic activity in the main export markets following the crisis in the Persian Gulf, persistently high interest rates in Western Europe, and – in the case of Finland – the collapse of the Soviet Union reduced exports in 1991. In Sweden, tax policy created a further shock when a long overdue reform of the income tax system was finally implemented in 1990–91. A reduction of the marginal tax rate applicable to interest deductions from 50 to 30 per cent finally made after-tax real interest rates positive, but it also meant a substantial negative shock to aggregate demand.[11] In their evaluation of the tax reform, Agell et al. (1998) estimate a negative effect on aggregate demand by around 1 per cent. Added to the autonomous forces already affecting domestic demand, these shocks gave major negative impulses to aggregate demand. GDP declined in both countries in 1991, by 6 per cent in Finland and by 2 per cent in Sweden (see Figure 2.1).

The shocks impacted on the monetary and financial systems in many ways. The exchange rate pegs were called into question, putting renewed upward pressure on domestic interest rates. In response, both countries tried to strengthen their fixed exchange rate commitment by changing the currency index that the exchange rate was tied to. Sweden moved from a trade-weighted basket to the ECU basket in May 1991, and Finland followed a month later. In fact, the Finnish action was forced by the Swedish move, which created speculation that Finland would follow suit and use the occasion to make a 'final' devaluation. No devaluation came, and for a while the market in Finland also calmed down.

Despite this temporary success on the exchange rate front, signs of financial distress were mounting. Plummeting corporate profitability weakened firms' capacity to service debt, and bankruptcies increased by some 50 per cent in both countries in 1991 from the already elevated levels of 1990. Bank earnings were squeezed by lost income from non-performing assets and declining fee income from new lending and trading activity. Declining collateral values increased the costs of bankruptcies to the lending banks (Figure 3.4).

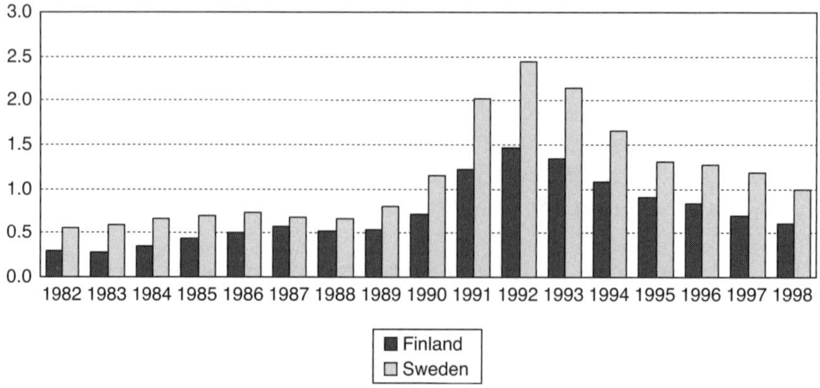

Figure 3.4 Bankruptcies per capita (thousands) in Finland and Sweden, 1982–98

3.4.3 Swedish Finance Companies the First Casualty

During the fall of 1989 one saw the first indications that the commercial property market had reached its peak in Sweden, and there were reports of increasing vacancies and difficulties in finding tenants at current rent levels. The stock market reacted rapidly and from its peak on 16 August 1989 the construction and real estate stock price index fell by 25 per cent in one year, compared with 11 per cent for the general index. Now there were also indications of potential credit losses among the finance companies, but nothing signaled expectations of a widespread financial crisis.

Reports early in 1990 about sizeable credit losses in some finance companies – such as *Infina* and *Obligentia* – went by without any effects on stock prices or on expectations more generally.[12] It was only in September 1990 that the mood suddenly changed when one of the finance companies, *Nyckeln* ('the Key'), with heavy exposure to real estate, found itself unable to roll over maturing commercial paper (*marknadsbevis*). This was a sort of 'run'; rather than actively running to the bank to withdraw deposits the holders of maturing *marknadsbevis,* otherwise routinely reinvesting, now refused renewed funding in the face of an imminent bankruptcy risk. The crisis spread to the whole market for *marknadsbevis,* which dried up in a couple of days. Surviving finance companies had to resort to bank loans. The crisis also spread to other segments of the money market with sharply increasing spreads between t-bills and certificates of deposit. In the next few months a number of other finance companies also went into bankruptcy.[13]

In this situation the banks, which had underwritten the commercial paper programs, had two options: either let the finance companies go bankrupt and take the losses right away or extend new lines of credit with the risk of higher losses further on. One example of the latter strategy is the rescue operation undertaken by *Nordbanken* to save the finance company *Gamlestaden* in the autumn of 1990. As the crisis deepened such a strategy proved less tenable. Several finance companies were allowed to go bankrupt, and now the crisis spread rapidly to the banks. Already in August 1990, *Nordbanken*, with the state as the main owner, reported unusually large credit losses. Total credit losses in the bank sector amounted to around 1 per cent of total lending in 1990, two to three times the level in earlier years.

3.4.4 Banking Problems and Exchange Rate Collapse in Finland

The crisis processes that followed were broadly similar, although the timing was somewhat different, with Finland in general leading Sweden. In Finland, problems came earnestly out into broad daylight on 19 September 1991, when *Skopbank* could not even obtain overnight funding and faced the risk of imminent closure. This was not allowed to happen, and the Bank of Finland took over the failing bank, which continued its operations under new management. The bank was split into three holding companies: one for ordinary banking operations, one for equity and real estate holdings, and one for the main industrial holding, the *Tampella* group. The Bank of Finland invested some FIM 3.5 billion in the operation in equity investment. The total commitment was substantially higher, estimated at the time at FIM 14 billion, although the final cost of the rescue operation was expected to be much smaller.

The *Skopbank* failure added to the general pessimism about the state of the economy, while other bad news continued to accumulate. Industrial production was declining, bankruptcies and unemployment increasing, and the public deficit increasing. Devaluation speculation started anew, and short-term interest rates shot up sharply from August 1991. In defense of the existing parities, the Bank of Finland sold foreign currency worth FIM 28 billion over two months from mid-August, leaving the currency reserve at only FIM 16 billion at the end of October.

In a final attempt to avoid devaluation, the labor market parties negotiated a rather extraordinary wage agreement that would have cut nominal wages by some 7 per cent. However, as powerful unions did not agree in the end, the agreement was never signed. Speculation increased further, and on 14 November 1991 the *markka* was devalued by 13 per cent. This brought short-term interest rates down by some 4 percentage points for a while, but longer-term rates were largely unaffected, the five-year bond rate remaining above 12 per cent.

3.4.5 From the *Skopbank* Take-over to a Full-blown Crisis

Skopbank was first considered a single rotten apple in the lot, rather than one of many; more than any other bank it had pursued a risky lending and investment strategy. However, the overall deterioration of the economy and particularly the continuing high interest rates progressively weakened all banks. The devaluation was an important element in this process. Although their currency positions were closed, banks were hurt by bankruptcies among firms with loans denominated in foreign currency. While large export companies could typically overcome an additional foreign debt burden through higher prices, companies operating in the depressed domestic market could not do so.

In early 1992, the Finnish government decided to reserve FIM 8 billion to bolster the capital base of the deposit banks across the board through a capital injection. Furthermore, a completely new authority, the Government Guarantee Fund (GGF), was established to 'safeguard the stability of deposit banking and depositors' claims'. The GGF was authorized to use up to FIM 20 billion for support operations. These decisions were largely considered – for example, in the financial press – very proactive and sufficient to guarantee the stability of the banking system. Interestingly, the Swedish authorities did not yet admit any reasons for similar precautionary measures. In Sweden the banking problems were still seen as isolated to a couple of banks and not to be handled as a systemic crisis.

It did not take long for new problems to emerge in Finland, particularly among the savings banks, as a large fraction of their loans turned non-performing. This reflected the generally weak quality of the loan stock, which had continued expanding even as late as 1991, and a high proportion of loans in foreign currency.[14] In addition, the savings banks had substantial investments in *Skopbank* shares, which had become practically worthless. In June 1992 the GGF committed FIM 7.2 billion to support some 40 distressed savings banks that were merged to form the Savings Bank of Finland (*SBF*). By September the whole *SBF* capital had already been wiped out, and by the end of the year a total of FIM 12.5 billion in bank support had been allocated to the SBF, now transformed into a joint stock company owned by the GGF.

In October 1992 yet another bank was failing. The *STS*-bank – a rather small commercial bank with close links to the trade unions – was taken over by one of the two largest commercial banks (*KOP*). The government took responsibility for the substandard assets of the failed bank, nominally worth FIM 3 billion. The overall credit and guarantee losses of the banking sector in 1992 amounted to about FIM 20 billion. Combined with weak net interest earnings and loss of fee income, the overall loss of the

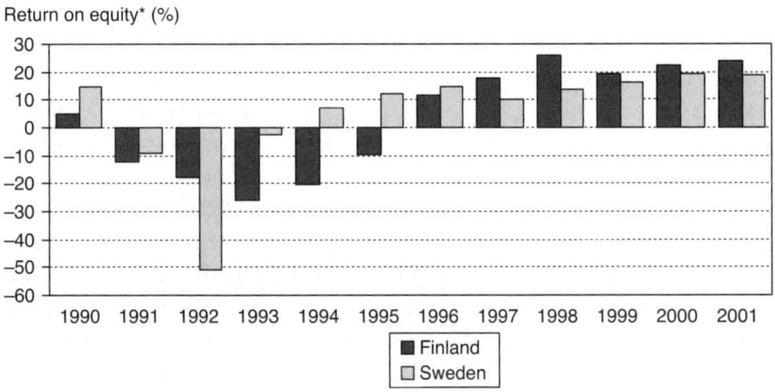

Note: Excluding asset management companies.

Figure 3.5 Net profit of the banking sector in Finland and Sweden, 1990–2001

year was also FIM 20 billion, reducing bank capital by almost 40 per cent. Three banks had been taken over by the state – *Skopbank*, the Savings Bank of Finland and the *STS*-bank – and the remainder of the banking system had become dependent on government support. By the end of the year almost all banks had accepted their share of the FIM 8 billion capital injection offered by the state (Figure 3.5).

As the banking crisis erupted, GDP continued to decline, unemployment shot up, central government borrowing increased unabated, and there were no signs of current account improvements. In this situation new pressures started to mount on the Finnish *markka* in the spring of 1992. Both short- and long-term interest rates increased, and the Bank of Finland had to sell foreign exchange to support the exchange rate.

After having calmed somewhat in the summer, pressures increased again in early September. Apart from the general economic decline, the budgetary situation and the general uncertainty about the sustainability of the ERM particularly brought pressure on the *markka*. With depleted foreign exchange reserves and no rapid improvements in sight, the Bank of Finland abandoned the peg on 8 September 1992. The currency immediately depreciated by some 12 per cent.

3.4.6 The Swedish Crisis Spreads to the Banks

In Sweden, bank credit losses accelerated during 1990 and 1991 to reach an annual rate of 3.5 per cent of lending by the end of 1991, and 7.5 per cent of lending at the peak of the crisis in the final quarter of 1992, about twice the operating profits of the banking sector. Over the period 1990–93, accumulated losses came to a total of nearly 17 per cent of lending.[15] The evolving crisis was closely connected with a sharp downturn in the real estate market, with prices of commercial properties in downtown Stockholm falling by 35 per cent in 1991 and by another 15 per cent the following year.[16] Lending 'related to real estate'[17] accounted for between 40 and 50 per cent of all losses, but only 10–15 per cent of all lending.

The fraction of lending going into real estate and the pace of lending expansion in previous years are the key factors that explain why some banks had larger credit losses than others. *Handelsbanken* – the only major bank to go through the crisis without the need for government support[18] – had the lowest rate of expansion and the lowest fraction of real estate loans, whereas *Gota*, with the largest losses, was at the other end of the scale.

The first signs that the losses caused solvency problems came in the fall of 1991, when two of the six major banks, *Första Sparbanken* and *Nordbanken*, needed new capital to fulfill their capital requirements. Just as in Finland, problems were at first seen to be limited to a couple of banks. In *Nordbanken* the state had to act in its capacity as the main owner. In December 1991, SEK 5 billion of new equity was injected into *Nordbanken*, 4 billion by the government and close to 1 billion by the private owners. The government also issued a guarantee to the owners of *Första Sparbanken* – a foundation – for a loan that enabled the bank to fulfill its capital requirement. Problems returned for these two banks already in the spring of 1992, leading the government to issue a new guarantee to *Första Sparbanken* and to transform the earlier guarantee into a subsidized loan at a cost of SEK 1.3 billion. In the case of *Nordbanken*, a major restructuring was decided by parliament in June 1992. The government was given a total limit of SEK 20 billion, part of which was used to bail out the private owners of the bank at a cost of SEK 2.1 billion, 20 per cent above the current stock market valuation. A 'bad bank', *Securum*, was founded and a quarter of *Nordbanken*'s credit stock, at an original book value of SEK 67 billion, was transferred to *Securum*.

During the spring of 1992, problems also surfaced in *Gota Bank*, the bank that in the end turned out to have made the largest losses. In April the bank's private owners put up new capital, but this lasted only a few months and on 9 September 1992 the holding company owning *Gota Bank* went bankrupt. It was only at this stage that the banking problems were dealt with as a systemic crisis. Sweden had no formal deposit insurance at the time, but now the government immediately announced that it guaranteed *Gota*'s liabilities. A similar guarantee, covering not only deposits but all forms of bank debt, was extended to all banks a few weeks later. Subsequently the state bought *Gota* at a price of one *krona*, but with recapitalization costing a total of SEK 25 billion.

3.4.7 The Swedish Currency Crisis

The banking crisis coincided in time with the European ERM crisis. The currency market unrest in the summer of 1992 spilled over with particular force on Sweden and Finland, not surprisingly given their legacies of high inflation and recurring devaluations. The immediate result was further interest increases; the *Riksbank* raised the overnight interest rate to 12 per cent in July and to 13 and 16 per cent in August. While rescuing the *krona* for the moment, it deepened problems for many bank customers and threatened to have adverse effects on Swedish banks' international funding. With more than 40 per cent of their lending in foreign currency, banks were heavily dependent on access to international financial markets, and with increasing signs of crisis, loan maturities shortened.

In early September 1992, the pound and the lira touched the lower limits of their currency bands and on 8 September the Finnish *markka* started floating. This led to speculation against the *krona* and on 9 September (the day of the *Gota* bankruptcy) the overnight rate was raised to 75 per cent. On 16 and 17 September, the UK and Italy left the ERM and the *Riksbank* now had to increase the overnight rate to 500 per cent to defend the *krona*. In this situation the general bank guarantee announced by the government (see below) played an important role in securing continued international funding for the Swedish banks. The *Riksbank* also provided liquidity by depositing a part of the foreign exchange reserves with the banks, thereby insuring bank liquidity against problems with international funding. During the fall the Swedish government presented some restrictive fiscal measures, making it possible to lower the overnight interest rate gradually to 11.5 per cent. But this brought only temporary relief. In November speculation against the *krona* resumed, and on 19 November the *krona* was left to float, leading to an immediate depreciation by 9 per cent the next day and by 20 per cent by the turn of the year.

The interaction between the currency crisis and the banking crisis is complex. The fact that the banking crisis started at least a year before the currency crisis with credit losses culminating in the fall of 1992 – before the fixed rate was abandoned – indicates that there was no strong direct link from currency losses to the banking crisis. In this regard the Swedish crisis process differs from that in Finland, where the 1991 devaluation had a direct impact on the debt service burden of the corporate sector, thereby adding to credit losses relatively early in the process. On the other hand, there was an indirect link, which was particularly important in Sweden, with the defense of the *krona* by high interest rates, causing credit losses and deepening the banking crisis.

During the 1980s, the Swedish private sector built up a large stock of foreign currency debt, estimated to be SEK 541 billion in September 1992 (35 per cent of GDP). Most of this was intermediated by the banking sector, whose net position in foreign currency was essentially balanced. The spot position was positive (SEK 20 billion), but the position on the forward market was minus SEK 65 billion.[19] This situation involved two risk elements for the banks. One was the liquidity risk: even if banks did not directly take excessive exchange risk, they faced the risk of foreign lenders refusing to roll over short-term credit lines. This mechanism contributed to deepening many other banking and currency crises (see, for example, Mishkin (1999a) on Mexico and Corsetti et al. (1999) on Asia). In the end, the liquidity support provided by the *Riksbank* played an important role in avoiding this risk.

The other risk element relates to bank customers. Whereas the banks themselves had a balanced position, many of their customers were heavily exposed in foreign currency. Indeed, profiting from the gap between domestic and foreign interest rates had been the main purpose of much of the borrowing. On aggregate, however, the private sector held foreign currency assets to offset the debt. Financial assets in foreign currency amounted to SEK 174 billion, making the net financial position in foreign currency minus SEK 367 billion in September 1992. Adding direct investments abroad and holdings of foreign shares made the total net position in foreign currency a trivial minus SEK 13 billion; that is, the balance sheet of the aggregate private sector was not very vulnerable to a Swedish devaluation. But the balanced average concealed an uneven distribution, with many small and medium-sized bank customers heavily exposed to devaluation. It is not known what share of currency positions was hedged, but it is believed to have only been a minor fraction.

The banking crisis and the currency crisis reinforced each other. As the precarious situation of the Swedish banks came to be recognized internationally during 1992, it became clear that the banks and many of their customers would not be able to survive an extended period of very high interest rates. This improved the odds of speculating against the Swedish *krona*, thereby leading to further interest increases, and in the end making it unavoidable to abandon the fixed parity.

3.4.8 Additional Bank Support and Stabilization

In the first months of 1993 the scale of the bank support became a major issue in Finland. A GGF decision to allocate almost FIM 5 billion to the

SBF at the end of 1992 had raised the total GGF support commitment to FIM 15 billion. Thus only some FIM 5 billion out of the originally authorized 20 billion would be left for further support. As no signs of overall improvement were seen, there was market concern about what would happen once the support resources were exhausted. As a consequence, the maturity of banks' foreign borrowing shortened substantially, and many lender banks cut their quotas – the same problems as encountered by Swedish banks in the fall of 1992, before the general government guarantee. Furthermore, the currency depreciated strongly again in the first months of 1993.

In this situation the parliament passed a resolution in February 1993, guaranteeing that Finnish deposit banks would meet all their financial commitments. This extended the 100 per cent deposit insurance to all bank liabilities, although the resolution was not stipulated by law as was the deposit insurance. The analogy with the Swedish bank guarantee introduced in late 1992 is immediate. Further, the parliament decided to commit more funds to bank support. The GGF support authorization was increased first by an additional FIM 20 billion in the spring of 1993 and later in two more steps to a total of FIM 80 billion by the end of 1993.

Towards the spring of 1993 the pressures in the financial markets started to recede in both countries. In Finland, short-term interest rates had been declining since the currency was left floating, and long-term rates had started to fall following a major budgetary package in October 1992 including expenditure cuts in the order of FIM 20 billion. But it was only after the bank support measures taken in February 1993 and the first signs of a more sustained improvement in the current account in the second quarter that the financial markets calmed down, with capital flows now turning towards *markka* assets. The exchange rate started to appreciate, while the Bank of Finland could simultaneously buy foreign currency, and interest rates continued to decline. The real economy also stabilized and from mid-1993 GDP started growing again and the increase in unemployment decelerated. Towards the end of 1993 even the central government borrowing requirement started to decline substantially.

Despite the overall improvement, further bank support measures were still needed. In August 1993 the two major commercial banks – *KOP* and *SYP* – were given GGF guarantees for raising tier-2 capital.[20] In November, the government also stepped in to protect the trust fund 'depositors' of a large co-operative retail chain (EKA). Those funds were not strictly deposits as defined in the Deposit Bank Act, and not covered by formal deposit insurance. Yet the government decided to guarantee the capital, although not the interests accrued.

Table 3.2a Bank support payments in Finland, 1991–96

		Value (billion FIM)
1991	*Skopbank*, equity etc. by the Bank of Finland	3.5
1992	All deposit banks, general capital injection	7.7
	Skopbank, additional equity capital	1.5
	Savings Bank of Finland/*Arsenal*, equity capital	10.0
1993	*STS*-bank, equity capital	3.0
	Skopbank, additional equity capital	1.0
	SBF/Arsenal, additional equity capital	7.1
1994	*Skopbank*, additional equity capital	0.5
	SBF/Arsenal, additional equity capital	6.2
1995	*SBF/Arsenal*, additional equity capital	8.0
1996	*SBF/Arsenal*, additional equity capital	3.8
Total payments		52.4

In addition, the restructuring of the *Skopbank* and the Savings Bank of Finland and the associated asset management company, *Arsenal*, continued with full force throughout 1993. The single largest restructuring measure of all took place in the autumn: the splitting up and sale of the Savings Bank of Finland (a more detailed account is given in Section 3.6). This ended the acute crisis management phase, but the restructuring of failed institutions and the associated disposal of assets required substantial public funding for several years to come (Table 3.2a).

Also in Sweden, financial indicators started to return to normal levels in 1993, with interest rates falling continuously during the year. By the end of 1993 both short- and long-term rates were down at around 7 per cent. The depreciation of the *krona* was halted in February 1993, but in contrast to the *markka* it was not strengthened until 1995. Lower interest rates eased the situation for the banks, and after 1993 no more government support was needed. From May 1993 a new government agency, *Bankstödsnämnden* (the Bank Support Agency), was coordinating all forms of bank support. Government payments to the banks are summarized in Table 3.2b. Out of a total of SEK 65 billion, only 3.1 billion went to the old bank owners: 1 billion in interest subsidies to *Första Sparbanken* and 2 billion in buying out the old owners of *Nordbanken*. By and large the government followed the principle of saving the banks but not their owners.

Table 3.2b Bank support payments in Sweden, 1991–94

Date	Event	Value (billion SEK)
1991	*Nordbanken*, new equity	4.2
1992	*Nordbanken*, bailout of old shareholders	2.1
	Nordbanken, new equity	10.0
	Securum, equity	24.0
1993	*Gota*, new equity	25.1
1994	*Första Sparbanken*, interest subsidy	1.0
Total payments		66.4

3.5 CRISIS MANAGEMENT AND RESTRUCTURING

When the crisis hit, it entailed a new experience for the active generation of bankers and regulators, both in Finland and Sweden. Previous bank failures in the 1920s and 1930s were ancient history. Not only did the bankers of the 1980s have little experience in handling large-scale credit losses, but regulatory institutions were also unprepared for the sort of massive problems that emerged. Thus, while the authorities tried to come to grips with what was going on, and what should be done about it, new organizational structures had to be created to handle an unprecedented intervention in the workings of the financial system.

3.5.1 Recognizing the Scale of the Problem Took Time

In Finland, the possibility of banking problems started to be recognized in late 1989. The Bank of Finland and the Bank Inspectorate put *Skopbank* under special surveillance, as it and the savings bank group finally started to constrain lending. The *Skopbank* CEO, the architect of the expansion strategy, committed suicide shortly afterwards, which was by many considered an admission that the bank was heading for disaster. At this stage the authorities actively tried to work out ways for the bank to reduce its risks and find additional private capital. This resulted in a restructuring program in 1990, part of which was the capital injection by the savings banks described above. No public money was involved at this stage.

With the onset of the general economic downturn in 1991, it became clear that private solutions would not suffice to keep *Skopbank* alive, and plans were made for a central bank intervention. However, it took an acute liquidity crisis before the central bank felt obliged to step in and take over the failing bank in September 1991. Subsequently, a working group was appointed by the prime minister at the end of 1991 with the task of assessing the situation and making proposals about the measures to be taken. The working group concluded in March 1992 – more than two years after the emergence of the *Skopbank* crisis – that serious problems extended to the banking system as a whole, and that extraordinary measures would need to be taken.

Sweden experienced a similar process of gradually recognizing that the crisis involved the banking system as a whole. In the early phase, when the finance companies were hit in 1989–90, the Bank Inspection Board (*Bankinspektionen*) was actively involved in discussions with the banks with the aim of finding private solutions that avoided the crisis spreading to the rest of the financial system. As a result the banks took over loans previously granted by the finance companies. Apart from this the role of the Bank Inspection Board was limited and the government acted primarily directly through the Finance Ministry. In the case of *Nordbanken*, the government was involved from the start for the obvious reason that it was the main owner.

For other banks private solutions were sought, as in Finland. In April 1992 the owners of *Gota*, who had invested new money to ensure that the bank could meet the capital requirements, declared themselves unwilling to make further investments. In this situation the bank signed a contract with a group of international insurance companies, which guaranteed *Gota* the right to borrow money to cover credit losses within a frame of SEK 13 billion. For the biggest savings bank, *Första Sparbanken*, the government had already issued a guarantee for losses up to a maximum of SEK 3.8 billion in 1991, a guarantee that was later transformed into a loan. The triggering event in recognizing that it was a systemic crisis was the bankruptcy of the holding company owning *Gota Bank* in September 1992. At that stage – which coincided with the currency crisis – it did not take lengthy deliberations of a working group to realize that the stability of the whole financial system was at stake.

In characterizing the government's 'emergency treatment', two things should be emphasized. The first factor is the decisiveness and broad political support once action was taken. The government made it clear that it guaranteed *Gota*'s obligations on the very day of the bankruptcy. The announcement of the general bank guarantee came only two weeks later with the support of all parties except a small populist party (*Ny demokrati*). Broad political support was particularly important, since the bank guarantee was so far just an announcement of a forthcoming bill to parliament; the formal decision in parliament came three months later. The second factor is that there was in principle no direct compensation given to the shareholders of the failed banks. Of course the general bank guarantee was a valuable asset provided free of charge. In fact, its existence probably saved one or more of the surviving banks from bankruptcy, and thereby indirectly part of the wealth of the shareholders. But the guiding principle was to rescue the financial system with a minimum of wealth transfer to the original shareholders.

3.5.2 Systemic Problems Motivated Action in Both Countries

Once the scale of the banking problems started to emerge, the stability of the financial system was seen as being under threat in both countries. Even though government actions were limited to individual banks, they were explicitly motivated by the threat that the failure of a large bank would pose for the stability of the financial system. This was the case with *Skopbank* in Finland[21] and *Nordbanken* in Sweden.[22] Similar arguments were used in the assessment of the aforementioned Finnish working group when discussing the consequences of further banking problems. But in addition to a general reference to the value of preserving financial stability, the working group emphasized the danger of a 'credit crunch'. The group argued that depletion of bank capital could force banks to cut down lending, even forcing customers to pay back debts in advance. Such a decline of credit supply would exacerbate the deflationary tendencies, even in the absence of additional bank failures.[23] In Sweden the potential impact on the real estate market was also emphasized. It was pointed out that a weak banking system would be unable to continue funding real estate holdings, with the risk of contributing to a downward price spiral impelled by fire sales. This version of a credit crunch argument appears to have featured more prominently in Sweden than the broader impact of a credit crunch on investment and consumption.

A practical conclusion from the perceived systemic threat was that no bank should be allowed to close operations. The absence of bank runs suggests that this policy was quite well understood by bank creditors, even if never officially spelled out by the authorities.[24] Still, liquidity problems occurred in both countries as some banks encountered difficulties in renewing funding in the international money market. This was a crucial factor in triggering bank support. In Sweden it led the *Riksbank* to deposit a good part of its exchange reserves with the banks in the fall of 1992. The purpose was to shield the banks, and their borrowers, from any immediate problems if foreign credit lines were to be cut off. Similarly in Finland, the broad guarantee resolution in early 1993 and the subsequent widening of GGF support authorization were particularly motivated by the need to safeguard a steady flow of foreign credit.

The difference in formal depositor protection between the two countries does not seem to have played any role. Even though all bank depositors were fully covered by insurance in Finland but not in Sweden, the authorities in both countries intervened in roughly the same manner. Perhaps the fact that Sweden did not have deposit insurance may have made the Swedish politicians more prone to issue an unlimited guarantee straight away once they acted in the fall of 1992, while the Finnish authorities took a more gradual approach.

3.5.3 The Main Policy Response: Capital Support and Guarantees

In principle, several policy options were available to deal with the looming banking problems. One was an expansionary macroeconomic policy. In particular, easing monetary policy would both help bank borrowers to meet their contractual commitments and lower bank costs of financing non-interest-yielding assets. A second approach would be to bolster bank profitability through targeted policy measures such as providing inexpensive central bank financing or changing fees and remaining interest rate regulations. A third option would be to reduce the costs of market financing through various guarantee schemes. Finally, capital bases could be strengthened by direct equity injections by the state.

Of these options, macroeconomic policy played an important role in both countries, in particular the exchange rate policy. Holding the exchange rate fixed for so long undoubtedly had contributed to aggravating the crisis, but conversely the depreciation that followed when the exchange rates started floating had an important expansive effect at a critical moment. As a result, interest rates came down immediately. Some targeted measures to boost bank profitability were also undertaken, but their significance was relatively small.[25] Instead, both countries came to rely heavily on capital injections and guarantees, Sweden putting more emphasis on the latter and Finland on the former.

3.5.4 Preferred Capital Certificates: A Finnish Innovation

Acting on the advice of the working group on bank problems, the Finnish government offered in March 1992 to inject FIM 8 billion into the deposit banks. The injection was allocated to the banks according to their risk-weighted assets and off-balance-sheet commitments. The instrument – preferred capital certificates – was specially designed to allow it to be included in Tier 1 capital while avoiding direct government ownership.

Preferred capital certificates could be used to cover losses along with other Tier 1 capital. The instrument carried an interest equal to the short-term money market rate for the first three years. Thereafter, the interest rate would increase progressively so as to create incentives for the bank to replace the instrument with equity. Should the bank be unable to pay the contractual interest for more than three years or should the bank's capital ratio fall under the statutory minimum, the government would be entitled to convert preferred capital certificates into ordinary shares with voting rights.

The basic idea was to bolster in a pre-emptive manner the banking sector's capital base across the board, thereby avoiding any loss of confidence in the banking system's solvency and any need for the banks to constrain lending due to lack of capital. Making the facility available to all banks was considered important in order to avoid distorting competition. A special instrument rather than new equity was considered necessary in order to make all banks willing to accept government involvement, and to make the capital injection easy to apply to all kinds of banks, some of which did not have share capital at all.

The preferred capital certificates worked broadly as intended. Almost all banks accepted the offer in the end,[26] and all banks not resorting to GGF support paid back the capital when the interest charge started to exceed the going money market rate. Thus the cost to the government was restricted to the lost interest revenue over a three-year period. Although the counterfactual is difficult to establish, it is very likely that at least one other bank – *KOP* – would have had to resort to GGF support in the absence of the general capital support.

3.5.5 Sweden: Direct Capital Support and Guarantees

Most of the Swedish government support went to the state-owned *Nordbanken* (Table 3.2b), mainly in the form of new equity with no strings attached. The amount of new equity went beyond what was needed to fulfill the capital requirement. A private majority owner would not have invested in *Nordbanken* the way the government did. Since this was a transfer from one pocket of the state budget to another pocket, it may be argued that it did not involve as severe moral hazard problems as support to a private bank would have entailed, although such concerns about the relation between owner and manager should not be neglected. In any case, this was clearly a selective subsidy reducing the cost of capital for *Nordbanken* relative to other banks. This selective support gave *Nordbanken* a competitive advantage over other banks, thereby strengthening the bank as a player in the future restructuring of the banking sector in the Nordic region.

In relation to privately owned banks, various forms of guarantees played the major role. These involved guarantees to the foundation that was the owner of *Första Sparbanken*, allowing the bank to obtain a loan on the open market. This guarantee was later transformed into a direct loan with favorable conditions. At a later stage, in 1993, the Bank Support Agency granted a special form of guarantee to *Föreningsbanken*, ensuring that the bank would be able to fulfill its capital requirements. If its capital were to fall below 9 per cent of the capital base, that is, dangerously close to the limit of 8 per cent, then the Bank Support Agency was committed to buy preferential shares with a yield corresponding to the market interest rate. Existing shareholders were given the right to buy back the preferential shares at face value until 1998. If this right was not exercised, the preferential shares should be transformed into regular shares with full voting rights. This construction had some similarities with the Finnish capital injection. It ensured that the government got its money back if the bank were in a position to survive. As it turned out, the guarantee was never used.

3.5.6 Handling of Failing Banks through Specially Created Institutions

In neither Sweden nor Finland were there pre-existing government institutions with a clearly defined task to handle failing banks. Key actors in both countries have testified to the improvised nature of many of the measures taken in the early stages of the crisis.[27] In Sweden, the Financial Supervisory Authority was in charge of bank supervision, but almost all measures taken during 1991 and 1992 were handled directly by the finance ministry. In Finland, as noted above, the first bank failure was taken care of by the central bank. As the scale of the banking problems became understood, special institutions were created in both countries to handle support to banks at the risk of failure or having failed.

In Finland, the special institution was the Government Guarantee Fund (GGF) created in April 1992. The fund was authorized to extend credit to the security funds of various banking groups, to guarantee such funding, to acquire shares and other equity capital in banks, to extend loans and guarantees to deposit banks, and so on. Originally, the decision-making powers were formally given to a board with representatives of the Ministry of Finance, the central bank and the bank inspectorate. In practice all major decisions were taken at the highest political level, and in February 1993 the formal decision authority was transferred to the government.

The GGF became the central body of bank support operations in Finland. The Bank of Finland sold its shares in *Skopbank* to the GGF, which from June 1992 onwards was responsible for the restructuring of this bank. The GGF also took over the failing savings banks, organized their merger into the Savings Bank of Finland and later restructured the bank. Similarly, non-performing loans and other assets of the *STS*-bank became the responsibility of the GGF. All these activities involved large amounts of capital injections, and the GGF became the main channel of public capital support to the banking sector.

In Sweden, the general bank guarantee was first announced in a press release issued by the government on 24 September 1992, following consultations with all political parties represented in parliament. It was only confirmed three months later by a formal decision in parliament. Handling of the guarantee was now moved from the finance ministry to a special authority, the Bank Support Agency (*Bankstödsnämnden*), which started operating in May 1993. It was staffed with civil servants headed by a director general, and overseen by a board of governors, some of whom had a background in business and banking. In contrast to Finland, formal decision authority was moved from the central government to an independent agency. The tasks of the Bank Support Agency involved the detailed scrutiny of the economic health of those individual banks that might be in need of government support. Aided by international consulting teams, the agency conducted in-depth analyses of the credit portfolios and future prospects of individual banks (all major banks except *Handelsbanken*). This resulted in a special agreement with one of the remaining banks, *Föreningsbanken*, as mentioned above. In practice, the Bank Support Agency took few concrete decisions. By the time it was operative, bank profits were improving and the need for support disappearing.

3.5.7 Work-out of Bad Assets in Asset Management Companies

A major issue concerning the failing institutions was the handling of non-performing loans and other 'bad' assets. Unlike Norway, both Sweden and Finland chose to set up separate government-owned asset management companies. In Sweden, *Securum* was created in 1992 as a vehicle to remove bad loans from the balance sheet of *Nordbanken*. It was originally conceived by the management of the bank, not as an instrument to handle a general banking crisis but rather as an ingredient in the efforts to turn *Nordbanken* into a strong and profitable bank. In all, assets with a book value of SEK 67 billion were transferred to *Securum*. In January 1993 it started operating as an independent company, owned directly by the state to 100 per cent. Not being a subsidiary of *Nordbanken*, it was not subject to banking regulation. As a bank subsidiary it would, for instance, have been obliged to sell its assets as soon as market conditions permitted, and would not have had the right to purchase additional assets apart from those taken over as collateral. Now its freedom of action was only restricted by general corporate law.

Securum was run by a professional management team, which was given substantial independence by the owner. The company was capitalized in order to be able to operate with a long time horizon. Its assets consisted of a portfolio of non-performing loans, and the primary initial task was to rescue whatever economic values these contained. In an initial phase this involved taking decisions on whether to have the debtors file for bankruptcy or not. In most cases bankruptcy turned out to be the solution, resulting in *Securum* taking over the underlying collateral, mostly real estate assets. The company then faced the task of disposing of these assets. This involved, first, securing that the underlying economic activities were run efficiently; second, repackaging the assets in such a way that the potential market value was maximized; and, third, selling them at the best possible price.

Securum had to operate with an eye to the development of the real estate market. It was the owner of around 2500 properties with an estimated market value of SEK 15–20 billion, corresponding to between 1 and 2 per cent of all commercial real estate in Sweden. It was believed that putting all of this on the market immediately, for example, through auctions, would have led to large losses and depressed the real estate market even further. For this reason, *Securum* was heavily capitalized with the intent of guaranteeing its survival without further government support for at least ten years.

Assets were sold in three ways: IPOs (initial public offerings) on the Stockholm stock exchange, corporate transactions outside the stock exchange, and transactions involving individual properties. Most of the sales were carried out in 1995 and 1996, when the real estate market had started to recover but prices were still low by historical standards. The company was dissolved in the summer of 1997, after a much shorter period than the ten years envisaged when it was formed. Out of an initial equity of SEK 28 billion, 14 billion was repaid to the state.[28]

In Finland, the creation of asset management companies was a more contentious issue. It was widely agreed that the restructuring of the failing banks would be aided by separating the assets of dubious quality from ordinary banking business. Nevertheless, there were concerns that the transfer prices of the assets might be set too high so as to create hidden subsidies to the remaining 'good bank', which in principle could remain in private ownership. The issue became highly politicized, and in February 1993 the parliament rejected the proposal to use asset management companies as a vehicle of bank restructuring. However, as it became clear that such companies would only be used in the context of banks for which the government in any case bore a full financial responsibility, they were finally approved by the parliament in October 1993.[29] Once approved, asset management companies became a central vehicle of restructuring. In particular, *Arsenal* played a central role in the banking sector restructuring that took place.

Arsenal was established in November 1993 as a state-owned company with the task of taking care of substandard assets of the Savings Bank of Finland (SBF). For practical reasons, *Arsenal* in fact became the owner of the SBF with sound assets sold out to four other banks (see below). The book value of the assets transferred to *Arsenal* from the SBF originally amounted to FIM 39 billion, of which 16 billion were non-performing corporate loans, 8 billion non-performing household loans, 12 billion real estate holdings and 3 billion stocks. Later, *Arsenal* also took over the bad assets of the failed *STS*-bank (FIM 1.4 billion at the time of the transfer in 1995) and some real estate holdings of the former *Skopbank*.

The disposal of assets took place gradually for the same reasons as in Sweden. In particular, the property holdings were considered simply too large to be sold immediately in a depressed market. In fact, the disposal process was completed only in 2000. By the end of that year, the total losses of *Arsenal* amounted to FIM 20 billion, about 50 per cent of the original book value of transferred assets.

3.5.8 Bank Creditors Bailed out but not Owners

The very commitment to take whatever measures are needed to keep banking systems operational – such as the open-ended guarantee resolutions adopted in Finland and Sweden – invariably constitutes an implicit subsidy to the banks and their owners. The potential for receiving government support quite clearly creates moral hazard problems, giving banks incentives to take on excessive risks. This implies that the conditions of the support operations are very important. A general principle in both countries was that no bank creditors, including holders of subordinated debt, were allowed to suffer losses, but that bank owners should carry their full financial responsibility. Thus when the authorities took over a failing bank, the government also became the owner of the bank with nominal or no compensation to the earlier owners.

In practice there were exceptions to the rule of full ownership responsibility. In Finland, the most obvious one is the general capital injection. Even ex post, it constituted a transfer to the bank owners corresponding to the interest revenue lost by the government. The size of this subsidy was nevertheless relatively modest: FIM 1.2 billion to the banks that remained in private ownership, corresponding to less than 5 per cent of these banks' regulatory capital at the outset of the crisis. The principal owner of *STS*-bank – a foundation – was also paid FIM 75 million for its equity in the bank, whose net worth was clearly negative. Although some additional transactions make it debatable whether this represented a transfer from the government to the fund, the fact remains that an owner of a failing bank was compensated for relinquishing his or her ownership in a negative-net-worth bank.[30]

In Sweden, owners of a failing bank were also to some extent compensated. The owners of *Första Sparbanken* – a foundation – received an interest subsidy of SEK 1 billion. The private minority owners of *Nordbanken* were paid SEK 21 per share in the summer of 1992 when the market price was only SEK 18. The value of this subsidy amounts to SEK 300 million. Both of these cases reflect decisions taken early on during the crisis. In the case of the interest subsidy to *Första Sparbanken*, the government at a later stage tried to persuade the bank to pay it back, without success.

A potential for hidden government subsidies also existed in the sale of assets in the process of restructuring. In Finland, particularly the pricing of the 'sound' assets of *SBF* was questioned at the time of the split-up of the bank. In Sweden, there are similar issues with regard to the pricing of assets sold by *Nordbanken* to *Securum*, although this may simply be regarded as a transfer between two accounts in the governmental books. In practice it is of course not easy to determine what is the fair value in a highly distressed and illiquid market.

3.5.9 Strong-handed and Rapid Restructuring of the Banking Sector

The banking crises led to large-scale reorganizations of the banking systems, particularly in Finland but in many ways also in Sweden. In Finland the end result in fact resembles a likely market outcome in the sense that all failed banks ceased to exist. The good assets of *Skopbank*, the Savings Bank of Finland and *STS*-bank were sold to other banks and dubious assets were disposed of through asset management companies. In Sweden, on the other hand, the two banks that would have gone bankrupt in an unregulated market – *Nordbanken* and *Gota* – were allowed to survive and form the nucleus of the successful *Nordea* banking group.

The single most important restructuring action in Finland was the split-up and sale of the Savings Bank of Finland with the bad assets transferred to an asset management company and the good assets sold to the four domestic competitors in equal shares. In particular, all branch offices, including deposit accounts, were sold to the buying banks. As a result, most of the savings bank sector disappeared overnight. The split-up in equal shares was considered the only practical option, as foreign interest in acquiring the bank was small and no domestic bank was in a position to buy the whole of the *SBF*.[31] The crisis can also be seen as the main impetus for the merger of the two largest commercial banks, *KOP* and

SYP (*Unitas*), into *Merita Bank* in 1995. Particularly, *KOP* had suffered significant losses and seemed unable to restructure on its own.

The Swedish crisis was also followed by some restructuring efforts. Out of six major banks before the crisis, four now remain. If the market forces had been allowed free play, at least two banks would have disappeared, *Nordbanken* and *Gota*. In the case of *Nordbanken* this was prevented through government interventions securing the survival of a financially strong bank. *Gota*, on the other hand, was put up for sale after the government take-over. After some negotiations with domestic and foreign banks the government decided to sell *Gota* to *Nordbanken*. This bank would subsequently take the lead in international restructuring, resulting in the creation of a truly pan-Nordic banking conglomerate through a merger with *Merita Bank* in 1997 and later mergers with *Unidanmark* from Denmark and *Christiania Bank* from Norway. The result is a banking group, *Nordea*, which is by far the largest in the Nordic area.

In both countries the restructuring was accompanied by substantial cost cutting. Given that the Finnish banks had been less cost-efficient at the outset of the crisis, it is natural that the efficiency gains were larger in Finland than in Sweden. In Finland, the number of bank employees and branch offices declined by more than 50 per cent during the 1990s. In Sweden, the number of branch offices declined by over a third, but the number of employees declined only marginally. Both countries have been pioneers in introducing modern banking technologies. Apart from automated teller machines and points of sale, remote access banking in the form of telephone and internet-based services also spread faster in Finland and Sweden than in most other countries. As a result, at the end of the 1990s the Swedish and Finnish banking sectors employed the least personnel relative to population in the whole EU. In fact, Finnish banks seem to have surpassed Swedish banks in overall cost efficiency, measured by the ratio of total costs to total revenues. On the other hand, looking at the value of bank assets per employee, Swedish banks remain above and Finnish banks below the EU average. Between 1985 and 1995 the number of bank employees per ecu billion of assets decreased from 929 to 371 in Finland and from 205 to 137 in Sweden. Corresponding averages for the EU area were 507 and 241, respectively; see Ibañez and Molyneux (2001, Table 10).

3.5.10 Substantial Costs to the Public Sector

Substantial amounts of public funds were committed to bank support in both countries. In Finland, the total commitment was FIM 97 billion, of which 69 billion was in paid-out support and the rest in various kinds of legally binding guarantees. In Sweden, SEK 65 billion was paid out in support between 1992 and 1994. The total commitment under the general bank guarantee was in principle only limited by the value of total liabilities. Relative to the annual GDP at the outset of the crisis in 1991, the paid-out support amounted to 4.8 and 13.9 per cent in Sweden and Finland, respectively. The Swedish cost is clearly at the low end while the Finnish cost is relatively typical compared with fiscal costs in other countries. In a comprehensive sample of 40 banking crises studied by Honohan and Klingebiel (2003), the average fiscal cost is 12.8 per cent of GDP.[32]

The definition of fiscal costs is not clear-cut. One problem is the valuation of the guarantee commitments. Since they are not available on the market, they are difficult to price correctly. In practice they are typically ignored, that is, valued at zero, which is clearly not sensible. Another problem is that a considerable fraction of what is paid out is normally recovered at a later stage, making the final cost smaller. The question is when to close the books. This was particularly important in the Swedish case, where a large part of the support went to a government-owned bank that was subsequently partly privatized, and recoveries depended on the price development of *Nordea* shares. Closing the books in mid-1997 (when *Securum* was dissolved and the surplus returned to the government), Jennergren and Näslund (1998) arrive at a net cost estimate of SEK 35 billion in 1997 prices, corresponding to no more than 1.7 per cent of 1991 GDP. For Finland the final costs have been estimated at FIM 33 billion, or 6.5 per cent of 1991 GDP.[33]

While the fiscal costs may appear rather small put in the perspective of national income, they are certainly non-negligible compared with banking sector capital, particularly in Finland where the total cost amounted to over 60 per cent of the regulatory capital at the outset of the crisis. It is also worth remembering that the support operations aggravated the budgetary crises. Nevertheless, in comparison with other banking crises, the costs to taxpayers were in no way exceptionally high.

3.6 EFFECTS ON THE REAL ECONOMY

The mechanisms whereby financial crises can have real consequences remain controversial. A traditional monetarist view posits that a financial crisis is important only to the extent that it affects the money supply. A crisis that leads to bank runs and forces bank closures can cause a large decline in the money supply and disruptions in the payments system. These can substantially reduce aggregate demand. On the other hand, crises that do not reduce the money supply are seen as inconsequential for economic activity, even though they may involve bankruptcies in the non-financial as well as financial sectors and volatile asset prices. Schwartz (1986) calls such non-monetary crises 'pseudo crises'.

In this terminology the financial crises in Sweden and Finland were pseudo crises with no real consequences. Money stocks did not drop much, and there were no suspensions of banking operations or disruptions in the payments systems. The only real consequences could then be associated with the adverse effects of bank support policies as such, for example, the effects through public finances on public and private spending and longer-term effects on risk-taking incentives.

This narrow view of the significance of financial crises has been increasingly challenged. In the last two decades a large body of literature has emerged about the role of financial intermediation in economic activity. It emphasizes the role of the financial system in general and the banking system in particular in channeling funds from savers to investors in situations of asymmetric or incomplete information. Financial intermediation can be disrupted by crises, and such disruption can have adverse real consequences. Consistent with this view, Mishkin (1999b) defines 'financial instability' as a situation 'when shocks to the financial system interfere with information flows so that the financial system can no longer do its job of channeling funds to those with productive investment opportunities'. Such a failure naturally has negative real consequences, irrespective of what happens to the money supply.

3.6.1 Financial Factors Can Affect Real Outcomes in Several Ways

Financial intermediation can be disrupted in different ways by the type of events that took place in the early 1990s. One can distinguish between at least four channels. First, high interest rates not only dampen demand through the standard opportunity cost mechanism but also exacerbate adverse selection problems that create credit rationing; see, for example, Stiglitz and Weiss (1981). Thus rationing phenomena can become more serious, reducing aggregate demand.

Second, debt service problems and failures among non-financial and financial institutions alike increase uncertainty in financial markets. This makes it more difficult to assess risk, thereby increasing adverse selection problems. Further, one cannot exclude the possibility that bank managers' risk perceptions change, and that their risk assessment may become excessively cautious.

Third, weak borrower balance sheets affect creditworthiness. Low asset prices reduce the value of collateral that can be used to reduce credit risk.

Declining borrower net worth – whether associated with asset values or lower expected earnings – makes lending riskier. Variations in borrower net worth create a financial accelerator: lower net worth increases risk premiums and thus lending interest rates, in the extreme leading to credit rationing; see, for example, Gilchrist et al. (1996).

Fourth, weak intermediary balance sheets weaken lending capacity. Intermediaries themselves can suffer from the same sort of net worth problems as non-financial entities: banks cannot raise sufficient funds, as their depressed net worth makes them too risky borrowers. In addition, capital regulations may create a constraint even when no market pressures exist. The result can be a 'credit crunch', that is, a decline in credit supply due to lack of capital or insufficient net worth in the banking sector.

3.6.2 Aggregate Observations Broadly Consistent with a Financial Factor Story

The decline in aggregate demand and production during the crisis years was associated with a significant decline both in aggregate credit and in the importance of bank loans in relation to other sources of funds. In Finland, the ratio of total liabilities among non-financial enterprises to GDP declined from 65 per cent in 1992 to 40 per cent in 1995, and the share of bank loans in those liabilities fell from 52 per cent to 49 per cent. The pattern was similar in Sweden, where total liabilities fell from 126 per cent of GDP in 1992 to 83 per cent in 1995, and the fraction of bank loans among total liabilities decreased from 28 to 25 per cent.

This is consistent with the hypothesis that credit constraints became more important and contributed to reducing economic activity during the depression. However, declining credit volume could also be explained by weak credit demand owing to high interest rates and weak profitability prospects of firms and weak income expectations of households. Survey data lend some support to the hypothesis that financial constraints indeed played a role. In Finland a large proportion of firms reported financing difficulties during the crisis years. Responses to such survey questions can be interpreted in different ways, however. In particular, it is not easy to disentangle problems that are due to the borrowers' lack of creditworthiness from those that reflect the weakness of banks and other lenders. Nevertheless, the sharp increase in the proportion of firms in Finland reporting funding difficulties indicates a role for tighter financial constraints, be they on the side of borrowers or lenders.

Econometric analyses with aggregate time series data are also in line with the financial constraints story. In a study on quarterly data for all Nordic countries 1980–2002, Hansen (2003) finds that total lending of all credit institutions, along with house prices, has a strong predictive power for bankruptcies (Granger causes). For Finland, vector autoregressive models on monthly data from 1980 to 1996 reported in Anari et al. (2002) indicate that shocks to bank credit explain a significant proportion of GDP variation, even accounting for the effects of past GDP, money supply, consumer prices and exports. Similarly, Saarenheimo (1995) finds on quarterly data from 1970 to 1994 that bank credit impacts significantly on private fixed investment, allowing for the effects of money supply and interest rates. A problem with these studies is that what are referred to as credit shocks need not be supply shocks but could also represent autonomous changes in credit demand. However, this objection is not very strong, since credit shocks have a significant impact on output and investment, even when credit is allowed to affect investment and GDP only with a lag.[34]

Furthermore, a more structural analysis by Pazarbaşioğlu (1997) supports the idea that supply is indeed responsible for at least a part of the decline of credit in Finland in the early 1990s. Pazarbaşioğlu estimates a disequilibrium model of the Finnish credit market with monthly data from 1987 to 1996. Her results suggest that supply determined the amount of credit from the second half of 1991 to late 1992.

For Sweden, Hallsten (1999) studies the hypothesis of a lending channel for monetary policy within the framework of an *IS*/*LM* model extended with an equilibrium condition for the loan market. The model implies that the mix between bank loans and other sources of private sector funding should vary with the stance of monetary conditions, and further that this mix should have an impact on production, investment and consumption. Her study documents a pronounced decline in the share of bank loans out of various broader credit aggregates between 1991 and 1993. In a regression analysis on quarterly data from 1985 to 1995 she studies the impact of the mix between bank loans and other sources of funding measured in different ways. The general finding is that a reduced proportion of bank loans has a significantly negative impact on GDP.

3.6.3 Collateral Squeeze or Credit Crunch?

Aggregate relationships cannot say much about the nature of the link between financing problems and real outcomes, and even if credit shocks are identified as stemming from the supply side it is not obvious whether they reflect reduced credit supply to constant quality borrowers or weakened borrower creditworthiness. Using the terminology of Holmström and Tirole (1997), one has to distinguish between a 'credit crunch' and a 'collateral squeeze'. This is not easy in practice because, for instance, declining asset prices may simultaneously reduce the collateral values and lender net worth. Similarly, bankruptcies and associated credit losses deplete lender capital while also signaling an increased bankruptcy risk among other borrowers.

From a policy point of view, it is still crucial to know whether the main problem is lack of bank capital or weak borrower balance sheets. In the former case, bank support and restructuring could help, while such support might be rather ineffective in the latter case. Expansionary macro policy or targeted borrower support schemes would help only slowly if bank capital is the main constraint on credit expansion and would be much more effective if weak borrower net worth is the main issue.

The time series analysis for Finland by Pazarbaşioğlu (1997) attempts to find proxy variables for the two mechanisms. Borrower credit worthiness is proxied by market capitalization of listed companies, representing corporate net worth, and by the differential between the bank lending rate and the money market rate, indicating a risk premium. The availability of bank funding is proxied by the variance of bank share prices relative to the market average. It turns out that both borrower credit worthiness proxies obtain a significant coefficient with the expected sign. In contrast, the coefficient of the bank risk variable remains insignificant. Thus, collateral squeeze rather than credit crunch receives support. Nevertheless, the evidence hinges on the credibility of the proxy variables and must be considered rather weak.[35]

3.6.4 Borrower Balance Sheets Played a Role

Let us now look in some more detail at the connection between private sector balance sheets and consumption and investment. Starting with firm investment, there is evidence that weak firm balance sheets had a negative impact on fixed investment in Finland in the early 1990s. Honkapohja and Koskela (1999) show, for panel data on the 500 largest Finnish firms for the years 1986 to 1996, that investment spending was much more dependent on cash flow (positively) and on debt (negatively) for firms that on a priori grounds could be considered financially constrained than for non-constrained firms.[36] Furthermore, the effect of cash flow was stronger during the depression than in an average year. With somewhat different specifications but using essentially similar though shorter data, Brunila (1994) also found that investment depends positively on cash flow and negatively on indebtedness. The effects are stronger for non-manufacturing than for manufacturing firms, which may reflect differences in the nature of available collateral assets. Similar patterns are found in time series data. According to estimates by Kajanoja (1995), investment would have been 6 to 15 per cent higher in 1993 had the sector's debt ratio remained at the 1980 level. On the other hand, the changes in indebtedness do not seem to have contributed much to the rapid growth of investment in the late 1980s.

For Sweden, Hansen and Lindberg (1997) estimate the impact of financial constraints using an unbalanced panel of manufacturing firms that had been in existence for at least six years during the period 1979 to 1994. They capture borrowing restrictions by treating the marginal cost of capital as an increasing function of indebtedness. They find a significant, but quantitatively small, effect of indebtedness on the cost of capital, consistent with the importance of financial constraints.

All in all the evidence indicates that high debt levels tend to constrain investment. In particular, the Finnish results are in accordance with the idea that borrower balance sheets have a rather non-linear impact on investment. Marginal changes in indebtedness at low debt levels, particularly under favorable macroeconomic conditions, do not matter greatly, but at high debt levels increased indebtedness can be a significant constraining factor, particularly in bad macroeconomic circumstances. This is likely to have played a role at least in the Finnish financial crisis.

The evidence with regard to consumption is less clear-cut. In neither country have there been studies based on panel data for individual households, and we have to rely on aggregate time series. For Finland, Honkapohja and Koskela (1999) estimate a consumption function augmented by measures of net wealth and credit growth, and find that private consumption depends, apart from on disposable income, positively on net wealth and credit growth and negatively on the nominal interest rate.[37] This is in line with corresponding studies for Sweden by Berg and Bergström (1995) and by Agell et al. (1995). Clapham et al. (2002) confirm the existence of wealth effects for Finland, whereas their results tend to be weaker for Sweden. For Finland they find a stronger propensity to consume out of housing wealth than out of stock wealth, in accordance with recent evidence from US data by Case et al. (2005).

A further approach builds on the assumption that financially unconstrained households consume according to an intertemporally optimal consumption plan. If this is so, the marginal utility of consumption should follow a random walk, that is, in a time series regression the coefficient on (the marginal utility of) lagged consumption should be unity. Adding current income as an independent variable, its regression coefficient should indicate the fraction of total consumption that is limited by credit constraints. Employing such an Euler-equation approach, Agell and Berg (1996) and Takala (2001) find for Sweden and Finland, respectively, that private consumption has been sensitive to current disposable income, and that this sensitivity increased after 1991. The interpretation is that the fraction of credit constrained consumers increased during the crisis.

These findings are consistent with the idea that weak balance sheets played a role in the development of investment and consumption during the crisis years. However, these studies being basically single-equation ones, other interpretations are certainly possible. It is, for instance, conceivable that the presence of wealth effects and the significance of current cash-flow and income in Euler equations reflect that these variables are correlated with changes in the perception of risk, and hence intertemporal discount rates, or with factors affecting the supply of credit.

3.6.5 Weak Evidence for 'Credit Crunch' due to Insufficient Bank Capital

Inference of the role of bank balance sheets requires bank level analysis. Furthermore, to really distinguish between 'collateral squeeze' and 'credit crunch' one should ideally combine data on individual firms with those of individual banks. Unfortunately, a lack of data has largely prevented such analyses.

Kinnunen and Vihriälä (1999) examine how the likelihood that a firm terminated its operations in Finland in the early 1990s depended on firm characteristics and on whether the firm had a lending relationship with the most troubled part of the Finnish banking system, that is, the Savings Bank of Finland and *Skopbank*. The database consists of 474 small and medium-sized firms with accounting data and information about the bank from which the firm had outstanding credit. The results suggest that, even accounting for the effects of liquidity, current profitability, indebtedness, age and size, firms with a lending relationship with the SBF and *Skopbank* were more likely to close in 1992 than other firms that year or the same firms in other years. The statistical significance of the finding is not very strong, however.[38]

In a related study for Sweden, Bergström et al. (2002) examine the probability of default for a cross-section of all Swedish firms in 1991–93 with more than ten employees. The focus of the study is on the impact of being a client of *Securum*, that is, having at least one loan that was transferred from *Nordbanken* to *Securum*. The study shows that, apart from a number of standard indicators of financial health, being affiliated with *Securum* had a positive impact on the probability of the firm being liquidated or going bankrupt. Since *Securum* was a financially strong lender, unaffected by credit crunch, this result suggests that the behavior of other lenders was also unrestricted by balance sheet factors.[39]

Another study with Finnish data follows the widely used cross-sectional approach of examining how the rate of credit growth is affected by bank capital.[40] Vihriälä (1997, Chapter 4) estimates reduced form equations for loan growth of 313 individual savings and co-operative banks in the early

1990s. The study controls for demand factors using data on the economic conditions in the regions of operation of the banks and for borrower quality by the share of non-performing assets in each bank's loan stock.[41] There is no significant effect of bank capital on credit growth, a finding that is robust to various definitions of capital. Nor does a complementary analysis of bank issuance of subordinate debt suggest that capital constrains lending. On the other hand, borrower quality affected lending growth among the savings banks as in the collateral squeeze story.

As a whole, the Finnish evidence supports the conclusion that financial factors exacerbated the economic downturn in the early 1990s. This seems to stem mainly from weak borrower balance sheets. The lending behavior of banks may have contributed as well, but the evidence on this score is rather weak. The Swedish evidence is generally weaker, perhaps because the crisis was not as deep in Sweden as in Finland.

3.7 A COMBINATION OF FACTORS

The Finnish and Swedish banking crises share many features of the crises experienced elsewhere. Geographically, the closest case is Norway, but many similarities can also be seen with the crises of several developing countries.[42] In particular, the East Asian financial crises are rather similar in many respects.[43] These experiences and extensive research on them allow one to draw some broad conclusions about the factors that triggered the crises, contributed to their depth, and shaped the pattern of recovery. We will attempt to distinguish between triggering factors ('shocks'), on the one hand, and factors that affected responses to these shocks ('propagation mechanisms'), on the other. We conclude that the crises were due to the combination of extraordinary shocks and a propagation mechanism that was fundamentally altered as a result of financial deregulation.

3.7.1 Financial Liberalization and Credit Boom not the Whole Story

It is commonplace to claim that the key shock occurred several years before the crises: the deregulation of the financial markets in the mid-1980s. Such reforms were undertaken in many countries all over the world as financial systems moved away from pervasive controls and restrictions towards market systems. A wide array of conduct regulations were eased or lifted completely. Interest rates are now freely determined in the market, and intermediaries are no longer required to invest in certain preferred assets or prohibited from investing in other types of assets. New derivative markets substantially increase opportunities for shifting risk. Further, the abolition of a host of restrictions on the international mobility of corporations and capital has made financial markets in different countries much more closely integrated. Financial capital now flows freely and it is much easier for foreign institutions to enter into domestic markets.

Such reforms were as a rule followed by periods of increased activity in the financial markets. Securities markets expanded, with both the capital raised and secondary market transactions increasing strongly, and banks and other intermediaries expanded credit supply. Part of this was a reallocation of credit away from previously unregulated lending such as trade credits. But to a large extent it was a real credit expansion. Many countries, like Finland and Sweden, saw periods of exceptional credit growth.

Such credit booms often preceded financial crises. There is econometric evidence of a strong positive correlation between the degree of credit growth and the resulting indebtedness, on the one hand, and the occurrence of a banking crisis, on the other. For example, Demirgüç-Kunt and Detragiache (1998) found – in a panel analysis of 65 countries over the period 1980–94 – that, even after controlling for factors such as GDP growth, the real rate of interest and the existence of deposit insurance, the rate of credit expansion and the ratio of private sector credit to GDP had significantly positive impacts on the likelihood of a subsequent banking crisis. Kaminsky et al. (1997) reach similar conclusions based on a survey of seven studies on the role of credit in creating currency crises. In five of these studies there is a statistically significant effect of credit growth on the likelihood of a currency crisis. As we do not know of any crisis country – at least among developed countries – where the financial problems were not preceded by rapid credit growth, we conclude that financial deregulation facilitating a credit boom has been a necessary condition for a banking crisis.

But financial deregulation has been far from a sufficient condition. While financial liberalization in one form or another has occurred in basically all developed and many developing countries, it has been followed by a lending boom and a crisis in only a few. More importantly, only a minority of credit booms have ended in banking or currency crises with associated credit busts. Gourinchas et al. (2001) find that a credit boom, defined as a deviation of the ratio of private credit to GDP from a stochastic trend, was followed by a banking crisis in only 10 to 21 per cent of all cases, depending on the precise definitions of boom and crisis. Thus, in the vast majority of credit growth episodes, no banking crisis followed. The likelihood of a currency crisis was even smaller.

In general, liberalization alone does not create a boom–bust cycle like that experienced in Finland and Sweden, much less a banking crisis. This conclusion is in line with evidence discussed in Section 3.6 above, indicating that removing financial restrictions did not *per se* have a dramatic impact on household consumption and corporate investment in Sweden and Finland. This is not to say that the booms in the two countries were not triggered by the deregulations, but rather that the credit booms had a strong impact on aggregate demand only in combination with other macroeconomic disturbances and expansive macro policies. Furthermore, deregulation was instrumental in leading to a crisis only because of the absence of effective supervision or other institutional arrangements giving banks the right incentives vis-à-vis risk-taking.

3.7.2 External Macro Shocks Important, Particularly for Finland

Both Finland and Sweden are small open economies heavily exposed to external events. The years around 1990 were unusually turbulent with a series of negative international macro shocks. First, there was the increase in European interest rates following German reunification. This affected both countries more or less in the same way as it did other Western European countries, although countries with a high government debt – like Sweden – may have been hit harder than others.

Second, demand in the OECD area declined in response to the higher interest rates and the fallout of the crisis in the Persian Gulf. This demand shock also had a similar impact on most countries, albeit stronger on countries heavily dependent on foreign trade, like Finland and Sweden. Third, the ERM crisis initiated a general turmoil in exchange markets. Although general in nature, this shock was particularly important for small countries like Finland and Sweden, trying to defend fixed exchange parities increasingly removed from their fundamental values.

Finally, the Soviet Union collapsed and with it the Soviet export market. This specific shock hit Finland – traditionally having a large share of its trade with the Soviet Union – much more strongly than other countries. In fact, Finland was the only OECD country to experience declining overall export market growth in 1991.[44] As a result, the volume of goods and services exports declined by 6.6 per cent in Finland in that year. In Sweden the decline was 2.5 per cent.

A comparative analysis by Pesola (2001) using panel data for the four Nordic countries quantifies the shocks to aggregate demand occurring in the early 1990s. He finds external macro shocks to be of major importance in Finland but not in the other countries and estimates that the negative GDP surprise was much bigger in Finland than in Sweden or in Denmark or Norway. In 1991, Finnish GDP was 8 per cent below expectations, while the biggest Swedish negative shock occurred in 1993 – past the peak of the crisis – and was no more than 3 per cent.

3.7.3 Fiscal Policies were Pro-cyclical, but the Impact Uncertain

Other shocks derive from fiscal policy measures. For Sweden it is widely acknowledged that the boom in the late 1980s was exacerbated by an expansionary fiscal policy. It was only in 1990, when the crisis was well under way, that some contractionary fiscal policy measures were undertaken. When the crisis hit, there was a dramatic deterioration in the central government budget, from a surplus of 4 per cent of GDP in 1990 to a deficit of 12 per cent in 1993.

In Finland, fiscal policy also fueled rather than reined in economic expansion during the boom years. Taxes were cut in several steps, while attempts to reduce tax expenditures, such as the deductibility of interest expenses in household taxation, met with strong resistance. The high tax revenues induced by the booming economy kept surpluses significant, making it politically very difficult to tighten policy.

When the crisis hit, government finances deteriorated rapidly, as tax revenues declined, and various subsidy programs including bank support payments increased expenditure. Exploding deficits were forecasted unless expenditures were radically cut, and there was a discretionary tightening of fiscal policy in 1992 and 1993 through several expenditure and tax packages. This tightening reduced – at least as a direct effect – aggregate demand and thereby exacerbated the downward spiral. At the same time, however, interest rates started to come down, thus supporting growth. It is still a matter of substantial controversy as to how contractionary fiscal policies were during the depression (see, for example, Kiander and Vartia (1998)). In a situation where the solvency of the public sector is in question – as may quite well have been the case in both countries – it is also an open question whether budget cuts may not be expansionary in the end, as suggested by Giavazzi and Pagano (1990, 1996). A deeper analysis of the role of fiscal policy is, however, beyond the scope of this chapter.[45]

3.7.4 Pegged but Adjustable Exchange Rate Regime Fatal

The great majority of recent financial crises have occurred in countries with a pegged exchange rate regime of one sort or another. In this sense, Finland and Sweden in the early 1990s were similar to Mexico in 1994, the East Asian countries in 1997, Russia and Brazil in 1998, Turkey in 2000 and Argentina in 2000–01. This supports the new consensus view that a fixed but adjustable exchange rate regime is conducive to financial crises and not really sustainable (see, for example, Fischer (2001)).

The Finnish and Swedish crisis episodes are well in line with this general pattern. In the period when liberalization unleashed suppressed demand

and led to strong growth, market confidence in the existing parities remained relatively strong, although large and occasionally increasing interest differentials indicate that the probability of exchange rate adjustments was not zero. Nevertheless, the exchange rates were sufficiently credible for attempts to tighten monetary policy to be largely futile. Interest rates could not be raised sufficiently, as capital inflows responded strongly to higher short-term rates. Furthermore, many non-financial firms took large exchange rate risks by borrowing in foreign currency to benefit from interest differentials. Ironically, the authorities in both countries – supported by a large majority of the academic opinion – strongly emphasized that the era of recurring devaluations was over for good.[46] This historically exceptionally strong commitment to unchanging exchange rates presumably increased public confidence in the exchange rate, irrespective of underlying economic realities.

When the financial positions had become vulnerable and external shocks hit the economies, a confidence crisis was quick to unfold. Interest differentials vis-à-vis continental Europe had to increase, and coming on top of an international increase this combined to form a major interest rate shock hitting the decelerating economies. Naturally, this had a very strong negative effect on the highly indebted private sector.

In the end, the fixed rate regimes had to be abandoned in both countries. Although the resulting depreciations could be considered necessary for recovery, they involved a short-run deflationary effect through the impact on the domestic currency value of borrowing denominated in foreign currency. The magnitude of this effect depends on the currency position of the private sector. For Sweden, calculations made by the *Riksbank* indicate that the negative financial position in foreign currency was fully offset by positive holdings of shares and real assets. The Finnish private sector had relatively fewer foreign assets, and the overall net currency position was likely to be significantly negative. Therefore, the expansionary effects of the depreciation of the domestic currency may have been more subdued in Finland than in Sweden.

The processes leading to floating rates differed between the two countries, and this may have impacted on the macroeconomic developments and perhaps on the banking crises as well. Finland was first forced to devalue in late 1991 and then floated in September 1992 before the exchange market turbulence led several countries to leave the ERM. Sweden attempted to defend the exchange rate even after that, with extremely high short-term rates in the fall of 1992.[47] An earlier devaluation in November 1991 helped Finland's exports to start recovery earlier. However, the decision to devalue rather than float left the exchange rate regime still highly vulnerable to further speculations and thereby contributed to high interest rates. This, in combination with the windfall losses brought about via foreign currency loans, weakened the financial position of the domestic sectors in Finland, even before the turbulence and the inevitable floating in the autumn of 1992. It therefore seems that the Finnish approach to floating was more unfortunate from the point of view of the domestic sectors – and banks – than the Swedish one, with just a brief period of extremely high *krona* rates before floating. Be that as it may, with hindsight it seems obvious that both countries would have benefited from an earlier floating.

3.7.5 The First Downturn in a Recently Deregulated Economy

In retrospect the processes of deregulation that took place over a couple of years in the mid-1980s may appear inevitable; the time just seems to have been ripe. At the time, however, the swiftness of the process came as a surprise. As a result, many actors, not least among regulators and financial institutions, were ill-prepared for the new situation. But it did not take long for the financial sector to realize that the competitive environment was fundamentally different. Lending restrictions no longer conserved the relative positions of different institutions. Competition over market shares was unhampered, and did in fact develop vigorously. Even though banks remained quite profitable in the short term, underlying profitability and solidity did not in general improve and in many cases deteriorated as a result of the rapid rate of expansion.

It took longer for banks and regulators to learn to understand the nature of financial risks in the new situation. Up until 1990 credit losses had been running at minuscule levels for as long as any active banker could remember. Few had studied the banking history of the 1920s and 1930s, and little was learnt from the current crisis experience in nearby Norway. In practice, risk assessment followed routine procedures, at best. When the crisis was resolved some years later it was even found that standard documentation was lacking for many loans. In times of rapid expansion administrative matters had been given low priority. As a result, not only was there poor risk analysis of individual loans, but also banks had little overview of the portfolio of loans they were holding, such as the exposure towards a single borrower or a particular sector.

A conspicuous illustration of higher risk-taking is the treatment of real estate collateral. In both countries banks started accepting loans with ever higher loan-to-value ratios, even exceeding 100 per cent, presumably based on recent experience of an inflationary and regulated environment where prices were growing at high and stable rates. This environment was to change in two ways, both of which may have been difficult to predict.

The trend growth rate of nominal property prices was reduced as a result of lower inflation. Further, real estate prices became more volatile, as a result of the higher loan-to-value ratios.

The recession that started in both countries around 1990 was the first downturn after the deregulation. It hit a bank system with low solidity, high-risk loan portfolios and highly leveraged borrowers. This triggered dynamic responses that banks and regulators were quite unaccustomed to. In particular, the interaction between asset prices, collateral values and credit losses was a new phenomenon, or rather the rediscovery of a phenomenon well known decades ago to Irving Fisher (1933) and others. It was the combination of strong negative shocks and a fundamentally altered propagation mechanism that was at the heart of the crisis.

3.7.6 Supervisory Policies, Deposit Insurance and the Too-big-to-fail Doctrine

There are also grounds to believe that lax prudential regulation and supervision contributed to both the size and vulnerability of the credit boom of the late 1980s. For Finland, the careful analysis by Halme (1999) points to severe shortcomings of supervision, which for example allowed banks to report unrealistically strong capital positions and to lend against insufficiently secure collateral. For Sweden, Sjöberg (1994) documents that resources devoted to on-site bank inspections were cut in favor of tasks related to consumer protection rather than financial stability.

Bank risk-taking can undoubtedly partly be explained by a lack of understanding of how unregulated markets function. In particular, there is ample evidence that bankers did not fully understand how credit risks depended on inflation, asset values, interest rates and exchange rates. However, there are also good reasons to believe that distorted incentives played a role. There is evidence for both countries that banks with a weak capital base and profitability deliberately tried to resolve their problems through growth. This picture emerges both from insider accounts and from econometric analyses.[48]

In the academic literature many studies single out deposit insurance as a major cause of such distorted incentives, but this was of little importance for the Nordic crises. Sweden had no deposit insurance at all, and in Finland the marginal funding that the most expansive banks relied on – money market funding and bonds – was not covered by deposit insurance. More plausible is that providers of funds – even in a late stage of credit expansion – trusted that banks would not be allowed to fail given their central position in the payments systems. Such beliefs were also supported by actions and statements. One example is the special arrangement by the

Finnish central bank to alleviate the pressure on bank profits created by the high interest rates in 1986. Another Finnish example is that the central bank priced all bank CDs on par with its own CDs in market operations, implicitly treating them as free of credit risk.

3.7.7 The Bottom Line

The banking crises of Finland and Sweden in the 1990s stand out as extraordinary events both from an international perspective – in occurring in advanced market economies with strong public sectors – and from a historical perspective – in being the first major crises to hit these economies since the worldwide depression of the early 1930s. In this concluding section, we have isolated the factors that triggered the emergence of the crises and that explain the relatively speedy recoveries.

We conclude that there is not one explanation. The crises were due to the combination of several extraordinary shocks and serious mistakes, both in macro policies and in regulatory policies. The crises were preceded by a far-reaching financial liberalization in both countries. This may have been a necessary condition, but it was far from a sufficient cause for the crises. Neither can formal deposit insurance or other aspects of government regulation be blamed. The crises exacerbated macroeconomic problems primarily through their impacts on borrower balance sheets. However, evidence of a so-called credit crunch remains weak. Crisis management was fast and strong-handed. In both countries the financial sectors were substantially restructured and recovered from the crisis relatively quickly.

NOTES

1. We thank Ari Hyytinen and Thomas Hagberg for very competent research assistance. We are grateful to the Bank of Finland, *Sveriges Riksbank* and the Finnish Ministry of Finance for data.
2. See Jonung (1993) for an account of these meetings.
3. Hörngren (1989, Table 4.7).
4. This was done in two steps, taking effect in January 1991 and January 1992, raising the capital requirements on mortgage loans (except for owner-occupied housing) and mortgage-institution bonds to a maximum of 8 per cent.
5. See Kuusterä (1995) for documentation that this was indeed the case.
6. Larsson and Sjögren (1995, Table 3.1).
7. See Pettersson (1993) for an insider account of the strategic thinking within this bank.
8. Financial Stability Report, *Sveriges Riksbank*.
9. Wallander (1994, Tables A1 and A3).
10. The only exception was the savings bank group, which deliberately chose to pay the extra costs involved to gain market shares. Internal *Skopbank* documents quoted in Kuusterä (1995) reveal that the center strongly encouraged individual savings banks

to disregard the Bank of Finland recommendation of slowing down credit growth. Instead, the banks were advised to use the opportunity to capture market shares.

11. In Chapter 6 of this volume the pro-cyclicality of real interest rates is presented as a key ingredient in the Finnish and Swedish boom–bust cycle. The same holds for the boom–bust cycle in Norway as demonstrated in Chapter 7.
12. See Jennergren (2002) for a study documenting the lack of stock market reaction to the early reports of credit losses among finance companies.
13. This crisis bears some resemblance to the crisis for the British 'secondary banks' in 1973. Like the finance companies, they had thrived due to regulation and were put under competitive pressure when the operations of banks were deregulated. See Davis (1992, pp. 152–3).
14. There is evidence that the speed of credit expansion during the boom years had as such a clear negative impact on credit quality during the crisis. The savings banks that had the fastest aggregate credit growth also had the largest share of non-performing loans in all lending. Solttila and Vihriälä (1994) show that the speed of credit expansion during the boom is a much more important factor in explaining the later credit quality of individual savings banks than the sector composition of lending or share of loans denominated in foreign currency.
15. These numbers include provisions for future losses for loans that were still performing.
16. These are particularly uncertain estimates as the market dried up with few transactions making the empirical ground for the appraised values thinner than usual.
17. See Wallander (1994, Tables 4 and 5). The concept was defined by the Financial Supervisory Authority and includes loans to the real estate and construction industries but also other loans against real estate collateral.
18. *SE-banken* entered discussions with the Bank Support Agency, but they did not result in any direct support. The private owners invested new equity capital in the bank to ensure that capital requirements were fulfilled.
19. These figures are based on unpublished calculations within the *Riksbank*. We are grateful to Anders Lindström and Kerstin Mitlid for making these figures available to us.
20. The GGF decided in principle to guarantee the interest payments and the capital for ten years of the tier-2 instruments to be issued by the banks. In November the GGF also decided to guarantee the interest payments of the co-operative banks' guarantee fund. In the end none of these guarantees was used.
21. Bank of Finland Year Book 1991.
22. Government bill to Parliament 1991/92:153.
23. The term 'credit crunch' was adopted from the contemporaneous American discussion related to the slowdown of both economic activity and credit contraction. Particularly the article by Bernanke and Lown (1991) was often cited in this context.
24. There was, nevertheless, a run on the trust fund of the retail chain EKA in November 1992, forcing a temporary closure of the fund. The fund was not covered by any formal deposit insurance scheme. Furthermore, its small size and secondary importance in the financial system suggested that not bailing it out might be a real option. Yet the government decided to pay out to the 'depositors' their lost capital (but not interest accrued). In Sweden, *Gota Bank* lost 5 per cent of its deposits during one week in the spring of 1992. This 'mini-run' was apparently the result of statements made by the owner indicating doubts about the willingness to support the ailing bank further.
25. In Finland, interest rate regulation was used to increase by a percentage point the rate of interest on the stock of bank credit with low interest rates linked to the Bank of Finland base rate. A change in tax legislation was used to prevent this change from increasing deposit rates so as to widen banks' interest margins.
26. Some banks delayed accepting the offer until the end of the year, which suggests that the conditions put on the capital injection were considered at least somewhat difficult to accept by the banks.
27. See, for example, Ingves and Lind (1997 and 1998) for Sweden.
28. See Bergström et al. (2002) for a detailed analysis of *Securum*.

29. For this reason the pricing of transferred loans was less of an issue in Sweden where the 'selling' banks were already state-owned. The total book value of the loans was depreciated by SEK 14 billion in *Securum* shortly after the transfer, which indicates over-pricing. See Bergström et al. (2002, pp. 48–51).
30. The buyer of the 'good' parts of the bank (*KOP*) reimbursed the government the FIM 75 million after the deal.
31. A particular problem in selling the bank (good assets) to a single buyer was that it was considered difficult for a single buyer to keep deposits given the competition of other banks. In the split-up deal such competition was likely to be less serious. Competition was, furthermore, contractually limited through an agreement that the buying banks would not advertise deposit accounts for a few months.
32. See also Chapter 9 of this volume for a comparison between the Nordic crisis and the Asian financial crises.
33. The official estimate made by the Finnish government in its report to parliament in 1999 ('Valtioneuvoston selonteko eduskunnalle pankkituesta', 1999). The Swedish estimate uses the interest rate on 12-month t-bills to bring all cash flows forward to 1 July 1997. The Finnish estimate is not quite comparable as it does not include any discounting or interest expenses.
34. In neither study is the effect of a credit shock sensitive to the ordering of variables in the Choleski decomposition. Credit shocks matter even when there is no contemporaneous effect from credit to investment or GDP or money.
35. One can question particularly the appropriateness of the variable used to proxy for the lending capacity of banks. It does not reflect the capacity of the non-listed banks (savings banks and co-operative banks). Yet, it was the savings banks, if any, that should have suffered from lack of bank capital. The proxy also overlooks any potential effects of capital regulation. One can also question the conclusions based on the borrower creditworthiness variables. Net worth is inherently a firm level issue, and an aggregate measure may quite well proxy for something other than the individual firms' net worth positions. Furthermore, the coefficient of the interest differential turns out to be unstable over time.
36. A firm was classified as financially constrained if it could not meet the interest payments on its debt by profits in the previous period.
37. The authors interpret the finding that the nominal rather than the real rate of interest affects consumption as evidence of liquidity constraints.
38. The critical coefficient has a t-value of 1.83, implying a marginal significance level of 6 per cent.
39. This is not the only possible interpretation. It may be that *Securum* was more ruthless than other lenders, because by construction it had a limited lifespan and no long-term borrower relations to worry about.
40. These credit crunch studies were started by Bernanke and Lown (1991). A survey and critique of the early studies is provided by Sharpe (1995).
41. The share of non-performing assets can be considered as an indicator of borrower quality, because even in normal times most lending goes to existing customers. In a financial crisis situation adverse selection problems are likely to tie borrowers even more closely to their existing lending banks. On the other hand, non-performing assets represent a loss potential not fully accounted for by loan loss provisions. This is problematic because they can thereby also capture the effect of expected changes in bank capital. However, if this effect dominates, one would expect the capital ratio and the share of non-performing assets to have a roughly similar effect on lending. This is not the case.
42. See Chapter 7 in this volume for a discussion of the Norwegian experience. Despite many features in common with the other Nordic countries, Denmark did not experience a financial crisis, as analysed in Chapter 8 of this volume.
43. See Chapter 9 of this volume for a comparative analysis of the Nordic and Asian financial crises.

44. According to the *OECD Economic Outlook*, the export market for Finnish manufacturing declined by 1.2 per cent in 1991, while it increased by 4.3 per cent on average in the OECD area and by 2.2 per cent in Sweden. This was indeed a shock as export markets had been expected to grow robustly in 1991. The December 1990 *Outlook* predicted a market growth of 6.2, 6.0 and 5.7 per cent for Finland, the OECD and Sweden, respectively.
45. See Chapter 2 in this volume for a discussion of the role of fiscal policy.
46. In Finland the government in power in 1987–91 described its economic policy strategy as one of 'managed structural change' as opposed to the 'soft' devaluation-prone policies of earlier governments. Prior to the general election of spring 1991, the governing coalition furthermore made the 'stable *markka*' a central plank of its election platform. See Chapter 2 on the politics of the crisis.
47. The rates were so high that no financial system could sustain such pressures for more than a few days. The exorbitant rates were probably central to making the banking crisis acute in Sweden in the fall of 1992. In fact, the crisis in *Gota* occurred on 9 September, the very same day that the overnight interest rate was increased to 75 per cent.
48. For Finnish savings banks this is supported both by internal documents as shown by Kuusterä (1995) and by the econometric analysis of Vihriälä (1997). For Sweden, Pettersson (1993) provides an insider account based on his experience as CEO of *Första Sparbanken*.

REFERENCES

Agell, J. and L. Berg (1996), 'Does financial deregulation cause a consumption boom?', *Scandinavian Journal of Economics*, **98** (4), 579–601.

Agell, J., L. Berg and P.-A. Edin (1995), 'The Swedish boom-to-bust cycle: tax reform, consumption, and asset structure', *Swedish Economic Policy Review*, **2**, 271–314.

Agell, J., P. Englund and J. Södersten (1998), *Incentives and Redistribution in the Welfare State*, London: Macmillan.

Allen, F. and D. Gale (2000), 'Bubbles and crises', *Economic Journal*, **110**, 236–55.

Anari, A., J. Kolari, S. Pynnönen and A. Suvanto (2002), 'Further evidence on the credit view: the case of Finland', *Applied Economics*, **34**, 267–78.

Bank of Finland Year Book, various issues.

Berg, L. and R. Bergström (1995), 'Housing and financial wealth, financial deregulation, and consumption – the Swedish case', *Scandinavian Journal of Economics*, **97**, 421–39.

Bergström, C., P. Englund and P. Thorell (2002), *Securum. Vägen ut ur bankkrisen* (Securum, the road out of the banking crisis), Stockholm: SNS.

Bernanke, B. and C. Lown (1991), 'The credit crunch', *Brookings Papers on Economic Activity*, 2:1991, 205–47.

Brunila, A. (1994), 'Investment and financing considerations: evidence from Finnish panel data', Bank of Finland Discussion paper 4/94.

Case, K.E., J.M. Quigley and R.J. Shiller (2005), 'Comparing wealth effects: the stock market versus the housing market', *Advances in Macroeconomics*, **5** (1), 1–32.

Clapham, E., A. Hyytinen and K. Takala (2002), 'Household wealth, credit and consumption: evidence from Finland and Sweden', manuscript.

Corsetti, G., P. Pesenti and N. Roubini (1999), 'What caused the Asian currency and financial crisis?', *Japan and the World Economy*, **11**, 305–73.

Davis, E.P. (1992), *Debt, Financial Fragility and Systemic Risk*, Oxford: Oxford University Press.

Demirgüc-Kunt, A. and E. Detragiache (1998), 'The determinants of banking crises in developing and developed countries', *IMF Staff Papers*, **45**, 81–109.

Fischer, S. (2001), 'Exchange rate regimes: is the bipolar view correct?', *Journal of Economic Perspectives*, **15**, 3–24.

Fisher, I. (1933), 'The debt-deflation theory of great depressions', *Econometrica*, **1**, 337–57.

Giavazzi, F. and M. Pagano (1990), 'Can severe fiscal contractions be expansionary? Tales of two small European countries', *NBER Macroeconomics Annual*, 75–116.

Giavazzi, F. and M. Pagano (1996), 'Non-Keynesian effects of fiscal policy changes: international evidence and the Swedish experience', *Swedish Economic Policy Review*, **2**, 67–103.

Gilchrist, S., B. Bernanke and M. Gertler (1996), 'The financial accelerator and the flight to quality', *Review of Economics and Statistics*, **78**, 1–15.

Gourinchas, P., R. Valdés and O. Landerretche (2001), 'Lending booms: Latin America and the world', *Economía*, **1**, 47–89.

Hallsten, K. (1999), 'Bank loans and the transmission mechanism of monetary policy', in K. Hallsten, 'Essays on the effects of monetary policy', dissertation in economics 1999:2, Department of Economics, Stockholm University.

Halme, L. (1999), *Pankkisääntely ja valvonta. Oikeuspoliittinen tutkimus säästöpankkien riskinotosta* (Regulation and supervision of banks. A legal policy study of savings banks' risk taking), Bank of Finland Studies E:15.

Hansen, J. (2003), 'Financial cycles and bankruptcies in the Nordic countries', Sveriges Riksbank, Working paper no. 149.

Hansen, S. and S. Lindberg (1997), 'Agency costs, financial deregulation, and corporate investment – an Euler equation approach to panel data for Swedish firms', Working paper 1997:20, Department of Economics, Uppsala University.

Holmström, B. and J. Tirole (1997), 'Financial intermediation, loanable funds and the real sector', *Quarterly Journal of Economics*, **112**, 663–91.

Honkapohja, S. and E. Koskela (1999), 'The economic crisis of the 1990s in Finland', *Economic Policy*, **29**, 399–424.

Honohan, P. and D. Klingebiel (2003), 'The fiscal cost implications of an accommodating approach to banking crises', *Journal of Banking and Finance*, **27**, 1539–60.

Hörngren, L. (1989), *Kostnadsutveckling och konkurrens i banksektorn* (Cost development and competition in the banking sector), SOU 1989:16, Stockholm.

Ibañez, D.M. and P. Molyneux (2001), 'Financial restructuring in European banking and foreign expansion', paper presented at the Workshop on European Banks and the Brazilian Financial System, University of Oxford Centre for Brazilian Studies, 12 March.

Ingves, S. and G. Lind (1997), 'Loan loss recoveries and debt resolution agencies: the Swedish experience', in C. Enoch and J. H. Green (eds), *Banking Soundness and Monetary Policy. Issues and Experiences in the Global Economy*, Washington, DC: IMF.

Ingves, S. and G. Lind (1998), 'Om att hantera en bankkris' (Handling a banking crisis), *Ekonomisk Debatt*, **26**, 41–54.

Jennergren, P. (2002), 'The Swedish finance company crisis – could it have been anticipated?', *Scandinavian Economic History Review*, **50**, 7–30.
Jennergren, P. and B. Näslund (1998), 'Vad blev notan för skattebetalarna?' (What was the bill to tax payers?), *Ekonomisk Debatt*, **26**, 69–76.
Jonung, L. (1993), 'Riksbanken i regleringsekonomin. Mötena mellan riksbanken och affärsbankerna 1956–1973' (The *Riksbank* in the regulated economy. The meetings between the *Riksbank* and the commercial banks 1956–1973), in L. Werin, (ed.), *Från räntereglering till inflationsnorm* (From interest regulation to inflation norm), Stockholm: SNS Förlag.
Kajanoja, L. (1995), 'Aggregate investment and corporate indebtedness: some empirical evidence from Finland', Bank of Finland Discussion Paper 9/95.
Kaminsky, G., S. Lizondo and C. Reinhard (1997), 'Leading indicators of currency crises', IMF Working paper 97/79.
Keeley, M. (1990), 'Deposit insurance, risk, and market power in banking', *American Economic Review*, **80**, 1183–1200.
Kiander, J. and P. Vartia (1998), 'Suuri lama' (The great depression), Elinkeinoelämän tutkimulaitos (Research Institute of the Finnish Economy), B143.
Kinnunen, H. and V. Vihriälä (1999), 'Bank relationships and small-business closures during the Finnish recession of the 1990s', Bank of Finland Discussion Paper 13/99.
Kuusterä, A. (1995), *Aate ja raha. Säästöpankit suomalaisessa yhteiskunnassa 1822–1994* (Ideology and money. The savings banks in the Finnish society), Helsinki: Otava.
Larsson, M. and H. Sjögren (1995), *Vägen till och från bankkrisen* (The road to and from the banking crisis), Stockholm: Carlsson.
Mishkin, F.S. (1999a), 'Lessons from the tequila crisis', *Journal of Banking and Finance*, **23**, 1521–33.
Mishkin, F.S. (1999b), 'Global financial instability: framework, events, issues', *Journal of Economic Perspectives*, **13**, 3–20.
OECD Economic Outlook, various issues.
Pazarbaşioğlu, C. (1997), 'A credit crunch? Finland in the aftermath of the banking crisis', *IMF Staff Papers*, **44**, 315–27.
Pesola, J. (2001), 'The role of macroeconomic shocks in banking crises', Bank of Finland Discussion Papers 6/2001.
Pettersson, K.-H. (1993), *Bankkrisen inifrån* (The banking crisis from the inside), Stockholm: SNS Förlag.
Saarenheimo, T. (1995), 'Credit crunch caused investment slump? An empirical analysis using Finnish data', Bank of Finland Discussion Paper 6/1995.
Schwartz, A. (1986), 'Real and pseudo-financial crises', in F. Capie and G. Wood (eds), *Financial Crises and the World Banking System*, London: Macmillan.
Sharpe, S. (1995), 'Bank capitalization, regulation and the credit crunch: a critical review of the research findings', US Federal Reserve Board, Finance and Economics Discussion Series 95-20.
Sjöberg, G. (1994), 'Bank- och Finansinspektionens verksamhet 1980–1993' (The activities of the Financial Supervision Agency 1980–1993), in *Bankkrisen*, reports from *Bankkriskommittén*, Stockholm.
Solttila, H. and V. Vihriälä (1994), 'Finnish banks' problem assets: the result of unfortunate asset structure or too rapid growth?', Bank of Finland Discussion Paper 23/94.

Stiglitz, J. and A. Weiss (1981), 'Credit rationing in markets with imperfect competition', *American Economic Review*, **71**, 393–410.

Takala, K. (2001), *Studies in Time Series Analysis of Consumption, Asset Prices and Forecasting*, Bank of Finland Studies E:22.

'Valtioneuvoston selonteko eduskunnalle pankkituesta' (Government report to parliament on bank support) (1999), 16 November, Helsinki: Edita.

Vihriälä V. (1997), *Banks and the Finnish Credit Cycle 1986–1995*, Bank of Finland Studies E:7.

Wallander, J. (1994), 'Bankkrisen – omfattning, orsaker, lärdomar' (The banking crisis – magnitude, causes, lessons), in *Bankkrisen,* reports from *Bankkriskommittén*, Stockholm.

4. The crisis of the 1990s and unemployment in Finland and Sweden

Klas Fregert and Jaakko Pehkonen

INTRODUCTION

The unemployment figures during the early 1990s crises in Finland and Sweden had not been experienced since the Great Depression, and even now, about 15 years later, unemployment is still considerably higher, by any measure, than the normal post-World War II level. In this chapter, we investigate the character and the causes of the unemployment crises in Finland and Sweden and their aftermath. We ask whether the current high unemployment in these two countries is a legacy of the earlier crises. Any attempt at evaluating the cost of the crises must take into account this possibility. Long-term forecasts as well as policy analysis will also depend on how the present unemployment rates came about.

The chapter is divided into four parts. In Section 4.1, we present the unemployment outcome. We describe the size and timing for comprehensive as well as decomposed measures of unemployment. Through inspection of graphs, we look for indications of possible structural breaks that would indicate a change in the structural rate of unemployment. The purpose of the section is two-fold: to gain a sense of the welfare consequences of the unemployment crises in Finland and Sweden and to collect clues about the underlying causes.

In Section 4.2, we investigate the division into temporary and permanent effects by testing for structural breaks in Okun and Beveridge relations. In Section 4.3, we look at possible exogenous causes, again seeking indications of temporary versus permanent effects. Finally, in Section 4.4, we employ previously estimated empirical panel models to examine the contributions of the exogenous factors to the changes in the structural unemployment rate. We present separate estimates for the mid-1990s, late 1990s and early 2000s. They indicate that the structural rate has decreased in both countries, but has not returned to the levels of the 1980s.

4.1 THE UNEMPLOYMENT OUTCOME: SIZE AND TIMING

Figure 4.1 displays the open unemployment rates for 1980–2004 according to survey measures and OECD standardized measures. The main difference between the two data sets is for Sweden where the OECD way of defining unemployment adds between 1 and 1.6 per cent to the official figures. The OECD correction stems mainly from the exclusion of students looking for work in the labor force survey.

Finland and Sweden are alike in the timing of the rise in unemployment from the trough in 1990 to the peak in 1994. They differ, however, in the magnitude of the initial rise and in the evolution of unemployment

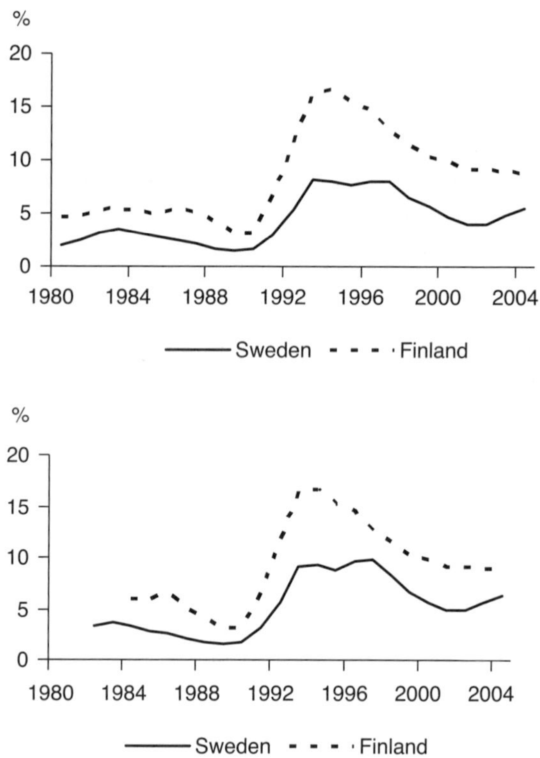

Source: *OECD Economic Outlook* (*Source OECD* web resource).

Figure 4.1 Official and standardized (OECD) unemployment rates, respectively, in Finland and Sweden 1980–2004

after the peak. The Finnish unemployment rate rose from 3 to 16 per cent compared with the 2 to 9 per cent increase in Sweden. Thus, the absolute increase in percentage points was roughly double in Finland (13 versus 7 percentage points). Regarding the timing of the recovery, Finnish unemployment has steadily decreased since the peak in 1994, while Swedish unemployment remained constant at between 9 and 10 per cent (standardized figures) between 1994 and 1997.

The official (open) unemployment rate is a narrow measure as it fails to account for the possibility that some workers left the labor force as a consequence of the crises of the 1990s. The participation rate, the labor force divided by the working age population, is shown in Figure 4.2. Compared with the average of the 1980s, the participation rate declined in both countries by about 5 percentage points: in Finland from 76 to 71 per cent and in Sweden from 80 to 75 per cent. Since 1994, the participation rate has increased slowly in Finland, while remaining roughly constant in Sweden. The coincidental timings of the decline in the participation rate and the increase in unemployment suggest that most of the decline was related to the deterioration in labor market conditions.

The people who left the labor force can be divided into participants in labor market programs, discouraged workers and others. Since participants in labor market programs and discouraged workers are directly linked to the labor market situation, a comprehensive measure of unemployment should include these two categories. Unfortunately, consistent data on the number of discouraged workers are not available for Finland. Therefore, two alternative measures that provide bounds on the possible size of the

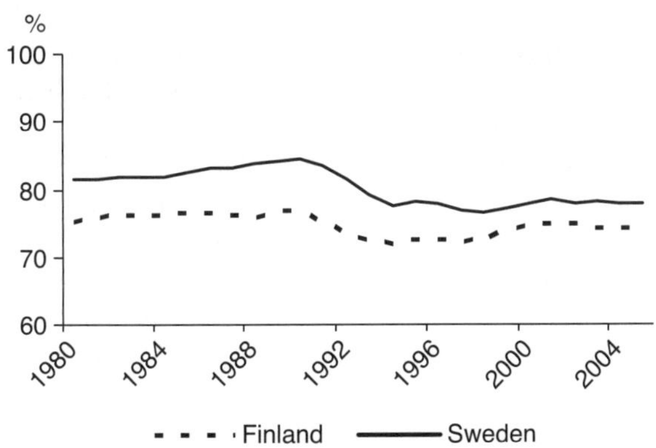

Source: *OECD Economic Outlook* (*Source OECD* web resource)

Figure 4.2 Labor force participation rate 1980–2004

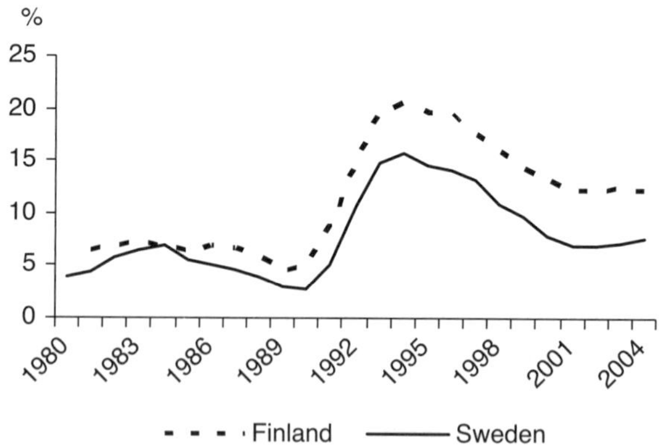

Sources: Finland: *Työpoliittinen aikakauskirja* (*Finnish Labour Review*), Ministry of Labour; Sweden: *Arbetskraftsundersökningarna* (*Labour Force Survey*), Statistics Sweden, SCB and Arbetsmarknadsverket (Swedish National Labour Market Administration), www.amv.scb.se (historisk statistik).

Figure 4.3 Total unemployment in Finland and Sweden, 1980–2004

total unemployment effect are used here: the sum of the openly unemployed and participants in labor market programs, and the non-employment rate.

Figure 4.3 shows total unemployment defined as the sum of the openly unemployed and labor market program participants. This measure removes most of the difference in timing observed in open unemployment in Figure 4.1 after the peak in 1994. Total unemployment steadily decreases in both countries after the peak. The explanation lies in the different timing of labor market programs. Finnish programs did not reach their peak of 4.8 per cent until 1997, while Sweden increased its programs more aggressively, reaching almost 6 per cent of the labor force in labor market programs in 1994.[1]

The non-employment rate, that is, one minus the ratio between employment and the working age population, is shown in Figure 4.4. This measure takes into account the changes both in the open unemployment rate and in the outflow from the labor force. Since part of the outflow from the labor force may be due to non-cyclical factors, such as increased enrollment in higher education, the change in the non-employment rate represents the upper limit of an increase in total unemployment. A difference in the timing of the recovery phase, seen in the open unemployment rate, is again evident: the recovery begins in Finland from the unemployment peak in 1994, whereas in Sweden the non-employment rate is constant until 1998. The difference in timing in Sweden between total unemployment and non-employment between 1994 and 1998 is due to a combination of an increase

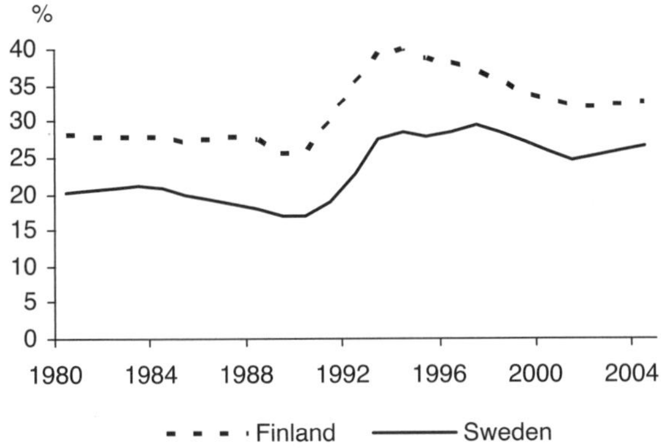

Sources: Finland: *Työpoliittinen aikakauskirja* (*Finnish Labour Review*), Ministry of Labour; Sweden: *Arbetskraftsundersökningarna* (*Labour Force Survey*), Statistics Sweden, SCB.

Figure 4.4 The non-employment rate in Finland and Sweden, 1980–2004

in discouraged workers and others that make up for the decrease in labor market program participants.

Since it is likely that most of the decrease in the participation rate is due to the labor market situation and as the effect is similar in both countries, the non-employment rate should give a better sense of the relative size of the underlying shocks than the open unemployment rate.[2] In Finland it rose by 15 percentage points, whereas in Sweden it increased by 10 percentage points. Thus by this measure, the Finnish crisis was 50 per cent worse than the Swedish crisis.[3]

We now turn to flow and duration statistics. Such data can give further insights into both the welfare consequences of the crisis and its underlying causes. The unemployment rate, or the non-employment rate, is at best an incomplete social welfare measure. Many would argue that an unemployed individual is harder hit than one who is employed. Furthermore, how hard the unemployed individual is hit depends on how long the unemployment spell lasts, one reason being that unemployment benefits are not perceived to compensate for the loss of income (even including increased leisure). Another reason is that unemployment may hurt long-term earnings potential. Finally, the psychic cost of being outside ordinary society can be high. All these costs increase with the length of the unemployment spell. Thus, the duration of unemployment spells is an important indicator in its own right. Duration is also closely related to the flow out of unemployment, or the job-finding rate, which makes it an alternative measure of the tightness of the labor market.

The maximum duration is 40 weeks in Finland and 27 in Sweden. Duration reached its peak in Finland in 1994, while it had already peaked in Sweden in 1992. The recovery phase is also slightly different. Duration decreased steadily after 1994 in Finland, albeit at a decreasing rate, whereas most of the decline in Sweden occurred after 1998. The Finnish duration continues to be considerably higher than in the 1980s, whereas Sweden has returned to close to the levels of the 1980s. The faster decrease in duration after 1998 in Sweden also implied a quick fall in the share of the long-term unemployed.[4]

Inflow rates are consistently higher in Finland. Since the unemployment rate is roughly equal to the inflow rate multiplied by duration (exactly equal in the steady state), we conclude that the permanently higher unemployment rate in Finland is due to a combination of longer duration and a higher inflow rate into unemployment. The Swedish inflow rate appears to have increased permanently and explains most of the permanently higher unemployment rate.[5]

What accounts for the differences in inflow rates and duration? To gain additional insight into this issue, we turn to estimates of job creation and destruction in Finland (Böckerman and Maliranta, 2001) and Sweden (Andersson, 1999).[6] The Finnish data cover the private non-farming sector, while the Swedish data refer more narrowly to the manufacturing sector. Job destruction was consistently higher in Finland during 1988–1996. Since international data show that roughly half of all worker reallocations depend on new jobs being created and old jobs disappearing, it seems likely that the higher rate of job destruction in Finland explains the difference in the inflow into unemployment. The job creation data show a difference in level (higher in Finland) as well as in timing. While job creation remained constant in Sweden during the crisis, it fell drastically in Finland. Thus, it seems the faster increase in duration in Finland during the downturn phase can be explained by the fall in the number of new jobs available for the unemployed.

To put the crises in the two countries into a broader perspective, they can be compared with previous crises. Unemployment in both countries reached record levels during the post-war period at more than double the previous peaks. In a cross-country perspective, the Finnish unemployment level is near the top, while Sweden's peak is at the bottom in the OECD in 1992. In a long-run perspective, Sweden's crisis is a long way from the Great Depression peak of 23 per cent, while Finland's crisis appears the worst during the century. Thus both countries' crises qualify as extreme crises when compared with their own post-war history, but only the Finnish crisis qualifies in an international perspective.[7]

Did the two crises differ from previous crises with respect to their broad

Table 4.1 Real wages and output: percentage change in unemployment and real output from through to peak

	1990s: percentage changes			Next highest: percentage changes		
	Unemployment	GDP	Real labor cost	Unemployment	GDP	Real labor cost
Finland	13.5	−6.8	7.9	5.6	3	13.9
Sweden	6.8	−3.4	4.3	1.5	2.7	−3.6

Note: The change in unemployment is the absolute percentage change.

Source: *OECD Economic Outlook* 1960–2000.

macroeconomic development? Table 4.1 presents the basic price and quantity developments as measured by real labor costs and real GDP. GDP fell in both crises during the 1990s by about the same proportion relative to the absolute change in unemployment, in contrast to the previous crises when GDP grew. Real labor costs rose in both countries during the crises of the 1990s. The counter-cyclical real wage development is consistent with a fall in aggregate demand being propagated into a fall in real GDP.

We summarize our findings for the downturn and the recovery as follows:

The downturn The two crises are alike in their initial timing as far as unemployment is concerned: both began in 1991 and peaked in 1994. Finland's crisis was deeper in both absolute and relative terms for all unemployment measures. A likely proximate explanation is the corresponding steep decrease in job creation in Finland, which did not occur in Sweden.

The recovery Finland appears to have been in a recovery process since its peak in 1994 while Sweden's unemployment appears to have remained at the peak level until 1998. After 1998, the two countries also differ in that the inflow into unemployment and duration of spells of unemployment continued to decrease in Finland, whereas the recovery in Sweden is due mainly to a sharp decrease in the latter.

4.2 DID THE CRISES CAUSE PERMANENT INCREASES IN UNEMPLOYMENT?

Since unemployment rates have been going down in both Finland and Sweden since their peaks in 1994, it is conceivable that they will return to their average levels of the 1980s. In that case, the structural rate of unemployment will not have changed. On the other hand, any such adjustment appears to have been slow, so it is also conceivable that unemployment will remain high for a long time, possibly never returning to its pre-crisis level. In this case, the structural rate of unemployment will have increased. We examine these two possibilities formally by estimating bivariate Okun and Beveridge relations with structural breaks to allow for a shift in the mean of unemployment at the time of the crises as well as changes in the dynamics.

4.2.1 Okun's Law

Okun's law is an empirical law stating that an increase in the GDP gap (cyclical GDP) is associated with a certain decrease in unemployment. Given a stable relation, we can estimate the structural (natural) rate of unemployment as the rate that is consistent with a zero GDP gap. Here we test for a change in the structural unemployment rate, by testing whether the relation shifted in the 1990s. We choose the simplest possible specification for the Okun relation consistent with previous empirical work. In particular, we adopt unemployment as the dependent variable and the GDP gap as the independent variable. We capture slow adjustment by adding one lag of unemployment as an explanatory variable.[8] We allow for a structural break by adding an intercept dummy and a slope dummy for the lagged unemployment term. The slope dummy also allows for a change in the dynamics. Thus the estimated regression is:

$$u_t = \alpha_0 + \alpha_1 D_t^{1990s} + \alpha_2 u_{t-1} + \alpha_3 D_t^{1990s} u_{t-1} + \alpha_4 Gap_t + \varepsilon_t$$

where u is the unemployment rate, Gap the output gap and D_t^{1990s} is a dummy equal to one for 1992–2004, and zero otherwise. The coefficient on the lagged unemployment term is α_2 in the 1980s and $\alpha_2 + \alpha_3$ in the 1990s. The associated long-run relation, 'the Okun curve', is found by setting $u_t = u_{t-1} = u^*$, and $\varepsilon_t = 0$:

$$u = \frac{\alpha_0 + \alpha_1 D_t^{1990s}}{1 - \alpha_2 - \alpha_3 D_t^{1990s}} + \frac{\alpha_4}{1 - \alpha_2 - \alpha_3 D_t^{1990s}} Gap = u^* + u^{cyclical}$$

If either one of the dummies is statistically significant (by itself or with the other), there is a significant shift in the Okun relation. The structural rate of unemployment is found by setting the GDP gap equal to zero.

The results are given in Table 4.2.[9] The intercept dummies in the two countries are not statistically significant. The dummy is close to zero

Table 4.2 Okun's law 1980–2004: unemployment dependent variable

	Independent variable										
			u_{t-1}					Structural rate			
	c_{1980s}	c_{1990s}	1980s	1990s	Gap_t	*Adj.* R^2	*D.W.*	u_{st}^{1980s}	u_{st}^{1990s}	Δu_{st}
Finland	4.17	4.83	0.23	0.48	−0.40	0.98	1.59	5.4	9.3	3.9
p-value	0.00	0.51	0.17	0.16	0.00					0.000
Sweden	1.07	2.10	0.46	0.57	−0.31	0.96	1.06	2.0	4.9	2.9
p-value	0.04	0.12	0.03	0.59	0.00					0.000

Note: *p*-value for the 1990s dummy and slope effects refers to the extra effect. The *p*-value of the difference in the structural rate refers to a Wald test of the null hypotheses of no difference between the 1980s and 1990s:

$$H_0: \frac{\alpha_0 + \alpha_1}{1 - \alpha_2 - \alpha_3} = \frac{\alpha_0}{1 - \alpha_2}$$

in Finland, while it increased in Sweden. The slope dummies indicate a slower response of unemployment to a shock in the GDP gap or the error term for both Finland and Sweden, but the effect is only statistically significant for Finland.

The estimated change in the structural rate of unemployment is 3.9 per cent for Finland and 2.9 per cent for Sweden. Both changes are statistically significant (<1 per cent) by the Wald test. Thus, the two dummies are statistically significant together for Sweden, although insignificant by themselves.

According to the estimates, both countries have been close to their estimated long-run relations for the period 1995–2004. This finding, together with the fact that the GDP gap was positive between 1998 and 2002, implies that unemployment has been below the structural rate in the late 1990s for both countries.

4.2.2 The Beveridge Curve

The Beveridge curve is a bivariate relation that can be used in an analogous fashion to Okun's law to test for a change in the structural unemployment rate. Arguably, it is more attractive than the Okun relation since it can be derived from reasonable micro foundations that explicitly focus on the matching process.[10]

In an analogous specification to the Okun relation, we attempt to distinguish between cyclical movements and a horizontal shift in the curve which indicates a change in the structural rate of unemployment. Thus, we estimate the following dynamic equation:

$$\ln u_t = \alpha_0 + \alpha_1 D_t^{1990s} + \alpha_2 \ln u_{t-1} + \alpha_3 D_t^{1990s} \ln u_{t-1} + \alpha_4 \ln v_t + \varepsilon_t$$

where v is the vacancy rate (vacancies divided by the labor force). The Beveridge curve is estimated in logarithms to allow for a convex shape. The coefficient α_1 measures the change in the intercept and the coefficient α_3 measures the change in the effect of lagged unemployment, that is, a change in the dynamics.[11] The associated long-run relation, 'the Beveridge curve', is found by setting $\ln u_t = \ln u_{t-1} = \ln u$, and $\varepsilon_t = 0$:

$$\ln u = \frac{\alpha_0 + \alpha_1 D_t^{1990s}}{1 - \alpha_2 - \alpha_3 D_t^{1990s}} + \frac{\alpha_4}{1 - \alpha_2 - \alpha_3 D_t^{1990s}} \ln v \Leftrightarrow u = e^{\frac{\alpha_0 + \alpha_1 D_t^{1990s}}{1 - \alpha_2 - \alpha_3 D_t^{1990s}}} \cdot v^{\frac{\alpha_4}{1 - \alpha_2 - \alpha_3 D_t^{1990s}}}$$

If either one of the dummies is significant, there is a shift in the Beveridge curve.

Table 4.3 gives the results.[12] The estimated coefficients on lagged unemployment indicate a change in the dynamics towards slower adjustment in Finland but not in Sweden. The 1990s coefficient on lagged unemployment in Finland is both statistically and economically different from the 1980s coefficient. The intercept dummy is higher for Sweden in the 1990s, but not significantly higher. The estimate of the change in the structural rate

Table 4.3 The Beveridge curve 1980–2004: ln(unemployment) dependent variable

	Independent variable									
			$\ln u_{t-1}$					*Structural rate*		
	c_{1980s}	c_{1990s}	1980s	1990s	$\ln v_t$	*Adj.* R^2	*D.W.*	u_{st}^{1980s}	u_{st}^{1990s}	Δu_{st}
Finland	1.53	1.33	−0.15	0.33	−0.47	0.98	2.34	4.6	10.4	5.8
p-value	0.00	0.51	0.27	0.01	0.00					0.013
Sweden	0.28	0.48	0.55	0.53	−0.47	0.98	1.67	3.0	4.2	1.2
p-value	0.00	0.19	0.00	0.81	0.00					0.006

Note: p-value for the 1990s dummy and slope effects refers to the extra effect. The p-value of the difference in the structural rate refers to a Wald test of the null hypotheses of no difference between the 1980s and 1990s:

$$H_0: \frac{\alpha_0 + \alpha_1}{1 - \alpha_2 - \alpha_3} = \frac{\alpha_0}{1 - \alpha_2}$$

of unemployment, the horizontal shift of the Beveridge curve, depends on what is considered a normal level of vacancies. A reasonable estimate is the mean for the whole period 1980–2000. The shift in Finland is 5.8 percentage points, which is higher than the Okun estimate (3.9). The shift in Sweden is 1.2 percentage points, which is considerably lower than the Okun estimate (2.9). The shift in Sweden is, however, not precisely estimated with high *p*-values for the dummy effects.

Given the degree of agreement across approaches and the statistical significance of the changes, we conclude that it is probable that a large shift in the structural unemployment rate occurred in both Finland and Sweden during the 1990s. A conservative estimate is that the structural rate of unemployment doubled in both countries in the 1990s.

4.3 STRUCTURAL CHANGES IN THE LABOR MARKET

This section describes the evolution of possible factors behind the change in the structural unemployment rate. We first look at changes in the composition of employment across sectors and types of contracts, which may be linked to different long-run unemployment risks. We then consider institutional developments of the labor market, including changes in employment protection, unemployment insurance, active labor market policies, wage bargaining and taxes. Such factors, shown to affect the structural rate of unemployment as well as the speed of adjustment to shocks, are used in the panel data tests in Section 4.4.

4.3.1 Relative Labor Demand Shifts

Data and previous literature suggest that the following changes are connected with the crisis.[13] In Sweden, there was a rather substantial cyclical increase in part-time work from 1991 to 1994, part-time work showing a rise of up to 2 percentage points over the four-year period. Presumably, this work-sharing dampened the rise in unemployment in Sweden. However this did not happen in Finland. In Finland, in turn, the share of temporary employment went up by about 2 percentage points over the first years of the crises. In Sweden, the opposite happened: the share of temporary employment declined in 1990 and 1991. There was a small cyclical increase in the share of public sector (state and local) employees in both Finland and Sweden during the downturn phase. In any case, public sector employment decreased absolutely in both countries and hence did not act as a buffer. In Finland, public sector employment has shown a steady rise since 1994, attaining the peak level of the year 1990 in 1998. In Sweden, public sector employment is still about 10 per cent lower than in 1990.

There was a permanent decline in the share of employment in construction in both countries, especially in Finland where employment decreased by almost 50 per cent. This decline is, at least to some extent, linked to the boom–bust cycle in the construction sector as described in Chapter 2. The cycle left a legacy of new buildings, especially office space, with a resulting decrease in the demand for new buildings. Demand had still not recovered in 2004. Construction is typically a sector with relatively high unemployment. So the decline in this sector should reduce the structural rate of unemployment in the long run, but may cause higher mismatch and thus higher unemployment in the medium run.

There was a permanent increase in the share of temporary work contracts in both countries, with an increase from a constant level in Finland and a reversal from a decline in Sweden. Ceteris paribus, this increases the structural rate as the inflow to unemployment increases. Holmlund and Storrie (2002) note the concurrent permanent increase in the inflow rate in Sweden and attribute 50 per cent of this increase to the increased use of temporary contracts. Their prime candidate explanation is that the recession increased uncertainty and thereby gave incentives to both employers and employees to accept temporary contracts, while they rule out large effects from the legislative changes that occurred in this period. The Finnish case appears to be similar. Over the period 1993–2004 about 60 per cent of new contracts were temporary. This behavior suggests hysteresis: the recession triggered a temporary increase, but the effect was permanent.

Some trends appeared to be unaffected by the crises. The declining (increasing) trend in the share of agriculture and forestry (services) continued in the 1990s and in the 2000s in both countries. Part-time work decreased throughout the 1980s and 1990s in Sweden, while increasing in Finland, seemingly converging at around 12 per cent. To conclude, the only structural change in labor market demand that appears to be connected with the crises in both Finland and Sweden, and with the potential for increasing the structural unemployment rate, is the increasing share of temporary employment.

4.3.2 Employment Protection Legislation

The purpose of employment protection legislation (EPL) is to make it harder to fire employees. Theoretically EPL has an ambiguous effect on structural unemployment. On the one hand, EPL makes it more risky for employers to hire new employees and thus the outflow from unemployment decreases, which in turn increases unemployment. On the other hand, EPL decreases unemployment through several possible channels. First, EPL reduces the number of unfair dismissals and thus the inflow into unemployment. Second, EPL creates incentives for on-the-job training, which increases the outflow rate from unemployment, as it becomes easier for better-trained workers to find new jobs. Third, EPL increases on-the-job search by increasing the incentive for the employer to give advance warning of firing. This reduces the inflow from employment as well as increasing the outflow from unemployment.[14]

We use the measures on the strictness of EPL in Finland and Sweden provided by the OECD for the late 1980s, late 1990s and early 2000s.[15] Both countries are in the middle of the distribution in all periods, with Finland ranking 12 and Sweden 16 in the late 1990s, compared with highest strictness ranking of 26. Both countries have increased flexibility since the late 1980s. According to the absolute change in the index, the change towards flexibility from the late 1980s to the late 1990s was marginal in Finland (2.3 to 2.0) and substantial in Sweden (3.5 to 2.2). The international rankings for both countries have, however, fallen and Finland and Sweden have both become relatively stricter.

Finland is on a similar level to Sweden, that is, both are middle-ranked countries in the regulation of both regular and temporary jobs. With respect to collective dismissals regulation, Finland is less stringent than Sweden. There were some changes in Finland towards greater flexibility in the late 1990s. These mainly occurred in the regulation of permanent work. In particular, there is now more flexibility in local arrangements regarding working time. Furthermore, the period of notice in the case of individual dismissals has been reduced from one month to two weeks if employment has lasted less than one year. Collective temporary layoffs are now possible at 14 days' notice and the new Co-determination Act cut the negotiation period from three months to two months. On the other hand, there are more restrictions on temporary work. In essence, workers with successive contracts are, to a limited extent, entitled to the same benefits as workers in permanent jobs.

Sweden's ranking in employment protection for regular jobs reflects, on the one hand, strict rules on length of notice and, on the other, liberal rules for redundancy pay (none) and liberal reasons for collective dismissal. The changes in Sweden towards greater flexibility have occurred in the regulation of temporary work.[16] First, private temporary work agencies were allowed from 1993. These companies provide brokerage services and, most importantly, rent out temporary workers. They were supplying 24 000 employees (0.6 per cent of the labor force) by the year 2000. Second, the restrictions on temporary work contracts were relaxed in 1997 to allow for temporary work contracts for no specific reason (such as temporary workload, or temporary vacancies).[17] The employer is restricted to no more than five such contracts and for any individual their accumulated length may not exceed 12 months during a three-year period.

4.3.3 Active Labor Market Policy

Like employment protection legislation, active labor market policies (ALMPs) have several potential effects, which go in different directions. At the macro level, ALMPs may increase real wages, and hence unemployment, by diminishing the current threat of unemployment. At the micro level, there are two opposing effects. First, ALMPs may diminish search activity and so lead to longer duration of unemployment. Second, ALMPs may increase the chance of employment through better training. Empirical studies suggest that ALMPs lower the structural unemployment rate although the estimates are not robust – in many cases they depend on the inclusion of Sweden in the data set.

Finland spends considerably less on ALMPs than Sweden, when measured by expenditures on ALMPs in relation to GDP. The total amounts spent on unemployment (active and passive measures) are, however, roughly of a similar order, due to higher unemployment in Finland. Total spending, as well as its composition in passive and active measures, returned to its pre-crisis level in the early 2000s.[18] Thus, there has been no significant structural change in ALMPs that potentially could explain a change in structural unemployment. This does not, however, rule out possible effects due to changes in the composition of programs, since a number of new programs were introduced in both Finland and Sweden during the 1990s. For example, Finland introduced a part-time work supplementary benefit and a job-sharing program, following a trainee work scheme with labor market subsidy launched in 1993. In Sweden, several new subsidized youth trainee programs were introduced.

The possible impact of active labor market policies on structural unemployment can be evaluated by measures that control for cyclical effects. One such measure, the so-called accommodation ratio, is calculated as the share of active labor market policy participants in total unemployment.[19] The measure implies that Finland has had a less ambitious approach to active measures than Sweden. On average, the accommodation ratio has been less than 30 per cent in Finland and about 40 per cent in Sweden. The accommodation ratio diminished considerably in both countries in the early 1990s, after a previous upturn in the mid-1980s. In addition, Finland has gradually approached the Swedish level:

the gap of about 20 percentage points in the accommodation ratios in the 1980s and early 1990s plummeted to about 5 percentage points in the early 2000s.

The proportion of persons in ALMPs in training programs (not including youth trainee programs) has remained fairly constant in Finland between 35 and 40 per cent, whereas in Sweden it has been strongly counter-cyclical, coming down from a peak of about 60 per cent in 1990 to around 20 per cent in 2004. During the downturn, a large fraction of new entrants into ALMPs entered non-education programs, including work schemes.

To sum up, ALMPs increased during the crisis in both Finland and Sweden, but then swiftly were reduced to below their pre-crisis levels. Otherwise no permanent changes appear to have occurred in the general composition of ALMPs. In both Finland and Sweden, the focus has been on temporary jobs in state offices and municipalities and placement in the private sector.

4.3.4 Unemployment Insurance

The theoretical literature emphasizes the adverse effects of unemployment benefits: they generate unemployment by reducing the cost of unemployment. This raises the reservation wage, leading to longer search periods, thus lengthening the average duration of unemployment spells. This traditional view has received empirical support. However, in many cases unemployment effects are unclear and depend on the institutional arrangements of the labor market. For example, the magnitude of the effect tends to vary with the structure of the benefit system, including duration, type (flat or means-tested) and eligibility conditions. Furthermore, the financing of benefits seems to affect the outcome.

In Finland, unemployment benefits consist of three components: earnings-related unemployment allowance, basic unemployment allowance and, from 1996 onwards, labor market subsidy. Earnings-related benefits are administered by trade unions. In 2005, this system covered about 50 per cent of those receiving benefits. Labor market subsidies and basic unemployment allowances are both administered by the Social Insurance Institute. In 2005, the average daily compensation for a member in an insurance fund was about 45 euros. In the case of a fixed benefit, it was 24 euros.[20]

The system is basically the same in Sweden. There is an earnings-related system administered by trade unions and a fixed allowance for those not qualified, due to lack of previous membership and work experience, administered by the government. Also coverage and rates are comparable: in Sweden about 60 per cent of the unemployed are covered by the earnings-related system and the fixed government allowance accounts for about 60 per cent of the average union member's allowance.

In both Finland and Sweden, the replacement ratio has diminished since it peaked in 1992.[21] Thus the changes in the unemployment benefit system have worked in the direction of lowering the structural rate of unemployment. In Finland, the increase in the relative share of unemployed individuals receiving the fixed allowance explains the largest part of the decline in the average replacement rate. In Sweden, the reduction has been caused by a combination of lower percentage compensation for earnings-related benefits, caps on earnings-related benefits and an increase in wages.

4.3.5 Wage Bargaining System

The degree of centralization of wage bargaining has been linked both to the degree of nominal wage sluggishness and to the equilibrium level of the real wage, and thus also to structural unemployment. The effect of the degree of wage co-ordination on the structural rate of unemployment is linked to the bargaining strength of the labor unions. Strong unions with wide membership, as is the case of Finland and Sweden, tend to raise wages and thus increase unemployment. If, however, unions can co-ordinate their actions and agree on wage moderation, the adverse effects of their behavior are mitigated. In an economy with large and powerful unions, there is an economic rationale for the co-ordination of wage bargaining.

According to Calmfors (2001, Table 2), both Finland and Sweden moved towards decentralized wage bargaining in the mid-1990s. He considers them both intermediate countries, although Sweden has gone a bit further than Finland. The centralization/co-ordination index, varying from 0 (no centralization) to 1 (complete centralization), changed from 0.58 to 0.47 in Finland between the periods 1983–87 and 1993–97. In Sweden, the index decreased from 0.49 to 0.39. In the late 1990s wage bargaining in Finland became, once again, more centralized. Between 1996 and 2005 there was only one year with decentralized bargaining, namely the year 2000. Sweden moved towards informal wage co-ordination through general agreements on the procedural rules for wage bargaining, starting in 1996 in the industrial sector, and extending thereafter to other sectors. Furthermore, a new government mediation institute was set up in 2000. Studies of wage formation suggest that it has been stable in Sweden and therefore that informal rules have replaced previous formal co-ordination; see Holmlund (2006) and Nymoen and Rödseth (2003).[22]

The shift towards decentralized wage bargaining in Finland in the mid-1990s and Sweden over the 1990s suggests that the speed of adjustment to shocks decreased and that the structural rate of unemployment went up.

In this view, the shift towards more decentralized wage bargaining in the early 1990s, while both countries were hit by the largest downturn in the post-war period, were indeed ill-timed.

4.3.6 Tax and Price Wedges

The theoretical literature suggests that tax and price wedges affect employment and unemployment. The wedge between the real cost of a worker to the employer and the real consumption wage of the worker is composed of payroll taxes, income taxes, consumption taxes and the price of imported goods. Higher consumption or income taxes, or a rise in the price of imported commodities, require higher nominal wages to sustain the same after-tax purchasing power. Similarly, higher payroll taxes increase real labor costs. A higher wedge leads to inflationary pressures and to a rise in structural unemployment if workers attempt to maintain their living standards. This is true at least in the short run. In the long run, the impact of a higher wedge will depend on how the tax burden and changes in the price of foreign commodities ultimately affect real labor costs.

Taxes that affect the cost of labor are high in Finland and Sweden by EU standards. During the 1990s employer costs were almost double the take-home pay of the employee, taking into account the payroll, income and value-added taxes.[23] Both in Finland and Sweden, the tax wedge grew in 1992–96. It remained stable over the period 1997–2000, finally slowly declining towards its pre-crisis level in 2001–05. In Finland, the tax wedge continues to be above the pre-crisis level and the increase in it coincided with the rise in unemployment. Although the causality is not clear, the adverse effects of the increase in the tax wedge on unemployment cannot be ignored.

Tax reforms lowered the Swedish tax rate temporarily in the early 1990s. As in Finland, there was a modest decline in the tax wedge in the early 2000s. The price wedge went up after 1991 in both Finland and Sweden due to currency depreciation, but then moved back slightly. The price wedge remains lower than it was in the 1980s.

To sum up, neither the tax wedge nor the price wedge is a likely candidate as a major cause of the increase in unemployment in Sweden, although temporary effects cannot be ruled out. In Finland, the negative effects of the increases in the price and tax wedges in the early 1990s are likely to be stronger and last longer than in Sweden.

4.3.7 Summary

The evidence on the evolution of the institutional determinants of structural unemployment points in different directions. Comparing the early

1990s with the early 2000s indicates that there are two factors in both countries that imply a lower structural unemployment rate: decreases in the replacement rate and union bargaining power.[24] The comparison of the late 1990s to the early 2000s suggests an increase in the structural unemployment due to an increase in the tax wedge. Similarly, an increase in active labor market policies in the first part of the 1990s, measured by the share of ALMPs in GDP, suggests a lower structural rate for the early 1990s but a higher rate for the late 1990s and early 2000s. An alternative ALMP measure, active spending per unemployed person, in turn indicates a higher structural unemployment rate for all the post-crisis years. As above, this applies in both countries. Numerical summary estimates of employment protection, union and employer co-ordination and union coverage, both for Finland and Sweden, remain unchanged over the period, although there were signs of a change towards decentralized bargaining in the mid-1990s in both countries, particularly in Sweden.

4.4 EVIDENCE FROM PANEL DATA STUDIES

This section surveys the empirical evidence on the link between structural unemployment and its causes in Finland and Sweden. We begin by reviewing existing estimates. This will be followed by an account of new estimates for the 1990s and early 2000s, carried out by updating and utilizing the results of existing models. This augments the bivariate evidence reported earlier. Our analysis may provide an insight into this issue and thus lessons for policy.

4.4.1 Existing Estimates

The empirical evidence stems both from panel studies that exploit variation across time and countries and from single-country studies that only exploit the variation across time. Typically, panel studies use reduced-form unemployment equations with several explanatory factors. Single-country studies generally use only univariate or bivariate regressions. Below we classify previous empirical studies according to the data. First we review panel data evidence and then country evidence.[25]

The panel studies considered are Scarpetta (1996), Elmeskov et al. (1998), Layard and Nickell (1999) and Blanchard and Wolfers (2000).[26] In these studies estimates are derived from the parameters of a reduced-form unemployment rate equation. The set of explanatory variables typically includes proxies for unemployment benefits (level and/or duration), active labor market policies (expenditures per GDP or per person), bargaining structures (measured by co-ordination, union density and coverage), employment protection (length of notification, severance payments), tax wedge (labor, income and consumption tax rates) and cyclical fluctuations that control for deviations between structural and actual unemployment (measured either by change in inflation, output gap or interest rate or by time dummies). In all cases the data are annual and typically consist of at least two cross-sections, generally one from the early 1980s and one from the early 1990s. The most recent data are used in Blanchard and Wolfers (2000) where the last cross-section ends in 1995/1996. The number of countries included in the studies varies from 15 to 21.

The results of the study by Scarpetta (1996) suggest that structural unemployment increased in the European OECD countries by approximately 4 percentage points from the early 1970s to the mid-1990s. In the US, it rose by 1 percentage point. For Finland and Sweden the estimates are considerably higher at 11 and 3.7 percentage points, respectively. In both cases the increase is mainly attributed to higher unemployment benefits and militant labor unions. As the study focuses on change over a long time period, it is not well suited to the Finnish and Swedish cases, where the change occurred in the early 1990s, as opposed to the early 1980s in the case of the other OECD countries.[27]

The results of Elmeskov et al. (1998) indicate that structural unemployment increased in Europe on average by 1.5 percentage points from the mid-1980s to the mid-1990s. In the US, it fell by 1 percentage point. According to the study, Finland and Sweden have both performed extremely badly. In Finland, the structural unemployment rate has risen by more than 10 and in Sweden by more than 4 percentage points. In both cases, the rise stems mainly from unidentified country-specific factors.

The results of Layard and Nickell (1999) indicate that structural unemployment increases with higher unemployment benefits, stronger trade unions, higher taxes and a higher homeowner-occupier rate. Wage co-ordination between unions and employers and active labor market policies, in turn, decrease unemployment. Estimates of the structural unemployment rate for 1991–95 are 9 per cent for Finland and 3 per cent for Sweden. The difference is almost entirely due to one factor: the extent of active labor market policies. At the Finnish level of active labor market policies, Swedish unemployment would be around 5–6 percentage points higher.

Blanchard and Wolfers (2000) construct country-specific time series for shocks (productivity, real interest, shifts in labor demand) and allow for interactions between shocks and institutions. They conclude that interactions account rather well for the rise and heterogeneity in the evolution of actual unemployment in Europe. Crude estimates of the structural unemployment rate for the early 1980s in Finland and Sweden are 5 and 2 per cent, respectively. For the mid-1990s, the corresponding numbers are 16.0 and 4.5.

The time series evidence by and large accords with the findings from the panel studies. In short, the results for Finland indicate that the structural unemployment rate in the mid-1990s was in the range 7–12 per cent. The highest estimates are reported by Holm and Somervuori (1997), the lowest estimates by Kiander and Pehkonen (1999), OECD (2000) and Rasi and Viskari (1998). The OECD results imply that the NAIRU (non-accelerating inflation rate of unemployment) rose significantly from the mid-1980s to the mid-1990s. The results for 1999, in turn, suggest that the NAIRU had fallen about 1.5 percentage points from its highest level.

Forslund (1995), Apel and Jansson (1999), OECD (2000) and Hjelm (2003) provide estimates on structural unemployment in Sweden. Forslund (1995) estimates equations for wages, prices and trade balance. OECD (2000), Apel and Jansson (1999) and Hjelm (2003) apply the method of unobserved components to data on unemployment, inflation and output. In short, the results indicate that structural unemployment in Sweden rose by about 2–3 percentage points in the early 1990s, the average estimate for the mid-1990s being about 5 per cent.

4.4.2 Causes and Updates

Table 4.4 summarizes the evidence on causes underlying changes in unemployment for the early 1990s. The purpose of the exercise is to investigate the performance of the existing models in explaining the observed decline in the Finnish and Swedish unemployment rates since the mid-1990s. The contributing factors are divided into six main groups: taxes, benefits, unions, active labor market policies, shocks and other factors. Estimates have been calculated by multiplying impact coefficients with the change in the average values of the independent variables between 1985–89 and 1990–94.[28]

In Finland, the rise in actual unemployment in the early 1990s is mainly accounted for by shocks and unidentified country-specific factors. On average, they indicate an increase of about 6–7 percentage points in the structural unemployment rate; see Table 4.4. The highest estimates are by Scarpetta (1996) and Elmeskov et al. (1998), who attribute the rise in unemployment to the rise in output gap, indicating an increase of around 4.5 percentage points. Layard and Nickell (1999) associate the increase in unemployment to falling inflation, the estimate being about 3 percentage points. The estimate of Blanchard and Wolfers (2000), in turn, consists of an increase in the interest rate, a decrease in total factor productivity and an adverse labor demand shift over the period. Institutional variables

Table 4.4 Contribution of different factors to the change in unemployment in the early 1990s in Finland and Sweden (percentage points between 1985–89 and 1990–94)

Study	(1) Taxes	(2) Benefits	(3) Unions	(4) ALMPs	(5) Others	Sum: 1–5	Shocks
Scarpetta (1996)	0	0.3/0.1	0.5/0.1	0/0	2.0/0.1	2.8/0.3	4.9/2.9
Elmeskov et al. (1998)	0.2/−1.3	0.2/0.1	0.9/0	0.2/1.1	3.6/0.8	5.0/0.7	4.6/2.6
Layard and Nickell (1999)	0.3/−0.9	0.2/0	0.2/0	0.3/0.6	0.3/0.1	1.2/−0.2	2.9/−0.1
Blanchard and Wolfers (2000)	0.1/−0.4	0.1/0	0.1/0	0.1/0.3	0/0	0.4/−0.1	3.0/0.1

Note: – = not considered in the study; 0 = considered, but an insignificant effect/no change in explanatory variable. In Layard and Nickell (1999), the dependent variable is lnU. We evaluate the effects at $u = 5$ per cent (2.5 per cent) which is the average unemployment rate of the 1980s in Finland (Sweden). Shocks are as follows: in Scarpetta (1996), interest rate (0.3/0.3) and output gap (4.6/2.6); in Elmeskov (1998), output gap (4.6/2.6); in Layard and Nickell (1999), change in inflation (2.9/0); in Blanchard and Wolfers (2000), interest rate (1.0/1.3), productivity (1.4/–1.6) and labor demand shift (0.6/0.4). 'Others' includes country-specific effects plus all other impacts by unreported factors.

(taxes, unions, benefits and active labor market policies) play a substantial role, although they are less significant than cyclical factors. Altogether the institutional variables indicate an increase of 1 percentage point in Finnish structural unemployment.

In Sweden, as in Finland, the main evidence points towards shocks. The highest estimates are, again, by Scarpetta (1996) and Elmeskov et al. (1998), suggesting an increase of around 3 percentage points in the unemployment rate. The absence of an adverse effect of shocks in Layard and Nickell (1999) and Blanchard and Wolfers (2000) is due to two factors: there is no change in inflation[29] and the effect of the increase in the real interest rate is counterbalanced by a positive change in productivity of approximately the same magnitude. As in Finland, modest adverse effects stemming from higher benefits, union activity and unidentified factors are reported in Scarpetta (1996) and Elmeskov et al. (1998). A decrease in structural unemployment due to a lower tax wedge is reported by Layard and Nickell (1999), Blanchard and Wolfers (2000) and Elmeskov et al. (1998). They all, however, indicate a corresponding rise in structural unemployment due to a decrease in the extent of active labor market policies.[30]

We have done the same exercise for the late 1990s and the early 2000s.[31] In both countries there are two distinct factors that, according to the empirical studies, should have lowered unemployment over the period, namely, the fall in the replacement rate and unionization. In Finland, the average replacement rate decreased by about 9 percentage points, from 56 to 47 per cent. In Sweden, the maximum replacement rate dropped from about 87 per cent in the early 1990s to 69 per cent in the early 2000s. Union density, in turn, fell by about 8 percentage points in Finland and 5 in Sweden. A lower level of active labor market policies, in turn, should have increased unemployment in both countries over both periods. The relative decline in expenditures on active labor market policies since the mid-1990s has been about 20–50 per cent, depending on how the extent of active policies is measured. The evolution of the tax wedge, and thus its impact on unemployment, varies across the periods. In the late 1990s, the wedge increased in Finland and Sweden, rising by about 12–13 percentage points. In the early 2000s, it declined by 7 percentage points in both countries.

The increase in the tax wedge imposed upward pressure on unemployment over the late 1990s in both Finland and Sweden. The estimates are, however, rather imprecise, varying from zero to 3 percentage points; see column 1. These adverse effects are largely offset by a decline in unemployment benefits and union power; see columns 2 and 3. In the early 2000s taxes were lowered in both countries, resulting in a substantial decrease in unemployment. A continuing decline in unemployment benefits and union density over the period 2000–04 enhanced this positive trend. Depending on the study, these institutional variables predict a fall in the unemployment rate of about 1 percentage point in both countries. These positive effects are partly offset by a decline in the extent of active labor market policies. Cuts in active expenditures increased unemployment in both Sweden and Finland by about 0.5 percentage points in the early 2000s.[32]

As in the early 1990s, cyclical factors have an important role in explaining the evolution of unemployment in the late 1990s and early 2000s. Their role is somewhat stronger in Finland than in Sweden. The decline in real interest rates was particularly marked, from about 6 to 2 per cent over the period in both countries. This boom–bust–recovery cycle shows up in the output gap and inflation. The output gap of a magnitude of about 4–6 per cent of GDP disappeared in both Finland and Sweden. This happened without an increase in inflation, indicating that the actual unemployment rate exceeded the structural unemployment rate.

All things considered, the evidence of the panel data models over the period 1990–99 is somewhat mixed.[33] Two studies, Elmeskov et al. (1998) and Layard and Nickell (1999), indicate that adverse developments in institutional factors increased structural unemployment considerably in the late 1990s, while one study, Blanchard and Wolfers (2000), suggests a moderate increase and one study, Scarpetta (1996), a substantial decrease in structural unemployment. Excluding Layard and Nickell (1999), the role of cyclical factors is coherent over the period: the models imply that positive shocks reduced unemployment by approximately 2 percentage points in Finland and 1 percentage point in Sweden.

The evidence for the early 2000s suggests that the unemployment rate declined by about 2 percentage points in Finland such that about 60–70 per cent of the decline stems from cyclical factors and the rest from structural factors. In Sweden, these estimates are of similar magnitude. These predictions underestimate the observed evolution in unemployment in Finland, where the unemployment rate fell from about 16 per cent in 1992–94 to about 11 per cent in 1995–99 and then further to around 9 per cent in 2000–05. In Sweden, the corresponding fall was about 2 percentage points, from about 7 per cent to about 5 per cent in the late 1990s and then further to around 4 per cent. To sum up, the ability of the reviewed panel data models to account for the observed fall in Finnish and Swedish unemployment is not more than satisfactory, although the predictions are clearly on the right side.

4.5 SUMMARY

The two crises are alike in their initial timing, both beginning in 1991 and peaking in 1994. Finland's crisis was deeper in both absolute and relative terms for all the unemployment measures. The non-employment rate, which takes into account the changes both in the open unemployment rate and in the outflow from the labor force, provides an upper limit on the increase in total unemployment. The non-employment rate increased in Sweden by 10 percentage points whereas in Finland it rose by 15 percentage points. By this measure, the Finnish crisis was 50 per cent worse than the Swedish crisis.

Sweden had a quick recovery until 1995, after which unemployment remained constant until 1998, whereas Finland was in a recovery process for the rest of the 1990s. After 1998, when unemployment also decreased in Sweden, the two countries differ in that the inflow into unemployment and the duration continue to decrease in Finland, whereas the recovery from 1998 in Sweden was due solely to a sharp decrease in duration. One legacy of the crises shows up in the share of temporary employment, which rose substantially in both countries in the 1990s.

The time series analyses indicate that there was a large shift in the structural unemployment rate in both Finland and Sweden. Our findings suggest that the structural unemployment doubled in both countries in the early 1990s. These findings accord with those of previous studies, which imply, on average, a rise of about 4–6 percentage points for Finland and 2–4 for Sweden. Although empirical estimates of structural unemployment are likely to be uncertain when economies are subject to large shocks, as in Finland and Sweden in the early 1990s, the existing evidence implies that the crises of the 1990s in Sweden and Finland had long-lasting, if not permanent, effects on the labor market. Given the shelter afforded by various institutional arrangements, it comes as no surprise that adverse shocks (such as the rise in real interest rates) may have long-lasting effects on unemployment.

The estimates imply that structural unemployment remained roughly constant in both Finland and Sweden over the late 1990s. The impact of higher taxes was offset by lower replacement rates. For the early 2000s, the evidence suggests a modest decrease in structural unemployment, mainly due to lower rates of taxation, a lower replacement rate and diminishing union power in both countries. As a whole the results indicate that much of the decline in open unemployment in the late 1990s and early 2000s was due to positive demand shocks.

Overall the evidence on the factors explaining the evolution of unemployment remains vague. This applies both to our findings reported as well as to the evidence reported in previous studies. It appears that the rise in unemployment and its persistence at a high level was mainly due to aggregate demand shocks, several small effects stemming from changes in institutions combined with lagged adjustment (hysteresis). The hysteresis explanation, in particular, shows up in the estimates for the late 1990s: adjustment towards the unemployment levels of the late 1980s is slow in both countries in spite of increasing aggregate demand and enhanced incentives to accept job offers. Finland and Sweden are thus prime candidates for the thesis put forward by Blanchard and Wolfers: a negative demand shock together with rigid institutions leads to long-lasting effects.

NOTES

1. Time series are shown in Fregert and Pehkonen (2008, Figure 4).
2. Data from the Swedish labor force survey give an indication of how important the discouraged worker effect is. The 7 percentage points decline in the participation rate between 1990 and 1994 is roughly equal to 400 000 people. At the same time, the number of discouraged workers increased by about 140 000. Thus at least a third of the decrease in the participation rate was due to the discouraged worker effect. At the same time, participation in labor market programs increased by 170 000 between 1990 and 1994. Thus, roughly 25 per cent of the decrease in the participation rate (90 000/400 000) was due to other reasons.

3. See Chapter 5 in this volume for a comparison of the deepest crises hitting Finland and Sweden.
4. Time series of duration and long-term unemployment are shown in Fregert and Pehkonen (2008, Figures 6 and 7).
5. Time series are shown in Fregert and Pehkonen (2008, Figure 8).
6. Time series are shown in Fregert and Pehkonen (2008, Figure 9).
7. Data are given in Table 1 in Fregert and Pehkonen (2008). Böckerman and Kiander (2002) provide a detailed account of labor market adjustment channels during the great depressions of the 20th century in Finland. See also Chapter 5 in this volume.
8. Gylfason (1997) estimated versions of Okun's law for Sweden with lagged unemployment.
9. The Okun relations are graphed in Fregert and Pehkonen (2008, Figure 10).
10. Blanchard and Diamond (1989) provide theoretical underpinnings for the Beveridge curve and introduce it as a tool for distinguishing between different shocks. Other empirical applications that use the Beveridge curve to distinguish between structural and cyclical shocks are, inter alia, Jackman et al. (1990) and Nickell and van Ours (2000).
11. Jackman et al. (1990) estimated Beveridge curves for 14 countries for the period 1971–88 with unemployment as the dependent variable and the vacancy rate and lagged unemployment as independent variables, all in logarithmic form.
12. The Beveridge relations are graphed in Fregert and Pehkonen (2008, Figure 10).
13. Data are given in Fregert and Pehkonen (2008, Figures 13 to 16).
14. See OECD (2004) and Nickell and van Ours (2000) for recent empirical accounts.
15. See OECD (2004, Table 2.A2.4.).
16. Besides these changes, reform of labor legislation was on the political agenda in Sweden during the 1990s. In 1994, the Employment Protection Act (*Lagen om anställningsskydd*) of 1974 was also changed in several respects by the center-right government. However, the change had only lasted for a year, when the Social Democrats took power. The most important change was allowing two persons to be exempt from the seniority principles governing firing in small companies (less than ten employees). In 1994, the maximum duration of temporary work contracts was extended to 12 months, but it is estimated that the new law had practically no impact during the short time it was in force. The exemption from seniority was reinstated in 2000 by the Social Democratic government as part of a deal with the Green Party.
17. Holmlund and Storrie (2002) provide a detailed discussion of temporary work in Sweden. As mentioned above, they argue that these legislative changes have had little effect.
18. The time series are shown in Figure 17 in Fregert and Pehkonen (2008).
19. This measure is used, inter alia, by Forslund and Kolm (2000). It can be given two interpretations. First, it measures the willingness of policy-makers to accommodate unemployment by ALMPs. Second, it measures the individual's chance of ending up in an ALMP program. The time series are shown in Figure 18 in Fregert and Pehkonen (2008).
20. The labor market subsidy and the basic benefit are means-tested and paid for an unlimited period. Earnings-related benefit is paid for a maximum of 500 days. Those who turn 59 before the benefit expires are entitled to an extension until the age of 60. Before 2005 (1997), the age limit for the extension of benefits was 57 (55).
21. Time series are given in Fregert and Pehkonen (2008, Figure 20).
22. See also Marjanen (2002) and Ahtiainen (2007) for an account of Finnish bargaining in the 1990s.
23. Time series are given in Fregert and Pehkonen (2008, Figure 21).
24. We provide data on the explanatory variables in Fregert and Pehkonen (2008, Appendix 1).
25. Detailed information is given in Fregert and Pehkonen (2008, Tables 8–10).
26. Recent studies also include Daveri and Tabellini (2000). Unfortunately, we were not

able to derive their estimates of structural unemployment for Finland and Sweden. Their study, however, provides evidence on the role of taxes, unions and benefits in the rise of unemployment in these countries.
27. The panel, in fact, excludes data for Finland for 1992-93.
28. See Appendix 1 in Fregert and Pehkonen (2008) for the period means and Appendix 2 for the coefficients. In the case of Elmeskov et al. (1998), we divide the country-specific effects reported in the study into shocks and 'others' using the OECD's output gap estimates (a shock) and reported impact coefficients. In the case of Blanchard and Wolfers (2000), we ignore the interaction terms since the Finnish and Swedish economic institutions are alike in many respects. See Appendix 3 in Fregert and Pehkonen (2008), which shows that this simplification does not affect the results, since the implied range of effects across these two countries is small.
29. In Sweden, the inflation effect depends on how the periods are divided. For example, the use of end-period values (1989 versus 1994) implies a decrease in inflation of about 3 percentage points and thus an increase in unemployment of about 0.6 percentage points.
30. The tax effects show up more strongly in the time series studies than in the panel data studies. This result may reflect the fact that both unemployment and taxation (both of which showed an increase in the 1990s) are determined simultaneously by a third factor, which is not captured by time series analysis. On the other hand, with the exception of Blanchard and Wolfers (2000), the panel data studies report considerable country-specific, and thus unidentified, factors which are absent from the time series studies.
31. See Tables 12 and 13 in Fregert and Pehkonen (2008).
32. The results on the role of active policies are imprecise and in most cases depend on the inclusion of Sweden in the data set; see, for example, Layard and Nickell (1999), Blanchard and Wolfers (2000) and Daveri and Tabellini (2000).
33. Furthermore, in many cases the confidence intervals of the estimates are wide and the results depend on the inclusion/exclusion of certain variables/countries. This issue is well documented in Staiger et al. (1997).

REFERENCES

Ahtiainen, L. (2007), 'The coverage of collective agreements in Finland in 2004', Työpoliittinen tutkimus, no. 328, Ministry of Labour, Helsinki.

Andersson, F. (1999), 'Job flows in manufacturing in Swedish manufacturing 1972–1996', The Office of Labour Market Policy Evaluation, Working paper, no. 4, Uppsala.

Apel, M. and P. Jansson (1999), 'System estimates of potential output and NAIRU', *Empirical Economics,* **24**, 373–88.

Blanchard, O. and P. Diamond (1989), 'The Beveridge curve', *Brookings Papers on Economic Activity*, 1989:1, 1–76.

Blanchard, O. and J. Wolfers (2000), 'The role of shocks and institutions in the rise of European unemployment: the aggregate evidence', *Economic Journal,* **110**, c1–c33.

Böckerman, P. and J. Kiander (2002), 'Labour markets in Finland during the great depressions of the twentieth century', *Scandinavian Economic History Review*, **50**, 55–70.

Böckerman, P. and M. Maliranta (2001), 'Regional disparities in gross job and worker flows in Finland', *Finnish Economic Papers*, **14**, 84–103.

Calmfors, L. (2001), 'Wages and wage-bargaining institutions in the EMU – a survey of the issues', *Empirica*, **28**, 325–51.

Daveri, F. and G. Tabellini (2000), 'Unemployment, growth and taxation in industrial countries', *Economic Policy*, **30** (April), 47–104.

Elmeskov, J., J. Martin and S. Scarpetta (1998), 'Key lessons for labour market reforms: evidence from OECD countries' experiences', *Swedish Economic Policy Review*, **5**, 205–52.

Forslund, A. (1995), 'Unemployment: is Sweden still different?', *Swedish Economic Policy Review,* **2**, 15–58.

Forslund, A. and A. Kolm (2000), 'Active labour market policies and real wage determination – Swedish evidence', IFAU Working paper, no. 7, Uppsala University.

Fregert, K. and J. Pehkonen (2008), 'Causes of structural unemployment in Finland and Sweden 1990–2004', Working paper 2008:14, Department of Economics, Lund University.

Gylfason, T. (1997), 'Okun's law and labour market rigidity: the case of Sweden', Occasional Paper 79, SNS, Stockholm.

Hjelm, G. (2003), 'Simultaneous determination of NAIRU, output gaps and structural budget balances: Swedish evidence', National Institute of Economic Research, Working paper no. 81.

Holm, P. and E. Somervuori (1997), 'Structural unemployment in Finland', Discussion Papers no. 136, Government Institute for Economic Research, Helsinki.

Holmlund, B. (2006), 'The rise and fall of Swedish unemployment', in M. Werding (ed.), *Structural Unemployment in Western Europe: Reasons and Remedies*, Cambridge, MA: MIT Press, pp. 103–32.

Holmlund, B. and D. Storrie (2002), 'Temporary work in turbulent times: the Swedish experience', Working paper no. 2002:1, Uppsala University.

Jackman, R., P. Pissarides and S. Savouri (1990), 'Labour market policies and unemployment in the OECD', *Economic Policy,* **11**, 449–90.

Kiander, J. and J. Pehkonen (1999), 'Finnish unemployment: observations and conjectures', *Finnish Economic Papers*, **12**, 94–108.

Layard, R. and S. Nickell (1999), 'Labour market institutions and economic performance', in O. Asherfelter and D. Card (eds), *Handbook of Labor Economics*, vol. 3, Amsterdam: North-Holland, pp. 3029–84.

Marjanen, R. (2002), 'The content and realization of wage settlements in the period of income policy', Research Institute of the Finnish Economy, B 188, Helsinki.

Nickell, S. and J. van Ours (2000), 'The Netherlands and the United Kingdom: a European unemployment miracle', *Economic Policy*, **30**, 135–80.

Nymoen, R. and A. Rödseth (2003), 'Explaining unemployment: some lessons from Nordic countries', *Labour Economics*, **10**, 1–29.

OECD (2000), 'Revised OECD measures of structural unemployment', in *Economic Outlook*, no. 68, Paris: OECD.

OECD (2004), *Employment Outlook*, Paris: OECD.

Rasi, C.-M. and J. Viskari (1998), 'The time-varying NAIRU and potential output in Finland', Bank of Finland, Discussion Papers, no. 6, Helsinki.

Scarpetta, S. (1996), 'Assessing the role of labour market policies and institutional settings on unemployment: a cross-country study', *OECD Economic Studies,* **26**, 43–98.

Staiger, D., J. Stock and M. Watson (1997), 'The NAIRU, unemployment and monetary policy', *Journal of Economic Perspectives*, **11**, 33–59.

5. How costly was the crisis in Finland and Sweden?

Thomas Hagberg and Lars Jonung

INTRODUCTION[1]

In the 1990s the world economy was hit by a series of unusually deep crises, the first of which occurred in 1991–92 in Finland and Sweden. The depression in these two Nordic countries has much in common with those that occurred later in the decade in Mexico, South-East Asia, Russia, Brazil and Turkey. Although the downturn in economic activity in the early 1990s in Finland and Sweden is commonly regarded as exceptionally severe – associated with deep and lasting effects on the economy, institutions and policies of both countries – we lack systematic comparisons between the crises of the 1990s and other major episodes of crisis or depression.

This chapter adds to our understanding of the turbulent 1990s by comparing the cost of the depression of the 1990s with the costs caused by the major crises since the 1870s in the two Nordic countries. We adopt an approach developed by IMF (1998) and extended by Bordo et al. (2001) where the cost of a crisis is estimated in terms of output growth foregone. In these two studies the output losses of a large number of crises are compared across countries and time. Here, by contrast, we focus only on the experience of Finland and Sweden, calculating the cost of crises using three measures: loss of real income growth, loss of industrial production growth and loss of employment growth. We cover the experience of World Wars I and II as well.

This chapter is organized in the following way. We first identify all major crises that have occurred in Finland and Sweden since the 1870s. Second, we calculate the costs of crises in terms of real income, industrial production and employment foregone. Next, we briefly describe each crisis and consider its costs. Third, we compare the Finnish and Swedish records with each other and with the international pattern. The last section summarizes.

5.1 IDENTIFYING MAJOR CRISES

How do we identify a crisis? When should a downturn in economic activity (a recession) be classified as a crisis? There is no straightforward answer to these questions, as there is neither a commonly accepted definition nor a common theory of crises.[2] Here we define a crisis as 'an exceptionally sharp decline in economic activity', hence, the larger the decline in real income (GDP) growth, the deeper the crisis. This simple rule of thumb will guide us in the following sections.

We identify the episodes that should be classified as crises in Finland and Sweden using the following strategy. As a first step, we investigate which selection of years researchers and other observers have defined as crisis years in the economic history of the two countries. Next we examine how a number of key macroeconomic time series have evolved from the early 1870s to the late 1990s. We identify the years with the largest declines in the growth of real income (GDP), industrial production and employment. Lastly, we compare how well these episodes correspond to the classification of crises made in previous research. By combining these two sources of information, we arrive at a crisis chronology from which we calculate the cost of crisis.

Our chronology covers the deepest downturns or recessions that have hit the Finnish and Swedish economies in the past 130 years. Thus, a crisis is synonymous with a depression in our analysis. Finland and Sweden have also experienced minor banking and currency crises with no or little impact on real activity. Such episodes are not covered by our chronology.

5.1.1 The Crisis Record of Finland

The judgment of economic historians and economists

Comparing the most severe depressions in Finland since the 1870s, Hjerppe (1989) finds the depressions during the two world wars to have been the most severe. The crises of the 1870s and the 1930s also had significant, long-lasting negative effects, while the oil crises of the 1970s (OPEC I and II) were milder. Heikkinen and Kuusterä (2001) identify the following economic crises in Finland during the 20th century: 'World War I and its aftermath' (1914–19), 'the Great Depression' (1929–32), 'the latent crisis of the turbulent fifties' (1953–58), 'the stagflation years' (1975–77) and 'the deregulation crisis' (1990–93).

Herrala (1999) examines financial crises in Finland since 1862. These have generally occurred at the same time as depressions. He classifies as major depressions the crisis of the 1870s, World War I, the Great Depression of the 1930s and the crisis of the 1990s. He also identifies major economic shocks that did not lead to banking problems. These shocks occurred during the 1880s, the international financial crisis of 1907, World War II, 1952–53 and the OPEC crises.

Judging from these sources, the most severe downturns in the Finnish economy during the last 130 years occurred during the 1870s, World War I, the 1930s and the 1990s. Other periods, such as World War II, the 1950s and the oil crises of the 1970s, are also classified as periods of dismal economic performance.

Key macroeconomic time series

Figure 5.1 shows the annual percentage change in real income (GDP) in Finland for the period 1872–1996. According to our definition, an economic crisis is associated with a sharp and exceptionally large decline in economic activity. Therefore, our chronology should include those years with significant decreases in these series.

All the downturns classified as crises by economic historians and economists are associated with significant declines in real income. For World War II also a sharp drop is registered. During the 1950s and the OPEC crises, however, growth did not fall markedly. Industrial production has fluctuated more than real income. Its largest drops are recorded during the same periods as for real income, namely the crisis of 1877–78, the two world wars, the 1930s and the 1990s. The first OPEC crisis is associated with a minor decline, as are the early 1950s.[3]

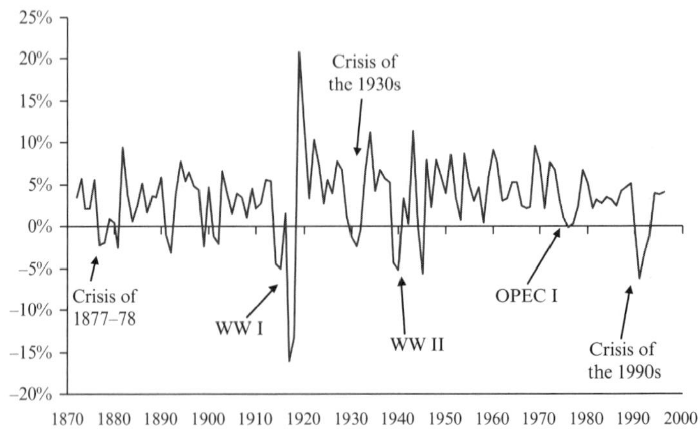

Source: Jonung and Hagberg (2005).

Figure 5.1 Real income 1872–1996 in Finland (annual percentage change)

Employment has not fluctuated as much as the two production series, but an identical pattern is discernible. The largest declines during peacetime conditions occurred during the crises of the 1990s and the 1930s. The crisis of 1877–78 saw the largest decrease during the period prior to World War I. OPEC I resulted in declines similar to those that occurred during the non-crisis years of the 1960s.[4]

The evidence from the time series confirms the identification made by economic historians and economists of the periods 1877–78, the 1930s, the 1990s and the two world wars as crisis episodes. The downturns in economic activity experienced during OPEC II and the latent crisis of the 1950s were not much more severe than 'ordinary' cyclical downturns. OPEC I, by contrast, was associated with a prolonged decline in employment and reductions in production growth. For this reason we also include OPEC I in our chronology. To summarize, the major economic crises in Finland over the last 130 years have been those of 1877–78, the 1930s, the 1990s, OPEC I and the two world wars.

5.1.2 The Crisis Record of Sweden

The judgment of economic historians and economists

In a study of business cycles and economic policies in Sweden, Lundberg (1953) classifies 1920–22 and 1931–33 as crisis years. Thirty years later, Lundberg (1983) examines four major crisis periods: the early 1920s, the early 1930s, and OPEC I and II. Lindgren (1993) focuses on the financial aspects of the crises of 1877–78, the early 1920s and the 1990s. Jonung (1994) compares quantitatively the crises of the early 1920s and the early 1930s, the OPEC crises and the crisis of the early 1990s. Jonung (1999) contrasts economic policies and outcomes during the OPEC crises and the crisis of the 1990s. Contemporary observers also classified 1907–08 as crisis years; see, for example, Cassel (1908) and Sveriges *Riksbank* (1909). Hagberg and Walldov (2000) treat 1907–08 as a period of crisis, as does Schön (2000).

The literature on Sweden's economic and financial history thus identifies seven major crises: 1877–78, 1907–08, the early 1920s, the early 1930s, OPEC I and II, and the 1990s. The two world wars, when Sweden remained neutral, are not commonly analysed as crisis years.

Key macroeconomic time series

As regards the statistical evidence, Figure 5.2 displays the annual percentage changes in real income in Sweden, 1872–1996. This figure confirms the judgment of economic historians. All crises except OPEC II are associated with a sharp reduction in the level of real income. However, the largest falls

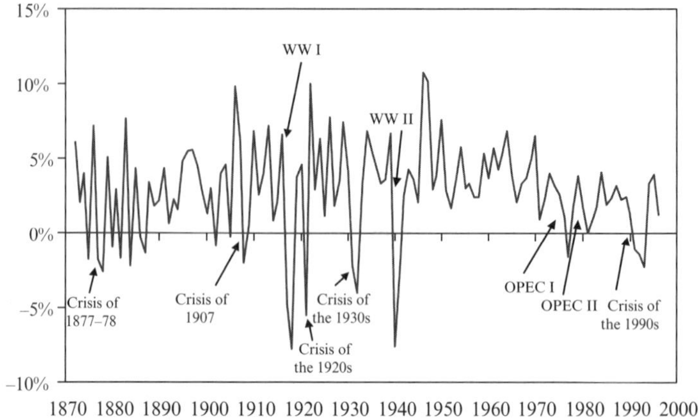

Source: Jonung and Hagberg (2005).

Figure 5.2 Real income in Sweden 1872–1996 (annual percentage change)

in real income did not occur during these episodes but at the end of World War I and at the beginning of World War II. Prior to World War I, several years display absolute declines in real income although they have not been classified by economic historians as crisis years. OPEC II does not stand out as a major crisis – real income growth remained positive – although contemporary observers, including Lundberg (1983), regarded it as such.

The evolution of industrial production is in accordance with the assessments by economic historians and economists.[5] The largest declines occurred during the seven major crises mentioned above and during the two world wars. Employment declined during these crises, most noticeably during the crises of the 1920s, the 1930s and the 1990s as well as during World War II. The OPEC crises saw barely any decline in employment, probably reflecting the impact of accommodative fiscal, monetary and labor market policies applied in the 1970s.[6]

Taken separately, data on annual changes in real income, industrial production and employment are not entirely consistent with the crisis chronology found in the work of economic historians. Significant declines in these aggregates have occurred during years other than those classified as crisis years. Put together, however, the figures give us no reason to contest the judgment of the economic historians. The two world wars are often not considered to have been economic crises but they stand out as being periods of exceptionally sharp swings in economic activity. For this reason we also include them in our sample.

To conclude, we select the following years to be studied as crises in Sweden: 1877–78, 1907–08, the early 1920s, the early 1930s and the early 1990s, the two OPEC crises and the two world wars.

5.2 DEFINING THE COST OF A CRISIS

What is the cost of a crisis? The answer depends on whether the intention is to study the fiscal costs or the costs to the economy as a whole. The fiscal costs, that is, government support to industries or commercial banks and other types of financial institutions, should be viewed as transfers from taxpayers to a specific group of actors within the economy, such as depositors in the case of a banking crisis, and thus not necessarily as a cost to society at large (see, for example, Caprio and Klingebiel, 1996).[7] The cost to society of a crisis should be measured in terms of foregone output or foregone output growth. The IMF (1998) suggests a measure of output loss for estimating the costs of crises to the economy which has been widely adopted, for instance by Aziz et al. (2000) and Bordo et al. (2001).[8] We build here on this approach by focusing not only on the loss of real income (GDP) but also on the loss of industrial production and employment to get a broad picture of the costs of crises.[9]

The output loss – or more precisely the loss in output growth – as defined by the IMF approach is calculated by totalling the differences between the trend growth rate of real income (GDP) and the actual growth rate from the start of the crisis until the growth rate of the series returns to trend rate. The estimated loss in output growth is thus dependent not only on how the series measured evolves during the crisis but also on how the trend rate is defined and the exact dating of the start and end of the crisis. Let us look at these two aspects of the estimation procedure.

First, the trend should ideally reflect the development of real income growth had the negative shock/crisis not occurred. It is impossible to carry out such a counterfactual analysis accurately. In the literature on output loss the usual solution to this problem is to simply assume that the economy would continue to grow at a rate equal to the average growth rate prior to the crisis. In IMF (1998) a three-year trend is used. Bordo et al. (2001) adopt a five-year trend. One major criticism of this method is that output growth prior to crises tends to be unsustainably high. Thus the output loss will overstate the severity of the crisis; see, for example, Mulder and Rocha (2000, p. 5). A five-year trend, such as the one we use below, should therefore be preferred to a three-year trend.

Since we are interested in the relative severity of the crisis of the 1990s, the absolute value of the output loss would matter only to the extent that the size of the cost of crisis is affected differently by the assumed trend rate across the crises we study. However, we conclude that this is not the case when a set of other trend rates are used.[10]

Second, turning to the dating of the start and the end of a crisis, we note that the longer a crisis lasts, the larger the output loss will be. Determining the points in time between which the loss should be calculated is thus of crucial importance. In studies such as Aziz et al. (2000), Bordo et al. (2001), Hoggarth et al. (2002) and IMF (1998), the aggregate output loss has been used to measure the real effects of financial crises. As we are studying economic crises, defined as periods with severe decreases in aggregate economic activity, and not crises in a single sector of the economy, the beginning is defined simply as the first year in which a large decline in the aggregate growth rate is recorded. The loss is then calculated until that year in which the growth rate once again equals or exceeds the trend rate.

Formally, the cost of crisis is calculated as

$$\textit{Loss in output growth} = \sum_{t=t_0}^{t_n} (y^* - y_t)$$

where y^* is the trend and y_t is the observed (actual) percentage change in real income. The loss in growth is calculated during the period when $y_t < y^*$. The loss of industrial production and of employment is calculated in the same way. Table 5.1 summarizes the estimates of the cost of the deepest crises for Finland and Sweden measured in this way.

5.3 BRIEF ACCOUNTS OF THE CRISES

Both Finland and Sweden are commonly regarded as small and open economies during the period we are studying. Given this openness and thus the importance of international trade to the two economies, it should not come as a surprise that the economic crises in Finland and Sweden occurred during periods of international economic slowdown. As seen from Table 5.1, economic crises have also often coincided in the two countries. In this section we present short descriptions of the crises and their costs.

5.3.1 The Crisis of 1877–78

After the Franco-German war in 1871, the European economy boomed, raising the demand for Finnish and Swedish exports. In Finland, this caused a speculative boom in forest land. When the price of forest products began to decline later in the decade, the country was driven into a severe

Table 5.1 The costs of Finland's and Sweden's most severe crises in terms of foregone growth in real income, industrial production and employment relative to a five-year trend (percentage points)

Crisis of:	1877–78	1907	1920s*	1930s	1990s	OPEC I	OPEC II	WW I	WW II
1. Loss of real income									
Finland	24.2	no crisis	no crisis	24.3	26.4	17.8	no crisis	57.8	32.4
Period below trend	*1877–81*	–	–	*1929–32*	*1990–93*	*1975–78*	–	*1914–18*	*1939–42*
Average loss per crisis year	*4.8*	–	–	*6.1*	*6.6*	*4.5*	–	*11.6*	*8.1*
Sweden	11.3	11.2	9.6	17.7	13.0	9.9	1.9	21.2	25.6
Period below trend	*1877–78*	*1908–09*	*1921*	*1931–33*	*1990–93*	*1976–78*	*1980–82*	*1917–19*	*1940–45*
Average loss per crisis year	*5.7*	*5.6*	*9.6*	*5.9*	*3.3*	*3.3*	*.6*	*7.1*	*4.3*
2. Loss of industrial production									
Finland	72.2	no crisis	no crisis	46.4	21.4	27.7	no crisis	98.6	72.2
Period below trend	*1876–79*	–	–	*1930–33*	*1990–92*	*1975–78*	–	*1914–18*	*1939–42*
Average loss per crisis year	*18.1*	–	–	*11.6*	*7.1*	*6.9*	–	*19.7*	*18.1*
Sweden	14.7	17.3	19.8	30.9	17.0	13.5	5.3	40.9	36.6
Period below trend	*1877–78*	*1908–09*	*1921*	*1930–33*	*1990–93*	*1976–78*	*1980–82*	*1917–19*	*1940–45*
Average loss per crisis year	*7.4*	*8.7*	*19.8*	*7.7*	*4.3*	*4.5*	*1.8*	*13.6*	*6.1*
3. Loss of employment									
Finland	5.9	no crisis	no crisis	16.4	24.0	6.1	no crisis	11.0	no loss
Period below trend	*1878–79*	–	–	*1929–32*	*1990–94*	*1975–78*	–	*1914–18*	–
Average loss per crisis year	*3.0*	–	–	*4.1*	*4.8*	*1.5*	–	*2.4*	–
Sweden	3.1	1,2	8.4	10.9	16.6	2.1	1.9	1.0	10.3
Period below trend	*1877–79*	*1908–09*	*1921–22*	*1931–33*	*1990–94*	*1976–78*	*1981–83*	*1917–18*	*1940–41*
Average loss per crisis year	*1.0*	*.6*	*4.8*	*3.6*	*3.3*	*.7*	*.6*	*.5*	*5.2*

Notes: The costs are calculated by summing the differences between the trend growth rate and the actual growth rate from the first year of recession until growth returns to trend.
*A two-year trend (for 1919–20) is used to calculate the loss of real income and industrial production during the crisis of the 1920s in Sweden.

Source: Jonung and Hagberg (2005).

depression. Bankruptcies increased markedly, especially in the sawmill industry, and real income started to decrease in 1877 (Herrala, 1999, p. 10). The recovery did not start until 1882. This crisis was later dubbed 'The Long Depression' (Hjerppe, 1989, p. 56). Domestic demand growth spurred the recovery, while exports remained depressed (Hjerppe, 1989, p. 47).

In Sweden, the railway industry expanded dramatically during the boom of the early 1870s. However, as the economy started to contract, the demand for transportation fell. It soon became evident that a bubble had burst. With large portfolios of railway bonds and thus strong exposure to the railway industry, many financial institutions suffered substantial losses. By the end of 1877 a major financial crisis was looming. The problems in the financial sector were reflected in the money stock. In 1878–79 it fell by more than 10 per cent (Jonung, 1975).

The combination of a domestic financial crisis and declining international demand caused a fall in economic activity. Real income declined for two years in a row, in 1877 and 1878. Industrial production fell by almost 9 per cent in 1878. Although labour market conditions worsened considerably, employment fared better, with almost no change in the number of employed recorded. The recovery began as early as 1879, when financial stability was restored and international demand increased. However, the 1880s have been characterized as a protracted recession (Heckscher, 1960, p. 296). Prices fell, export growth was weak and Sweden experienced large-scale emigration.

The crisis of the 1870s was more costly in Finland than in Sweden. Loss of real income was more than twice as high in Finland: 24.2 percentage points compared with 11.3 in Sweden, due to the longer duration of the crisis in Finland (Table 5.1). However, average loss per year was larger in Sweden.

Industrial production in Finland was particularly hard hit. However, the industrial sector was smaller in Finland than in Sweden and consequently this did not affect the aggregate economy to the same degree. The loss of industrial production in Sweden amounted to 14.7 percentage points, accumulated over two years – 1877–78 – whereas the loss in Finland was about five times that figure. Employment was less affected than production in both countries. In Finland a 5.9 percentage point loss of employment is recorded for the years 1878–79. The Swedish decline in employment started a year earlier. The total loss was a moderate 3.1 percentage points.

5.3.2 The Crisis of 1907[11]

International financial tension emerged in 1906 with financial crises in Italy and Japan. Gold scarcity forced the Bank of England to raise its discount rate to halt gold flows to the US.[12] The US eventually became the centre of the international crisis of 1907. The American economy entered a recession during the spring of 1907. During the summer the copper market collapsed. The banking sector came under stress. In October the Knickerbocker Trust Company went bankrupt. This sparked a severe banking crisis in New York, resulting in bank runs and declining money supply (Friedman and Schwartz, 1963; Wicker, 2000). The ensuing financial unrest and recession spread quickly throughout the industrialized world.

Finland did not suffer severely from the international downturn. It maintained its financial stability, though a decline in exports lowered industrial output. The large agriculture sector fared well and real income growth remained positive.

Sweden, on the other hand, was hit much harder than Finland. The financial system played an important role in the transmission of the international downturn into the Swedish economy. During the preceding boom, commercial banks had increased domestic lending and financed the credit growth by short-term borrowing on the international capital markets, especially in Germany. During the international turmoil in the fall of 1907, it became increasingly difficult to renew foreign loans. Almost 50 per cent of short-term foreign debt had to be repaid.

The *Riksbank*, the Swedish central bank, stepped in as a lender of last resort and allowed commercial banks to rediscount bills to obtain foreign currency. This action by the *Riksbank* limited the extent of the banking crisis, though 16 banks went bankrupt or were reconstituted (Schön, 2000, pp. 263–4). As new credit became increasingly costly to obtain, industries such as building and construction fell into a slump. Iron, mining and forestry were also hit hard whereas the paper and pulp industry fared better.

The international recovery started in 1908, but in Sweden worsening labour market conditions, culminating in a general strike in 1909, hampered growth. More than 300 000 workers were involved in the strike and more than 11 million working days were lost (Jörberg, 1961, p. 307). It was not until the second half of 1909, when the strike had ended, that the Swedish economy started to recover. In 1910 growth returned to positive figures and a boom began that would last almost uninterrupted until the outbreak of World War I.

Though the crisis in Sweden began during the latter part of 1907, growth rates for that year remained positive. The subsequent two years, on the other hand, show a contraction of economic activity. The loss of real income during 1908–09 was 11.2 per cent and the loss of industrial production 17.3 percentage points. Employment was not affected as much as production. Only small reductions in the number of employed persons were recorded during 1908–09. The total loss amounted to 1.2 percentage points (Table 5.1).

5.3.3 The Crisis of the 1920s

A strong international boom, fuelled by pent-up demand from the war, expansionary economic policies and speculative stock buying, started at the end of World War I (Aldcroft, 1994, pp. 25–6). Inflation continued to increase. In 1920, the leading economic powers adopted contractionary monetary policies. The overriding goal was to return to the gold standard, preferably at the pre-war parity exchange rate. The deflation required to reach this goal was the prime cause of the slump that followed. The international recovery did not start until 1922, when deflation ceased.

Finland, which had suffered during World War I by virtue of being a grand duchy of the Russian Empire and in the civil war following the declaration of independence in 1917, had experienced high inflation. Prices rose by more than 800 per cent between the outbreak of war in 1914 and 1920 (Haavisto and Jonung, 1995, p. 253). This record rendered a return to the pre-war exchange rate for the Finnish currency politically difficult. Thus, a deflationary policy was not adopted. By this choice Finland was able to avoid a sharp downturn and growth remained positive.

In Sweden inflation during the war years was high, but not as high as in Finland. After a long debate it was decided that the *krona* should be brought back to its pre-war gold parity, which required the adoption of tight monetary policies. The effects were staggering. Between 1920 and 1922 wholesale prices fell by almost 60 per cent and consumer prices by 30 per cent. By the end of 1922 the *krona* had returned to the pre-war rate, though Sweden did not officially return to the gold standard until 1924.

The tightening of monetary policies was not the only reason for the severe deflation that occurred during the early 1920s, but it was the primary cause. Other contributory factors included falling international prices due to deflationary policies in other countries (Boksjö and Lönnborg-Andersson, 1994, p. 19; Lundberg, 1983, p. 68; Fregert and Jonung, 2004).

The fall in domestic prices as well as the international slump pushed the Swedish economy into its deepest peacetime recession. In 1921 real income fell by 5.5 per cent and industrial production by almost 16 per cent. The crisis was deep but short-lived. Recovery was well under way in 1922, when GDP grew by 10 per cent and industrial production by 17 per cent, in spite of a severe banking crisis that culminated in that year.

As the crisis in Sweden was brief in time, the cumulative loss of real income – totalling 9.6 percentage points – turned out lower than during any of the other major crises although the average loss per crisis year was the highest (Table 5.1). However, the loss of industrial production was relatively high. For the first time, a crisis in Sweden resulted in significant loss of employment. The deflation led to large increases in real wages during 1921, which contributed to a total loss of employment of 8.4 percentage points.

5.3.4 The Crisis of the 1930s

The great stock market crash in New York in October 1929 is often taken as the start of the worst international recession on record. Over the course of three years, the real income of the leading economic power, the US, fell by more than one third. The depression spread – through finance and trade – to the rest of the world, including Europe, where it eventually became extremely severe. The default of the largest Austrian commercial bank *Kreditanstalt* in 1931 sent a financial shock wave through the continent, which ultimately forced several countries, notably Britain, to abandon the gold standard in September 1931. Countries that left the gold standard early and let their currencies devalue fared better than those that stayed on longer (Eichengreen, 1992).

In Finland the depression started a few years earlier than in most of Europe. Real income growth peaked in 1928. In that year a crop failure, which led to an increase in imports, and growing competition from the Soviet Union in the sawn goods market created a substantial trade deficit. A year later the overheated building industry collapsed as the money market got tighter and a three-year-long decline in GDP commenced (Hjerppe, 1989, p. 48; Herrala, 1999, p. 12). Private consumption fell considerably – four times as much as GDP – during the depression (Heikkinen and Kuusterä, 2001, p. 33).

The recovery that began in 1932 has been attributed both to the abandonment of the gold standard in late 1931 and to flexible wages. The *markka* depreciated markedly after Finland was forced off the gold standard. This benefited the export-oriented sawmill, pulp and paper industries (Heikkinen and Kuusterä, 2001, p. 34). The private sector was also helped by nominal cuts in wages that were so large that, in spite of the deflation, real wages decreased in several industries (Böckerman and Kiander, 2002). The Finnish economy recovered strongly. Growth was rapid throughout the 1930s.

The Finnish economy started to contract in 1929 with losses of real income recorded until 1932 of a total of 24.3 percentage points. Industrial production started to fall a year later and did not return to its pre-crisis trend until 1933, resulting in a loss of industrial production of 46.4

percentage points. The employment loss amounted to 16.4 percentage points in 1929–32 (Table 5.1).

The Great Depression hit the Swedish economy in late 1931. Falling exports reduced aggregate demand, employment and industrial production. The international reserves of the *Riksbank* declined due to capital outflows. Sweden was forced to abandon the gold standard and allow the *krona* to float in September 1931, shortly after the pound left the gold standard. A policy of price stabilization was adopted. The depreciation that followed allowed Sweden to isolate itself from the international economic turmoil. Thus, both Finland and Sweden adopted a floating exchange rate at an early stage of the depression, alleviating the negative effects of the international downturn.

At first, the decline in economic activity did not pose a major threat to the financial system. However, the death of the financier Ivar Kreuger set off a series of bankruptcies in the spring of 1932. Several large banks were heavily involved in Kreuger's businesses and suffered considerable losses, in particular the *Skandinaviska Banken*. The government intervened to secure the stability of the banking system. Depositors suffered no losses from bank failures, though the financial unrest aggravated the depression. The Swedish economy made a rapid recovery, starting in 1933. In 1934 real income grew by almost 7 per cent and industrial production by more than 19 per cent. The boom continued until the outbreak of World War II.

The Swedish economy fared better than the Finnish in terms of the cost of the crisis and also in terms of the average loss per crisis year. Real income started to decline in 1931 and returned to trend in 1933, making the cumulative loss 17.7 percentage points. Industrial production was depressed a year longer than real income. Between 1930 and 1933 the cumulative loss was 30.9 percentage points. Loss of employment was recorded for three years, amounting to a total loss of 10.9 percentage points.

5.3.5 The Crisis of the 1990s[13]

The early 1990s were turbulent years. The iron curtain came down, the Soviet empire imploded and the Gulf War erupted. The industrial world entered a recession, triggered by rising oil prices and rising real interest rates in Europe due to the re-unification of Germany. The *Bundesbank* responded to the expansionary fiscal policy in Germany by increasing its interest rate. In autumn 1992 and summer 1993, the recession culminated in Europe with the ERM crisis.

The Finnish economy grew throughout the 1980s after recovering from the OPEC crises of the 1970s and early 1980s. However, signs of an overheated economy began to show in the latter part of the 1980s, when real income growth accelerated, asset prices rose rapidly and inflation rates started to increase. The boom was fuelled by the deregulation of financial markets. Bank credit rose sharply and Finland received large capital inflows. Terms of trade improved owing to the fall in energy prices and the increase in prices in the forestry sector, a most important Finnish export industry. Fiscal policies were expansionary as well, thus contributing to the bubble (Honkapohja and Koskela, 2001, pp. 56–60).

The boom in Finland ended in 1990. A switch to tighter policies to defend the fixed exchange rate of the *markka*, along with rising international interest rates, led to a sharp increase in the real rate of interest. Asset prices plummeted and a period of debt deflation set in. A financial crisis erupted. Exports weakened further as a result of the collapse of trade with the imploding Soviet Union in 1991. The *markka* came under severe pressure as the depression grew deeper. In November 1991, the government enforced a devaluation of the currency (Pekkarinen and Vartiainen, 2001, p. 332). In September 1992, the peg became unsustainable and the Bank of Finland had to let the *markka* float.

The depreciation of the Finnish currency started the turnaround in 1993. The recovery was export-led, while the domestic sector remained depressed for a few years longer (Honkapohja and Koskela, 2001, p. 65). During the remainder of the 1990s the economy grew rapidly and new industries emerged. The structure of the economy changed fundamentally. The old forestry and engineering industries became less important, while high-tech sectors such as the mobile phones industry dominated the recovery process (Kalela et al., 2001, p. 8).

The Finnish economy started to decline in 1990 and real income did not return to its pre-crisis trend until 1994, with a cumulative loss of real income of 26.4 percentage points. Industrial production was somewhat less affected by the crisis than the rest of the economy, with a loss of 21.4 percentage points during 1990–92. Employment declined by the same proportion but over a longer period. Between 1990 and 1994 the cumulative loss of employment was 24 percentage points (Table 5.1).

The Swedish economy followed roughly the same path as the Finnish. In Sweden the credit market was deregulated in 1985, leading to a rapid increase in the demand for and supply of credit. High inflation rates and inflationary expectations combined with the design of the tax system gave rise to very low real interest rates, often negative ones. The result was a 'financial hothouse' with sharply increasing asset prices (Jonung and Stymne, 1997).

In 1990, the introduction of a tax reform combined with higher international interest rates and falling inflation created a sharp and sudden increase in the real rate of interest, bursting the bubble and setting off a process of balance sheet adjustment with strong signs of debt deflation. The financial sector was put under severe stress and Sweden was soon plagued by a banking crisis and a currency crisis at the same time. The depression led to a sharp increase in unemployment. Government expenditures increased while tax revenues stagnated, leading to huge budget deficits. The *Riksbank* was eventually forced to let the *krona* float in November 1992. As a result of the consequent depreciation and lowering of interest rates, an export-led recovery slowly took hold.

The Swedish economy was hard hit by the crisis of the 1990s. It was one of the most severe downturns in the 20th century (Table 5.1). Still, Sweden was less affected than Finland by the real effects of the crisis. Between 1990 and 1993 the loss of real income was 13 percentage points and of industrial production 17. Employment continued to decline for a year longer than the two other measures. Between 1990 and 1994 job losses totalled 16.6 percentage points.

5.3.6 The OPEC crises

The 1970s saw the end of the fairly stable economic environment that had existed in the industrialized world after World War II. The Bretton Woods system broke down, inflation and unemployment rose and the world economy was hit by two severe oil price shocks known as the OPEC crises or OPEC I and OPEC II.

In Finland inflation increased sharply in 1975 and the economy slowed down. Though no significant decline in real income was recorded, growth came to a halt in 1976–77 and industrial production fell (Heikkinen and Kuusterä, 2001, p. 37). Economic polices were made anti-inflationary. Bilateral trade with the Soviet Union, from where Finland imported a great deal of oil, softened the recession. As the cost of oil increased, so did Finnish exports to the Soviet Union (Hjerppe, 1989, p. 50).

The recovery of the Finnish economy was facilitated by the devaluations of the *markka* in 1977 and 1978. Real wages also declined during 1977–78 and 1980–81 due to modest nominal increases and high inflation rates (Heikkinen and Kuusterä, 2001, p. 39). Real income growth increased strongly in 1979 and remained high during the second oil price shock.

In Sweden, full employment emerged as the main policy goal for monetary and fiscal policies during the early 1970s. Hence, as oil prices rose sharply during 1973–74, an expansionary fiscal policy was adopted in an attempt to 'bridge over' the expected recession. As a result, prices and wage costs increased faster domestically than internationally. To compensate for the worsening terms of trade, fiscal policy was made still more expansionary. However, the recession was held off for only a short time. Industrial production declined in 1975 and, notwithstanding a short recovery in 1976, continued to decline in 1977–78. Real income was not as affected as industrial production. It fell only in 1977.

In 1977 the incompatibility of expansionary domestic policies and the fixed exchange rate of the *krona* became evident. The *krona* was devalued in two steps in 1977. During the remainder of the 1970s the government adopted a tight fiscal policy and the economy started to recover.

As oil prices began to rise again during the autumn of 1979, the Swedish economy slumped into a recession. Once again, industrial production was worse hit than the rest of the economy. Real income in fact continued to grow, except in 1981. Belief in expansionary fiscal policies had disappeared as a result of the experience in OPEC I. Now more focus was put on monetary policy. Two pre-emptive devaluations were carried out during 1981–82. These, in combination with the international economic recovery, ended the OPEC II crisis and laid the foundation for the boom of the 1980s. Eventually this boom turned into a bust in the early 1990s.

Though the costs of the OPEC crises are lower than those of the other crises examined here, substantial losses were recorded in both countries. In Finland during OPEC I, the real income loss amounted to 17.8 percentage points, loss of industrial production to 27.7, and the loss of employment to 6.1 percentage points. All these losses occurred in 1975–78. As mentioned above, the second oil price shock later in the decade did not give rise to any notable decline in economic activity in Finland.

In Sweden, the OPEC I crisis resulted in a 9.9 percentage point loss of real income during 1976–78. Industrial production started to decrease a year earlier. By the end of the crisis the production loss was 13.5 percentage points. The policy goal of full employment seems to have been successful: the employment loss was modest.

The OPEC II crisis was milder than OPEC I in terms of the loss of real income, which totalled only 1.9 percentage points. Industrial production also fared better during OPEC II. Total loss of industrial production was 5.3 percentage points, after which growth rates returned to their pre-crisis trend in 1982. Once again employment did not suffer as much, with a loss in employment of only 1.9 percentage points in 1981–83.

5.3.7 World Wars I and II

Wars are not commonly analysed as periods of economic crisis. However, the disturbances and reallocations in Finland and Sweden associated with the world wars gave rise to the strongest negative impulses that have hit economic life in the two countries over the last century.

In Finland one immediate negative effect of the outbreak of war in 1914 was the closing of the important export markets in the West. This was somewhat alleviated by an increase in Russian demand for Finnish products, in particular for war material. Fortification works in southern Finland by the Russian army kept Finnish employment high. Finnish real income fell in both 1914 and 1915 (Heikkinen and Kuusterä, 2001, p. 30). Furthermore, Finland, at that time a grand duchy in the Russian Empire, was forced to accept roubles in return for its exports to Russia at an overvalued rate. This, exacerbated by the fact that Finland had left the gold standard at the beginning of the war, sparked an inflationary trend, followed by a speculative boom (Haavisto and Jonung, 1995; Herrala, 1999, p. 11).

In 1917, when Russia imploded, exports came to an end and Finland plunged into the worst recession of the period under study. The civil war, which broke out at the beginning of 1918, made matters worse. Peace brought a rapid recovery, with national income growing by more than 35 per cent in 1919–20 – a performance that has been attributed to the undervalued currency and the fact that Finnish export firms cooperated rather than competed with each other (Heikkinen and Kuusterä, 2001, pp. 31–2).

Finland was drawn into World War II when the country was attacked by the Soviet Union late in 1939. GDP fell in both 1939 and 1940, but growth then remained positive until the end of the war, largely because financial stability was maintained, which was not the case during World War I (Herrala, 1999, p. 19).

Sweden, like many countries, left the gold standard at the outbreak of war in August 1914 and adopted a paper standard. Though Sweden was not one of the belligerents, the war affected the Swedish economy strongly. Monetary policy became expansionary, driving up the rate of inflation during all the years of the war. At an early stage, quantitative restrictions on foreign trade were introduced, especially on exports of foodstuffs (Larsson, 1991, p. 68). During the first years of the war, demand for Swedish exports was high and the current account showed large surpluses, sparking a speculative boom. In 1918 the stock market set a volume record that was not to be broken until 1980 (Lindgren, 1993, p. 253).

When Germany unleashed its unrestricted U-boat warfare, foreign trade became increasingly difficult, leading to falling industrial production and real income during 1917 (Larsson, 1991, p. 69). A crop failure in 1918 brought the country to the brink of famine and led to severe political unrest. The armistice in November 1918 opened up foreign trade, setting off a post-war boom with rising industrial production and real income in 1919.

The government played a more active role during World War II than it did in World War I. Extensive regulation of financial markets, the housing market and product markets was imposed at an early stage. World War II affected the Swedish economy strongly. Real income fell substantially during the first years of the war. During World War I Germany was able to pay for its imports from Sweden by selling its Swedish assets. These were depleted long before the outbreak of World War II, during which Sweden consequently faced a smaller demand for its exports (Schön, 2000, p. 359).

Given Finland's direct involvement in the two wars, it is not surprising that its economic losses were much larger than Sweden's. Real income declined throughout World War I. Notwithstanding the short recovery in 1916, the economy did not return to its pre-war trend until 1919. The loss amounted to 57.8 percentage points. Industrial production was even worse off, with a staggering loss of 98.6 percentage points, most of which occurred during the latter part of the war. Employment, though depressed during the war, fared better, probably owing to the demand for manpower in the war industries. Total loss of employment amounted to 11 percentage points.

The Swedish economy was better off in the early part of World War I. Except for a short downturn in 1914, the economy grew rapidly until 1917, when a sharp depression began. The loss of real income between 1917 and 1919 was 21.2 percentage points and the loss of industrial production 40.9 percentage points. In spite of this decline, employment remained high, the loss amounting to 1 percentage point.

World War II gave rise to smaller economic losses than World War I in Finland. Its real income loss was 32.4 percentage points between 1939 and 1942 compared with the pre-war trend, and the loss of industrial production was 72.2 percentage points between 1940 and 1942. For employment, by contrast, no loss is recorded, though employment rates did fluctuate markedly. In Sweden the loss of real income was almost as dramatic as during World War I, at 25.6 percentage points between the years 1940 and 1945. Industrial production lost 36.6 percentage points. Employment also declined, causing a loss of 10.3 percentage points at the beginning of the war, between 1940 and 1941.

5.3.8 Summary

Finland and Sweden are economically alike in many ways. They are small, open economies with similar industrial structures, heavily dependent on international trade. They border each other geographically. For these reasons it is not surprising that economic crises have occurred at roughly the same times during the last 130 years. Sweden has been more prone to crisis, having had three deep crises more than Finland – those of 1907–08, the 1920s and OPEC II. In the deep crises common to both countries, Finland has, however, suffered greater losses in terms of real income, industrial production and employment. Measured in this way, Sweden has the better record.

It is outside the scope of this study to explain why real income, industrial production and employment evolved as they did during the various crises. However, we can give the arithmetical reasons for the difference in losses between the two countries. The larger losses in Finland are due to longer crisis periods below trend than in Sweden rather than to larger absolute percentage declines in the time series. The reasons for this are twofold. First, during all crisis periods examined here except World War I, the Finnish pre-crisis trends have been higher than the Swedish trends. Second, the recoveries in Finland have been slower than in Sweden.

5.4 HOW COSTLY WAS THE CRISIS OF THE 1990S?

Judging from the calculations presented in Table 5.1, the crisis of the 1990s in Finland and Sweden was costly in terms of output, industrial production and employment foregone compared with the record of all major crises during the past 130 years.

In Finland, the loss in real income in the 1990s was the largest of any peacetime crisis. In Sweden, only the crisis of the 1930s caused a larger loss in real income than the crisis of the 1990s. These income losses were not so much an effect of falling industrial output as of exceptionally large declines in other sectors of the economy. Loss of industrial output remained moderate in both countries compared with the other major crises. Employment in the two countries, however, was particularly hard hit during the 1990s. The cumulative employment loss is the greatest on record, much higher than during the Great Depression of the 1930s.

The impact of the two oil crises was quite different. OPEC I stands out as a crisis in both countries, though deeper in Finland than in Sweden. OPEC II, on the other hand, did not create a crisis in Finland, and caused only minor losses in Sweden. This is most probably because policy-makers learnt from OPEC I how to handle OPEC II. According to our estimates, the two world wars stand out as the most costly of all the episodes examined. As could be expected, Finland suffered more, as it was involved directly in the wars.

The crisis in Finland and Sweden in the 1990s is a unique episode. It was unusually deep and prolonged. It occurred after a long period of peacetime prosperity and growth, so long that policy-makers and the public thought that a deep depression could not happen again. It is probably partly because the crisis came as a surprise that it turned out to be so costly.

NOTES

1. We are indebted to Patrik Walldov for compiling data, constructing tables and drawing figures and to Michael D. Bordo, Jesper Hansson, Sakari Heikkinen, Risto Herrala, Riitta Hjerppe, Olle Krantz, Antti Kuusterä, David Mayes, Heikki Oksanen, Daniel Waldenström and Lars-Erik Öller for helpful suggestions.
2. See, for example, the introduction by Krugman (2000), where he notes that 'we know [currency crises] when we see them'. Similarly, in a comment on the work by Bordo et al. (2001), Rose (2001) suggests that 'the crisis literature is in crisis', arguing that empirical measures of the cost of crises may be a way of improving our knowledge of crisis. We take his view as a source of inspiration for our study of Finnish and Swedish crises.
3. For a figure showing annual changes in industrial production 1872–1996 in Finland, see Jonung and Hagberg (2005).
4. For a figure showing annual changes in employment 1872–1996 in Finland, see Jonung and Hagberg (2005).
5. See Jonung and Hagberg (2005) for a figure displaying annual changes in industrial production 1872–1996 in Sweden.
6. See Jonung and Hagberg (2005) for a figure displaying annual changes in employment 1872–1996 in Sweden.
7. However, fiscal costs may cause deadweight costs affecting the general economy, especially if the raising of social funds is subject to large marginal costs; see Hoggarth et al. (2002).
8. Hjerppe (1989) used similar methods to calculate the loss of production of Finnish depressions, 1876–1980. Her results are in line with those presented here.
9. The cost of crisis literature has recently been advanced by relating the cost of crisis to variables measuring, for example, the degree of leverage, the openness to trade, the quality of institutions, IMF support and the design of fiscal and monetary policy. See Barrell et al. (2004), Claessens et al. (2004) and Hutchison (2003).
10. Calculations based on alternative trends are displayed in the appendix to Jonung and Hagberg (2005). They show that the use of different trends changes the magnitude of the cost of crisis somewhat. However, as we are interested in comparing the crisis of the 1990s with other crises, the absolute magnitudes are of less importance. We are interested in the relationship between the losses estimated for the different crises. Here we find no major change. The relative severity of the crisis of the 1990s stands out as fairly stable. To sum up, our basic conclusions remain robust to the adoption of different trend rates.
11. This section is based on Hagberg and Walldov (2000).
12. Neal and Weidenmier (2003, pp. 497–501) argue that the initial cause of the international crisis of 1907 was the devastating earthquake that hit San Francisco in April 1906. British insurance companies, forced to pay out on earthquake insurance, started payments in October 1906. This outflow caused the Bank of England to raise the discount rate sharply. Later, when it lowered the rate in January 1907, it refused to discount any bills from the US. This step cut off the New York trust companies from their usual source of liquidity.
13. For an analysis of the financial crisis of the early 1990s in Finland and Sweden, see Chapters 2 and 3 in this volume.

REFERENCES

Aldcroft, D. (1994), *The European Economy 1914–1990*, London: Routledge.

Aziz, J., F. Caramazza and R. Salgado (2000), 'Currency crises: in search of common elements', IMF Working paper 00/67, March.

Barrell, R., E.P. Davis and O. Pomerantz (2004), 'Costs of financial instability, household-sector balance sheets and consumption', Discussion paper no. 243, National Institute of Economic and Social Research, London.

Boksjö, A. and M. Lönnborg-Andersson (1994), *Svenska finanskriser – orsaker, förlopp, åtgärder och konsekvenser (Swedish financial crises – causes, developments, measures and consequences)*, Uppsala papers in financial history, Uppsala.

Bordo, M., B. Eichengreen, D. Klingebiel and M.S. Martinez-Peria (2001), 'Is the crisis problem growing more severe?', *Economic Policy*, **32**, 51–82.

Böckerman, P. and J. Kiander (2002), 'Labour markets in Finland during the great depressions of the twentieth century', *Scandinavian Economic History Review*, **50**, 55–70.

Caprio, G. and D. Klingebiel (1996), 'Bank insolvencies: cross-country experience', World Bank Policy Research Working paper no. 1574.

Cassel, G. (1908), *Riksbanken under krisen 1907–1908 (The Riksbank during the crisis of 1907–1908)*, Stockholm: Hugo Grebers förlag.

Claessens, S., D. Klingebiel and L. Laeven (2004), 'Resolving systemic financial crises: policies and institutions', World Bank Policy Research Working paper no. 3377, August.

Eichengreen, B. (1992), *Golden Fetters: The Gold Standard and the Great Depression, 1919–1939*, Oxford: Oxford University Press.

Fregert, K. and L. Jonung (2004), 'Deflation dynamics in Sweden: perceptions, expectations, and adjustment during the deflations of 1921–1923 and 1931–1933', in R. Burdekin and P. Siklos (eds), *Deflation: Current and Historical Perspectives*, Cambridge: Cambridge University Press, Chapter 4.

Friedman, M. and A. Schwartz (1963), *A Monetary History of the United States 1867–1960*, Princeton, NJ: Princeton University Press.

Haavisto, T. and L. Jonung (1995), 'Off gold and back again. Finnish and Swedish monetary policies 1914–1924', in C. Feinstein (ed.), *Banking, Currency and Finance in Europe between the Wars*, Oxford: Oxford University Press, Chapter 8.

Hagberg, T. and P. Walldov (2000), 'Den finansiella krisen i Sverige 1907–08 – dess orsaker och verkan' (The financial crisis in Sweden 1907–08 – its causes and effects), mimeo, Stockholm School of Economics, Stockholm.

Heckscher, E.F. (1960), *Svenskt arbete och liv (Labour and life in Sweden)*, Stockholm: Albert Bonniers Förlag.

Heikkinen, S. and A. Kuusterä (2001), 'Finnish economic crises in the 20th century', in J. Kalela, J. Kiander, U. Kivikuru, H. Loikkanen and J. Simpura (eds), *Down from the Heavens, Up from the Ashes – the Finnish Economic Crisis of the 1990s in the Light of Economic and Social Research*, Helsinki: Vatt Publications, Chapter 2.

Herrala, R. (1999), 'Banking crises vs. depositor crises: the era of the Finnish Markka 1865–1998', *Scandinavian Economic History Review*, **49**, 5–22.

Hjerppe, R. (1989), *The Finnish Economy 1960–1985: Growth and Structural Change*, Helsinki: Bank of Finland.

Hoggarth, G., R. Reis and V. Saporta (2002), 'Costs of banking instability: some empirical evidence', *Journal of Banking and Finance*, **26**, 825–55.

Honkapohja, S. and E. Koskela (2001), 'The economic crisis of the 1990s in Finland', in J. Kalela, J. Kiander, U. Kivikuru, H. Loikkanen and J. Simpura (eds), *Down from the Heavens, Up from the Ashes – the Finnish Economic Crisis of the 1990s in the Light of Economic and Social Research*, Helsinki: Vatt Publications, Chapter 3.

Hutchison, M. (2003), 'A cure worse than the disease? Currency crises and the output costs of IMF-supported stabilization programs', in M. Dooley and J. Frankel (eds), *Managing Currency Crises in Emerging Markets*, Chicago, IL: University of Chicago Press.

IMF (1998), *World Economic Outlook*, May, Washington, DC: IMF.

Jonung, L. (1975), 'Studies in the monetary history of Sweden', dissertation, UCLA, Los Angeles.

Jonung, L. (1994), '1990-talets ekonomiska kris i historisk belysning' (The crisis of the 1990s in a historical perspective), Occasional paper, Stockholm: SNS förlag.

Jonung, L. (1999), *Med backspegeln som kompass – om stabiliseringspolitiken som läroprocess (Looking ahead through the rear-view mirror. Swedish stabilization policy 1975–1995)*, Ds 1999:9, Finansdepartmentet, Stockholm.

Jonung, L. and T. Hagberg (2005), 'How costly was the crisis of the 1990s? A comparative analysis of the deepest crises in Finland and Sweden over the last 130 years', European Economy, Economic Papers, no. 224, March, European Commission, Brussels, http://ec.europa.eu/economy_finance/publications/publication_summary698_en.htm.

Jonung, L. and J. Stymne (1997), 'The great regime shift: asset markets and economic activity in Sweden, 1985–93', in F. Capie and G. Wood (eds), *Asset Prices and the Real Economy*, London: Macmillan, Chapter 1.

Jörberg, L. (1961), *Growth and Fluctuations of Swedish Industry 1869–1912*, Stockholm: Almqvist and Wiksell.

Kalela, J., J. Kiander, U. Kivikuru, H. Loikkanen and J. Simpura (2001), 'Introduction', in J. Kalela, J. Kiander, U. Kivikuru, H. Loikkanen and J. Simpura (eds), *Down from the Heavens, Up from the Ashes – the Finnish Economic Crisis of the 1990s in the Light of Economic and Social Research*, Helsinki: Vatt Publications, Chapter 1.

Krugman, P. (2000), 'Introduction', in P. Krugman (ed.), *Currency Crises*, Chicago, IL and London: University of Chicago Press.

Larsson, M. (1991), *En svensk ekonomisk historia 1850–1985* (*A Swedish economic history*), Stockholm: SNS förlag.

Lindgren, H. (1993), 'Finanssektorn och dess aktörer 1860–1992' (The financial market and its participants 1860–1992), in B. Furuhagen (ed.), *Äventyret Sverige (The Swedish adventure)*, Arlöv: Bra Böcker, pp. 241–63.

Lundberg, E. (1953), *Konjunkturer och ekonomisk politik: utveckling och debatt i Sverige sedan första världskriget (Business cycles and economic policy: Development and debate in Sweden since World War I)*, Stockholm: SNS förlag.

Lundberg, E. (1983), *Ekonomiska kriser förr och nu (Economic crises: Then and now)*, Stockholm: SNS förlag.

Mulder, C. and M. Rocha (2000), 'The soundness of estimates of output losses in currency crises', unpublished manuscript, IMF.

Neal, L. and M. Weidenmier (2003), 'Crises in the global economy from tulips to today. Contagion and consequences', in M.D. Bordo, A.M. Taylor and J.G. Williamson (eds), *Globalization in Historical Perspective*, Chicago, IL and London: University of Chicago Press, Chapter 10.

Pekkarinen, J. and J. Vartiainen (2001), *Finlands ekonomiska politik – den långa linjen 1818–2000 (Finland's economic policy – the long term view 1818–2000)*, Stiftelsen Fackföreningsrörelsens institut för ekonomisk forskning, Stockholm.

Rose, A. (2001), 'Discussion of Bordo, M., B. Eichengreen, D. Klingebiel and M. Soledad Martinez-Peria (2001)', *Economic Policy*, **32**, 75–7.

Schön, L. (2000), *En modern svensk ekonomisk historia (A modern Swedish economic history)*, Stockholm: SNS förlag.

Sveriges Riksbank (1909), *Sveriges riksbank 1908 – Årsbok (Sweden's Riksbank 1908 – Yearbook)*, Stockholm: P.A. Norstedt.

Wicker, E. (2000), *Banking Panics in the Gilded Age*, Cambridge: Cambridge University Press.

PART II

The international context

6. The boom and bust cycle in Finland and Sweden in an international perspective

Lars Jonung, Ludger Schuknecht and Mika Tujula

INTRODUCTION[1]

Finland and Sweden experienced an intense boom in the late 1980s, followed by a sharp contraction in the early 1990s and an exceptionally long recovery roughly until the turn of the century. The intensity of this boom–bust cycle is unique in the economic history of the two countries – but it is not unique in an international context. Actually, a pattern of boom–bust is common to many countries in recent decades and, in this respect, Finland and Sweden are no exception. What is exceptional is that two such advanced welfare states as Finland and Sweden with a tradition of full employment and well-developed social systems could end up in such a deep financial crisis with an unprecedented decline in real output, a dramatic rise in unemployment and huge government deficits. The banking and currency crisis of the 1990s turned out to be one of the most severe ever to occur in these two Nordic countries – in some aspects the worst on record.[2]

For policy-makers, economists and the public the magnitude of the boom and bust of the 1990s came as a surprise.[3] The common view was that 'it couldn't happen here'. After the crisis, however, a large volume of research has dealt with various aspects of the boom–bust cycle: its effects on the financial system, on the fiscal stance and balances and on the real economy, and the role of economic policies in inducing and alleviating the crisis. As a rule this work has been focused either on the two countries' individual experience or on their joint record; hardly any systematic comparisons between the Finnish and Swedish boom–bust pattern and the international experience have been forthcoming.[4] The purpose of this chapter is to remedy this deficiency.

The chapter is organized in the following way. First, we describe the methodology on which our empirical work is based as developed by Jaeger and Schuknecht (2004). They devise a technique to separate boom–bust episodes from standard business cycle phases for a large number of countries. In this way they arrive at a dating of boom–bust episodes, which we adopt when calculating the average behavior of the variables that we study in this chapter.

Second, we present a brief explanation of the driving forces behind the boom–bust pattern in Finland and Sweden, based on the account of Chapters 2, 3 and 4 in this volume. We focus on the impact of financial deregulation combined with the defense of the fixed exchange rate policy in pushing the two countries first into a phase of overheating with rising inflation and loss of competitiveness, and subsequently into a deep financial crisis with falling output and rising unemployment. The twin crisis, the domestic banking crisis and the currency crisis for the Finnish *markka* and the Swedish *krona*, was eventually halted and resolved when the two currencies were allowed to float and the monetary stance could be relaxed. At the same time the strategy of the two central banks was changed, with inflation-targeting replacing the defense of the fixed exchange rate.[5] This brief summary of the boom and bust in the two Nordic countries helps us to identify a number of key variables, which we examine more closely in our cross-country comparisons.

Next, we examine the boom–bust pattern of key time series for Finland and Sweden compared with their international averages using our dating methodology. We focus on three areas: the financial system, the real sector and public finances. We find clear differences between the Nordic countries and the countries in our international sample. The boom–bust cycle was stronger in Finland and Sweden as measured by almost all the time series; in particular we find that the downturn and the recovery were much more pronounced.

6.1 METHODOLOGY FOR IDENTIFYING BOOMS AND BUSTS

Boom–bust cycles have attracted a growing interest from researchers in recent years, and there have been a number of theoretical and empirical studies on their causes and consequences. A major challenge is to identify empirically episodes of boom–bust, for which there is no commonly accepted method. See, for example, the work by Bordo and Jeanne (2004), one of the first attempts to measure boom–bust periods in a comparative setting. Borio et al. (1994), Borio and Lowe (2002), Detken and Smets (2004) and Helbling and Terrones (2003) apply different methods for constructing chronologies of booms and busts from various time series.[6]

We build our analysis on the results derived by Jaeger and Schuknecht (2004). They construct boom and bust phases in real aggregate asset prices by following a dating method initially proposed by Harding and Pagan (2002), based on the so-called triangular methodology. This technique identifies the peaks and troughs of the asset price series (their turning points). Then Jaeger and Schuknecht (2004) calculate the duration of the period from trough to peak (the upswing) and from peak to trough (the downturn) and the amplitude of the asset price changes over these periods. By multiplying duration and amplitude, they arrive at a ranking of asset price upswings and downturns, the largest quintile of which is referred to as boom–bust episodes. This enables them to separate booms and busts in asset prices from more normal asset price movements. Using this method, a boom does not necessarily need to be followed by a bust, and vice versa.

In this way they arrive at a classification of booms and busts in real asset prices for 16 industrialized countries for 1970–2002, including the seven major industrial countries (G7), Australia, Belgium, Denmark, Finland, Ireland, the Netherlands, Spain, Sweden and Switzerland as shown in Table 6.1. Altogether 20 boom and 20 bust phases are identified for this period. The duration of boom and bust phases usually ranges from five to seven years, quite a prolonged period compared with the normal business cycle.

Jaeger and Schuknecht (2004) find that nearly all countries included in their sample went through booms and busts in real asset prices in 1970–2002. Germany, Italy and Belgium are the only ones that did not face persistent and large asset price swings that qualify as a boom phase in this period, while the United States and Germany did not experience a bust. The booms are mainly concentrated in the second half of the 1980s (eight episodes) and in the 1990s (nine incidents), while the busts mostly took place in the early 1990s (eight or nine events) and to a lesser extent in the late 1970s/early 1980s (seven incidents altogether).

For the purpose of comparing boom–bust phases across industrialized countries with those of Finland and Sweden in the late 1980s and early 1990s, we adopt the dating of Jaeger and Schuknecht (2004) and calculate the average behavior for a number of macroeconomic variables deemed important to understand booms and busts. We examine a broader range of variables than they do. The computations are done in annual terms from $t - 5$ to $t + 6$, where $t = 0$ is the observation for the final year of the boom. Hence, $t - 5$ to $t = 0$ portrays representative developments during booms and $t + 1$ to $t + 6$ during busts. The calculations of the averages for industrialized countries exclude data for Finland and Sweden for the 1986–89 boom and the 1990–93 bust.

Table 6.1 Size distribution of identified boom–bust phases in real aggregate asset prices for industrialized countries, 1970–2002

Boom phases			Bust phases		
Country	Years	Cumulative price change(1)	Country	Years	Cumulative price change(1)
Japan	1979–90	358.0	Japan	1991–2002	−364.1
Sweden	1994–2000	329.6	Sweden	1977–85	−185.1
Finland	1994-2000	293.1	Ireland	1979–85	−173.3
Ireland	1994–2001	289.1	Italy	1991–97	−173.1
Spain	1985–90	249.4	Netherlands	1979–83	−163.0
Netherlands	1993–2000	237.2	Finland	1974–79	−155.1
United States	1995–2000	157.8	Finland	1990–93	−135.4
United Kingdom	1983–89	152.1	Spain	1991–95	−124.6
Switzerland	1983–89	110.9	Belgium	1980–85	−115.2
Finland	1986–89	92.2	Denmark	1977–82	−113.5
Denmark	1996–2000	90.6	Australia	1973–78	−113.4
United Kingdom	1995–2000	90.4	Spain	1979–82	−111.3
Australia	1996–2002	89.2	France	1991–96	−108.6
Sweden	1986–89	88.1	Sweden	1990–93	−108.0
Australia	1984–89	87.7	United Kingdom	1974–77	−106.3
Denmark	1983–86	85.9	Switzerland	1990–96	−104.0
Finland	1980–84	84.9	Japan	1974–78	−88.1
Spain	1996–2000	84.0	United Kingdom	1990–94	−86.1
France	1986–90	74.6	Italy	1981–85	−80.7
Canada	1985–89	74.3	Canada	1990–95	−80.2

Note: (1) Based on triangular approximation.

Source: Jaeger and Schuknecht (2004).

We do similar computations for Finland and Sweden covering the 1986–89 boom and the 1990–93 bust, where t = 0 is set at 1989. This year is often considered the peak year of the asset boom in Finland and Sweden before the financial crises struck.[7] Next, we plot in the same figure three time series: one for Finland, one for Sweden and one for the international average during boom–bust episodes. The duration of boom and bust phases usually ranges from five to seven years, quite a prolonged period compared with the normal business cycle.

6.2 THE BOOM–BUST CYCLE IN FINLAND AND SWEDEN, 1984–95

The evolutions of the economies of Finland and Sweden during the last decades of the 20th century are identical in many respects. As the causes and consequences of the boom–bust cycle in the two economies were identical, there are strong reasons to describe them as economic twins, as argued in Chapter 2 in this volume.

Prior to 1985, extensive credit market regulations restricted the level of interest rates and the supply of credit in both countries. The tax system favored borrowing, yet households and companies were severely restricted in their choice of loans. Consequently, large portfolio imbalances existed because of the prevailing system of nominal interest rates, inflation and tax rates. Both countries maintained fixed exchange rates for their currencies at this stage. Future devaluations were ruled out as an unviable strategy as the beneficial effects of the devaluations of the past had turned out to be short-lived, with rapid increases in wages and prices rapidly eliminating the gains in competitiveness thus obtained.

Around 1985 the domestic credit market was deregulated in both countries. Hardly any restrictive fiscal or monetary policy measures were taken in connection with or immediately following the financial deregulation. Consequently, lending from banks and other financial institutions in national and foreign currencies, in particular for property purchases, increased rapidly. The rate of inflation and inflation expectations increased. Real after-tax lending rates adjusted for inflation expectations were close to zero or negative for companies and households, which strengthened their demand for loans. Asset prices (prices on property, in particular commercial property, and shares) grew more rapidly than consumer prices.

The outcome was a strong boom in the Finnish and Swedish economies in 1988–89 with labor shortages, rising consumption, and falling savings ratios. The current account worsened as export performance weakened. Signs that the *markka* and the *krona* were overvalued emerged. The national budgets of the two countries turned into surplus during the peak on the back of property- and capital-based taxes as well as revenues from booming consumption and high wage growth. Public consumption and public expenditures grew rapidly during the boom as well.

In 1990–91 the boom in the real economy was halted and turned into a bust by a combination of factors. Real interest rates rose internationally as a result of the German monetary policy reorientation due to the consequences of the financing of the German reunion, putting strong upward pressure on Finnish and Swedish rates. The Swedish 1990–91 tax reform made borrowing less attractive and stimulated private savings, effectively raising real after-tax rates. In Finland stepwise limitations in the tax deductibility of mortgage rates in the early 1990s increased the after-tax cost of servicing debt.

Finnish and Swedish interest rates increased when attempts were made to defend the fixed exchange rate against recurring speculative attacks in 1989–92. As the Finnish and Swedish currencies became overvalued due to rapid domestic inflation, the export sector started to encounter rising problems. For Finland the collapse of trade with the Soviet Union contributed to domestic problems.

A rapid and less than fully expected decline in the rate of consumer price inflation and inflation expectations in 1990–92 contributed to a sharp rise in real interest rates. Asset price deflation surfaced when the value of real assets was reduced by rapidly rising real interest rates. Balance sheets turned fragile when asset values, primarily property prices, fell below collateral values. The number of bankruptcies increased extremely quickly. Asset price deflation showed a cumulative tendency. The sell-out of property forced down property prices, which, in turn, triggered new sales.

As the balance sheets of households and firms were eroded, large negative wealth effects were set in motion. The level of consumption declined. The savings ratio of households increased rapidly. Investments plummeted, in particular within the construction sector. Unemployment soared and employment decreased drastically. Tax revenues fell and public expenditures rose. The government budget deficit increased dramatically.

In 1992 the financial system of both countries was rocked to its foundations when the *markka* and the *krona* were exposed to major speculative attacks. The Finnish *markka* was set floating in September 1992. Two months later, in November 1992, Sweden followed suit. The floating of the domestic currencies eventually checked the downturn of the Finnish and Swedish economies. An upturn commenced in the following year and lasted for several years. The recovery was driven by the strong upturn in exports.

6.3 THE INTERNATIONAL PERSPECTIVE

The above brief account of the Finnish and Swedish boom–bust cycle – more fully developed in Chapters 2 and 3 – demonstrates that financial developments – credit growth, asset prices and real after-tax lending rates – were principal factors driving the boom–bust cycle in Finland and Sweden. The deregulation of the financial markets should properly be seen as the start of the cycle – the impulse that initiated the whole process. This impulse, emanating from the financial sector, impacted on the rest of the economy and on public finances. Of course, there was also feedback from the real economy and public finances into the financial sector. For this reason we will start our empirical analysis by studying the behavior of some financial variables in a comparative perspective. We will then move on to the real economy and to public finances.[8]

6.3.1 Financial and Price Developments

The international evidence demonstrates that several recent asset price cycles have started with a positive shock to the financial environment in the form of financial liberalization. Liberalization has triggered both a demand and a supply shock in credit as households and companies find it easier to borrow and banks and other financial institutions easier to lend. These events have impacted significantly on domestic credit developments, causing a rise in domestic credit growth and contributing to the emergence of and fueling of a boom. After the boom runs its course, high debt and valuation losses of assets undermine private and financial sector net worth, resulting in a fall in collateral values and a tightening of credit standards, which in turn make it more difficult to lend and borrow.[9] Thus we start by examining the behavior of the volume of credit over the asset price cycle.

Domestic credit

Figure 6.1, displaying the growth rate of domestic credit in Finland and Sweden and the international average, demonstrates first of all that credit growth was extremely volatile in the Nordic countries. During the boom 1984–89, growth was higher than the international average. Annual credit growth in Finland and Sweden peaked at about 30 per cent and 20 per cent respectively in the boom. During the subsequent bust, the decline in growth was much stronger in the Nordic countries. Growth became negative for several years while it remained positive internationally.

This large difference in credit developments between the two Nordic countries and the international average, especially in the downturn – which we will also find for other economic variables in the following – is due to the fact that Finland and Sweden experienced a full-fledged and very rapid twin crisis – a deep banking crisis and a currency crisis at the same time – which severely disrupted financial intermediation. This was not the case for most of the other episodes in our sample.

Asset prices

The international evidence from asset price cycles suggests that rapid domestic credit growth during the boom phase is primarily channeled through asset markets, in particular the market for real estate. This is consistent with what one would conjecture from the fact that real estate

Source: Appendix A in Jonung et al. (2005).

Figure 6.1 Domestic credit growth in boom–bust episodes (annual change in per cent)

demand in particular is strongly correlated with credit availability. Figure 6.2 shows that inflation-adjusted real estate price increases averaged almost 10 per cent annually over the boom years. This gain was partly reversed in the bust when price declines averaged about 5 per cent. Given the average length of upswings and downturns (about five years), this translates into average real increases of almost 50 per cent, most of which was reversed during the downswing.

Looking at Finland and Sweden, the volatile picture of credit dynamics of Figure 6.1 is clearly mirrored in the real estate market in Figure 6.2. In Finland in particular, real estate price increases were dramatic, reaching up to 30 per cent in 1988, the year before the peak. The subsequent downturn was also steeper in the Nordic countries than elsewhere with a maximum year-on-year decline of 20 per cent for Finland.[10] In both countries, the full capital gain in house prices was eliminated during the bust. Figure 6.2 also demonstrates that after Finland and Sweden adopted a floating exchange rate the fall in commercial and residential property prices was halted.

Real interest rates

Many observers of the Finnish and Swedish record have regarded the crisis as a result of a very sharp rise in real rates of interest – adjusted for inflation, actual or expected, and taxes – at the end of the 1980s.[11] Unfortunately, data on real after-tax rates are not available for most countries in our sample. However, when looking at the international

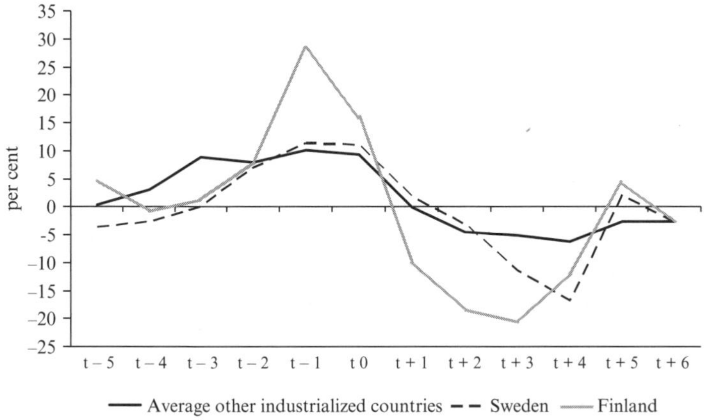

Source: Appendix A in Jonung et al. (2005).

Figure 6.2 Real estate prices in boom–bust episodes (annual change in per cent)

pattern of real interest rates (not adjusted for taxation), the dynamics of the monetary policy environment in Finland and Sweden are not very surprising (and are consistent with growth and output developments, as we will see later). Real interest rates tend to be somewhat higher internationally during the boom than during the bust. Nevertheless, there is also no interest rate tightening to speak of as the boom proceeds. The real rate falls during the international bust phase.[12]

This picture is markedly different from the experience of Finland and Sweden concerning the real after-tax lending rate. In the two Nordic countries, real after-tax rates were in decline after the deregulation until the end of the boom in Finland and were negative in Sweden during the full boom phase. These very low after-tax interest rates fueled the growth of credit in the boom years in the 1980s. Then real after-tax rates increased sharply in a few years, surpassing the international level, contributing to the bust and the downturn with its credit slump. In other words, Finland and Sweden featured a highly pro-cyclical monetary and fiscal policy environment.

As pointed out earlier, the pro-cyclical monetary policies in Finland and Sweden had their origin in a number of factors. Both countries pursued nominal exchange rate targeting policies, the hard currency strategy. With the easy credit policies of the late 1980s, interest rates could be kept very low. As inflation picked up, the *markka* and the *krona* became the subject of speculative attacks, forcing the Bank of Finland and the Bank of Sweden to raise domestic rates to high levels, and as the international financial environment became less favorable (notably in the context of German unification and the ERM crisis), real interest rates increased significantly. On top of that, changes in the Finnish and Swedish tax regimes at the height of the boom reduced incentives towards accumulating debt and had a strongly pro-cyclical effect on real after-tax rates.

Exchange rates

For open economies, the exchange rate is the central asset price, and thus a major determinant of macroeconomic performance. For the average of boom–bust episodes, the real effective exchange rate appreciates in the upswing. The resulting deterioration of external competitiveness is typically corrected in the downturn when the real effective exchange rate depreciates.

Again the pattern is similar, though more extreme, for the two Nordic countries during the bust phase. As mentioned above, during the boom, the exchange rate targeting combined with easy credit resulted in a stable nominal exchange rate. In an environment of rising unit labor costs (discussed below), this translated into an appreciating real effective exchange rate. This development was reversed fully when both countries floated their exchange rates in 1992, roughly at the end of the second year of the bust. While the depreciation of the domestic currency initially exacerbated the net wealth position of holders of foreign debt, it also facilitated the rapid rebound through a readjustment in relative prices and competitiveness in the tradable sector. The exchange rate behavior of the *markka* and the *krona* is thus crucial for the understanding of the boom–bust cycle and, in particular, for the quick emergence of Finland and Sweden from the bust phase. The recovery was driven by the sharp rise in exports.[13]

The net foreign asset position (the current account)

Another way of assessing and comparing the effects of booms and busts on the balance sheet position of an economy is to examine the net foreign asset position across countries. However, in the absence of such comprehensive data, the annual flows as reflected in the current account position of the balance of payments of countries can be used. Such data show a deterioration in the current account position for the average of boom–bust episodes and a subsequent correction of the imbalances in the bust. The average current account position turns from a small surplus to a deficit of almost 3 per cent of GDP at the end of the boom. By the end of the downturn, the imbalance was eliminated.[14]

This pattern is similar for Finland and Sweden except for the very final years of the observation period. Initially, the current account position deteriorated by 5 per cent of GDP in Finland and by 3 per cent in Sweden. This changed little until the depreciation of the domestic currency in 1992.

By the fourth year of the bust a dramatic improvement is recorded and the current account has remained in strong surplus ever since.

Our stylized facts on financial and price developments during boom–bust episodes across industrialized countries demonstrate a common pattern of strong credit growth and asset price growth in the boom. This picture is reversed in the subsequent bust. This pattern is more pronounced in the Finnish and Swedish cases, where the bust is deeper but also more short-lived compared with the international average.

6.3.2 Real Economic Developments

Real growth

Real economic growth deviations from trend in boom–bust episodes are typically much more persistent than in normal business cycles. The period of above-average growth in the boom and below-average growth in the bust normally ranges from five to seven years but it can be over ten years long. Growth averages about 4 per cent for all boom episodes (Figure 6.3). In the bust, growth initially falls steeply and averages around 1 per cent. This finding of persistence is consistent with the view that rising asset prices and easy money (credit) stimulate demand in the boom before a correction in asset prices undermines individuals' net worth and forces an extended period of subdued demand when balance sheets are adjusted. In

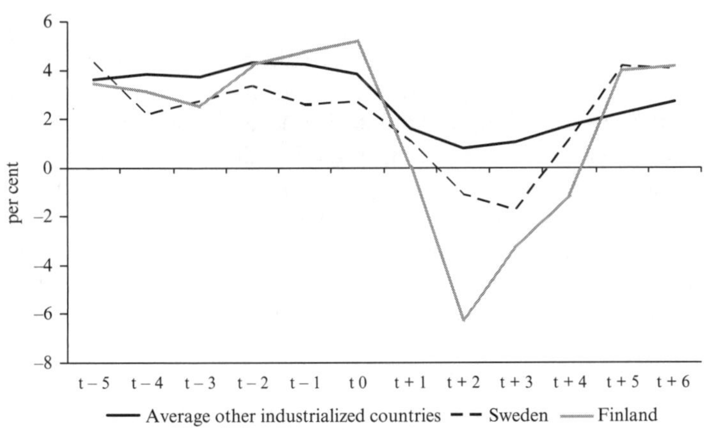

Source: Appendix A in Jonung et al. (2005).

Figure 6.3 Real economic growth in boom–bust episodes (annual change in per cent)

the boom, savings tend to fall, while consumption and investment rise. This boosts growth and also fuels the deterioration in the current account. In the bust the opposite happens as the private sector raises its savings, reduces its spending and, thereby, improves not only its wealth position but also the whole country's external accounts.

As regards growth in Finland and Sweden, the pattern is similar to those of other international episodes. However, due to lower trend growth, the growth curve, especially in Sweden, is shifted slightly downward. Nevertheless, the negative growth experienced by the two countries in the downturn is staggering.[15]

Output gaps

The data for output gaps reveal the extreme character of the Finnish and Swedish bust, giving rise to a similar pattern to that of real economic growth in Figure 6.3. The output gap declines for all countries in the boom and rises in the downturn. However, output gap developments are more volatile in the two Nordic countries. A positive gap of about 4 per cent is followed by a staggering output loss and negative output gap, measured at 6–8 per cent. A rapid rebound starts from the fourth year after the asset price peak. This recovery coincides with the crisis resolution and the exchange rate depreciation.[16]

Consumption and investment

The experience of boom–bust cycles reveals that they are typically accompanied by extreme private investment cycles and somewhat less pronounced private consumption cycles. Real private consumption growth was about 4 per cent for all countries and about 5 per cent in Finland and Sweden over the boom. Annual investment growth was about twice as high and peaked at 15 per cent in the Nordic countries just before the crash. The downturn featured a strong slowdown in consumption and a slightly negative investment growth rate for the average of all episodes. By contrast, the investment figures were distinctly negative for Finland and Sweden. In fact, the cumulative decline in investment over the bust was about 25 per cent in Sweden and a staggering 50 per cent in Finland.[17]

Exports

The previous findings on boom–bust episodes are consistent with developments in exports. As the tradable goods sector lost competitiveness, export growth remained constant or slowed down in Finland and Sweden as well as in the international context (Figure 6.4). The slowdown continued well into the bust and was only reversed when the depreciation restored competitiveness. The rebound in the Nordic countries was much sharper

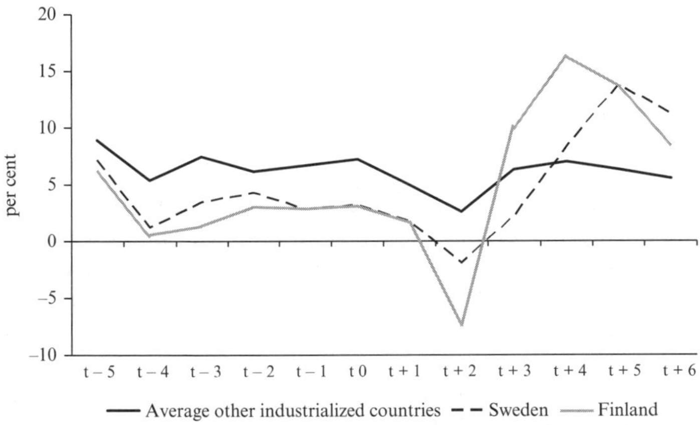

Source: Appendix A in Jonung et al. (2005).

Figure 6.4 Export in boom–bust episodes (annual change in per cent)

than the average of the other episodes and contributed significantly to the rebound of the real economy as a whole.

Import developments are also consistent with this picture: rapid import growth in the boom was followed by moderation in import demand and a period of zero or even highly negative import growth, reflecting the reversing fortunes of domestic import competing industries in the boom–bust countries. This only reversed with a lag when the export boom was already well under way and thus created new import demand from this sector and the recovering economy.

Employment

The relatively subdued employment growth in Finland and Sweden in the boom and the stark fall in employment in the bust stand out against the much more stable and balanced picture for the international average. The main reason for the modest employment growth during the boom in the Nordic countries is the fact that they were already operating at full employment when the boom started – in contrast to higher rates of unemployment in the industrialized countries in our sample. Thus the boom could not create much of an increase in employment – though it fell very sharply during the bust phase.

The sharp fall in Nordic employment reflects a marked restructuring of the Finnish and Swedish labor markets due to the financial crisis, in particular due to the collapse of the construction sector and the fact that the banking, manufacturing and public sectors shed labor as well.[18] In a historical perspective, the crisis of the 1990s made a stronger mark on employment than any other previous crisis.[19] Employment had not returned to its pre-crisis level ten years after the bust. Similarly, unemployment rates have remained high during the recovery phase.

Real labor costs

Real labor costs increase strongly during booms. Again this is consistent with the finding of booming consumption and housing investment and falling competitiveness (via rising labor costs and an appreciating real effective exchange rate). One way to measure this phenomenon is to look at the differential between real wages (compensation per employee) and productivity gains. For the average of all episodes, this figure is slightly positive, suggesting a small but persistent tendency to squeeze profits and to lose competitiveness. This process is reversed early in the bust, when productivity tends to rise faster than real wages.

For Finland and Sweden, we again observe a similar but more pronounced pattern. In the boom, real compensation rose much faster than productivity and, because of the fixed exchange regime, this led to a marked loss of profitability and competitiveness for the tradable sector. In the bust, real productivity-adjusted wages fell strongly, as wage restraint through both rising unemployment and depreciation took effect. This helped restore the profitability of the corporate sector and thus contributed to the strong turnaround.

This section on real economic developments demonstrates that Finland and Sweden follow broadly the same pattern as that of other boom–bust episodes in industrialized countries. Again the Nordic countries experienced more extreme fluctuations in these variables and the downturn appears to have been deeper and more short-lived.

6.3.3 Public Finance Developments

The behavior of fiscal aggregates illustrates the role of government in destabilizing as well as stabilizing the economy over boom–bust cycles. It reveals the role it has played in the underlying balance sheet cycle and thus how fiscal policy has impacted on aggregate demand through wealth effects. Changes in public debt reflect the design of discretionary fiscal measures and the workings of automatic stabilizers.

Fiscal balances

Unsurprisingly, fiscal balances tend to improve so much over extended boom periods that they are in surplus by the end of the boom. Jaeger and Schuknecht (2004) argue that this is mainly the result of strong revenue growth from tax bases that directly benefit from rapid asset price increases, like property taxes and taxable capital gains, and indirectly, through wealth effects on demand. This budgetary improvement masks the continued relatively strong expenditure growth experienced in many industrialized countries over boom episodes. In the downturn, revenue windfalls reverse while spending obligations through the workings of automatic stabilizers such as unemployment benefits increase faster, so that fiscal balances go quickly and deeply into the red.

This pattern was experienced in an extreme manifestation by Finland and Sweden in the second half of the 1980s. Given an asset-price-sensitive tax system, revenue windfalls increased, as shown by Eschenbach and Schuknecht (2004). Likewise, revenues from value added and wage-related taxes and social contributions rose sharply during the boom in consumption and the strong growth in wages, resulting in budget surpluses. These surpluses then turned into large deficits of 8–12 per cent of GDP within only a few years.

This pattern illustrates the sensitivity of fiscal balances to a major negative shock such as a financial crisis. It also reflects the fact that the financial crisis and bank failures spurred drastic government action. Corporate/bank bailouts together with increased welfare spending represented a partial socialization of the losses incurred by the private sector during the boom–bust cycle. Without these measures supporting the balance sheets of households and firms, the depression would have become even more severe. The policy of large budget deficits constitutes a clear case of tax-smoothing during an exceptional emergency such as the financial crisis.

Public debt

Public debt developments are consistent with and confirm the picture of the involvement of the public sector in the boom–bust cycles in Finland and Sweden via taxes and expenditure. This pattern is visible in the strong increase of public debt during bust episodes, much larger than the decline in public debt in the preceding boom. For all episodes, debt declines in the boom by an average of 10 per cent of GDP before rising in the bust by about 25 per cent of GDP. In Finland the debt increase was almost 50 per cent of GDP and in Sweden it was almost 35 per cent of GDP. In the case of Finland, a significant part of the rise in the debt-to-GDP ratio was related to the marked fall in nominal GDP and the depreciation of the Finnish *markka*.

Jaeger and Schuknecht (2004) also find that the maintenance of relatively strong expenditure growth in the boom and the additional pressures in the bust result in significant increases in the size of government – a ratchet effect. Moreover, government policies have at times exacerbated boom–bust cycles through pro-cyclical discretionary fiscal measures. In

Sweden the budget surplus created by the boom was taken as an excuse for reducing taxes. The tax reform in Sweden that reduced debt-friendly tax incentives at the height of the boom contributed to subsequent balance sheet problems and thus to the severity of the downturn. As many have commented, the Swedish tax reform should have been instituted at the beginning of the boom – not at the end of it.

To sum up, we find an asymmetric participation of government in the 'profits and losses' of boom–bust episodes – due to the workings of automatic stabilizers and the direct financial support given to the financial system during the bust phase. In short, governments felt obliged to step in to socialize wealth losses made during the bust while not preventing the boom from developing by making fiscal and monetary policies contractionary. This was the case in Finland and Sweden in the early 1990s. The need to recapitalize the banking system was so large that the central bank did not and could not serve as a lender of last resort, as the solidity of the banking system was undermined. Instead, fiscal policy was used to support the financial system during the crisis.[20]

6.4 SUMMARY

We have compared the boom–bust experience in Finland and Sweden during the last half of the 1980s and first half of the 1990s with the average boom–bust pattern calculated for a sample of industrialized countries in the period 1970–2002. Two clear conclusions emerge.

First, the Finnish–Swedish experience is much more volatile than the average. In short, the boom as well as the bust is more intense in the two Nordic countries. This holds for practically every time series examined: growth of credit, asset price inflation, real interest rates, real effective exchange rates, real growth, output gaps, consumption, investment, exports, employment, productivity, government budget deficits and government debt. Second, the bust and the recovery in the two Nordic countries diverge far more from the international pattern than the boom phase does. The bust is much deeper, and the recovery comes earlier and is more rapid than in the countries of our international sample.

How should we explain this highly volatile character of the Finnish and Swedish boom–bust episode? The prime determinant must be identified as the design of monetary, fiscal and regulatory policies in the 1980s and 1990s. In the mid-1980s, the Finnish and Swedish financial systems were deregulated, allowing for an extremely rapid increase in the supply of credit. During the long period of financial regulation, real rates of interest had been kept low or often negative by a combination of direct controls of nominal interest rates, high inflation and a progressive tax system allowing for deduction of interest payments on loans. Once the restrictions on commercial bank lending were abolished as part of the financial deregulation, households and firms were able to rapidly build up their debt at extremely low real rates. Actually, the real rate was still negative during several years of the boom phase. The monetary and fiscal authorities initially took no steps to raise the real rate when the process of credit expansion set in. Both monetary and fiscal policies were pro-cyclical during the boom.

Eventually, the low or negative rates were replaced by high and rising rates at the end of the 1980s, which contributed to and reinforced other developments turning the boom into a bust. When the bust came, monetary and fiscal policies actually enforced the downturn as well. Several factors contributed to this highly pro-cyclical policy, most prominently the defense of the fixed exchange rate. For a short time in September 1992, the overnight rate of the Swedish *Riksbank* was set at 500 per cent. The cost of borrowing was increased by changes in the tax system in both countries.

Once the two countries abandoned the defense of the fixed exchange rate and allowed floating rates in the fall of 1992, the downward slide was halted. The floating of the currency caused a sharp depreciation of the *markka* and the *krona*, which soon revived the export sector. The floating also allowed the central banks to lower nominal interest rates. Thus, the boom–bust pattern in Finland and Sweden 1985–95 was strongly driven by a financial liberalization and the design of monetary policy which caused very sharp swings in the real rate of interest, which were transmitted via the financial sector to the real sector, first causing a strong boom and subsequently a sharp bust. Thanks to their dependence on international trade, the Nordic countries were able to stage a rapid recovery by means of the sharp depreciation of the currencies. The export share of both countries increased significantly after the crisis.

To sum up, Finland and Sweden display a prominent boom–bust pattern for the period 1985–95 – more prominent than in the other industrialized countries in our sample. The development of the Finnish and Swedish economies should properly be regarded – and thus studied – as a highly representative example of a full-fledged boom–bust cycle.

NOTES

1. We would like to thank Claudio Borio at the BIS for making data available to us. The construction of this data set is described in Appendix I in Borio et al. (1994). We are indebted to Claudio Borio, Michael D. Bordo, Thomas Hagberg, Timo Hirvonen, David Mayes, Heikki Oksanen and Sari Sontag for constructive comments, and to Karel Havik for work with the figures. This chapter is an abridged version of Jonung et al. (2005).

2. See Chapter 5 in this volume for a comparison of the costs in terms of lost output, industrial production and employment of the six deepest crises in Finland and Sweden during the period 1870–2000. Chapter 5 demonstrates that the crisis of the 1990s was Finland's most severe, as measured by the loss in output, and in Sweden it was the longest crisis on record. The cumulative loss in employment was the biggest ever – much worse than during the depression of the 1930s in both countries.
3. This is clear from the memoirs by and interviews with policy-makers in Finland and Sweden. See the account in Chapter 2 in this volume.
4. An exception is Chapter 9 in this volume comparing the Nordic crises with the Asian crises of the late 1990s.
5. Eventually Finland adopted the euro in 1999 while Sweden maintained its national currency after the euro referendum in 2003.
6. See also Chapter II in *World Economic Outlook* of April 2003 and Chapter IV of April 2004 for an analysis of credit booms in emerging markets (IMF, 2003, 2004). The approach of these chapters is extended by Helbling and Terrones (2004).
7. The peak was reached in 1989 or in 1990 depending on which measure of economic activity is used. Here we focus on asset price movements. As asset prices peaked in 1989, we select that year as the peak year.
8. Appendix B in Jonung et al. (2005) displays the boom–bust pattern of additional aggregates.
9. See the financial accelerator literature, for example, Bernanke et al. (1999). Drees and Pazarbasioglu (1998) give an excellent account of the Finnish and Swedish boom–bust cycle from this perspective. See also Chapter 3 in this volume. The role of credit in the boom–bust cycle in Nordic countries is stressed by, among others, Borio et al. (1994).
10. Prices of commercial property were still more volatile than those of residential property. Price movements were also more volatile in cities than in rural areas.
11. See, for example, Chapter 2 in this volume.
12. See Jonung et al. (2005) for further documentation.
13. See also Jonung et al. (2005) and Chapter 2 in this volume.
14. Data for the current account balance are shown in Jonung et al. (2005).
15. The collapse of the trade between Finland and the former Soviet Union made the recession deeper in Finland. The role of the Soviet trade is discussed by Kiander and Vartia (1998).
16. Data for the output gap is available in Jonung et al. (2005).
17. Figures for the consumption and investments are shown in Jonung et al. (2005).
18. See Chapter 4 in this volume.
19. See Chapter 5 in this volume.
20. Here we have compared the pattern in Finland and Sweden with the international pattern of boom–busts for industrial countries using the methodology of Jaeger and Schuknecht (2004). A comparison of the Nordic pattern with those of a sample of 28 emerging countries demonstrates that the boom–bust episode in the two Nordic countries has many similarities with those of emerging markets. See Chapter IV in *World Economic Outlook* (IMF, 2004). The similarity between the Nordic lending boom and the lending booms preceding the Asian crisis are striking. See Collyns and Senhadji (2003) and Chapter 9 in this volume.

REFERENCES

Bernanke, B., M. Gertler and S. Gilchrist (1999), 'The financial accelerator in a quantitative business cycle framework', J.B. Taylor and M. Woodford (eds), in *Handbook of Macroeconomics*, vol. 1, Amsterdam: North-Holland.

Bordo, M. and O. Jeanne (2004), 'Boom–busts in asset prices, economic instability, and monetary policy', in R. Burdekin and P.L. Siklos (eds), *Deflation; Current and Historical Perspectives*, Cambridge: Cambridge University Press, Chapter 5.

Borio, C. and P. Lowe (2002), 'Asset prices, financial and monetary stability: exploring the nexus', BIS Working paper, no. 114, Basel.

Borio, C., N. Kennedy and S.D. Prowse (1994), 'Exploring aggregate asset price fluctuations across countries', BIS Economic Papers, no. 40.

Collyns, C. and A. Senhadji (2003), 'Lending booms, real estate bubbles, and the Asian Crisis', in W. Hunter, G. Kaufman and M. Pomerleano (eds), *Asset Price Bubbles: The Implications for Monetary, Regulatory, and International Policies*, Cambridge, MA: MIT press, Chapter 8.

Detken, C. and F. Smets (2004), 'Asset price booms and monetary policy', ECB Working paper, no. 364, ECB, Frankfurt.

Drees, B. and C. Pazarbasioglu (1998), 'The Nordic banking crisis. Pitfalls in financial liberalization', IMF Occasional Paper, no. 161, Washington, DC: IMF.

Eschenbach, F. and L. Schuknecht (2004), 'Budgetary risks from real estate and stock markets', *Economic Policy*, **19**, 313–46.

Harding, D. and A. Pagan (2002), 'Dissecting the cycle: a methodological investigation', *Journal of Monetary Economics,* **49**, 365–81.

Helbling, T. and M. Terrones (2003), 'Asset price booms and bust – stylized facts from the last three decades of the 20th century', paper presented at ECB Workshop on Asset Prices and Monetary Policy, 11–12 December.

IMF (2003), 'Real and financial effects of bursting asset price bubbles', chapter II of the *World Economic Outlook*, April, International Monetary Fund, Washington, DC.

IMF (2004), 'Are credit booms in emerging markets a concern?', chapter IV of the *World Economic Outlook*, April, International Monetary Fund, Washington, DC.

Jaeger, A. and L. Schuknecht (2004), 'Boom–bust phases in asset prices and fiscal policy behavior', IMF Working paper 04/54, Washington, DC.

Jonung, L., L. Schuknecht and M. Tujula (2005), 'The boom–bust cycle in Finland and Sweden 1984–1995 in an international perspective', European economy. Economic Papers, no. 237, December, European Commission. Brussels, http://ec.europa.eu/economy_finance/publications/publication550_en.pdf.

Kiander, J. and P. Vartia (1998), 'The depression of the 1990s in Finland: a Nordic financial crisis or a result of the collapse of the Soviet Union', in T. Myllyntaus (ed.), *Economic Crises and Restructuring in History: Experiences of Small Countries,* St. Katharinen: Scripta Mercaturae Verlag.

7. The boom and bust cycle in Norway

Erling Steigum

INTRODUCTION[1]

The Norwegian 1991–92 banking crisis was a dramatic manifestation that something had gone terribly wrong after the financial deregulation in the mid-1980s. With as short a time lag, Finland and Sweden experienced similar boom–bust cycles, banking crises and speculative attacks following their financial deregulations in the 1980s. Shortly after the crises in Finland, Norway and Sweden, several emerging market economies have been hit by financial crises involving speculative attacks on fixed (pegged) exchange rates and depressions in the wake of financial liberalization and lending booms, for example in Mexico, East Asia and Argentina.[2] The recent financial crisis which originated in the United States shows that even advanced market economies are not immune to the destructing forces of boom–bust cycles and financial crises.

Lending booms triggered by financial deregulation do not have to end in a crisis, however. On the contrary, cross-country studies suggest that although a lending boom typically follows financial liberalization, most lending booms end with a 'soft landing' and no financial crisis; see for example Gourinchas et al. (2001). Therefore, an important question is why did financial deregulation in Finland, Norway and Sweden end in systemic banking crises?

This chapter reviews the Norwegian boom and bust cycle and 1991–92 banking crisis. The Norwegian experience was quite similar to what happened in Finland and Sweden shortly afterwards; see Englund (1999), and Chapters 2 and 3. There are interesting differences though. Most noteworthily, the economic crisis in Norway was not as severe as those in Finland and Sweden.[3] It also took a much longer time for the banking crisis to materialize in Norway after the peak of the business cycle. Another difference is that the Norwegian government made a positive net profit from using taxpayers' money to rescue the banking sector; see Moen (2004). It is also worth noticing that the speculative attack on Norway's fixed exchange rate took place after those in Finland and Sweden, whereas the Norwegian boom–bust cycle and banking crisis were leading the corresponding events in Finland and Sweden by one to several years.

A crucial question is why did the previously very stable Norwegian economy become so unstable in the 1980s and early 1990s? To address this question, we take a closer look at important macroeconomic shocks as well as factors that may explain a change in the propagation mechanism of business cycles *after* the financial deregulation. We also discuss the role of fiscal and monetary policy, in particular the pro-cyclical monetary policy due to the fixed exchange rate regime. In addition, there are also more specific questions that we intend to address in what follows:

- Was the financial deregulation policy poorly designed?
- Does widespread bank management failure explain the banking crisis?
- Could the prudential supervision authorities have prevented the banking crisis?
- Was there a credit crunch?
- How successfully did the government handle the banking crisis in 1991–92?
- How significant was the speculative attack on the Norwegian currency (the *krone*) in December 1992?

A well-known difficulty when addressing questions about the relative importance of various factors and causes is the *identification problem.* It is not sufficient just to look closely at what happened, because the data are consistent with several reasonable stories explaining the events that unfolded. Ideally, one needs a good structural quantitative model to run counterfactual experiments. Actually, some studies have used macroeconometric models of the Norwegian economy to analyze business cycles in the 1980s and 1990s; see for example Johansen and Eika (2000). However, existing large-scale macroeconometric models have also been subject to critique. In particular, the practice of identifying shocks through exclusion restrictions may not be consistent with economic theory on how shocks are influencing the economy.[4] There is also another problem with large-scale macroeconometric models estimated on data before the financial deregulation. Typically, important behavioral equations tend to break down. Indeed, the dramatic drop in the savings rates of households in Finland, Norway and Sweden was impossible to predict in advance with econometric consumption functions estimated on pre-crisis data. Previously estimated investment equations were not performing satisfactorily during the boom–bust cycle.

The identification problem could be regarded as a failure of economic theory in general, and previous macroeconomic research in particular. Before the Nordic crisis, almost no attention was paid to lending booms and financial crises in macroeconomic theory, apart from the destabilizing role of bank runs for the supply of inside money as emphasized by Milton Friedman and others.[5] This theoretical void may explain why nobody foresaw the strong business cycle impulses released by the financial deregulation and the escalating problems in the Nordic banking sector. Since then, an upsurge of international theoretical and empirical research has cast new light on financial instability and contagion, as well as the interactions between the financial sector, asset markets and the real economy during boom–bust cycles.[6] Although many questions remain unsettled, the recent literature gives a far better basis for understanding the main causes of the Norwegian problems than what was the case in the early 1990s.

Recent empirical research on data after the boom–bust cycle has brought forward new information about interest sensitivity of aggregate demand and the effects of monetary policy. In the 1980s, the conventional wisdom among Norwegian economists was that the real rate of interest did not matter much for private consumption and investment. Therefore, monetary policy was considered to be ineffective. This view has now changed completely.[7]

In 2001, the central bank of Norway, *Norges Bank,* received a new set of guidelines for monetary policy, involving an operational inflation target of 2.5 per cent. Already in January 1999, however, *Norges Bank* began to set its interest rates in accordance with an inflation-targeting framework for monetary policy.[8] The interest rate setting of *Norges Bank* appears to have significant and predictable effects on aggregate demand, just as in other inflation-targeting countries. This information about the interest rate sensitivity of aggregate demand in Norway allows us to look back on the Norwegian boom–bust cycle with a better understanding of the role of the pro-cyclical monetary policy. It is indeed likely that the real interest rate was much more important for aggregate demand than perceived by Norwegian economists in the 1980s.

And finally, we now know a great deal more about what happened in the other Nordic countries. This helps us to look for common explanatory factors as well as to account for interesting differences. Such comparisons reduce the identification problem. However, more formal quantitative analysis of the Nordic business cycles and interactions between the real and the financial sectors must be left for future work.

Most of the previous research on the Norwegian crisis has focused on the banking sector and the causes of the banking crisis; see for example Steffensen and Steigum (1991), Johnsen at al. (1992), Steigum (1992), Berg (1993, 1998), Drees and Pazarbaşioğlu (1998) and Vale (2004) as well as books on the two largest commercial banks in Norway by Knutsen et al. (1998), dealing with *Christiania Bank og Kreditkasse*, and Lie (1998), focusing on the recent history of *Den norske Creditbank*, the largest Norwegian bank in the 1980s. Studies that have looked more closely at macroeconomic policies and the boom–bust cycle include Steffensen and Steigum (1991), Steigum (1992), Hove and Moum (1997) and Drees and Pazarbaşioğlu (1998). Although there is agreement on a number of issues, a strong consensus in regard to the importance of the fixed exchange rate policy for the boom–bust cycle and the banking crisis has not yet emerged.

For example, the study by Drees and Pazarbaşioğlu (1998) on the Nordic banking crises does not explicitly discuss the role of the fixed exchange rates for the pro-cyclical monetary policy, but criticizes the governments for too expansionary fiscal policies, inadequate prudential supervision and poorly prepared financial deregulations.[9] In contrast, in this chapter we argue that the fixed exchange rate policy and the pro-cyclical monetary policy are crucial in explaining the astonishing macroeconomic instability in Norway after the deregulation of credit markets and capital accounts. This combination undermined the stability of the Norwegian economy and made it very vulnerable to credit supply shocks and external interest rate shocks. It is unlikely that a systematically tighter fiscal policy or attempts to move fiscal policy counter-cyclically could have prevented a boom–bust cycle in Norway after the financial deregulation.

In the next two sections, we take a closer look at macroeconomic instability in the Norwegian economy after 1980, with emphasis on the critical years 1984–92. Section 7.3 deals with the financial deregulation and the lending boom. In Section 7.4 we discuss the change in the behavior of banks. Section 7.5 considers boom–bust cycles and the role of the fixed exchange rate, and in Section 7.6 we review the macroeconomic shocks and the fiscal policy responses. Monetary policy and the rate of inflation are the topics in Section 7.7, and in Section 7.8 we discuss the real estate price bubble in the light of recent economic theory. Section 7.9 discusses the resolution policies of the Norwegian government, and in Section 7.10 remaining issues are addressed. The conclusions are summarized in Section 7.11.

7.1 MACROECONOMIC INSTABILITY

In the post-war period up until the beginning of the 1980s, aggregate output and employment fluctuations in Norway were remarkably small, significantly smaller than in the rest of the OECD. Surprisingly, in the 1980s the amplitude of the Norwegian business cycle became much larger than before. Why did this happen in one of the most stable economies in the OECD?

Let us start with Norway's economic policies in the 1970s. Due to the emerging petroleum sector, OPEC I in 1973–74 had a strong positive wealth effect as well as a resource movement effect in Norway as oil revenues increased substantially. This shock triggered a rapid increase in aggregate demand, real appreciation, inflationary pressure and large current account deficits. The overly expansionary policies in the 1970s prevented unemployment from rising in the short run, but this policy approach was not sustainable. In 1977–78 measures were taken to reduce excess demand and the current account deficit. However, the attempts to increase competitiveness by devaluation (in 1978) and price and wage controls (in 1978–79) could only temporarily hold back inflation. At the beginning of the 1980s, many problems not addressed adequately in the 1970s re-emerged, involving difficult challenges for Norwegian economic policy. The most important challenges were:

- a considerable foreign debt
- a new oil price shock (OPEC II) in 1979–80 and large exposure to oil price risk
- double-digit inflation and increasing unemployment
- the fixed exchange rate policy not being credible, because of the inflationary bias in economic policy and lack of central bank independence
- a politically regulated nominal interest rate and a subsequent negative after-tax real interest rate
- a selective credit policy framework involving quantitative regulations of credit flows and increasing chaos on the credit market
- underdeveloped capital markets and strong political intervention in investment allocation
- a tax system giving powerful incentives to borrow rather than to invest in financial assets, as well as providing very strong incentives to invest in capital goods and to choose excessively high debt–equity ratios.

The legacy from the 1970s also included ideas and beliefs about the economy and economic policy that were not supportive of stability and growth. An ambitious quantitative planning and regulation approach to economic policy dominated economic policy thinking. There was a correspondingly strong skepticism in the political system towards increasing the role of markets. Industrial policy was geared to support industries threatened by market forces, not to promote competition, economic efficiency and productivity growth. The majority view among politicians was that interest rates in particular should not be left to the markets, but should be kept at 'low' levels that involved significant negative after-tax real interest rates for households and firms. Loanable funds were supposed to be regulated and allocated to politically important sectors, and there was a widespread belief that sufficient fiscal spending would always guarantee full employment.

Macroeconomic volatility increased during the 1980s. To obtain a sharper focus on the domestic business cycles, it is useful to look at the sector Mainland-Norway, excluding the petroleum and shipping sectors. The latter sectors were fairly small in 1970, but, due to the rapid growth of the petroleum sector in the following decades, they now amount to more than one-quarter of total GDP in Norway. Employment in these highly capital-intensive export sectors is quite small, however, and their output levels are not directly related to the Mainland business cycle. Employment fluctuations in the private Mainland sector were large, characterized by strong but short-lived growth in 1985–87 and a long period of decline from 1988 to 1993. Interestingly, private Mainland employment never returned to the same level as in 1987, due to crowding out by public sector employment.

In 1982–83, the Norwegian economy was hit by the downturn in the international economy. Then a spectacular lending boom took place in 1984–87, followed by a sharp cyclical downturn in 1988–89. Norway's Mainland economy continued to be weak. *Statistics Norway* has identified the fourth quarter of 1992 as the business cycle trough, more than six years after the previous peak. The rate of unemployment peaked in 1993. The recession was the worst since the 1930s, but not as deep as in Finland and Sweden in the first half of the 1990s. After 1993, economic growth and employment picked up and a new boom gradually built up. The strength of the Norwegian economy in 1993–98 came as a positive surprise as many had expected an increase in the structural rate of unemployment to a much higher level than before the recession.

7.2 THE CRITICAL YEARS, 1984–92

The period 1984–92 turned out to be a nightmare for Norwegian policymakers.[10] In 1984 and 1985 the financial deregulation process was speeded up considerably as all quantitative regulation on lending was removed, triggering a lending boom funded by short-term borrowing from abroad and (at a later stage) short-term loans from *Norges Bank*. Private consumption, investment and asset prices increased dramatically.

The government lost its majority in the parliament (*Stortinget*) in the 1985 election, and in the spring of 1986, after a dramatic fall in the oil price, the central wage settlement resulted in huge wage increases and shorter working hours. In 1986, the rate of (registered) unemployment was 1.8 per cent and declining. The current account went from +4.8 per cent of GDP in 1985 to –6.2 per cent in 1986, and the rate of inflation was increasing. There were large capital outflows and heavy speculation against the *krone* in the fall of 1985 and spring of 1986. In order to prevent the money market rate from increasing, *Norges Bank* sterilized by supplying short-term loans to the banking system on a grand scale. The new Labor government that came to power in May 1986 immediately devalued the *krone* by 9 per cent, followed by an increase in the interest rate and a fiscal restraint program. The huge wage increases happened after the dramatic oil price decline, which reduced Norway's terms of trade by about 25 per cent. Even at the time it was obvious that the wage increases were excessive. The labor market organizations responsible for the wage settlement probably wanted devaluation in order to prevent the wage settlement from destroying the international competitiveness of Norwegian industry. Thus, the devaluation in May 1986 could be interpreted as monetary policy accommodation driven by private sector expectations.

The business cycle peaked in the third quarter of 1986. The labor market was extremely tight in 1987 (1.5 per cent unemployment) and the rate of inflation was 8.7 per cent. The government decided to bring down inflation gradually to the average of its trading partners, realizing that it was no longer feasible to devalue the *krone* to give temporary relief to industry as had been done in the past on several occasions. In December 1986, the government delegated to *Norges Bank* the responsibility to set its interest rates such as to defend the fixed exchange rate, defined in terms of a currency basket. The bank did this successfully and after less than three years there were no longer signs of expectations of devaluation of the money market interest rates. In 1988 and 1989 wage regulation laws were passed to speed up the disinflation process. In 1988, Norway went into a recession and unemployment increased. From Figure 7.1 it is evident that the rate of inflation did in fact come down fairly quickly. During 1989–95, inflation was in fact lower than the average inflation rate of Norway's trading partners.

The macroeconomic story from 1986 to the end of the decade was the familiar story of disinflation through restrictive macroeconomic policies, and a recession. Although the strength of the cyclical downturn in 1988–89 came as a surprise, the idea of bringing down inflation quickly by establishing the credibility of the fixed exchange rate received wide support from Norwegian economists. It is quite possible, however, that many households, firms and banks did not expect that future inflation and wage increases were going to be much lower than in the previous 15 years, or that the strong tax incentives to borrow and spend were about to be

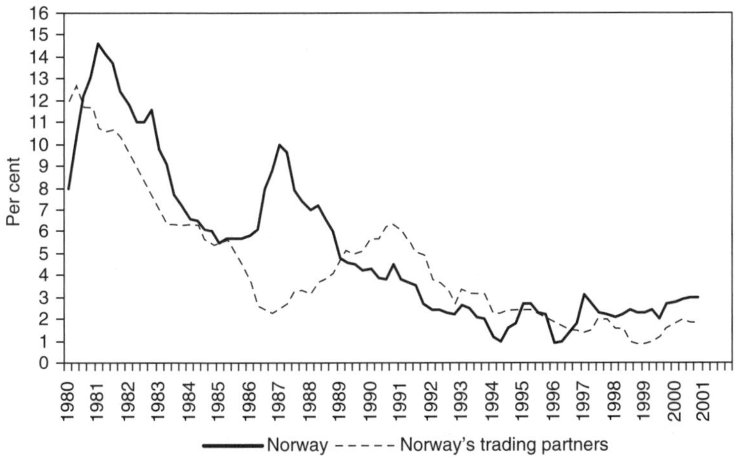

Source: National Budget 2001.

Figure 7.1 Inflation (CPI), Norway and Norway's trading partners, 1980–2001

reduced significantly. Even by the end of the 1980s, most banks probably had no idea of what was going to happen to their industry.

In 1990, a peg to the *ecu* replaced the currency basket. Soon, Finland and Sweden made the same decision. Since the German interest rate was high due to the effects of the German unification, this decision implied that monetary policy in the Nordic countries had to be even tighter than before. Before 1989, the German money market interest rate had been significantly lower than the US money market rate, but at the beginning of the 1990s the German rate climbed far above the US rate. Monetary policy was geared to the fixed exchange rate and could not be tailored to the Norwegian business cycle. Consequently, it became increasingly tight and pro-cyclical in the late 1980s and early 1990s due to German monetary policy. We shall come back to the role of monetary policy in Section 7.7 below.

The problems in the banking sector started in 1987 and increased through 1988–89. First it appeared that the problems could be handled by mergers and support from the banking industry's own deposit insurance funds.[11] In 1991, however, to everybody's surprise, a systemic banking crisis broke out, involving all the large commercial banks. The government quickly supplied new equity capital to stabilize the financial system. A more detailed account of the banking crisis and the resolution policies will be given in Section 7.9. Finally, in December 1992, after the previous attacks on the currency pegs of Finland and Sweden, the Norwegian currency was also attacked. After some defense, *Norges Bank* let the currency float. A new economic recovery started in 1993.

7.3 FINANCIAL DEREGULATION AND THE LENDING BOOM

After World War II, a 'low interest policy' was pursued in several European countries. However, hardly any country stuck to a policy of permanent interest and credit regulations for such a long time and with such determination as Norway.[12] During the 1960s and 1970s, the government developed a 'credit budget' framework for macroeconomic planning, involving special government lending institutions ('state banks') responsible for different sectors like the housing sector, manufacturing, agriculture and fisheries. The idea was both to control aggregate demand (jointly with fiscal policy), and sectoral investment allocation by means of a housing building permit system, regulation of the bond market and credit flows from private and public financial institutions, and regulation of cross-border capital movements.[13] Borrow-and-spend incentives of households and firms were strong due to tax rules that allowed unlimited tax deductions for nominal borrowing costs. Credit rationing was widespread, however. When inflation and marginal tax rates increased in the 1970s, the nominal interest rate was lagging behind.[14] The average real after-tax rate of interest therefore declined dramatically, sometimes as far down as –8 per cent. The interest regulation policy also generated powerful incentives to channel credit outside the regulated credit market by numerous shadow market operations. Over time, new innovative ways of circumventing the regulations triggered new regulatory measures.

From November 1978, the large commercial banks gained better access to international money market borrowing due to a new regulation requiring the sum of spot and forward foreign exchange operations of banks to be zero.[15] At the beginning of the 1980s, the growth of the *eurokrone* market, financial innovations and increasing flexibility of the shadow credit market made it much more difficult for the authorities to constrain the underlying market forces by quantitative credit regulations. In 1981–83, the credit ceilings in the credit budget were exceeded by nearly 30 per cent on average. By now it was fairly obvious that the old credit policy framework was not sustainable.

This perception appears to be the main reason why the authorities decided to abandon the former credit policy framework in the fall of 1983. *Norges Bank* believed that the regulations were not very effective anyway. The financial deregulation was therefore not expected to have significant macroeconomic effects. The new policy followed a general international trend towards deregulation of financial markets as well as other sectors. By this time, the government had already removed interest rate regulations in the bond market and opened up the Norwegian stock market to foreign investors. Moreover, housing prices had already been deregulated a few years back, permitting market forces to determine prices of houses and apartments in second-hand markets without the former system of cost-based price ceilings.

The abandonment of credit regulations took place in 1984 and 1985. After an unsuccessful attempt to re-regulate in 1986, the process of financial deregulation of domestic credit and bond markets was completed in 1988. By 1990, the remaining regulations of international capital movements had also been removed. The main idea behind the new policy was to replace quantitative credit regulations by indirect measures, such as liquidity reserve requirements. It turned out, however, that such requirements – although reducing bank profitability – were not sufficient to prevent the banks from rapidly increasing their lending. Moreover, due to disagreements within the ruling center-right coalition, the government did not terminate its policy of giving interest guidelines for the lending rates of banks until the fall of 1985. These targets were often too low in relation to money market rates, squeezing the profit margins of banks. The after-tax real rate of interest was quite low in 1984–86. In December 1986 *Norges Bank* increased the interest rate to defend the fixed exchange rate. This was too late to prevent inflation from shooting up in 1986–87 as a result of the positive output gap, the wage settlement shock of 1986, and the devaluation of May 1986. The increase in the real interest rate was not forthcoming until 1988, but then the lending boom was fading, the recession was underway, and real estate prices were heading downward.

An important element of the deregulation that swiftly increased competition in the customer market for credit was the abolishment of the regulation of new branch establishments. This stimulated banks to open up branches in new geographic areas. From 1983 to 1986, the commercial banks in Norway increased their number of branches by 15 per cent, and the savings banks by 5.5 per cent. Moreover, in the period 1983–87, the number of employees increased by 28 per cent in the savings banks and by 19 per cent in the commercial banks. When the business cycle turned downwards, the overcapacity in the Norwegian banking industry was evident. From 1987, the number of employees in the private banking industry began to decrease.

The new deregulation policy triggered an unprecedented growth in bank lending.[16] Nominal bank lending increased by about 30 per cent in each of the years 1984, 1985 and 1986, but the Norwegian data for 1984 partly reflect

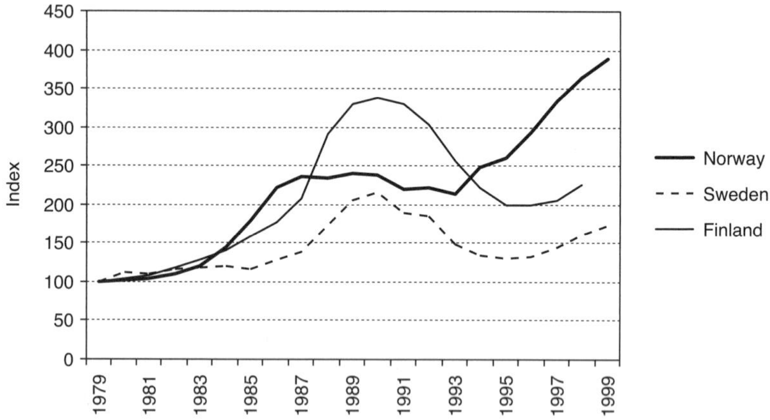

Source: OECD.

Figure 7.2 Real stocks of bank loans in Norway, Sweden and Finland, 1979–99 (1979 = 100)

that loans previously held outside the banks' balance sheets were taken 'back' when credit regulations were abolished. Figure 7.2 compares the growth of real bank loans in Finland, Norway and Sweden. Norway's real bank credit expansion was more short-lived than Finland's, which reached much larger proportions. The Swedish bank credit expansion looks marginally smaller than the Norwegian, but the Swedish loan data do not reflect lending from finance companies in the boom. Indirectly, this lending exposed the banks to substantial real estate price risk through bank guarantees. Taking the latter loans into consideration, the Swedish credit expansion was probably larger than the Norwegian as well. Another difference is that in Norway the subsequent credit contraction was not as severe as in Finland and Sweden. From 1987 to 1993, the stock of real loans from Norwegian banks only declined marginally (Figure 7.2). Thus, the credit contraction effect of the banking crisis in 1991–92 in Norway is very small compared with what happened to the real stock of loans from Finnish and Swedish banks. The rapid growth of real bank loans in Norway after 1993 is partly a reflection of the strong recovery of the Norwegian economy (Figure 7.2).

7.4 BAD BANKING

The credit market deregulation quickly changed the competitive environment and released aggressive competition for market shares in the credit market and strong aggregate growth of loans to households and firms. Most banks became much more willing to increase lending, often by venturing into new geographical areas. The expansionary lending behavior of banks may also be related to increased competition from non-bank financial institutions like finance companies that were less regulated than the banks before the deregulation of the credit market. The former had already for some time taken advantage of their freedom by increasing their market shares in the shadow credit market, partly by introducing 'bad banking' practices involving excessive risk-taking and poor managerial control over lending decisions. The finance companies were the first financial institutions to report alarming losses in 1986 and 1987, even before the cyclical downturn of the Norwegian economy.[17]

The large commercial banks also increased their activities outside Norway considerably. *Den norske Creditbank*, the largest bank in the 1980s, adopted an aggressive growth strategy in the early 1980s; see Lie (1998). After the credit market deregulation, *Den norske Creditbank* feared that *Christiania Bank* would grow faster and eventually succeed in overtaking it. A race started between the two to become the biggest bank in Norway. A significant change in behavior occurred in both banks. During its rapid expansion up until 1987, *Den norske Creditbank* had decentralized lending decisions, often to inexperienced and newly recruited staff that were given strong incentives to 'sell' new loans. At the same time its previous systems of internal control and credit evaluation broke down. Inadequate accounting systems gave the management wrong signals about profitability. For example, due to interest rate regulations, it was common to charge a fee at the time a new loan was granted, the effect of which was to boost short-run profits in rapidly expanding branches. Often the managers of such branches were promoted before the loans turned bad. Such problems were probably widespread in the Norwegian banking industry. *Den norske Creditbank* was the first of the large Norwegian banks to realize the downside of an aggressive growth strategy. Its losses were considerable from 1987 onwards. In 1990 it was merged with *Bergen Bank*. The new bank, *Den norske Bank*, was rescued by the government in 1991 and subsequently nationalized; see Section 7.9 below.

Since *Den norske Creditbank* was the biggest and most advanced bank in Norway in the 1980s, it probably acted as a role model for other banks. Also the aggressive behavior of *Christiania Bank* may have influenced the behavior of managements of other banks. Many other Norwegian banks (commercial banks as well as some savings banks) probably copied the aggressive behavior of the two leading banks, believing that this was the appropriate way to behave and survive in the new competitive environment.[18] Interestingly, the opposite turned out to be true: the survivors were

Table 7.1 Bank loan market shares of commercial banks in Norway, Sweden and Finland (loans in per cent of total year-end assets)

Year	Norway[a]	Sweden[b]	Finland[c]
1980	56.5	66.3	55.4
1985	57.8	71.7	58.8
1990	59.3	72.9	66.6
1995	58.8	93.2	69.8

Notes:

[a] There are two types of Norwegian banks: commercial banks and savings banks.

[b] Before the banking crisis, three types of Swedish banks existed: commercial banks, savings banks and cooperative banks. The cooperative banks disappeared as a result of the banking crisis. In 1990, the market share of cooperative banks was 5.1 per cent.

[c] There are three types of Finnish banks: commercial banks, savings banks and cooperative banks. The market share of savings banks dropped from 17.7 per cent in 1990 to 3.9 per cent in 1995 as a result of the banking crisis. In 1995, the market share of cooperative banks was 26.3 per cent.

the smaller and more conservative savings banks that did not try to copy the behavior of the fast-growing banks.

The large commercial banks played a crucial role in the Norwegian banking crisis in 1991–92. Table 7.1 shows that in 1980 the market share of commercial banks in the Norwegian bank loan market was 55 per cent, about the same as in Finland, but somewhat lower than in Sweden (66 per cent). After the deregulation of the credit markets in the 1980s, the market shares of commercial banks increased in all three countries, but less in Norway than in Finland and Sweden. In 1990, the market shares of commercial banks were 66.6, 59.3 and 72.9 per cent in Finland, Norway and Sweden, respectively. The national differences in market shares of commercial banks increased in the period 1990–95. The market shares further increased in Finland and Sweden, but fell in Norway.

The particular vulnerability of Norwegian commercial banks is related to low bank profitability in general. Profits before tax of Norwegian commercial banks turned negative already in 1987, and gradually deteriorated until the collapse in 1991–92 as a result of mounting losses that triggered the government rescue operation. The commercial banks in Finland and Sweden experienced a drop in profits before tax to about –2 per cent in the crisis year 1992, compared with –4 per cent in Norway in 1991. The Norwegian banking crisis was to a greater extent a commercial banking crisis than in Sweden, and particularly to a much greater extent in Finland, where the losses of the savings banks were staggering. There were large differences among Norwegian savings banks. Some medium-sized and large savings banks adopted an aggressive growth strategy very similar to what most commercial banks did, and eventually needed support from the deposit insurance fund and the new Government Bank Insurance Fund to survive. Many small savings banks did not attempt to expand beyond their traditional geographical area and thus avoided large losses.

Norwegian commercial banks were poorly capitalized when the loan market was deregulated in 1984–85. In 1983, capital and reserves were less than 5 per cent of total assets, compared with 6 per cent in Swedish and 7 per cent in Finnish commercial banks. One reason for the low capital share in Norwegian commercial banks was that they could replace equity by subordinated loan capital. This was done on a large scale. Moreover, the capital adequacy requirement had been reduced from around 10 per cent in the 1960s to 6.5 per cent in 1985.

Even without the benefit of hindsight, it is surprising that the top management of the large commercial banks did not worry about the risks involved in the aggressive growth strategies that they adopted. The low capital base and low profitability certainly called for concern about risks. Interview evidence strongly suggests, however, that there was a widespread belief that fast growth was profitable and the risk manageable (Johnsen et al., 1992). Some top bank managers may also have believed that the credit market deregulation was temporary. It then made sense to increase market shares before regulations were reintroduced.

A possible reason for the collective misperception of the high risk involved in fast expansion of lending may be that the bank losses used to be extremely small during the post-World War II period. Under the old credit policy framework, interest and credit regulations forced banks to ration credit to the least risky customers. This effectively protected banks from excessive risk-taking. Since entry was regulated and profit margins were comfortable, it was then very profitable and almost without risk for one bank to grow at the expense of others. It is possible that the expansionist banks brought with them their perception of 'growth without risk' under the old credit regulation regime into the new competitive environment that was established in 1984–85. Apparently, they did not perceive that the risk involved in rapid expansion of lending in a deregulated credit market was much higher because many other banks tried to grow or protect their market shares too. This line of reasoning does not easily explain why the performance of the Norwegian commercial banks was significantly poorer than those of the commercial banks in Finland and Sweden, however.

Another hypothesis is that the incentive systems shaping the behavior of bank managers stimulated rational herd behavior.[19] Interview evidence supports the hypothesis that many banks copied the aggressive lending behavior of *Den norske Creditbank* and *Christiania Bank* (Johnsen et al.,

1992). Moreover, insiders opposing the expansionary lending policies of the expansionist banks were often punished by means of degradation and negative social sanctions. It is therefore possible that the conformist pressure in the banking community was so strong that herd behavior was rational even among those who understood that the growth strategies were dangerous and counterproductive.

7.5 UNDERSTANDING BOOM–BUST CYCLES

The strength of the boom in 1985–87, the sharp decline in economic activity in 1988–89 and the following period of weak economic performance in 1989–92 were all great surprises for Norwegian economists and policy-makers alike. Apparently, after the financial deregulation, the Norwegian economy did not behave as it used to do and, despite attempts to use fiscal policy to stabilize aggregate demand, aggregate demand fluctuated widely.

We noted above that the after-tax real interest rate increased sharply towards the end of the 1980s, being low in the boom and high during the recession and its aftermath. There are strong theoretical reasons to believe that the sensitivity of consumption and investment demand to the (after-tax) real interest rate also increased as a result of the deregulation of the credit market. First, changes in the real interest rate trigger substitution effects as the relative price of future consumption changes. Second, when the indebtedness increases as a result of the lending boom, the income effects of changes in the real (after-tax) interest rate become larger, making indebted households and firms more vulnerable to increases in the real interest rate. And finally, changes in the real interest rate affect asset prices and household wealth. The fall in real estate prices gives rise to negative wealth effects in private consumption and makes it unprofitable to build new physical capital. Also in Finland and Sweden the after-tax real interest rate was low during the lending boom and very high during the economic crisis. It is therefore likely that the real interest rate played a crucial role in propagating the boom–bust cycles in all these three Nordic countries.

Another mechanism that became more important after the financial deregulation was the automatic tendency of the trade balance to correct itself over time. During the lending boom, the savings rate of Norwegian households dropped to about –5 per cent, and the government was deeply worried about the large current account deficits. However, households and firms could not spend more than their incomes forever, but had to satisfy their intertemporal budget constraints and reduce future spending. Therefore, the fact that households and firms intended to service their debts in the future would have an automatic stabilizing effect on the trade balance even in the absence of any fiscal policy restraint. What was not fully understood at the time was that households and firms could only temporarily increase spending as a result of increased credit availability. Therefore, the large current account deficit in 1986 could not be permanent. Moreover, it was likely that – as a consequence of financial deregulation – the long-run increase in the real rate of interest would reduce the share of gross investment in GDP, strengthening the current account in the medium term.

In retrospect, is it difficult to understand what caused the boom–bust cycles in Finland, Norway and Sweden in terms of mainstream macroeconomic theory? Let us see how far we can get with a simple story of the business cycle propagation mechanism of an exchange rate pegging country that deregulates its credit market and the capital account. When the fixed exchange rate is credible, neither the real interest rate nor the real exchange rate will move to counteract the effects of increasing or declining aggregate demand. Monetary policy must be used to keep the exchange rate fixed to the anchor countries (Germany in this case). Therefore, the nominal interest rate will closely follow the German interest rate, making it impossible for the central bank to set its interest rates for counter-cyclical purposes, or prevent fluctuations in the rate of inflation. Only fiscal policy may reduce fluctuations in aggregate demand, if the timing is right, but in practice a tightening of fiscal policy may come too late in the boom and could even make the bust worse.

Let us look at the effects of a positive demand shock in private investment and consumption. As we will argue in more detail below, the sudden change from credit rationing to easy credit in Norway in 1984–85 had a tremendous effect on private demand for consumption and investment. The monetary policy accommodation of the surge in aggregate demand is likely to increase housing and stock prices as well, stimulating consumption and investment demand further. Asset price increases could also turn into asset price bubbles in the stock market and the markets for real estate. Such bubbles appear to be important in most boom–bust cycles that involve financial crises.[20] We will return to the question why such bubbles build up and burst in Section 7.8. Another mechanism that usually adds to the demand pressure is the negative effect of increased inflation on the real interest rate during the boom. In the bust phase, this effect could be destabilizing, as a fall in wage and price inflation leads to an increase in the real interest rate.

Our simple story of a booming small open economy with a fixed exchange rate can explain why excess demand for goods and labor builds up in a lending boom and ignites wage and price inflation. It also explains why stagnant demand and high unemployment could continue for years if the real exchange rate is overvalued and low inflation (or deflation) leads to a high real interest rate. Falling asset prices, collateral squeeze, debt deflation and possibly also a credit crunch could also explain why a country could fall into a depression. It is then likely that a speculative attack would put an end to the fixed exchange rate policy. To make the story of the boom–bust cycle complete, however, we also need to consider the macroeconomic shocks that initiate the boom, burst the asset price bubbles and trigger the drop in aggregate demand, as well as fiscal policy. Without unfortunate shocks, lending booms do not have to turn into a recession and financial crisis.

7.6 SHOCKS AND MACROECONOMIC POLICIES

Let us now consider the shocks that started the boom. In previous Norwegian business cycles, international (particularly European) business cycle impulses have been important. This was not the case in the boom and bust of the 1980s, however. A quantitative analysis by Eika and Lindquist (1997) concludes that international impulses had a marginal stabilizing effect on the Norwegian economy through non-oil exports in the 1980s. Bjørnland (2000b) finds that after 1980 non-oil exports lag the Mainland cycle, implying that non-oil exports cannot have been an important driving force of Norwegian business cycles. The Norwegian boom therefore appears to have been homemade.

Could the high oil price in 1979–85 account for the boom? The world oil price increased sharply in real terms in 1979 and 1980 (OPEC II), and then declined gradually before the dramatic oil price decline in 1986. There are two main effects of a high oil price on the Norwegian economy. The first is the negative effect from the world economy, hitting non-oil exports in particular. The second is the aggregate demand effect of a more expansionary fiscal policy and increased investment spending in the petroleum industry. It is very difficult to quantify these effects, particularly what the government's fiscal policy would have been if OPEC II had not happened. A quantitative analysis by Eika (1996) suggests that in the period 1982–93 petroleum investment did in fact exacerbate macroeconomic fluctuations. For example, in 1988 petroleum investment dropped by more than 20 per cent as a result of the lower oil price, hitting the economy adversely in the midst of a recession. Another quantitative analysis by Eika and Magnussen (1997) argues that the total effect of the high oil price on Mainland GDP and employment was positive. This analysis suggests that OPEC II had a partially stabilizing effect in the business cycle downturn in 1982–83 but made a positive contribution to the next boom. According to these calculations, the increase in aggregate demand also increased real product wages and reduced the international competitiveness of Norwegian Mainland industry. Bjørnland (2000a) finds similar although somewhat smaller effects, using a VAR-model that distinguishes between shocks to aggregate demand, to aggregate supply and to oil prices.

Even though the high oil price in 1979–85 probably induced a more expansionary fiscal policy after OPEC II, it is unlikely that fiscal policy and petroleum investment played major roles in the boom of 1984–86. The changes in fiscal policy and petroleum investment were far from sufficient to explain the dramatic increase in private consumption and real investment in the boom. The sudden fall in the rate of household saving in 1985 and 1986 is particularly difficult to explain in terms of a fiscal stimulus at the beginning of the 1980s.

It is a reasonable hypothesis that a credit supply shock caused by deregulation and a change in lending behavior of banks and other financial institutions is the main cause of the dramatic increase in private consumption and investment in 1985 and 1986. The story is straightforward. First, the real rate of interest is very low, but loans are rationed, and there is excess demand for credit. When the banks are allowed to expand their lending, many households and firms want to consume and invest more. Thus, they increase their borrowing and spending. Aggregate demand increases, asset prices go up, the economy booms, excess demand for labor builds up, and wages and prices take off. This story is consistent with the fact that the savings rates of households suddenly dropped in all the Nordic countries (Figure 7.3). The fall in the savings rate was greatest in Norway, where it dropped by almost 10 percentage points from 1984 to 1986, despite normal growth in disposable income. Private consumption increased by a staggering 15 per cent in real terms during 1985 and the first half of 1986.

The consumption booms in Finland, Norway and Sweden are not typical for boom–bust cycles in other parts of the world. In a cross-country study of 39 middle-income countries that have experienced twin crises (both a currency crisis and a banking crisis), Tornell and Westermann (2002) find that in most cases consumption did not deviate much from trend during the boom.

Is it possible to explain the dramatic increase in private consumption in any other way than a shift from substantial credit rationing to extremely easy access to credit? An alternative hypothesis is that a wealth effect, not a shift from credit rationing to easy credit, explains the drop in the savings rate of households. The wealth of Norwegian households did indeed increase in 1984–86, particularly housing and stock wealth.[21] However,

Source: National accounts.

Figure 7.3 Household saving rates in Norway, Sweden and Finland (per cent of disposable income), 1980–95

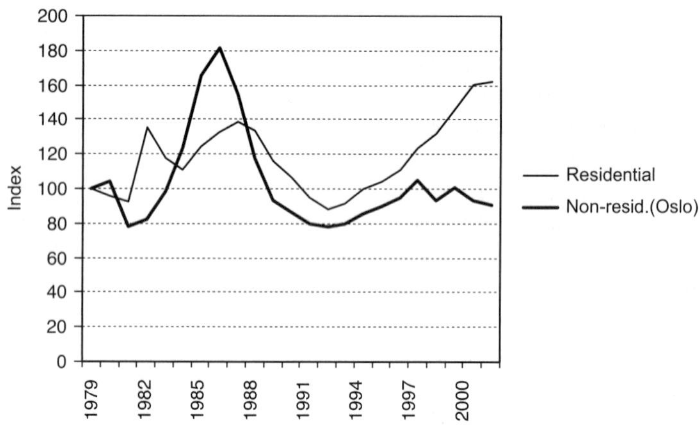

Source: *Norges Bank*. The series have been deflated by the CPI.

Figure 7.4 Real price of real estate, Norway, 1979–2001 (1979 = 100)

as illustrated in Figure 7.4, the real price of housing increased even more in 1981–82 (due to deregulation of the housing market) than in 1984–86. There was almost no decline in the savings rate following the housing price increase in 1981–82. Moreover, the quantitative effect of the stock market boom on household wealth was probably quite small. Therefore, the fall in the savings rate in 1984–86 was too large to be explained solely in terms of a conventional wealth effect.[22] In addition to a wealth effect, the new access to credit allowed households to reduce the forced saving inherent in the old credit-rationing regime.

The sudden change in lending behavior triggered by the deregulation of the credit market could thus be understood as an unprecedented credit supply shock that had a strong effect on aggregate demand.[23] The fact that domestic expenditure increased enormously in the business cycle upturn in 1984–86 fits well with our story that the credit supply shock mainly propagated through aggregate demand, which increased both Mainland output and the current account deficit. Although we cannot exclude the possibility that the increased availability of credit also had an aggregate supply effect, the fact that the rate of unemployment declined to 1.5 per cent in 1987, along with a wage explosion and large current account deficits, is strong evidence in favor of the hypothesis that the aggregate demand channel was dominant. The really great surprise in 1985–86 (and even today) was the strength of the effect of the shock.

Also the recession and the increase in unemployment after 1987 appear overwhelmingly to have been driven by aggregate demand. Aggregate expenditure dropped sharply from 1987 to 1989, and then grew only slowly until 1993. Again, Mainland GDP did not fall to the same extent as aggregate demand, as part of the effect showed up as a strengthening of the current account. Why did aggregate demand decline so much after 1987? Let us first consider the role of fiscal policy.

In 1985 the surplus of the government was 9 per cent of GDP and the current account surplus 5 per cent. In 1986, the current account turned into a 6 per cent deficit. A closer examination of the data reveals that lower exports of petroleum accounted for 53 per cent of the deterioration of the current account from 1985 to 1986, 32 per cent was due to increased imports, and 15 per cent to a decline in exports other than petroleum. Even if the oil price shock reduced the government's revenues substantially, we see that the surpluses were still 5 per cent in 1986 and 1987, declining slowly as a result of the automatic fiscal stabilizers.

When the new Labor government took over in May 1986, it justified the need for a fiscal policy restraint with the following strong words:

> Norway is now in the most serious situation of crisis. The country faces profound problems involving a huge weakening of the balance of payments and a consumption level that we as a nation cannot afford. The problems have been increasing during the last year, and were enhanced by the dramatic drop in the oil prices. (National Budget 1987)

Still, in 1986 the share of private consumption in total GDP was only 52.3 per cent, and Norway's total (net) saving was 10.2 per cent of disposable income. Compared with most other industrialized countries,

Norway's rate of saving was substantial, even after the oil price had dropped in 1986.[24] Therefore, in retrospect, the government's fear of permanently excessive private consumption and structural current account deficits appears to have been exaggerated. As discussed above, strong demand growth financed by lending is not sustainable, as households and firms have to satisfy their intertemporal budget constraints and cut future spending. Moreover, the high rates of investment in 1985 and 1986 were clearly part of the reason for the weakening of the current account. The high investment rates in the petroleum sector and in sectors producing non-traded goods were unlikely to be permanent. With a significant government surplus even after the oil price decline, it was therefore not obvious why the government should increase net taxes in order to curb the real income growth of households that were already heavily indebted.

The preliminary data used by the government underestimated the fall in the savings rate in 1985, however. It was also a new and difficult situation for the government to handle. The boom was mainly a result of a credit supply shock, but such a shock had not been observed before, at least not after World War II. Since the data revealed that private consumption had increased sharply, and that the economy clearly was in a state of excessive aggregate demand, it was not surprising that the government wanted a fiscal restraint directed towards constraining household income and private consumption.[25]

According to the finance ministry's own fiscal policy indicator, the fiscal restraint in the three years 1986–88 summed up to 4.5 per cent of Mainland GDP. The effects were, however, stronger if the effects of local government spending are accounted for as well. The latter effects usually come with a longer time lag than the effects of changes in central government spending and taxation. The government also reduced – in several steps – the rate at which borrowing costs could be deducted from the income tax. The most significant steps occurred in 1988 and as an element in the 1992 tax reform.[26] Together with a rising German interest rate and falling inflation, the change in the tax rules increased the after-tax real rate of interest from about zero in 1987 to more than 7 per cent in 1992. It is likely that the increase in the real rate of interest had a strong negative effect on aggregate demand and housing prices in the period 1988–93.

Table 7.2 reports key data on household income and consumption during the period 1984–92. In the boom years of 1985–86, real household income before net taxes grew faster than real disposable income due to automatic stabilizers. Very strong consumption growth triggered a dramatic decline in the savings rate. In 1987, the fiscal policy restraint reduced real disposable income by 0.9 per cent, while real income before taxes and transfers increased by 1.7 per cent. In this year, household consumption

Table 7.2 Household income and consumption (annual growth in per cent), Norway, 1984–92

Year	Real income before net taxes	Real disposable income	Household consumption	Consumption of goods	Rate of saving (per cent)
1984	3.5	4.0	3.3	2.6	5.1
1985	3.1	2.3	9.9	12.7	−1.9
1986	4.0	2.3	5.0	4.1	−4.7
1987	1.7	−0.4	−0.9	−3.7	−4.7
1988	−0.3	1.7	−2.2	−5.2	−1.3
1989	−2.3	1.9	−0.7	−2.2	1.1
1990	0.1	2.1	0.6	1.4	2.2
1991	1.8	3.4	1.3	1.4	4.3
1992	2.4	3.9	2.2	1.3	5.9

Source: National accounts.

declined due to a sharp fall in household purchases of goods. It is very likely that a weaker demand for goods such as cars and furniture would have set in even in the absence of higher net taxes in 1987. In 1985 and 1986, the purchases of consumer durables had increased enormously to a level that was clearly not sustainable. In the recession years of 1988–89, before-tax real income declined, but the automatic stabilizers generated a low positive growth of disposable real income.

Household consumption declined for three years, particularly consumption of goods, which fell by 11 per cent from 1986 to 1989. In 1990 a slow recovery in consumption started, and in 1992 the rate of saving of households recovered to 5.9 per cent. Fiscal policy became gradually more expansionary at the beginning of the 1990s, boosting household disposable income. According to a quantitative analysis by Bowitz and Hove (1996), fiscal policy was turned around too late to have a significantly counter-cyclical effect in the years 1989–91.[27] There can be no doubt that fiscal policy was expansionary in 1992 and 1993.

7.7 MONETARY POLICY

As in Finland and Sweden, previous high inflation and devaluations had undermined the credibility of Norway's fixed exchange rate policy at the time of the financial deregulation. The labor market organizations had reasons to expect that, from time to time, the government would devalue the *krone* with the intention of regaining lost competitiveness.[28] Lenders and borrowers also had reasons to expect continued inflation. Thus, after the fall in the oil price at the beginning of 1986, speculation against the *krone* was intense. When the new Labor government devalued the *krone* by 9 per cent in May 1986, it soon realized that, if the disinflation policy was to succeed, it was necessary to terminate the previous policy of improving the cost competitiveness of Norwegian industry through accommodative devaluations.

The question of whether the currency should be fixed or flexible had not been a political issue in Norway, however, even though the growing dependence on oil revenues could have been used as a sound argument for exchange rate flexibility to absorb terms-of-trade shocks and dampen the effects of other asymmetric shocks.[29] An important reason for the popularity of a fixed exchange rate for the *krone* was the Scandinavian-style wage formation system in Norway, according to which the manufacturing industry exposed to international competition should act as a wage leader. In securing agreement on the right nominal wage consistent with satisfactory cost competitiveness, a fixed exchange rate was perceived as a great advantage for the centralized wage bargaining process. A fixed exchange rate has therefore always been strongly recommended by the labor market organizations, but in years of excessive wage increases accommodative devaluations have been welcomed too.

If the exchange rate was to be fixed, it was necessary to leave the setting of interest rates to *Norges Bank* to bolster credibility. In the period 1987–89, this new monetary policy framework worked well in bringing inflation down (Figure 7.1). In 1989, the difference between the Norwegian and European interest rates was quite small, and all devaluation expectations seemed to have disappeared. In 1990, the center-right government removed the remaining regulations on international capital flows and replaced the currency basket with a currency peg to the *ecu*. There was one serious problem that only gradually became evident, however: German monetary policy had become very tight in the early 1990s due to the inflationary consequences of the German unification. Hence, Norwegian monetary policy had to be tight too, just as in Finland and Sweden. Therefore, the real interest rate increased substantially after the rate of inflation had come down to a level below that of Norway's trading partners. In the aftermath of the recession in 1988–89, monetary policy became increasingly tight.

Figure 7.5 illustrates the pro-cyclical monetary policy by comparing two versions of the Taylor rule with the money market interest rate (NIBOR). The two versions differ in that the Taylor interest rate (forward) is based on an estimate of expected inflation whereas the Taylor rate is calculated on the basis of observed inflation. The Taylor interest rates give an indication as to which interest rate would be appropriate for bringing inflation

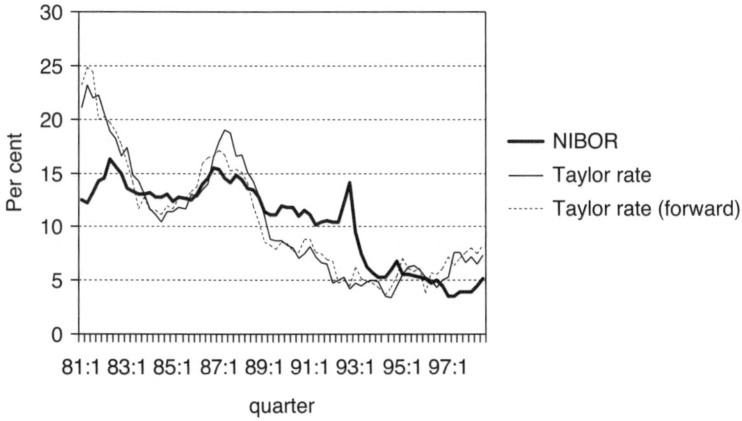

Source: Sveen (2000). The Taylor rate (forward) is based on data for expected inflation replacing actual inflation.

Figure 7.5 Money market interest rate (NIBOR) and Taylor interest rates, 1981–98

down to a 2.5 per cent inflation target. If the Taylor rates are higher than the money market rate, the method suggests that monetary policy in that particular quarter was too expansionary. Likewise, if the Taylor rates are lower than the money market rates, monetary policy was too tight, hurting the real economy more than necessary to bring inflation down.

One problem with this method is that we do not know whether the Taylor rule would in fact have brought inflation down in the 1980s. It is likely, for example, that the strong tax incentives to borrow and spend required a higher money market rate to bring down inflation than the Taylor interest rate. Since the tax rules were gradually changed to reduce these incentives in the period 1987–92, this bias in the Taylor rule was probably greater during the lending boom in 1984–86 than at the time of the banking crisis in 1991–92. Another problem is that the Taylor rule is estimated from US data in a period where the public expected future inflation to be low. In Norway it was probably a long time before the public began to expect low inflation to prevail, perhaps not until the beginning of the 1990s. If the public believes that future inflation is going to be much higher than 2.5 per cent, an optimal monetary policy strategy for bringing inflation down might require a higher interest rate than the Taylor rate. This is an additional reason for arguing that – during the lending boom – the Taylor rate underestimates the interest rate needed to bring inflation and expected inflation down to 2.5 per cent.

Figure 7.5 suggests that monetary policy was very tight in 1989–92, that is, the years before and during the banking crisis. In this period, tax incentives to borrow were gradually reduced, the rate of inflation was falling, and it is likely that the expected rate of inflation had already come down quite a bit. We are therefore confident that the large differences between the NIBOR and the Taylor rate (forward) in Figure 7.5 do indeed reflect that monetary policy was very tight in the period 1989–92.

Figure 7.5 is, however, less clear-cut about monetary policy during the lending boom. Since monetary policy in 1985 contributed to an increase in inflation from 5.7 per cent in 1985 to 7.2 and 8.7 per cent in 1986 and 1987, respectively, it is likely that the Taylor rate illustrated in Figure 7.5 underestimates the interest rate necessary to bring inflation further down in the boom years. In the period 1989–92, the Taylor rates were substantially below the NIBOR, particularly in 1992. In the second half of 1992, for example, the difference between the NIBOR and the Taylor rate (forward) was 8.4 percentage points (an average of quarterly observations), suggesting an extremely pro-cyclical monetary policy. Fortunately, the gap between the interest rate and the Taylor rate become almost closed when the German interest rate fell during 1993. Still, the previously tight monetary policy moved the inflation rate significantly below 2.5 per cent in 1994.

As discussed above, the interest rate sensitivity of aggregate demand had increased as a result of the effects of financial deregulation in the 1980s. It is therefore likely that high after-tax real interest rate in 1989–92 is an important explanatory factor behind the weak aggregate demand, slow economic growth and increasing unemployment in Norway during this period. The high real interest rate also helps to explain why housing prices declined for many years after the cyclical downturn in 1988–89, and why the banking crisis became systemic.

After the Swedish devaluation in November 1992, the Norwegian *krone* came under increased pressure. *Norges Bank* defended the *krone* by raising interest rates, but eventually gave in to the pressure and let the *krone* float on 10 December 1992. The final decision on the change in exchange rate policy was made by the government. It would have been possible to defend the *krone* longer, but it was considered not worth the cost. The ensuing depreciation turned out to be quite small, however, about 4 per cent. Four years later, the value of the Norwegian *krone* was even temporarily stronger than before the attack in 1992. It is difficult to find convincing fundamental factors that could explain the speculative attack in a conventional way. Inflation was quite low, government finances were good, the banking crisis had already been handled quite efficiently, and the current account had shown a surplus for several years. Moreover, the speculative attack was much less significant for the real economy than in Finland and

Sweden, where the currencies were clearly overvalued before the speculative attacks there.

It is quite possible that the basis for the attack was self-fulfilling expectations (Obstfeld, 1996). Several countries had been attacked 'successfully' before the November 1992 attack on the Swedish *krona*. Given Norway's recent history of inflation and accommodative devaluations, speculators had reasons to believe that the government would devalue rather than accept a high interest rate for an extended period of time. In retrospect, it was fortunate that *Norges Bank* did not defend the *krone* for an even longer period of time. Instead of following Sweden and introducing inflation-targeting, as the *Riksbank* did in January 1993, the government preferred a new policy of managed float according to which *Norges Bank* should raise or lower its interest rates whenever the exchange rate was considered to be too weak or too strong. This monetary policy did not work well in the boom years 1996–98, however, because monetary policy turned pro-cyclical and contributed to excess aggregate demand. Exchange rate targeting was practically abandoned in 1999 when *Norges Bank* began to set its interest rates in accordance with an inflation-targeting framework for monetary policy, a framework that was formalized in 2001.

7.8 THE REAL ESTATE PRICE BUBBLE

Empirical studies of financial crises around the world strongly suggest that financial liberalization, rapid credit expansion and bursting asset price bubbles are crucial factors that propagate boom–bust cycles and financial crises; see for example Kamsky and Reinhart (1996, 1999) and Demirgüç-Kunt and Detragiache (1998). Allen and Gale (2000) offer a theory of asset price bubbles based on a credit market failure, and Bernanke and Gertler (1989), Bernanke et al. (1996), Holmström and Tirole (1997) and Kiyotaki and Moore (1997), among others, have analyzed how such market failures may hurt the real economy. The crucial element in the model of Allen and Gale (2000) is an agency problem preventing lenders from observing how the funds are invested. The debt contracts then gives rise to a risk-shifting problem, as borrowers can shift downside risk on to the lenders when buying risky assets.[30] When investors behave according to these incentives, the equilibrium asset price will be high relative to the 'fundamental' value of the asset. In other words, an asset price bubble is created. This theory predicts that the size of the bubble will depend on both the availability of credit now and on expectations of future expansion of credit. Financial deregulation usually increases the availability of credit and could therefore start an asset price bubble. The bursting of the bubble could be due to a real shock that reduces asset returns or a change in monetary policy that makes credit less available. Allen and Gale (1999) suggest that the collapse of the Norwegian asset price bubble was due to the 1986 oil price shock, which triggered fiscal and monetary tightening.

In Norway the prices of real estate were far more important for aggregate demand than stock market prices, which dropped sharply but temporarily in 1987. Relative prices of housing and non-residential real estate (deflated by the CPI) are shown in Figure 7.4. The relative price of non-residential real estate in Oslo increased substantially during the lending boom, peaked in 1986 and then fell sharply to about the same level in 1992 as in 1982. The data suggest a non-residential real estate price bubble fed by the credit supply shock, which busted when economic policy was changed after the oil price shock in 1986. The fact that this relative asset price did not increase during the next boom in the 1990s also indicates that a real estate price bubble emerged in conjunction with the lending boom.

The relative housing price behaved strikingly differently. First it increased as a result of the deregulation of the housing market at the beginning of the 1980s. During the lending boom, the price rose further (after a temporary decline), but much less than the relative price of non-residential real estate. After 1987, it started a dramatic decline, which is not comparable with what happened during the boom. Then, in the next boom in the 1990s, the housing price climbed to a much higher level than the former peak in 1987. It is not obvious that the increase in the housing price during the lending boom could be characterized as a bubble. The theory of Allen and Gale (2000) predicts that the risk-shifting problem is more likely to be serious when firms with limited liability (rather than households) borrow to invest in real estate and other risky assets. In Norway and in most industrialized countries, households are stuck with the debt even if the collateral values of housing decline to a lower level than the debt. This suggests that large price bubbles are more likely in stock markets and markets for commercial real estate.

Concerning the dramatic decline in the real housing price in 1987–93, the high after-tax real interest rate probably played a crucial role (Figure 7.4). This also explains why the relative price increased so much in the years after the real rate of interest came down in 1993. It is also likely that the large decline in relative housing prices had a significant negative wealth effect on private consumption as well as a negative effect on investment in new homes.

7.9 RESOLUTION POLICIES

In some of the most expansionist banks and financial institutions, low profits and weakening of capital bases were already felt in 1987, before the sharp cyclical downturn in the following years. In 1988–89, several smaller banks got into trouble and had to be merged with larger banks or receive capital injections from the two deposit insurance funds for savings banks and commercial banks. By the end of 1990, the deposit insurance fund for the savings banks was almost empty. It was also becoming increasingly clear that the banking sector would need government support.

In March 1991, the Government Bank Insurance Fund was established, capitalized with NOK 5 billion, to secure the interests of depositors and bolster the general confidence in Norwegian banks. The mandate of this fund was to provide support loans to the two bank guarantee funds. During the summer of 1991, the deposit insurance fund of the commercial banks was empty, and on 14 October 1991 *Christiania Bank*, Norway's second largest bank, announced that its entire equity capital was lost. The government publicly declared that it would support the bank with sufficient share capital. It injected an additional NOK 6 billion into the Government Bank Insurance Fund and established a new fund, the Government Bank Investment Fund, which should supply capital to the banking industry at commercial terms and help banks to raise private equity capital. The capital of the latter fund was NOK 4.5 billion.

In December 1991, the Government Bank Insurance Fund injected new capital into another large commercial bank, *Fokus Bank*. As a result of high losses and a lack of confidence by private investors, the old share capital in *Christiania Bank* and *Fokus Bank* was written off to zero, making the government (through its Bank Insurance Fund) the sole owner of the two banks.[31] By the end of the year, Norway's largest bank, *Den norske Bank* (a recent merger of *Den norske Creditbank* and *Bergen Bank*) also reported a need for capital injections from the government. This rescue operation implied that the old private share capital was written off by 90 per cent. New reported losses in 1992 further reduced the value of the old share capital to zero, leaving the government as the sole owner of the biggest bank in Norway in addition to *Christiania Bank* and *Fokus Bank*. Ironically, the financial deregulation – which was intended to be an important step towards a greater role for decentralized market allocation of credit and financial assets and less government intervention in the banking sector – ended in a nationalization of the three largest commercial banks. Some further capital injections into the banking sector took place in 1992 and 1993; see Wilse (2004) for details.

The Norwegian banking crisis was without doubt a systemic one. The three largest commercial banks that were rescued by the government accounted for about half of the entire stock of bank loans to the domestic non-financial sector before the crisis (Vale, 2004). Still, at the peak of the banking crisis in the fall of 1991, non-performing loans were only 9 per cent of total bank loans. Compared with the East Asian crisis seven years later, for example, the share of non-performing loans in the Norwegian banking crisis was small. In Korea and Thailand, the shares of non-performing bank loans were about 30–40 per cent (Vale, 2004).

State ownership in the Norwegian banking sector was gradually reduced after the banking crisis. By the end of 1995, *Fokus Bank* was fully privatized. In 2000, the remaining government share holdings in *Christiania Bank* were sold to the Swedish bank *MeritaNordbanken* (later *Nordea*). However, the government wanted to retain a state ownership share in *Den norske Bank*. This share was 47.8 per cent before a merger with *Union Bank of Norway* in December 2003. The parliament decided that the government's ownership share of the new bank, *DnB NOR*, should be 34 per cent by the end of 2004. The main justification for retaining a government ownership share in the largest bank in Norway was to make sure that the bank would maintain its corporate headquarters in Norway.

Calculations by Moen (2004), based on estimated present values of fiscal costs and revenues at the end of 2001, show that the Norwegian government made a positive net revenue from rescuing and supporting the banking sector in the late 1980s and early 1990s. Table 7.3 reports some details from this analysis. Looking first at total fiscal costs and revenues at the bottom of Table 7.3 (the lines marked 3 and 4), the gross fiscal cost is NOK 51.1 billion when risk-adjusted interest rates are applied and NOK 39.7 billion if risk-free interest rates are used to calculate present values in 2001. In both cases, the present value of net revenues to the government is positive. It is estimated at NOK 5.8 billion using risk-adjusted interest rates and NOK 13.4 billion when risk-free interest rates are applied. This corresponds to 0.4 and 0.9 per cent of GDP in 2001, respectively. Included in revenues is the value of the government's remaining shares in the commercial banks in 2001, NOK 14.8 billion. Also the costs of *Norges Bank*'s subsidies and losses from liquidity loans to crisis banks are included in total fiscal costs; see the lower part of the table.

Looking at the upper part of Table 7.3, it is remarkable that the government rescue of the three large commercial banks, as well as *Sparebanken NOR* (a large savings bank), in each case yielded positive net revenue to the government in present value terms. The calculations show that the most profitable investment was the capital injection in *Den norske Bank*.

Why were no private investors willing to invest in the Norwegian commercial banks during the banking crisis? The main reason was that the risk was considered too high for potential private wealth owners. In 1992, the outlook for commercial banks and for the Norwegian economy was bleak compared with what actually happened in the rest of the 1990s. In 1995, a calculation based on market prices of bank shares indicated that the net

Table 7.3 The Norwegian government's rescue of the banking sector: fiscal cost and revenue (present values per 31 December 2001, billion kroner*)*

Government capital injections	Gross fiscal cost of investment[a] (outgoing payments)	Revenue (incoming payments)	Net revenue
Den norske Bank	20.89	31.54[b]	10.65
Christiania Bank	17.36	19.24	1.88
Fokus Bank	2.58	2.59	0.01
Sparebanken NOR	2.05	3.02	0.97
Other banks	0.60	0.43	−0.17
1. Sum	43.48	56.82	13.34
Other fiscal costs and revenues	Other fiscal costs	Revenue	Net revenue
Norges Bank's subsidies and losses	5.61	0.06	−5.55
Support to the savings bank's Deposit			
Insurance Fund	1.89	–	−1.89
Administration	0.1	–	−0.1
2. Sum	7.6	0.06	−7.54
3. Total (the sum of 1. and 2.)	51.1	56.9	5.8
3. in per cent of GDP in 2001	3.4	3.8	0.4
4. Total fiscal costs and revenue (using a risk-free interest rate)	39.7	53.4	13.7
4. in per cent of GDP in 2001	2.6	3.5	0.9

Notes:

[a] A risk premium of 4 percentage points has been added to the risk-free interest rate.

[b] Including the market value of the government's shares per 31.12. 2001, 14.8 billion *kroner*.

Source: Moen (2004).

fiscal cost would be positive.[32] It was therefore not really surprising that in Norway private investors were not willing to inject new capital on a scale sufficient to rescue the large commercial banks in 1991–92. However, from 1995 to 2001, the value of the government's bank shares increased substantially.

The Norwegian government's resolution policies were quite efficient. Given the government's explicit willingness to inject new capital, the banks could continue their operations and keep their lines open to the

Table 7.4 Real lending, the real interest rate and the real economy, Norway, 1990–95 (per cent)

Year	Real domestic credit growth	Real growth of bank lending	Real after-tax interest rate	Growth in relative housing price	Real GDP growth	Real Mainland GDP growth
1990	1.6	3.9	4.6	−8.2	2.1	1.1
1991	−3.7	−5.0	5.3	−10.6	3.6	2.0
1992	−5.8	−5.9	7.3	−7.4	3.3	2.3
1993	−4.6	−2.0	5.4	3.7	2.7	2.8
1994	−0.3	4.5	4.5	9.4	5.3	3.8
1995	1.4	6.1	3.1	4.5	4.4	3.5

Source: National accounts and *Norges Bank*.

international money markets. Compared with what happened in Finland and Sweden, the real economy was not declining in 1991–93, but economic growth was picking up; see Table 7.4. Due to strong growth of oil production, GDP was growing significantly faster than Mainland GDP in 1990–95, but even Mainland GDP was growing by 2.0 and 2.3 per cent in 1991 and 1992, respectively.

It is not possible to identify a credit crunch just by looking at aggregate data, but given the positive and increasing growth rate of Mainland GDP it seems unlikely that the quantitative importance of a credit crunch, if any, was great. Vale (2002) studies inventory behavior in a sample of 669 small firms and looks for behavioral differences between customers of 'problem banks', that is, banks which had received new capital from the government, and others. He does not find that the inventory behavior differed, although variables such as unused lines of credit and short-term debt to suppliers seem to matter for inventory behavior. In an empirical event study of stock prices of large firms, Ongena et al. (2003) do not find significant effects for customers of distressed banks.[33]

We note that the real after-tax rate of interest was particularly high in 1991–93 and that the real housing price was declining in 1990–92. It is therefore reasonable to interpret the negative real bank lending growth in 1991–93 in Table 7.4 mainly as a reflection of non-performing loans, falling collateral values and a declining demand for credit.

How successful was the government's handling of the banking crisis? According to Allen and Gale (1999), the Nordic governments' quick and extensive interventions were very appropriate. In particular, they compare Norway and Japan, concluding that: 'The [Norwegian] government's prompt action in restoring the banking system meant that it was quickly able to revert to performing its normal economic function. The return to robust economic growth in turn reinforced the recovery in the banking system.'

Contrasting this with the handling of the banking problems in Japan, they argue:

> Perhaps because in a number of dimensions other than asset prices, such as bank profitability, the severity of the crisis was not that great, the reaction of the Japanese government was initially in stark contrast to what happened in Norway. With the exception of modest financial assistance in 1995 to deal with the problem of housing companies affiliated to banks (the *jusen*), the government did not provide funds. This meant that banks slowly had to make provisions for bad loans from operating income and unrealized profits on stock holdings. In Japan the presumption was that economic growth would return and this would solve the banking problem. With the benefit of hindsight, it appears that the direction of causality is the opposite of that assumed in Japan. A solution to the banking problem is necessary to restore economic growth.

Allen and Gale (1999) do not discuss, however, whether the resolution policies in Norway were superior or inferior to those in Finland and Sweden. They emphasize that, although the details differ, 'the effect was the same in the sense that the macroeconomic impacts of the banking collapse were short-lived and the economies resumed growing again quite quickly'.

The Swedish model of bank crisis resolution, issuing blanket guarantees covering all liabilities of banks and establishing an asset management company to buy and resolve distressed loans, has perhaps been considered to be a more proper role model for other countries than the Norwegian model.[34] A potential problem with the Norwegian model is that the new government-owned banks could grow at the expense of banks that did not receive new capital from the government. The Norwegian government was well aware of this problem, however. In the first years after the banking crisis, the Government Bank Insurance Fund used its power as an owner to force the nationalized banks to focus on cost cutting and consolidation rather than on growth and market shares. A closer study of the behavior of the government-controlled banks and a comparative analysis of the banking industries in Finland, Norway and Sweden are important topics for future research.

7.10 REMAINING ISSUES

In the introduction we raised a number of questions of which only some have been addressed so far. It is now time to address the remaining ones.

The first question we asked was whether the financial deregulation itself was poorly designed and prepared. As mentioned above, Drees and Pazarbaşioğlu (1998) argue that the governments in Finland, Norway and Sweden failed 'to minimize the adjustment costs in the aftermath of the financial deregulation'. In retrospect, there can be no doubt that the Norwegian government was not prepared for the overwhelming lending boom after the financial deregulation. Hardly anybody foresaw the strong forces released by the deregulation. The government therefore did not perceive the need for preparatory measures in time. There seems to be broad consensus that the tax reforms that reduced the favorable tax treatment of interest payments should have been implemented before the deregulation of the credit market, instead of after the lending boom. It is almost impossible to know what difference this would have made to the course of events, but it would certainly have increased the after-tax real interest rate at an earlier stage.

One issue that has been debated intensively in Norway is the policy of government interest guidelines that distorted the structure of interest rates up until 1986, particularly the banks' lending rates in relation to the money market rate. This was not the case in Finland and Sweden. Thus, it is not clear how much this mattered for the course of events in Norway. Moreover, the government also decided on *Norges Bank*'s interest setting before December 1986, the effect of which was an expansionary monetary policy in 1985 and 1986. In retrospect, the responsibility for interest setting should have been delegated to *Norges Bank* before the credit market deregulation, but a large majority in the parliament was in favor of the 'low interest rate policy' and wanted the government to set interest rates, even the money market rate. Although the fixed exchange rate policy limited the scope for monetary policy in 1984, it would have been possible to increase the interest rate in the fall of 1985 and in 1986 to support the *krone*, which was under speculative pressure. It is also possible that such a monetary policy could have prevented the devaluation in May 1986 and accelerated the disinflation. To what extent a higher interest rate in the last months of 1985 and in 1986 could have changed the behavior of banks and households is an open question. In such a scenario the banks would have been forced to borrow more from abroad at a higher interest rate instead of borrowing from *Norges Bank*. Since the exchange rate was fixed and international capital mobility was high, however, it is unlikely that *Norges Bank* could have prevented a boom–bust cycle. The experience of Finland and Sweden suggests that the fixed exchange rate would have triggered a strongly pro-cyclical monetary policy in 1989–92 even if the fixed exchange rate had been defended successfully in 1986.

The second question we posed in the introduction was the following:

does widespread bank management failure (including moral hazard problems) alone explain the banking crisis? In other words, would a banking crisis have happened even under a flexible exchange rate regime that would have permitted a counter-cyclical monetary policy in 1989–92? No doubt some bank losses were primarily due to management failure, for example the huge losses in foreign branches.[35] Prior to 1985, Norwegian banks were prevented from establishing branches in different regions of the country. Those banks that expanded their lending in new regions suffered the greatest losses, due to young and inexperienced local branch managers with ambitious growth targets. However, the depressing effects of the high real interest rate on aggregate demand, real estate prices and the profitability of firms must also have been important. The large banking problems in Finland and Sweden after the recession and collapse in asset prices suggest that a significant share of the losses of Norwegian banks in 1991 and 1992 were triggered by high real interest rates and the decline in collateral values. Although many banks were in a vulnerable position due to the failure of the expansionist strategies pursued in the 1980s, it was not inevitable that the result would be a systemic banking crisis.

Another issue in relation to the financial deregulation process is the capital adequacy requirements of banks and the role of bank supervision. When the credit market was deregulated, capital requirements were lax, as the government had yielded to strong pressure from the banking industry. From today's perspective, the capital requirements were far from adequate, but neither the banks nor the financial supervision authority perceived the vulnerability of the banks before it was too late. The governments in Finland, Norway and Sweden are criticized by Drees and Pazarbaşioğlu (1998) for their failure to see the need to strengthen prudential safety-and-soundness regulations and adapt them to the new competitive environment. In Norway, the bank supervisory office was merged with the insurance supervisory body in 1986. The new Financial Supervisory Authority (*Kredittilsynet*) suffered from a shortage of expertise that could match the expertise of the large commercial banks. Furthermore, increased attention was being devoted to the developing capital markets and less devoted to monitoring the banking system. Routine on-site inspections were reduced as more priority was given to document-based supervision. Given its competence and focus, it was therefore hardly possible for *Kredittilsynet* to influence the behavior of banks during the lending boom.[36]

It is an open question how much a strong bank supervision authority would have mattered for the lending boom. It is quite possible, however, that if capital adequacy requirements had been the same as today from the start, the extent of the Norwegian banking crisis would have been much smaller, and perhaps would not have been systemic. In Denmark, bank capital adequacy requirements were much higher than in Norway. Moreover, there was no sudden deregulation of financial markets in Denmark in the 1980s as in Finland, Norway and Sweden. Denmark avoided a banking crisis despite having a fixed exchange rate. According to Chapter 8 dealing with the Danish record, a cautious fiscal policy that bolstered the credibility of the fixed exchange rate was also important in explaining why macroeconomic and asset price fluctuations were smaller in Denmark than in the other Nordic countries.

7.11 CONCLUSIONS

Why did the previously very stable Norwegian economy become so unstable in the 1980s and early 1990s? In the introduction we argued that answering this question is crucial for understanding the financial and economic crisis. A reasonable hypothesis, given the developments in Finland and Sweden as well as in East Asia in the late 1990s, is that the main cause was the combination of a fixed exchange rate and a rapid financial deregulation.[37] This policy forced the Nordic central banks to keep very high real interest rates at a time when the Nordic economies needed demand stimulus to fight recession. In addition, the postponement of many problems in the 1970s involved enormous challenges for Norwegian economic policy at the beginning of the 1980s. Economic policy mistakes in the 1970s, OPEC II and the international downturn had increased the rate of inflation to 13 per cent at the beginning of the 1980s. The rate of unemployment was increasing as well. It was hardly possible to bring inflation down to a low level without a cyclical downturn.

Norway was hit by several severe asymmetric shocks in the 1980s. First, the liberalization of the credit market caused a credit supply shock and a lending boom. Then the oil price shock in 1986 triggered a fiscal policy restraint and a policy of gradual disinflation. And finally, the German interest rate shock made monetary policy very pro-cyclical at the beginning of the 1990s.

Why did the deregulation of the credit market trigger such a large credit supply shock in Norway? Several factors contributed. First, the credit regulation policy had lost its legitimacy among the large banks, which had been very focused on fast growth at the beginning of the 1980s. It is also important that the deregulation of the credit market occurred rather quickly, increasing the degree of competition in a short period of time. At the same time, credit rationing of households had been quite extensive, and the previous deregulation of housing prices had already increased housing wealth considerably. The willingness of households and firms to increase borrowing was therefore quite large.

The most striking difference between Norway, on the one hand, and Finland and Sweden, on the other, is in the timing and depth of the economic and banking crises. The Norwegian economy did not plunge into a depression as those of the two other countries did. It was hit by a cyclical downturn in 1988–89, but the recession and decline in real estate prices did not trigger a banking crisis at once. However, for several years after the initial downturn, real after-tax interest rates increased, asset prices continued to decline, unemployment increased, and there was no sign of a recovery. The timing of events suggests that the strongly pro-cyclical monetary policy after the initial cyclical downturn was instrumental for the weak macroeconomic performance, the sustained fall in asset prices and the banking crisis. In the case of Finland and Sweden, the banking crisis happened in the midst of a severe economic crisis, and less than a year after the Norwegian banking crisis. The bust came much more quickly in Finland and Sweden, and asset prices declined more rapidly. Since all the three countries were hit by the same interest rate shock originating from Germany, it is likely that this shock was crucial in explaining why the banking crises in all three countries happened at about the same time.

Why did Norway get away with a milder economic downturn and a smaller banking crisis than Finland and Sweden? Probably the reasons for the relatively stronger macroeconomic performance of the Norwegian economy are also the reasons for the less severe banking crisis. One factor is the oil price shock in 1986, which prevented a longer-lasting boom and slowed down asset prices, borrowing, consumption and investment years before the German interest rate shock. The governments in Finland and Sweden did not receive a corresponding 'early warning', as the oil price shock was to Norway. On the contrary, the oil price shock improved the terms of trade for these two countries and paved the way for an international business cycle upturn that stimulated the booms in both Finland and Sweden. Another factor was the large increase in oil production that strengthened the Norwegian current account and government revenues after 1989. This permitted a more expansionary fiscal policy during the banking crisis. In Finland and Sweden, fiscal policy was expansionary during the boom, and after the bust the room for fiscal stimulus was small. Still, fiscal policy was more restrictive (pro-cyclical) during the crisis in Finland than in Sweden.

Looking back on economic policy and events in the 1980s and early 1990s, it is easy to see that the Norwegian government did not get the timing of its policy measures right. However, given the political constraints and the information available when the policy decisions were made, it is hard to imagine how any government could have got the timing right. Postponing financial deregulation was not an attractive option either. In our opinion the main problem was that monetary policy was tied to defending the fixed exchange rate and therefore was pro-cyclical in the boom as well as in the recession. The German monetary policy after the unification was really unfortunate for all the Nordic countries. It is difficult to imagine that a more active fiscal policy could have prevented a boom–bust cycle in Norway as long as the exchange rate was fixed. The macroeconomic shocks were simply too large for counter-cyclical fiscal policy to succeed when monetary policy was strongly pro-cyclical. Under a flexible exchange rate regime, however, monetary policy could have been used along with fiscal policy to counteract the boom–bust cycle. Still, the challenges for macroeconomic policy would have been overwhelming.

NOTES

1. Thanks are due to Bjørn Skogstad Aamo, Hilde Christiane Bjørnland, Arne Braaten, Øyvind Eitrheim, Svein Gjedrem, Finn Hvistendahl, Arne Jon Isachsen, Per Richard Johansen, Lars Jonung, Jan Tore Klovland, Kai Leitemo, Arild Lund, Thorvald Moe, Hermod Skånland, Henning Strand, Øystein Thøgersen, Bent Vale, Pentti Vartia and Erling Vårdal for useful comments. The responsibility for remaining errors and omissions is mine. This research has been supported by 'Fondet for bank og finansstudier', BI Norwegian School of Management. This chapter is an updated version of Steigum (2004).
2. For a comparison between the East Asian and Nordic crises, see Chapter 9 in this volume.
3. See Jonung and Stymne (1997) and Chapter 5 in this volume.
4. For an alternative VAR-analysis of Norwegian business cycles, see Bjørnland (2000a, 2000b, 2004). This analysis highlights the asymmetric nature of the oil price shocks for Norway.
5. A notable exception is Minsky (1977). Minsky's financial instability hypothesis plays an important role in Kindleberger's (1978) famous review of historical episodes of financial crises. It is fair to say that post war Keynesianism downplayed Keynes's own ideas about financial instability due to shifting expectations, uncertainty and speculation. Also the debt-deflation hypothesis by Irving Fisher (1933) was largely ignored until its revival in the 1990s. In the older literature on trade cycles, however, financial instability and banking crises played a much more prominent role; see Haberler (1958). According to John Stuart Mill (1867), trade and credit cycles have basically moral and psychological causes, leading to speculation in commodities often backed by 'irrational extension of credit'. He claimed that a sudden increase in the demand for credit would occur quite regularly (about every ten years), followed by destruction of credit. The credit cycle upturn breeds optimism which turns into 'recklessness' and leads to a crisis. Also Marshall and Marshall (1879) emphasize the relationship between economic crises and 'reckless' extension of credit.
6. Examples of more recent studies are Bordo and Jeanne (2004), Bordo et al. (2001), Bordo and Murshid (2003), Goodhart (2003) and Helbling and Terrones (2004). Particular attention has been given to asset bubbles in recent literature; see for example Allen and Gale (1999, 2000), Shiller (2000), Hunter et al. (2003) and Caballero and Krishnamurthy (2006). As Shiller (2003) has observed in regard to asset bubbles, there

are divergent views among economists: 'Highly educated people seem to differ at fundamental levels.'

7. Eika and Hove (1994) report increased interest rate sensitivity of aggregate demand using data after 1986.
8. For an evaluation of Norwegian monetary policy and institutions, see Svensson et al. (2002).
9. In the concluding section they write the following about Norway, Sweden and Finland: 'Monetary policy was constrained by the fixed-exchange-rate regime, and the stance of fiscal policy was not tightened in a timely manner and to a sufficient extent.' They also emphasize that the Nordic governments did not take 'adequate measures to minimize the adjustment costs in the aftermath of the financial deregulation. The authorities failed to tighten prudential bank regulation and to create an adequate supervisory framework to take into account the substantial increase in banks' exposure to real estate lending in foreign currency. The favorable tax treatment of interest payments was not reformed until well after the credit boom.'
10. A center-right coalition majority government ruled in 1984 (it came to office in 1981). It lost the majority in the general election in 1985, but continued to rule. It lost support from the Progress Party in May 1986, however, and a Labor minority government took over. The Labor Party lost the 1989 general election and a new center-right government came to power. This minority government was very short-lived, and a new Labor minority government came to office in 1990.
11. There were (and still are) two deposit insurance funds, one for the commercial banks and one for the savings banks. They are funded by annual contributions from member banks. Membership is compulsory.
12. For a discussion of the roots of the Norwegian low interest rate policy and credit controls, see Steigum (1980). These policies were important elements of a quantitative macroeconomic planning approach to economic policy that received strong academic support from leading economists at the University of Oslo in the 1960s and 1970s.
13. For an early macroeconomic analysis of credit regulations in a combined credit multiplier and income–expenditure framework, see Johansen (1958). Steigum (1983) offers a non-market-clearing analysis of interest rate regulation and capital rationing.
14. An increase in the level of nominal interest rates in 1977–78 failed to increase the real interest rate permanently due to rising inflation.
15. This change was motivated by a growing demand from the oil companies to buy Norwegian *kroner* forward from Norwegian banks to pay taxes to the Norwegian government on specific dates. The banks therefore needed to borrow US dollars to cover their foreign exchange risk.
16. Estimating a small, dynamic Bernanke-Blinder model on data up to the mid-1990s, Bårdsen and Klovland (2000) find a credit channel of monetary policy in Norway due to government regulation of credit flows and interest rates.
17. The losses were more than 1 per cent of year-end loans in 1986 and 2 per cent in 1987. The losses of finance companies reached a maximum in 1989, after which many of them were restructured or went out of business. Building on evidence from the UK secondary banking crisis in 1973–74, Revell (1986) argues that supernormal profitability due to bank cartel arrangements stimulates aggressive competition from other financial institutions. The latter increase their market shares by introducing bad banking practices involving excessive risk-taking and speculation (such as short-term money market funding of long-term assets). This competition may explain why some banks also began to take more risks to protect their market shares.
18. An extreme example of bad banking is the bank that let a firm selling yachts grant loans on its behalf. The firm could even grant loans to new customers in this innovative way during weekends, when it was impossible to control their creditworthiness. Not surprisingly, both the firm and the bank soon went out of business, the latter by merging with a large commercial bank that was rescued by the government in 1991.
19. See, for example, Scharfstein and Stein (1990) and Banerjee (1992).

20. See, for example, Helbling and Terrones (2003) and Chapter 6 in this volume.
21. Traditionally, the Norwegian stock market has been small in relation to GDP and share holdings by households have been quite low. Due to a high share of homeowners in Norway, housing wealth is much more important for households than stock market wealth.
22. Eitrheim et al. (2002) estimate a consumption function on Norwegian data in which a household wealth variable plays an important role along with income. They estimate a long-run wealth elasticity of 0.27, which is much stronger than conventional wealth effects in life-cycle models. The strength of this empirical effect could indicate that it picks up the effect of a shift from credit rationing to easy access to credit.
23. Using a macroeconometric model of the Norwegian economy, Hove and Moum (1997) conclude that the credit supply shock had a very strong effect on private consumption and aggregate demand in 1985–87.
24. The negative oil price shock itself called for a long-run fiscal restraint due to the fall in government wealth. In a dependent economy theoretical framework, Steigum and Thøgersen (2003) show that optimal fiscal policy involves temporary deficits and a low neutral real rate of interest if sectoral adjustment is costly and time-consuming. In the Nordic countries, the real rate of interest became very high as a consequence of the fixed exchange rate policy, however, triggering an intertemporal coordination failure.
25. The stabilization policy package also included measures to constrain private investment, but they were probably not very important quantitatively.
26. In the early 1980s, a tax commission recommended a tax reform that would have reduced the tax incentives to borrow. This recommendation was not followed up until the new Labor government took over in May 1986.
27. The measurement of fiscal policy impulses is sensitive to whether local government spending is included or not. If this is included, as in Bowitz and Hove (1996), it took a longer time before fiscal policy turned expansionary than if one uses the cyclically adjusted fiscal policy indicator of the Ministry of Finance to measure changes in fiscal policy.
28. It was the government, not *Norges Bank*, that made the final decisions in regard to the currency basket and devaluations of the *krone*.
29. Norway revaluated the *krone* in 1973 to reduce inflationary pressure. However, this step was unintentionally seen by the labor unions as a signal to increase wages, and the real exchange rate appreciated substantially after the wage settlement in 1973. This unfortunate experience may explain why exchange rate flexibility was not an issue in the economic policy debate in Norway until the late 1990s.
30. Deposit insurance or implicit guarantees from the government to bail out banks would add to the problems highlighted in this theory, but are not essential elements in it.
31. An amendment to the banking law permitted the government to write down the value of the old shares to zero in order to ensure that the old shareholders were covering losses before taxpayers' money was invested.
32. The present value of the total fiscal costs and revenues at the end of 1995 was NOK 28.6 and NOK 20 billion, respectively, yielding a net fiscal cost of NOK 8.6 billion (Moen, 2004).
33. Several studies have employed stock price data to search for contagion effects during the Norwegian banking crisis; see Kaen and Michalsen (1994), Clare and Priestley (2002) and Andrade et al. (2004). The answer seems to be yes, but the contagion appears to be temporary.
34. For a cross-country overview of various resolution mechanisms of systemic financial crises, see Calomiris et al. (2005). This study includes Sweden, but does not consider the resolution of the Norwegian banking crisis. In a recent paper, Laeven and Valencia (2008) express some doubts about the effectiveness of asset management companies set up to manage distressed assets.
35. Norwegian banks also lost a lot of money in the fish farming industry. The problems in this export industry were not directly related to the business cycle in Mainland Norway.

Most banks did not pay sufficient attention to the risks involved and failed to charge appropriate risk premiums.

36. In 1987, *Kredittilsynet* tightened the accounting rules of banks in order to prevent banks from postponing loss provisions. It has later been argued that if old accounting practice had been continued, the old shareholders of *Den norske Bank* would not have lost their entire capital, and the nationalization could have been avoided. This argument is controversial, however. Even if the argument had been correct *ceteris paribus*, laxer accounting rules could have disguised the underlying problems associated with the risky growth strategies for many bank managements, postponing the restructuring and cost-cutting efforts of Norwegian banks.
37. Wohlin (1998) argues that the root of the Swedish banking crisis was the fixed exchange rate policy after the financial deregulation.

REFERENCES

Allen, F. and D. Gale (1999), 'Bubbles, crises, and policy', *Oxford Review of Economic Policy*, **15**, 9–18.

Allen, F. and D. Gale (2000), 'Bubbles and crises', *The Economic Journal*, **110**, 236–55.

Andrade, I.C., A.D. Clare and R. Priestley (2004), 'The extent of real economy contagion effects during the Norwegian banking crisis', unpublished manuscript, Department of Financial Economics, BI Norwegian School of Management.

Banerjee, A.V. (1992), 'A simple model of herd behavior', *Quarterly Journal of Economics*, **107**, 797–817.

Berg, S.A. (1993), 'The banking crises in the Scandinavian countries', in *Bank Structure and Competition 1993*, Chicago, IL: Federal Reserve Bank of Chicago.

Berg, S.A. (1998), 'Bank failures in Scandinavia', in *Preventing Banking Crises*, Washington, DC: EDI Development Studies, The World Bank.

Bernanke, B. and M. Gertler (1989), 'Agency costs, collateral, and business fluctuations', *American Economic Review*, **79**, 14–31.

Bernanke, B., M. Gertler and S. Gilchrist (1996), 'The financial accelerator and the flight to quality', *Review of Economics and Statistics*, **78**, 1–15.

Bjørnland, H.C. (2000a), 'The dynamic effects of aggregate demand, supply and oil price shocks. A comparative study', *The Manchester School of Economic Studies*, **68**, 578–607.

Bjørnland, H.C. (2000b), 'Detrending methods and stylized facts of business cycles in Norway – an international comparison', *Empirical Economics*, **25**, 369–92.

Bjørnland, H.C. (2004), 'The role of the exchange rate as shock absorber in a small open economy', *Open Economies Review*, **15**, 23–43.

Bordo, M.D. and O. Jeanne (2004), 'Boom–busts in asset prices, economic instability, and monetary policy', in R. Burdekin and P.L. Siklos (eds), *Deflation: Current and Historical Perspectives*, Cambridge: Cambridge University Press.

Bordo, M.D. and A.P. Murshid (2003), 'Globalization and changing patterns in crisis transmission', in W.C. Hunter, G.G. Kaufman and M. Pomerleano (eds), *Asset price bubbles: the implications for monetary, regulatory and international policies*, Cambridge, MA: MIT Press.

Bordo, M.D., B. Eichengreen, D. Klingebiel and M.S. Martinez-Peria (2001), 'Is the crisis problem growing more severe?' *Economic Policy*, **16** (32), 51–82.

Bowitz, E. and S.I. Hove (1996), 'Business cycles and fiscal policy: Norway 1973–93', Discussion Papers, 178, Statistics Norway.

Bårdsen, G. and J.T. Klovland (2000), 'Shaken or stirred? Financial deregulation and the monetary transmission mechanism in Norway', *Scandinavian Journal of Economics*, **102**, 563–83.

Caballero, R.J. and A. Krishnamurthy (2006), 'Bubbles and capital flow volatility: causes and risk management', *Journal of Monetary Economics*, **53**, 35–53.

Calomiris, W., D. Klingebiel and L. Laeven (2005), 'Financial crisis policies and resolution mechanisms. A taxonomy from cross-country experience', in P. Honohan and L. Laeven (eds), *Systemic Financial Crises. Containment and Resolution*, New York: Cambridge University Press.

Clare, A. and R. Priestley (2002), 'Calculating the probability of failure of the Norwegian banking sector', *Journal of Multinational Financial Management*, **12**, 21–40.

Demirgüç-Kunt, A. and E. Detragiache (1998), 'Financial liberalization and financial fragility', Working paper, 98/83, Washington, DC: International Monetary Fund.

Drees, B. and C. Pazarbaşioğlu (1998), 'The Nordic banking crises: pitfalls in financial liberalization?', IMF Occasional Paper, no. 161, Washington, DC: International Monetary Fund.

Eika, T. (1996), 'Utbygging av petroleumssektoren og konjunkturforløpet 1973–93' (Expansion of the petroleum sector and business cycles 1973–93), *Økonomiske analyser*, 3/96, Statistics Norway, pp. 10–16.

Eika, T. and S.I. Hove (1994), 'KVARTS: Modellen bak prognosene' (KVARTS: the model behind the forecasts), *Økonomiske analyser*, 94/9, Statistics Norway.

Eika, T. and K.-G. Lindquist (1997), 'Konjunkturimpulser fra utlandet' (International business cycle impulses), *Rapporter*, 97/2, Statistics Norway.

Eika, T. and K.A. Magnussen (1997), 'Virkninger av den høye oljeprisen i 1979–85' (Effects of the high oil price in 1979–85), *Økonomiske analyser*, 8/97, Statistics Norway.

Eitrheim, Ø., E.S. Jansen and R. Nymoen (2002), 'Progress from failure – the Norwegian consumption function', *The Econometrics Journal*, **5**, 40–64.

Englund, P. (1999), 'The Swedish banking crisis: roots and consequences', *Oxford Review of Economic Policy*, **13**, 80–97.

Fisher, I. (1933), 'The debt deflation theory of the great depressions', *Econometrica*, **1**, 337–57.

Goodhart, C.A.E. (2003), 'The historical pattern of economic cycles and their interaction with asset prices and financial regulation', in W.C. Hunter, G.G. Kaufman and M. Pomerleano (eds), *Asset price bubbles: the implications for monetary, regulatory and international policies*, Cambridge, MA: MIT Press.

Gourinchas, P.O., O. Landerretche and R. Valdes (2001), 'Lending booms: Latin America and the world', NBER Working paper, no. 8249.

Haberler, G. (1958), *Prosperity and Depression*, London: George Allen & Unwin.

Helbling, T. and M. Terrones (2003), 'Asset price booms and busts – stylized facts from the last three decades of the 20th century', paper presented at ECB Workshop on Asset Prices and Monetary Policy, 11–12 December.

Holmström, B. and J. Tirole (1997), 'Financial intermediation, loanable funds, and the real sector', *Quarterly Journal of Economics*, **112**, 663–91.

Hove, S.I. and K. Moum (1997), 'Fra kjøpefest til ledighetskø. Kredittliberalisering, konsumutvikling og konjunktursvingninger 1983–93' (From spending frenzy to the unemployment line), *Økonomiske analyser*, 8/97, Statistics Norway.

Hunter, W.C., G.G. Kaufman and M. Pomerleano (eds) (2003), *Asset Price Bubbles: The Implications for Monetary, Regulatory, and International Policies*, Cambridge, MA: MIT Press.

Johansen, L. (1958), 'The role of the banking system in a macroeconomic model', *International Economic Papers*, no. 8. First published in 1956 (in Norwegian) as 'Bankenes rolle i en makroøkonomisk modell', *Statsøkonomisk Tidsskrift,* **70**, 1–26.

Johansen, P.R. and T. Eika (2000), 'Driving forces behind business cycles in the 1990s', *Economic Survey*, 10, 3/2000 (Statistics Norway).

Johnsen, T., T. Reve, E. Steigum, F. Sættem, C. Meyer and E. Høyland (1992), *Bankkrisen i Norge* (*The banking crisis in Norway*), SNF-rapport 29/92, Centre for Research in Economics and Business Administration (SNF), Bergen.

Jonung, L. and J. Stymne (1997), 'The great regime shift: asset markets and economic activity in Sweden, 1985–93', in F. Capie and G.E. Wood (eds), *Asset Prices and the Real Economy*, London: Macmillan.

Kaen, F.R. and D. Michalsen (1994), 'The effects of the Norwegian banking crisis on Norwegian bank and non-bank stocks', *Journal of Multinational Finance*, **7**, 83–111.

Kamsky, G. and C. Reinhart (1996), 'Banking and balance-of-payments crises: models and evidence', Working paper, Washington, DC, Board of Governors of the Federal Reserve.

Kamsky, G. and C. Reinhart (1999), 'The twin crises: the causes of banking and balance-of-payments problems', *American Economic Review*, **89**, 473–500.

Kindleberger, C.P. (1978), *Manias, Panics and Crashes*, New York: Basic Books.

Kiyotaki, N. and J. Moore (1997), 'Credit cycles', *Journal of Political Economy*, **105**, 211–48.

Knutsen, S., E. Lange and H.W. Nordvik (1998), *Mellom næringsliv og politikk. Kredittkassen i vekst og kriser 1918–98* (*Between business and politics. Kredittkassen during growth and crises 1918–98*), Oslo: Universitetsforlaget.

Laeven, L. and F. Valencia (2008), 'Systemic banking crises: a new database', IMF Working paper 08/224 (October).

Lie, E. (1998), *En storbank i vekst og krise. Den norske Creditbank 1982–90* (*A large bank during growth and crisis. Den norske Creditbank 1982–90*), Oslo: Universitetsforlaget.

Marshall, A. and M. Marshall (1879), *Economics of Industry*, London: Macmillan.

Mill, J.S. (1867), 'Credit cycles and the origin of commercial panics', *Transactions of the Manchester Society*, Manchester.

Minsky, H.P. (1977), 'A theory of systematic financial instability', in E.I. Altman and A.W. Sametz (eds), *Financial Crisis: Institutions and Markets in a Fragile Environment*, New York: Wiley, pp. 138–52.

Moen, H. (2004), 'The present value of central government investments in and support to Norwegian banks', in T.G. Moe, J.A. Solheim and B. Vale (eds), *The Norwegian Banking Crisis*, Norges Bank's Occasional Papers, no. 33, Oslo.

Obstfeld, M. (1996), 'Models of currency crisis with self-fulfilling features', *European Economic Review*, **40**, 1037–47.

Ongena, S., D.C. Smith and D. Michalsen (2003), 'Firms and their distressed banks: lessons from the Norwegian banking crisis (1988–91)', *Journal of Financial Economics*, **67**, 81–112.

Revell, J. (1986), 'The complementary nature of competition and regulation in the financial sector', in E.P.M. Gardener (ed.), *UK Banking Supervision: Evolution, Practice and Issues*, London: Allen & Unwin.

Scharfstein, D. and J. Stein (1990), 'Herd behavior and investment', *American Economic Review*, **80**, 465–79.

Shiller, R.J. (2000), *Irrational Exuberance*, Princeton, NJ: Princeton University Press.

Shiller, R.J. (2003), 'Diverse views of asset bubbles', in W.C. Hunter, G.G. Kaufman and M. Pomerleano (eds), *Asset price bubbles: the implications for monetary, regulatory and international policies*, Cambridge, MA: MIT Press.

Steffensen, E. and E. Steigum (1991), 'Penge- og kredittpolitikk, konjunkturer og bankkrise' (Monetary and credit policy, business cycles and banking crisis), in A.J. Isachsen (ed.), *Penger, kreditt og valuta*, Oslo: Universitetsforlaget.

Steigum, E. (1980), 'Norsk penge- og kredittpolitikk i perspektiv' (Perspectives on Norwegian monetary and credit policy), *Sosialøkonomen*, **34** (10), 15–22.

Steigum, E. (1983), 'Capital shortage and classical unemployment', *International Economic Review*, **24**, 461–73.

Steigum, E. (1992), 'Financial deregulation, credit boom and banking crisis: the case of Norway', Discussion Paper, 15/92, Norwegian School of Economics and Business Administration, Bergen. Translated into Finnish and published in *PTT Katsaus*, **4**, 10–31 (1992).

Steigum, E. (2004), 'Financial deregulation with a fixed exchange rate: lessons from Norway's boom–bust cycle and banking crisis', in T.G. Moe, J.A. Solheim and B. Vale (eds), *The Norwegian Banking Crisis*, Norges Bank's Occasional Papers, no. 33, Oslo, Chapter 2.

Steigum, E. and Ø. Thøgersen (2003), 'Borrow and adjust: fiscal policy and sectoral adjustment in an open economy', *International Economic Review*, **44**, 699–724.

Sveen, T. (2000), 'Tayloring the Norwegian interest rates', essay 3 in 'Five essays on credibility, monetary policy rules and inflation targeting', doctoral dissertation, Norwegian School of Economics and Business Administration, Bergen.

Svensson, L.E.O., K. Houg, H.O. Solheim and E. Steigum (2002), *An Independent Evaluation of Monetary Policy and Institutions in Norway*, Centre for Monetary Economics, Norwegian School of Management BI, Oslo.

Tornell, A. and F. Westermann (2002), 'Boom–bust cycles in middle income countries: facts and explanation', CESifo Working paper, no. 755, July.

Vale, B. (2002), 'Firms' inventory investments, financial condition and banking crisis', in I. Hasan and W.C. Hunter (eds), *Research in Banking and Finance*, vol. 2, Amsterdam, London and New York: Elsevier Science.

Vale, B. (2004), 'The Norwegian banking crisis', in T.G. Moe, J.A. Solheim and B. Vale (eds), *The Norwegian Banking Crisis*, Norges Bank's Occasional Papers, no. 33, Oslo, Chapter 1.

Wilse, P. (2004), 'Management of the banking crisis and state ownership of commercial banks', in T.G. Moe, J.A. Solheim and B. Vale (eds), *The Norwegian Banking Crisis*, Norges Bank's Occasional Papers, no. 33, Oslo, Chapter 6.

Wohlin, L. (1998), 'Bankkrisens upprinnelse' (The origin of the banking crisis), *Ekonomisk Debatt*, **26**, 21–30.

8. How did Denmark avoid a banking crisis?

Claus Vastrup

INTRODUCTION[1]

The financial situation of Danish commercial banks deteriorated in the late 1980s, and the problems peaked in the early 1990s. This was the first time since the Second World War with more than isolated problems in financial institutions, but the problematic situation never developed into a systemic crisis comparable to the banking crises in the other Nordic countries. Denmark did not experience bank failures to the same extent as Finland, Norway and Sweden as only a couple of small banks went bankrupt. Nor did the unfavorable conditions in the financial sector upset the macroeconomic situation in Denmark as the banking problems did in the other Nordic countries.

This chapter explains how Denmark avoided a banking crisis like those of the other Nordic countries in the early 1990s even though Denmark was affected by the same European economic environment as its Nordic neighbors, that is, high economic growth in 1988–89, mixed performance and tensions in 1990–91 when Germany was unified, and the European recession and exchange rate crisis in 1992–93. The chapter is arranged as follows. First, I review some results from the literature on banking crises. Second, an overview of the problems of the Danish banking sector 1984–94 is given. Third, I search for microeconomic contributions to an explanation of the Danish record. Here the Danish record is compared with those of the other Nordic countries. Next, Danish macroeconomic developments are reviewed and interpreted. Finally, my conclusions on Denmark, relative to the other Nordic countries, are given.

8.1 EMPIRICAL EVIDENCE ON BANKING CRISES

There is no single, widely accepted definition of a financial crisis. One definition suggests that a 'financial crisis is a disruption to financial markets in which adverse selection and moral hazard problems become much worse, so that these markets are unable to efficiently channel funds to those who have the most productive investment opportunities' (Mishkin, 2001; see also 1999). Such crises go together with an increase in the number of insolvencies, higher interest rates (or margins) and more uncertainty among some or most participants in the financial markets. A banking crisis is a financial crisis where the banking system is at the center of the disruptions.

Following the resurgence of banking crises in the 1990s, several studies have tried to find explanatory variables or indicators of these crises, some using data from both developed and emerging markets and some using data only from emerging markets. The explanatory variables can be divided into macroeconomic variables and microeconomic variables related to the banking system. Often, the interaction of more variables explains or increases the probability of a banking crisis. Further, the possibility of multiple equilibria in relevant models makes it more difficult to explain and predict banking crises. It follows that it is also difficult to explain the absence of a banking crisis.

Many macroeconomic studies find that a low or declining rate of economic growth, a reduction in a high level of inflation, a high real interest rate and turbulence in the foreign exchange markets may explain crises in the banking sector. In addition, the list of explanatory variables includes a preceding strong expansion in bank lending ('a credit boom'), low reserves (or high level of loans) relative to the liabilities (or deposits) of the banking system, precipitous financial liberalization, inadequate prudential supervision, and weaknesses in the legal and institutional framework. See Eichengreen and Arteta (2000) and Gorton and Winton (2002) for a review of historical episodes and early empirical evidence and Demirgüc-Kunt and Detragiache (2005) for a more recent review.

Theory and empirical results suggest that the connection between exchange rate regimes and banking crises depends on the source of the shocks. Conversely, the effects of shocks vary with the exchange rate regime. Accordingly, and contrary to assertions by advocates of fixed and flexible rates alike, it is not easy to find clear evidence on the relation between exchange rate regimes and banking crises, at least not for developing countries. See Eichengreen and Arteta (2000).

Banking crises generally precede currency crises while financial liberalization often precedes banking crises, according to Kaminsky and Reinhart (1999). In addition, a recent study by Domac and Peria (2003) using a comprehensive cross-country dataset including both developed and developing countries for the past two decades finds that a pegged exchange rate regime diminishes the likelihood of a banking crisis, at least for developing countries. However, once it occurs, the costs associated with a crisis appear to be larger in countries with a fixed rather than a flexible exchange rate.

The costs of banking crises to society can be substantial, in terms of unemployment, loss of output and government expenditures. Hoggarth et al. (2002) conclude that the average cumulative output losses of a banking crisis are 15–20 per cent of annual GDP, usually much higher in the event of a twin crisis, defined as a banking and a currency crisis occurring simultaneously. Honohan and Klingebiel (2003) find that government losses depend significantly on whether the policies of the crisis resolution have been strict or accommodating, the latter being far more costly. In addition, Chapter 5 in this volume concludes that the Finnish and Swedish twin crises of the early 1990s were very costly seen in an historical perspective.

Hutchison's (2002) study of 90, including 18 Western European, countries over the period 1975–97 makes a distinction between banking distress and banking crises, where the first includes the latter, which are defined to be only the large disruptions with systemic failures and risks in the banking sector. Regarding Western Europe, the study has less success in predicting banking crises (only four cases, namely Finland, Norway, Sweden and Spain) than banking distress. However, the results suggest that these banking crises in Europe 'were not so much related to legal and institutional characteristics as to macroeconomic and, perhaps, idiosyncratic factors' (Hutchison, 2002, p. 381). The legal and institutional characteristics referred to are bank regulation and supervision, accounting standards and other characteristics of the financial system, which are usually assumed to 'bear directly on the extent to which government guarantees and moral hazard translate into higher risk-taking on the part of banks' (Hutchison, 2002, p. 369).

The characteristics used by Hutchison (2002) do not include bank capital (or capital requirements for banks). However, differences in this respect between Denmark and the other Nordic countries in the 1980s and the early 1990s were important. Further, leaving out bank capital is contrary to the idea in many analytical models of bank lending and deposit assigning capital requirements an important role in the determination of prudent bank behavior.

Hellmann et al. (2000) analyze the interaction between the regulation of capital requirement and the public control of deposit rates in a dynamic context. One motivation is that empirical observations suggest that liberalizations of financial markets are often followed by financial crises. The authors show that increasing capital requirements will reduce the banks' incentives to take excessive risks or to gamble by putting their equity at risk. Further, competition among banks has a negative effect by harming their franchise values, that is, the discounted stream of future profits, thus encouraging gambling by banks. Accordingly, a competitive situation without (or with low) franchise values but with a high (cost of) capital requirement for the banks can be improved upon by adding a public regulation in the form of a ceiling for deposit rates (or another relevant regulation). The purpose should be to decrease competition and increase the franchise values of the banks. An improvement of welfare will then follow from a decrease in the size (and cost) of the capital requirement leaving unchanged the original level of gambling. Consequently, if a (optimal) ceiling for deposit rates is abolished, the capital requirement for banks should be increased to keep gambling or risk-taking constant. None of the Nordic countries did so when they abolished their regulation of bank deposit rates in the early 1980s.[2]

Bolt and Tieman (2004) use a dynamic model where banks compete for customers by setting acceptance criteria for the granting of loans. They find that more stringent capital requirements lead to stricter acceptance behavior. As in Hellmann et al. (2000), more competition among banks following a change to less stringent capital requirements leads to more risky bank behavior. Again, for a given risk of bank failure there is a trade-off between the capital requirement and the degree of competition.

Boyd and De Nicoló (2005), introducing moral hazard on the part of the borrower-entrepreneurs, show that if banks take the behavior of their customers into account when setting the interest rates for loans, more competition (with lower interest rates) leads to less risky activity by banks. They conclude that neither the analytical nor the empirical literature lends strong support for a positive relationship between competition and risk-seeking by banks. Moving further, Schaeck et al. (2006) present evidence that a more competitive banking system is less prone to systemic crises also when controlled for concentration and the regulatory environment.

Morrison and White (2005) analyze a general equilibrium model with moral hazard and adverse selection on the part of banks. They examine the role of a regulator in the auditing of the banks and in setting capital requirements to prevent crises. The capital requirements on their part determine the size of the banks and restrict the banks to being smaller than otherwise optimal. They show that if public confidence in the regulator's (or the accounting procedures') ability to detect bad banks is sufficiently high, crises will never occur. On the other hand, if the reputation of the regulator is poor, the regulator has several policy options with respect to the capital requirements. Other things being equal, poor regulators (or accounting procedures) must always pursue a tighter capital regulation policy than good regulators (or procedures). In addition, an independent shift from optimism to pessimism in the agents' expectations of the quality of the applicants for banking licenses may trigger a crisis of confidence, but again only if the reputation of the regulator is poor.

The overall conclusion is that banking crises are costly, but in most cases are not caused by a single factor. The explanation for a crisis seems to involve the interaction between factors related to macroeconomic instability and factors related to the banking system such as a credit boom, low bank reserves, poor accounting procedures and in most cases a low level of bank capital.

8.2 BANKING PROBLEMS IN DENMARK 1984–94

In the period 1984–94, the number of banks in Denmark decreased by roughly 70, from about 270 to 202 banks. The number of banks that went out of business was higher as slightly less than 20 new banks were established during this period. A total of 142 banks were involved in 75 mergers or acquisitions. According to an estimate by the Danish Financial Services Authority, 40 of these mergers and acquisitions involved an equal number of banks with crisis symptoms. The mergers of these crisis-ridden banks were with other and better capitalized banks. The banks closed without being acquired by or merged with other banks accounted for less than 10 per cent of the balances of all banks. Only five smaller banks (including three very small co-operative banks) went bankrupt without having their activities transferred to other banks. Only 37 per cent of the deposits (owned by 7 per cent of the depositors) of these institutions were lost; the rest were refunded by the deposit insurance scheme. Between 1/3 and 2/3 (approximately) of the capital of the five banks was lost. Some of the lost capital was the property of the co-operative banks. It is reasonable to assume that the merger activity of the period made the overall banking sector more resilient as the number of bank failures was reduced and concentration in the banking system increased.

The number of bankruptcies corresponds to the number of public rescue operations in the period, but not all of the banks rescued in this way went into bankruptcy. The rescue operations took place in 1984, 1987 and 1993–94.[3] In 1992, the Danish central bank formally announced that it was prepared to support the second largest bank with liquidity, following rumors of bankruptcy. The liquidity scheme might have discouraged speculators from attempting a 'bank run', but the most important reassurance at the time was probably the simultaneous declarations by the central bank and the Financial Services Authority that the rumors were unfounded. The bank never made use of the liquidity scheme, which was terminated in 1995.

A prime source of information on the reasons for the bank failures and other changes in the banking structure is the annual accounts of the Danish banks. The banks in total had an overall surplus before taxes in only half of the years 1984–94. In 1986, a deficit was due primarily to losses on bond and equity holdings. In 1990 and 1991, the deficits were minor, but the losses and loss provisions on lending increased to a high level. In 1992, the losses on bond and equity holdings together with higher losses and loss provisions on lending added up to the highest deficit of the period on the overall accounts of the banks. In 1993, the losses and loss provisions were still very high, but a decline in long-term market rates of interest turned both the result of bond (and equity) holdings and the overall result of the banks into a surplus. In 1994, the losses and loss provisions on lending declined and, even though the banks incurred some losses on bond and equity holdings, the overall result was zero. In short, the problems had passed away.

The Danish banks had the highest deficit in 1992 and the highest losses and loss provisions in the years 1991–93. The accumulated losses and loss provisions for the three years were a little more than 9 per cent of total bank lending and a little above 5 per cent of GDP. This made 1991–93 the most problematic period for the banks after the Second World War. Nevertheless, the total public support (excluding repayments) for Danish banks in crises over the three years was only 0.4 per cent of GDP. The greater part of the support was a loan to a bank fully repaid later. Almost no deposits were lost. Most of the costs of the banking problems were paid by the banking sector itself. Except for the banks directly involved, this happened after the government put some pressure on other banks to do so. However, as most of the problems were solved within the banking sector and without major disruptions to outsiders, the situation of Danish banks in the early 1990s should be classified not as a banking crisis but as a banking distress.[4]

The registered losses and loss provisions of Danish banks in the period 1991–93 were at the same level compared with GDP as in Norway, but smaller than in Finland, and much smaller than in Sweden. Compared with bank balances, the Danish loss and loss provisions were smaller than in Finland, Norway and Sweden. Further, public support for the Danish banks was far less than for the banks in any of the other Nordic countries. Seen in this perspective the banking sector financed more losses and loss provisions in Sweden (6.4 per cent of GDP) and Denmark (4.8 per cent) than in Norway (2.0 per cent) and Finland (1.7 per cent) (Table 8.1). As almost no Danish banks went bankrupt, it follows that the banks were more highly capitalized in Denmark than in at least Finland and Norway, where most of the banking sector had to be taken over by the government.[5]

Table 8.1 *Losses, loss provisions and public support for commercial banks in the Nordic countries, 1991–93*

	Losses and loss provisions 1991–93				Public support 1991–93(1)	
	In billions, national currency units	In per cent of lending	In per cent of GDP	In per cent of balances	In billions, national currency units	In per cent of GDP
Denmark(2)	44.5	9.1	5.2	4.5	3.9	0.4
Sweden	151.6	17.9	10.5	10.1	65.0	4.1
Norway	39.2	8.4	5.6	6.6	25.0	3.6
Finland	46.4	13.1	9.8	6.2	38.6	8.1

Notes: Accumulated figures.
(1) Actual support paid out; for Sweden and Denmark until end of September 1994, for Denmark repayments excluded.
(2) Excluding the Faroe Islands.

Source: Danish Ministry of Economic Affairs (1994).

The same kind of reasoning and results apply to the Swedish banking sector compared with Norway and Finland, even if part of the Swedish banking had to be supported by public funds. A comparison of Danish and Swedish banks, which were the best capitalized of the Nordic banks, is not possible from the information given.

8.3 MICROECONOMIC DEVELOPMENTS IN DENMARK

Except for the capitalization of banks relative to their losses and loss provisions, it is possible to mention only very few, if any, banking-specific circumstances or microeconomic factors known from the literature that, fully developed or in a more unfavorable situation, might have caused a banking crisis in Denmark in the early 1990s. I review these factors in this section.

An insurance scheme for bank deposits was first set up following the bankruptcy of a minor bank in 1987. In the period under review, ordinary deposits were insured up to DKK 250 000 per depositor and some special deposits in total. The scheme was and is financed by contributions from the banks only, but when the bill setting up the scheme was introduced in the parliament, comments close to a government guarantee were given. In principle, excessive risk-taking due to this government guarantee might have taken place in the early 1990s. On the other hand, the high level of bank capital and reserves of Danish banks (see below) and the moderate and restricted coverage of the deposit insurance scheme make it unlikely that moral hazard would have induced banks to make highly risky loans to a great extent. In fact, only small amounts were refunded by the deposit insurance scheme in the early 1990s. However, the Danish Financial Services Authority used the scheme as an argument for its interventions and proposals to merge banks exposed to crises.

All entries on the balance sheets of Danish banks (including bonds and equities) are at market values for 'a going concern'. Losses and loss provisions are deducted from the accounts of the individual customer not only when a loss is realized or registered (bankruptcy, collection of debt and so on) but until 2005 as soon as a loss was recognized as a possibility. Loss provisions are transferred to a special off-balance-sheet account. As from 1994, the two kinds of loss provision (realized/registered and recognized) are registered separately. If no longer necessary, a loss provision shall be cancelled and the original account re-established.

Loss provisions by banks are made (at least until 2005) at an earlier stage in a downturn and more comprehensively in Denmark than in the other Nordic countries. Therefore, the off-balance-sheet accounts for loss provisions in Denmark, ceteris paribus, are larger or of better quality, that is, with a smaller probability of eventually having to be written off. In addition, the size of the losses and the loss provisions depends on the point of time when a realized loss is formally registered as a loss, no longer being registered as a loss provision, but in this respect no differences are to be expected between the Nordic countries. The different rules and practices make the de facto differences for losses and loss provisions between Denmark and the other Nordic countries even larger than registered in the recessions of the early 1990s (as in Table 8.1). Consequently, the de facto capitalization of the banks was higher in Denmark than in the other Nordic countries (or at least in Finland and Norway).

A bank's ability to incur losses (and loss provisions) without going bankrupt depends on the gross income and the registered capital (including the formal reserves) of the bank. In this respect, the Danish banking law was changed in 1989 to accommodate the new EU (and Basel 1) rules on capital adequacy requirements. Accordingly, the Danish rules changed radically from the beginning of 1991. The new basis for calculating the capital requirements was the assets on and off the balance sheet of the banks weighted to some extent according to their risk. As from the beginning of the same year, the possibility was introduced of using supplementary capital for banks.

The new basis for capital requirements was on average about 30 per cent lower than the former basis (the total balance of the banks). Therefore, the solvency ratio was 11.7 per cent in 1991 according to the new rules compared with about 8 per cent in mid-1990 according to the former rules. Further, the capital requirement was reduced from 10 per cent of the new basis in 1991–92 to 9 per cent in 1993–94, and further to its present level of 8 per cent in 1995. Therefore, the formal excess capital of the banks was 1.7 per cent in 1991. This ratio gradually increased to 3.5 per cent in 1993 as the banks issued new capital and in particular reduced their assets weighted according to risk.[6] In general, Danish banks experienced no problems with the official capital adequacy requirements either before or after the changes of the rules.

The microeconomic factors that are the most important in explaining why Denmark avoided a banking crisis in the early 1990s are probably two. First, Danish banks had at least de facto more capital, due to more stringent rules for loss provisions and capital requirements, than banks in the other Nordic countries. Second, Danish banks had smaller actual losses and loss provisions, at least compared with Finnish and Swedish banks. Probably, the smaller losses were due to the more favorable overall economic conditions in Denmark at the end of the 1980s and in the early 1990s.

8.4 MACROECONOMIC DEVELOPMENTS AND POLICIES IN DENMARK

Following the turbulent 1970s, the second OPEC increase of oil prices in 1979 and the international recession in the following three years turned the Danish economy into a recession with negative growth rates in 1980–81 and increasing and unusually high unemployment reaching more than 8 per cent in 1982–83. At the same time, the current account was in deficit with 3–4 per cent of GDP (Figure 8.1). As Denmark had experienced deficits since 1963, the net foreign debt was about 30 per cent of GDP in the early 1980s. Part of the debt was the consequence of the deliberate government policy in the latter part of the 1970s of trying to increase employment through an expansionary fiscal policy and to improve the current account by several devaluations of the Danish currency. Therefore, in the early 1980s inflation was running at an annual rate of more than 11 per cent. At the same time, the spread of the interest rate against Germany was 10–12 per cent for long-term bonds. The absolute level of the Danish interest rate on the same bonds reached more than 20 per cent in 1982 (Figure 8.2). Compared with those of the other Nordic countries in the early 1980s, the Danish recession was deeper and the unemployment was higher.

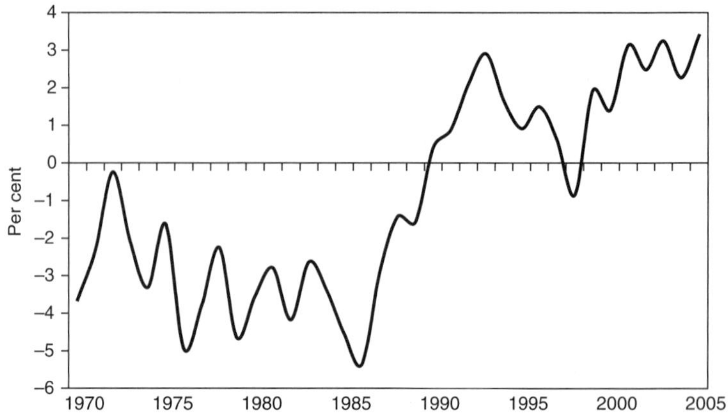

Figure 8.1 The current account of Denmark, 1970–2005 (per cent of GDP)

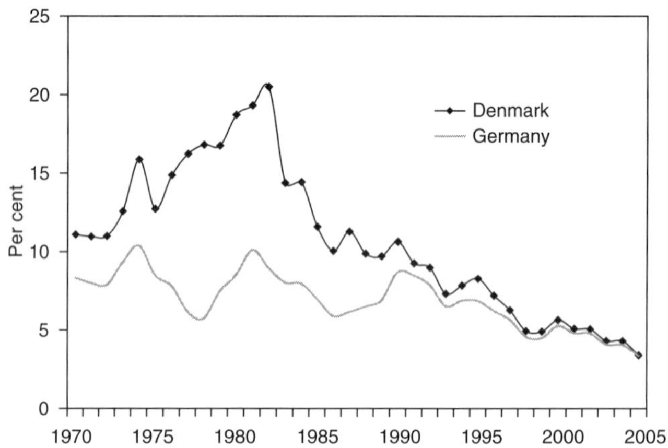

Figure 8.2 Nominal long-term interest rates in Denmark and Germany, 1970–2005 (per cent)

The recession and the very high interest rates made it possible for the Danish government and the Danish central bank in 1980 to terminate more than ten years of quantitative regulation of the credit market. The quantitative regulation of the commercial banks had been initially in the form of absolute limits for the total lending of individual banks. The central bank set the limits and the original purpose was to reduce both the economic activity and the market interest rates. However, the quantitative limits on bank lending increased the margin between the lending rates and the deposit rates of the commercial banks. Consequently, the limits on bank lending were later augmented with individual maxima for the commercial banks (determined by the history of the individual bank) for the margin between their average lending rate and their average deposit rate. Further, the two regulations were later augmented with individual maxima for the average deposit rate of the individual bank, which were even later substituted by individual maxima for the average lending rate of the individual bank.

Following the termination of the quantitative regulation of bank lending in 1980, the authorities abolished all the regulations on the interest rates of the banks in 1981. In addition, most of the quantitative regulations on new lending of the mortgage institutions were cancelled. Thus, Denmark liberalized its financial markets and its banking sector about five years earlier than Finland, Norway and Sweden. See Chapters 3 and 7 in this volume.

In the autumn of 1982, a new Danish government declared its adherence to a fixed exchange rate policy (within the EMS). Subsequently, the parliament suspended the general regulation of nominal wages according to changes in an index of consumer prices. In 1983, fiscal policy was tightened, and the exchange rate was kept unchanged although some other EMS countries, among them France, devalued their currencies. Subsequently, the interest rate on long-term bonds declined from more than 20 per cent in 1982 to almost 14 per cent in 1983 as especially the commercial banks increased their bond holdings (Figure 8.2). At the same time, the authorities abolished most restrictions on foreign capital movements, but, due to already existing even if restricted possibilities for capital movements, the fall in the market interest rates was the consequence of the new credibility of the fixed exchange rate policy rather than the free movements of capital between the domestic and foreign capital markets. An improvement in the international conditions, the lower interest rates and expectations of stability and improved general conditions following the tightening of fiscal policy all led to a strong increase in domestic demand and production. Inflation fell rapidly and strongly from above 11 per cent in 1981–82 to 4 per cent in 1986. In the same period unemployment fell by 3.5 percentage points and reached a low level of 5 per cent in 1986, which was only a little above the level of 1979, the year of the second OPEC increase of oil prices (see Vastrup (1989) for an explanation).

The higher level of domestic demand in 1986 increased the deficit on the current account to 5.5 per cent of GDP (Figure 8.1). The net foreign debt rose to almost 40 per cent of GDP. Therefore, the government and the parliament decided to tighten fiscal policy partly by reducing the tax rate for deductions in taxable income made on net interest expenditure on debt owned by private persons by slightly over 20 percentage points. The fiscal policy was rather tight in the following years. In 1990, a small surplus appeared on the current account for the first time in more than 25 years. The improvement of the current account continued until 1993 when a surplus of 3 per cent of GDP was registered.

Overall, the current account improved by more than 8 per cent of GDP from 1986 to 1993. In the same period, Denmark's competitive position did not improve – among other reasons, due to devaluations of the Finnish and Swedish currencies. Consequently, unemployment in Denmark gradually increased. When international economic conditions deteriorated in 1992–93, unemployment reached more than 9 per cent of the labor force. Due to the high and increasing unemployment and following a change towards a somewhat looser fiscal policy in 1992, a new government turned to an expansive fiscal policy in 1993 and particularly in 1994. The GDP growth rate picked up to 5.5 per cent, which was the highest in Europe for 1994 (except for Ireland), and the highest rate in Denmark for a long time. The fiscal expansion was supported by a decline in both the short-term and long-term interest rates. In the following six years, unemployment fell by more than half to almost 4 per cent. This happened without the emergence of deficits on the current account, except for 1998.

The Danish currency was part of the currency crisis of the EMS in 1992–93. In early 1993, the fixed exchange rate of the Danish currency came under pressure on the foreign exchange markets following an Irish devaluation in January the same year. This was shortly after the above-mentioned change of government in Denmark. However, the pressure on the exchange rate of the Danish currency disappeared following the central bank's increase of the over-night rate of interest to 90 per cent per annum, a coordinated intervention on the exchange market by Denmark and other EMS countries and finally a declaration by the new government that the fixed exchange rate policy would be maintained.

In the summer of 1993, further currency speculation took place within the EMS, mostly due to economic tensions in the market between France and Germany. In August 1993, the EMS countries suspended the fixed exchange rates among European currencies, in practice switching to floating exchange rates (fixed exchange rates with a very wide band). The suspension included the Danish currency, which immediately depreciated by 8–9 per cent against the *Deutschmark*, but afterwards gradually appreciated towards its former parity. The Danish exchange rate stabilized close to its former parity against the *Deutschmark* at the end of 1993. In the following years stability prevailed except for a few periods with minor unrest on the currency market.

8.5 WHY DID DENMARK TURN AROUND?

The Danish economy was in a precarious situation in the very early 1980s. Unemployment was high, deficits on the current account were large, inflation was running high, the currency had been devalued several times and the interest rate was very high. For these reasons and due to an expansionary fiscal policy and public sector deficits, Danish economic policy faced a serious credibility problem.

Credibility returned gradually from 1982–83 when fiscal policy was tightened and the fixed exchange rate policy was re-established. These policy changes were introduced, even though unemployment was high and Denmark had large deficits on the current account, because they were necessary to re-introduce a stable assignment of policy instruments, requiring a given instrument to be assigned to the target upon which the instrument has the relatively greatest impact.

For a small, open economy with a pegged exchange rate, a stable assignment implies that demand management (that is, fiscal policy) has to be assigned to focus on the current account, and expenditure switching (that is, changes in wage setting and the structure or flexibility of the labor market) shall be assigned to focus on (domestic) production and employment. In addition, the credible fixed exchange rate policy removed the inflation and devaluation bias of the previous years. The peg could serve as a nominal anchor as the exchange rate had no longer to take care of the (poor) domestic employment situation, instead tying the Danish rate of inflation in the long run to that of the other EMS countries, in short to the German inflation.

Fiscal policy was not tightened any further when the deficit on the current account increased in 1985. As economic developments were misinterpreted and the (re-)established assignment was not fully understood, the government tried for a short while by law to set an upper limit of 2 per cent for the annual increase in wages. This was too low given the employment situation. Instead of the current account improving as intended, both domestic demand and employment increased together with the deficit on the current account. When this was realized, fiscal policy was tightened in the course of 1986 so that the proper assignment and economic stability were re-established. The mistake was a short one, but long enough for the growth rate of nominal wages to increase.

From 1987 onwards, restrictive fiscal policy steadily turned the deficit on the current account into a surplus. Unemployment increased, but the assignment was stable and without the former devaluation bias. In 1993–94, the surplus on the current account (or rather the stability in the foreign exchange market due to the proper assignment) made it possible to relax fiscal policy. The declared purpose was to increase employment, but the financial markets, judged by the low spreads of the Danish against the German interest rate, were convinced that fiscal policy would be used not again to pursue an (excessive) employment target in a situation of conflict, but (only) to stabilize the current account in accordance with the proper assignment. Credibility prevailed and, following gradual reform of the labor market, cautious demand management reduced unemployment in the second part of the 1990s to a level below that of most other European countries.

Summing up, fiscal policy has been the only macroeconomic policy instrument used actively and the fixed exchange rate has been the anchor of the price level since the early 1980s. In a situation of conflict between internal and external stability, fiscal policy has had an external orientation at least since 1986. In the later stage of the process towards both stabilization of the current account/foreign debt and full employment, the newly established credibility of the fixed exchange rate policy allowed fiscal policy to turn expansionary in 1993–94 due to the large surplus on the current account. Without being recognized widely at the time, the fiscal expansion of 1993–94 ended the period of distress in the financial sector.

8.6 DID MACROECONOMIC FORCES CAUSE INSTABILITY IN THE FINANCIAL SECTOR?

There is no indication that the European currency crises in 1992–93 and Denmark's short-term deviation from the fixed exchange regime impacted on the stability of either the Danish economy or the Danish banking sector. Due to a tight monetary policy and the regulation of Danish banks, only the private non-banking sector and the government carried out foreign borrowing necessary to finance the foreign debt accumulated during the long period with deficits on the current account. Mainly domestic deposits and domestic borrowing funded the banks. In addition, following a reduction in the rate of increase of nominal wages since the late 1980s, the profit margins of the firms in the non-banking sector were in no serious need of a devaluation of the Danish currency. As foreign and especially domestic demand increased due to the fiscal expansion of 1993–94, the commercial banks were able to reduce their losses and loss provisions.

In a longer perspective, the fixed exchange rate and the external orientation of fiscal policy have been instrumental in bringing about macroeconomic stability in Denmark after the precarious situation in the early 1980s. Probably, the economy would have performed worse had Denmark had a floating or semi-fixed exchange rate with the possibility of the government (and the central bank) devaluing the currency now and then. As Denmark is a small, open economy, both regimes would have exposed the many industries depending on foreign markets to volatility in production and employment and all industries to volatility in the value of their foreign debt, due to speculation in the foreign exchange and other financial markets. The weight of this argument is increased by the lack of stability and the inflation-devaluation bias of a small, open economy with a record of deficits on the current account since 1963 and several devaluations in the late 1970s and early 1980s.

Even if other kinds of shocks to the economy have occasionally emerged and could have been destabilizing with less than a firmly fixed exchange rate, financial shocks and speculation would have caused important disturbances for a small, open economy with foreign debt and an inflation-devaluation bias like the Danish economy. This was an important argument at the time for having a fixed exchange rate towards a stable currency like the *Deutschmark*, that is, using the exchange rate as the nominal anchor. The external orientation of fiscal policy from the mid-1980s was a necessary condition for the overall stabilization and for the fixed exchange rate, but probably the external orientation of fiscal policy alone would not have been sufficient to bring about overall stability with the exchange rate being flexible or pegged but adjustable.

The two most important threats to the stability of the banking system from a macroeconomic point of view emanated from the low rate of economic growth from 1987 to 1993 and the reduction of real property prices in the same period. The growth rate of GDP was positive in all the years (except in 1993), but on average a little below 1 per cent per year. Accordingly, even if the rate of economic growth was low and unemployment increased, the economic growth rate was rather stable. This stability reduced the number and the size of unforeseen events.

The price deflation of owner-occupied housing and real property in general was probably a greater threat to the stability of the financial sector. The prices of the first category peaked in 1986 and declined in nominal terms until 1993, but only slowly by an average of 2 per cent per year. The prices of non-residential buildings developed even more gradually with a maximum in 1989. The decline in the prices of real property caused troubles for the mortgage institutions, especially those exposed to the housing market, but the problems only showed up for a few of the commercial banks. Consequently, the small and gradual reduction in the property price did not lead to a general or systemic crisis in the Danish banking sector. The independent mortgage institutions took most of the losses.

The different development of property prices in Denmark and the other Nordic countries is probably a very important factor in explaining the divergent developments in the banking sector across the Nordics. The volatility of property prices was lower in Denmark than in the other Nordic countries, especially in Finland and Sweden.[7] These divergences are due to a large extent to differences with respect to macroeconomic policies, the exception being the reductions in the tax treatment of private net interest expenditure, often closely related to the prices of owner-occupied houses and dwellings. The reduction of this tax rate was more cautious in Denmark than in the other Nordic countries.

As mentioned above, the quantitative restrictions on bank lending were lifted in Denmark in 1980. The same happened in 1981 to various restrictions on the commercial banks' setting of their interest rates. Liberalizing restrictions on lending before the restrictions on the margin between the deposit and lending rates might have given rise to an increase in bank lending. However, the immediate reactions were minimal, as the restrictions were not binding, largely due to the recession at the time of liberalization. The annual growth rate of bank lending was almost unchanged at 10 per cent in the three years 1980–82.

The growth rate of bank lending increased gradually to 28–29 per cent in 1985–86. This happened in a period with falling interest rates and a booming economy. Therefore, part of the increase in bank lending was a 'normal' reaction to the business cycle and part of it a catching-up process to re-establish a proper share for the business of commercial banks in the financial system. The catching-up part of the explanation is supported by the fact that domestic lending by banks increased from about 30 per cent of GDP in 1980–82 to 42 per cent of GDP in 1986 and stabilized around that level throughout the rest of the 1980s.

Even with such a catching-up in the level of bank lending, it is reasonable to assume that the ten years of market-based lending after 1980–81 were sufficient for the commercial banks to have normalized fully the credit rating of customers. Bank loans of low quality due to the previous restrictions gradually disappeared before the end of the 1980s. Therefore, the big losses and loss provisions in the early 1990s were not a postscript to the credit restrictions of the 1970s. Rather, the losses and loss provisions of Danish banks in 1991–93 were the consequence of a long period with low economic growth and the standard rules at the time requiring banks to be cautious and make loss provisions as soon as a loss appeared as a possibility. This conclusion is supported by the fact that the annual growth rates for bank lending fell to between 5 and 10 per cent in the late 1980s and were zero or negative in the early 1990s.

The liberalization of the quantitative restrictions on bank lending is not a sufficient condition to explain a banking crisis according to the Danish experience. This is different from the conclusions found in Chapters 2 and 3 of this volume on the Swedish and Finnish experiences and the conclusions in Chapter 7 on the Norwegian experience of financial liberalization. In addition to the higher capitalization of the Danish banks, the reason for the different conclusions on this issue might be the difference between the timing of the liberalization relative to the business cycle in Denmark and the timing in the other Nordic countries. The Danish financial deregulation came in the middle of a recession and several years prior to the next period with almost no economic growth.

8.7 CONCLUSIONS

Even if Denmark in the early 1990s experienced considerable problems in the banking sector for the first time since the Second World War, the situation never deteriorated to the same extent as in the other Nordic countries. Denmark did not face a deep financial crisis. This relative stability can be explained by circumstances related both to the Danish banking sector and to Danish macroeconomic conditions and policies.

From 1980–81, the Danish central bank used neither quantitative restrictions for the lending of the commercial banks nor restrictions on their setting of interest rates for lending and deposits, as was the case in the 1970s. The high growth rates of bank lending in the mid-1980s were probably, but only partly, due to an adjustment process following the abolishment of these quantitative restrictions. However, the banks' credit rating and risk management had enough time to adjust to a credit market without restrictions before the fiscal tightening and low economic growth rates of the late 1980s and early 1990s caused banks' losses and loss provisions to increase.

Consequently, the losses and loss provisions of banks before and during the early 1990s were not due to any extraordinary problems following financial liberalization. In addition, the capitalization of Danish banks was rather high and at least de facto higher than in the other Nordic countries. New capital requirements of the EU (and Basel 1) were introduced in Denmark during the period with high losses and loss provisions. On average, the new capital requirements were less stringent than the former Danish requirements. For this reason as well, Danish banks were well capitalized and had more capital than banks in the other Nordic countries.

The macroeconomic situation in Denmark in the early 1980s was one of instability with high unemployment and high inflation, as expansionary fiscal policy had been used to increase (or stabilize) employment and the currency had been devalued on several occasions to reduce the deficits on the current account. From 1982–83 or at least from 1986, a new assignment of the instrument of macroeconomic policy gradually turned the economic situation into one of stability based on a credible fixed exchange rate.

Especially, it was important that a rather tight fiscal policy and low economic growth turned the deficit on the current account into a surplus, which happened in 1990. In 1993–94, a surplus on the current account allowed Denmark to expand fiscal policy gradually and to increase domestic demand and employment without going into a deficit on the current account (except for 1998). This expansion ended the period of high losses and loss provisions of the financial sector in the early 1990s.

In spite of the fact that the period from 1987 to 1993 displayed very low, but stable, economic growth and slowly declining real property prices, the overall stabilization of the Danish economy was a necessary condition for the long-run health of the banking sector. Seen from this perspective, the sources of the banking problems of the early 1990s were the economic shocks stemming from the worldwide increases in oil prices and the legacy of destabilizing economic policies of the late 1970s and the early 1980s. Even if the stabilization was postponed until the mid-1980s, the reason why Denmark avoided a banking crisis following these events was the cautious change over several years to a proper assignment of fiscal policy to the stabilization of the current account and the foreign debt.

A policy of a fixed exchange rate was (re-)introduced in 1982–83. This policy would not have been sustainable without the proper assignment of fiscal policy to the current account a few years later. Due to the foreign debt of the private sector, a less cautious policy with one or more devaluations or a more vigorous or prolonged tightening of fiscal policy would probably have increased the losses and the loss provisions of the Danish banks. This might have moved the Danish banking sector into a deep crisis as in the other Nordic countries.

NOTES

1. I am grateful to Richard S. Grossmann and Lars Jonung for valuable comments.
2. Repullo (2003) shows that risk-based requirement for bank capital without binding ceilings for deposit rates will ensure prudent bank behavior. However, it was only in the early 1990s upon the implementation of Basel 1 that (partially) risk-based requirement was introduced at least in Denmark. See VanHoose (2007) for a review of some of the literature on bank capital regulation. The results are ambiguous with respect to the connection between risk-taking and bank capital requirements.
3. See Danish Ministry of Economic Affairs (1995).
4. This was not the case for the commercial banks on the Faroe Islands, which are not included in the discussion in this chapter. The Faroe Islands experienced a severe

banking crisis in 1992–93 as most of its banking sector faced huge losses and loss provisions and received public support on a large scale. A merger between the two main banks resulted in a predominant bank, which eventually was taken over by the authority of the Faroe Islands due to high losses and loss provisions. The reason for the banking crisis was a considerable reduction in the catch of fish, the most important industry on the islands, followed by a reduction of house prices, partly due to emigration from the Faroe Islands.

5. See Chapter 3 on Finland and Sweden and Chapter 7 on Norway.
6. See Danish Ministry of Economic Affairs (1994).
7. See Chapters 2, 3 and 7 in this volume.

REFERENCES

Bolt, W. and A.F. Tieman (2004), 'Banking competition, risk and regulation,' *Scandinavian Journal of Economics,* **106**, 783–804.

Boyd, J.H. and G. De Nicoló (2005), 'The theory of bank risk taking and competition revisited', *Journal of Finance,* **60**, 1329–43.

Danish Ministry of Economic Affairs (1994), *Den danske pengeinstitutsektor* (*The Danish banking sector*), Copenhagen.

Danish Ministry of Economic Affairs (1995), *Redning af pengeinstitutter siden 1984* (*The rescue of banks since 1984*), Copenhagen.

Demirgüc-Kunt, A. and E. Detragiache (2005), 'Cross-country empirical studies of systemic bank distress: a survey', IMF Working paper 05/96.

Domac, I. and M.S.M. Peria (2003), 'Banking crises and exchange rate regimes: is there a link?', *Journal of International Economics*, **61**, 41–72.

Eichengreen, B. and C. Arteta (2000), 'Banking crises in emerging markets: presumptions and evidence', from Barry Eichengreen's website, Research Papers.

Gorton, G. and A. Winston (2002), 'Financial intermediation', NBER Working paper, no. 8928.

Hellmann, T.F., K.C. Murdock and J.E. Stiglitz (2000), 'Liberalization, moral hazard in banking and prudential regulation: are capital requirements enough?', *American Economic Review*, **90**, 147–65.

Hoggarth, G., R. Reis and V. Saporta (2002), 'Cost of banking system instability: some empirical evidence', *Journal of Banking and Finance*, **26**, 825–55.

Honohan, P. and D. Klingebiel (2003), 'The fiscal cost implications of an accommodating approach to banking crises', *Journal of Banking and Finance*, **27**, 1539–60.

Hutchison, M.M. (2002), 'European banking distress and EMU: institutional and macroeconomic risks', *Scandinavian Journal of Economics,* **104**, 365–89.

Kaminsky, G.L. and C.M. Reinhart (1999), 'The twin crises: the causes of banking and balance-of-payments problems', *American Economic Review*, **89**, 473–500.

Mishkin, F.S. (1999), 'Global financial instability: framework, events, issues', *Journal of Economic Perspectives*, **13**, 3–20.

Mishkin, F.S. (2001), 'Financial policies and the prevention of financial crises in emerging market countries', NBER Working paper, no. 8087.

Morrison, A.D. and L. White (2005), 'Crises and capital requirements in banking', *American Economic Review*, **95**, 1548–72.

Repullo, R. (2003), 'Capital requirements, market power and risk-taking in banking', CEPR Working paper, no. 3721.

Schaeck, K., M. Cihák and S. Wolfe (2006), 'Are more competitive banking systems more stable?', IMF Working paper 06/143.

VanHoose, D. (2007), 'Theories of bank behavior under capital regulation', *Journal of Banking and Finance*, **31**, 3680–97.

Vastrup, C. (1989), 'Economic policy and adjustment in Denmark', in M. Monti (ed.), *Fiscal Policy, Economic Adjustment, and Financial Markets*, Washington, DC: IMF, Chapter 3.

9. The Nordic and Asian crises: common causes, different outcomes

Ari Kokko and Kenji Suzuki

INTRODUCTION

During the spring and early summer of 1997, there was widespread speculation against the Thai *baht*. The currency was closely tied to a basket dominated by the US dollar. The gradual appreciation of the dollar after the early 1990s had made the Thai *baht* more expensive, weakened export competitiveness, and contributed to a current account deficit of around 8 per cent of GDP. Worsening the problems related to the increasingly overvalued currency, there were also severe troubles in the financial sector. Asset prices had risen rapidly with an export boom that started in the late 1980s, but both real estate and stock market prices had collapsed when GDP and export growth rates had begun to slow in the mid-1990s. This left banks and finance companies with masses of non-performing loans (although it was not known at the time how serious this problem was). Most banks and financial institutions were also heavily exposed to currency risk. The high domestic interest rate needed to maintain the fixed exchange rate had made it favorable to borrow abroad. The financial sector was largely financed by Japanese and European investors.

While it was clear to many foreign observers that a currency adjustment would be necessary – for instance, in its consultations with the Thai government, the IMF had pressed for action already from the beginning of 1996 – most Thai observers seemed to believe that there was no need for any devaluation. The *baht* had maintained a stable value against the dollar since 1984, and the fixed rate was thought of as an anchor for macroeconomic stability. The overall growth rate of the economy was still respectable, at about 6 per cent. Moreover, the Central Bank had demonstrated its willingness to defend the currency, both by raising the interest rate and by spending considerable amounts from the foreign exchange reserves to support its fixed value.

Yet, by early July 1997, it was no longer possible to defend the fixed exchange rate. The reason was simply that the currency reserves had run dry: with few foreigners willing to invest fresh dollars in the economy, the Central Bank had been forced to use most of its foreign exchange on investors wanting to reduce their holdings of *baht*. On 2 July 1997, the Thai Central Bank announced that the *baht* would no longer be tied to the US dollar. It was left to float, and the intention was to manage a controlled depreciation of the currency.

Actually, the *baht* sank like a stone. In the following six months, the *baht* lost more than half of its value as the price of a US dollar increased from 25 *baht* to 56 *baht*. The Bangkok Stock Exchange fell by more than 30 per cent in local currency over the same period. A Thai share portfolio that had cost 100 US dollars at the end of June 1997 could be bought for a mere 33 US dollars a year later. The cost of servicing foreign currency loans grew rapidly: nearly half of the lending stock of the Thai financial system was classified as non-performing in 1998.

The real effects were also significant. Economic growth, which had averaged nearly 10 per cent over the previous decade, collapsed. In 1998, GDP fell by more than 10 per cent. To handle the problems, the Thai authorities and the IMF jointly designed a comprehensive reform program featuring macroeconomic stabilization, restructuring of the banking system, and new laws and regulations to increase transparency and accountability throughout the economy. For instance, four commercial banks were nationalized, 56 out of 91 finance companies were liquidated and a new bankruptcy law was introduced. A short period of fiscal and monetary austerity was implemented to absorb the excess liquidity created as people withdrew their savings from the weakened bank system.

The crisis spread rapidly to the rest of the region. Within a few weeks after the collapse of the Thai *baht*, the currencies, banks and stock exchanges in the Philippines, Indonesia and Malaysia were infected with the Thai disease (known alternately as *Bahtulism* or the *Tom Yam* effect). Indonesia was particularly badly affected, with both economic and political problems following the banking and currency crisis. Seemingly stable economies, such as Singapore and Taiwan, were also shaken during the following months. In October 1997, Hong Kong's currency was attacked. Thanks to its massive foreign exchange reserves and support from China, Hong Kong fought off the attack, but the stock exchange fell by 50 per cent over the following months.

In November, it was South Korea's turn. There, the current account deficit and the short-term foreign debt were larger than in Hong Kong, and the defense of the currency failed. Both share prices and the value of the Korean *won* halved very rapidly. Just as Thailand and Indonesia had already done, South Korea was forced to turn to the IMF for help.

The Japanese economy, which had struggled with massive losses in the financial sector since the early 1990s when its stock market and real estate bubbles collapsed, was also hit by the regional crisis. Japan had been able to delay necessary financial and structural reforms for more than half a decade – the economy was not dependent on foreign capital and policy-makers did not have to worry much about foreign confidence and transparency – but a string of bankruptcies and a 2.5 per cent fall in Japanese GDP in 1998 revealed the depth of the problems.

Much of this description of the Asian crisis – in particular the Thai crisis – appears familiar for observers of the Nordic region. A similar boom-to-bust cycle took place in both Finland and Sweden between the early 1980s and early 1990s, culminating in the financial and currency crisis of 1992.[1] Like Thailand and several other Asian countries, both Finland and Sweden maintained fixed exchange rates which reduced the perceived investment risk and encouraged inflows of foreign capital. In both regions, the acute crisis was closely connected to the reversal of these capital flows. There were also significant similarities in the short-term measures taken to resolve the crisis and to reform and restructure economic institutions.

In fact, the Asian reform measures drew to a large extent on lessons learned from the Nordic crisis: from the summer of 1997, there was a steady stream of Asian study tours to Finnish and Swedish central banks, finance ministries and other institutions in the financial sector. However, there are notable differences between, on the one hand, Finland and Sweden and, on the other hand, the Asian countries when it comes to reforms and recovery in the medium term. While the Nordic countries managed to complete the necessary reform and restructuring programs, restore the health of the financial system, and return to 'normal' growth in about three or four years, developments in Asia were slower. None of the East Asian economies that were most severely hit by the crisis had recovered after three or four years, and none of them have still been able to reach the investment and growth rates they recorded before the crisis. Problems with non-performing loans (NPLs) and heavy corporate debt remained serious in several of the regional economies for many years after the crisis.

The purpose of this chapter is to provide a comparative analysis of the Nordic and Asian crises. To illustrate some general, or at least common, features of financial crises, it is useful to point to some similarities between the two crises. The next two sections, Sections 9.1 and 9.2, provide a brief summary of some of the causes and consequences of the Nordic and Asian crises. The description of the Nordic crisis focuses on Sweden – the Finnish crisis followed much the same course, although the domestic problems were aggravated by the substantial fall in exports resulting from the collapse of the Soviet Union.[2] Section 9.3 concludes with a discussion about reforms and recovery in Asia.

Apart from the point that the causes of the crises in the Nordic countries and East Asia are very similar, our main argument is that the relatively quick resolution of the Nordic crisis constitutes a special case. The typical course of events is more similar to that experienced in large parts of Asia. Reform and change are painful and are typically opposed by vested interests. The main question emerging from the comparison between the Nordic countries and Asia is therefore 'Why were the Nordic reforms so successful?'. We suggest that the keywords are EU membership, IT and political structure.

9.1 THE NORDIC CRISIS

In retrospect, it is possible to distinguish four stages of the Nordic financial crisis. As we will see later, the same stages reappear in several of the Asian economies.

First, there was a collapse of the real estate and stock markets. In Sweden, real estate prices had risen continuously for a period of 15 years, to a peak that was reached in 1989. Over the following five years, property prices fell by more than half. Three-quarters of the forty or so real estate companies listed on the Stockholm Stock Exchange during the 1980s encountered such serious problems that they went bankrupt or had to be restructured (*Affärsvärlden*, 1992, p. 9). The stock market bubble that had developed during the decade preceding the crisis also collapsed. Between 1980 and 1989, prices on the Stockholm Stock Exchange rose by 1144 per cent, compared with a world average of 333 per cent (*Affärsvärlden*, 1992, p. 79). Over the next three years, the index fell by 50 per cent.

Second, the financial market went into deep crisis. Weighed down by substantial credit losses from bad loans on real estate and for share purchases, three major banks – *Nordbanken, Första Sparbanken and Gota Bank* – went bankrupt, while the two largest banks, *SE-Banken* and *Handelsbanken*, saw their share prices fall by around 80 per cent. Some 200 of the 300 finance companies disappeared from the market. Total credit losses during the period 1990–93 are estimated at almost SEK 200 billion, or roughly 10 per cent of GDP (Lybeck, 1994, p. 23).

Third, there was a currency crisis. The fixed exchange rate, which was seen as an anchor for Swedish economic policy, could no longer be maintained, given that the overheating of the economy in the late 1980s had lowered competitiveness and the financial crisis had weakened the economy. Despite the stubborn defense of the *krona* – with overnight interest rates reaching 500 per cent in September 1992, several crisis packages intended to strengthen Sweden's international competitiveness, and the commitment of around US$ 30 billion in defense of the currency – the *Riksbank*, the Swedish Central Bank, was forced to abandon the fixed rate for the *krona* on 19 November 1992. Over the next few months, the floating *krona* fell by 25 per cent against the *Deutschmark* and 40 per cent against the US dollar.

The fourth part was a crisis in the real economy and in government finances. The banking crisis led to a tighter credit policy, with higher interest rates and stricter requirements for collateral. At the same time, the collapse in asset values led to a reduction in private consumption and a reduced willingness to invest on the part of companies. For example, the level of industrial investment halved between 1989 and 1993. The result was a fall in total demand in the domestic market, with a consequent reduction in the demand for labor. The stimulus from the export sector, which benefited from the depreciation, was not sufficient to 'restart' domestic demand for several years. Open unemployment rose from 1.1 per cent in June 1990, to 9 per cent three years later, and real GDP fell every year during the period 1991–93, by 6 per cent in all (Lybeck, 1994, p. 15; Bäckström, 1998). In Finland, the crisis was worsened by the simultaneous decrease in exports to the former Soviet Union. Finnish GDP fell by about 12 per cent between 1990 and 1993, and total employment dropped by about 15 per cent over the same period. This led in turn to problems with government finances in both countries. The rapid growth in unemployment increased state spending, at the same time as tax receipts fell. At its peak, during 1994, the Swedish public sector's budget deficit had grown to almost 12 per cent of GDP (Bäckström, 1998, p. 11). In Finland, central government debt grew from 10 per cent of GDP in 1990 to 60 per cent in 1994.[3]

9.1.1 Why was there a Crisis?

What were the reasons for these crises, the combined effects of which were almost as serious as the deep recessions of 1921–22 and 1931–33? The simple answer is that there was an asset bubble that inflated over a period of several years and then suddenly collapsed. The causes of the development of the bubble can be analyzed systematically. It is difficult to explain the timing of the collapse in an equally systematic manner. Once a sufficient number of market actors started doubting the sustainability of the high asset prices, the collapse was arguably unavoidable. However, with most investors wishing to stay in the market as long as prices might still rise, the precise onset of the collapse probably had more to do with specific news events than more fundamental market characteristics.

The causes of the growth of the bubble are found in the simultaneous increases in the supply of and the demand for capital and credit during the

1980s.[4] The most important factors on the supply side were the deregulation of the financial sector that began in the mid-1980s, and the government's expansive monetary and fiscal policies. The demand side was also stimulated by financial deregulation, since requirements for security were eased, which meant that the collateral value of property and other assets increased. The most important events on the demand side, however, were the devaluations of 1981 and 1982, which created a long-lasting economic boom and rapid increases in the demand for credits, from both business and the household sector.

9.1.2 Increased Supply of Credit

The deregulation of the Swedish financial market in 1985 led to a very substantial increase in the supply of credit. Both the liberalization of various lending restrictions – interest rates were freed and property could now be fully mortgaged – and the fact that banks were now permitted to compete fully with the finance companies, contributed to the credit expansion. Increased competition meant that banks and other financial institutions replaced their traditional strategy of minimizing risk and maximizing profitability on a fairly constant volume of loans with a new strategy, which involved chasing volumes and market shares.

In only five years, the indebtedness of the private sector increased from 100 per cent to 150 per cent of GDP. At the same time, the average lending risk also rose. For example, the first-mortgage loan institutions increased their loan ratio from 75 per cent to 85–90 per cent. Deregulation also supported the internationalization of the Swedish capital market, and an increasing share of bank lending was financed on the international interbank market. Almost one-third of the financing of the *Gota Bank* in 1990, for example, originated from foreign banks (Urwitz, 1998, p. 56). This introduced an important element of currency risk.

The activities of the finance companies were particularly risky. During the 1970s and the 1980s, the restrictions on the operations of commercial banks had created space for finance companies specializing in leasing, factoring and other 'new' forms of financing. Most people believed that the deregulation in 1985 would mean the end of the finance companies' golden age. On the contrary, their lending continued to grow. In the first year after deregulation, lending by the finance companies increased by one-third. In particular, the companies that expanded most were involved in lending for investments in securities and property, such as *Nyckeln* and *Gamlestaden*. Their operations were, however, more risky than those of the banks. The finance companies had weaker collateral than the banks: the majority of their property loans were last-mortgage loans. Furthermore, their borrowings were short-term – often it was the commercial banks that financed the finance companies – while their lending was long-term. With hindsight, it is obvious that this imbalance would become problematic.

However, from the borrowers' point of view, deregulation was clearly beneficial. Anyone who wanted to borrow to invest, to buy property, to buy a car, to make a trip abroad, or for any other form of consumption, no longer had to go cap in hand to the bank. Now it was the banks' turn to seek out and market their services to the customers.

The increase in private indebtedness was made possible by expansionary monetary and fiscal policies. Throughout the 1980s, Sweden had a fixed exchange rate regime, which meant that monetary policy could not be used to counteract a credit expansion. A more restrictive monetary policy would have involved higher interest rates, and an inflow of capital from abroad, which would have made it difficult to keep the exchange rate unchanged. Any tightening would have had to come from fiscal policy. No such proposals were, however, made. One reason was that the central government budget looked unusually strong in the mid-1980s, thanks to full employment and the economic boom. In addition, there seemed to be no political reasons for a tightening of policy (Wohlin, 1998, p. 28). The government's preference, with the imminence of the 1988 election, was for tax cuts and a guaranteed fifth week of vacation for all employees (*Affärsvärlden*, 1992, p. 25).

9.1.3 Increased Demand for Credit

On the demand side, the most important factor was the long-running economic boom that began with a pair of devaluations at the beginning of the 1980s. Profits in export industries doubled in both 1983 and 1984 and remained high over the following five years. Despite substantial investment, both at home and abroad, several of the leading export companies had problems with 'excess liquidity', which was invested in the share and money markets. The corporate demand for commercial property and financial investments contributed to the high level of asset prices.

The high level of current demand resulted in high wage increases. In combination with the fixed exchange rate, these cost increases would gradually lead to the erosion of industry's competitiveness and the bursting of the bubble. Before this happened, inflation had expanded the bubble even more. The real interest rate on borrowing (after tax deductions) fell continuously during the second half of the 1980s, from about 2 per cent in 1986 to minus 1 per cent in 1990. This contributed to reduce the households' financial savings during the period 1985–90, to a nadir of minus 8 per cent of GDP in 1990 (Bäckström, 1998, p. 14). Quite simply, households lived beyond their assets. As noted earlier, the indebtedness of the private sector increased from 100 per cent of GDP to 150 per cent of GDP.

9.1.4 The Crash

The Swedish bubble began to burst on 25 September 1990. A leading finance company, *Nyckeln*, announced that it expected credit losses of SEK 250 million for the year. As a consequence, the general public and the banks began to back off and refused to roll over the maturing securities of *Nyckeln* and the other finance companies, that is, the short-term assets that financed a large part of their long-term lending. *Nyckeln*, *Gamlestaden*, *Independent* and most other finance companies found themselves in an acute liquidity crisis, and struggled to obtain capital injections and guarantees from their shareholders, but their credit losses grew too rapidly. Several of the companies were forced into bankruptcy, and the great majority went into liquidation over the following years.

The cause of the credit losses was, naturally, that the rate of growth of asset values began to weaken. There were several concurrent reasons for this. The overheating of the economy had created a cost crisis and, given the fixed exchange rate, eroded the competitiveness of the export industries. Interest rates had begun to rise as a result of the reunification of Germany. Iraq's invasion of Kuwait in August 1990 had led to falls in many stock markets. Each of these factors on its own could have burst the bubble. Now they came almost together, and as the beginning of the recession became more obvious and the increases in interest rates reduced property prices even further, the banks also found themselves in a crisis. The situation was aggravated by a tax reform in 1991 which limited interest deductions for tax purposes and made it more expensive to borrow, putting even more downward pressure on asset prices. The new focus of economic policy on price stability (which can be illustrated by the unilateral linkage of the *krona* to the *ecu* in May 1991 and the defense of the *krona* in the following year) also contributed to raising real interest rates.

9.1.5 Bank Support and Recovery

All the large Swedish banks were affected by serious losses during the crisis. Six of the seven largest banks required capital injections from the state or from their shareholders. For instance, the government injected over SEK 16 billion into *Nordbanken* in 1991 and 1992. The growing credit losses were also a contributory factor in the currency crisis in autumn 1992, since the reduced international confidence in the Swedish banking system led to several banks having difficulty in managing their foreign borrowing. The loss of foreign credits not only led to a weakening of the *krona* when the inflow of foreign currency slowed but also threatened the liquidity of the financial system.

In September 1992, the government introduced a bank guarantee that meant that all creditors – apart from shareholders – were protected against loss. A special Bank Support Board, *Bankstödsnämnden*, was established to administer the guarantee. The aim was to avoid a liquidity crisis – the *Riksbank* deposited a great part of its foreign reserves in the banks – and to maintain or restore confidence in the Swedish banking system. For this latter aim, transparent accounting of problem credits was particularly important. It was presumably also important that bank support came before the fixed exchange rate was abandoned in November 1992. The currency crisis made the situation worse for most of the banks, both because interest rates were raised substantially and because the cost of foreign debt increased considerably with the depreciation of the *krona*.

The public bank support funds were used largely as a shareholder's contribution to *Nordbanken* and *Gota Bank* and to detach the delinquent loans of these banks into two separate asset management companies, *Securum* and *Retriva*. In all, the payment of bank support amounted to SEK 63.3 billion, which was balanced by the government's holdings and income from shares and equity in *Nordbanken*, *Securum* and *Retriva* with an estimated value of more than SEK 60 billion in July 1997 (Jennergren and Näslund, 1998, pp. 70–1).[5] The guarantees to the rest of the banking system, which amounted to more than SEK 84 billion, were not utilized.

The recovery was surprisingly quick. After 1993, no new commitments were made by *Bankstödsnämnden*, and the banking sector as a whole showed a profit as early as 1994 (Ingves and Lind, 1998, p. 54). One reason was that the banks' interest margins rose substantially. Other important reasons were that the tight economic policies caused real interest rates to fall and that an upturn in the international economic situation contributed to an expansion in the export sector. By 1995, the situation was arguably back to normal, at least in the financial sector.

Ingves and Lind (1998) believe that the emergency treatment and aftercare given to cure the Swedish crisis were comparatively successful for four reasons, which might also comprise the conditions for a rapid recovery in confidence for any financial system in crisis:

- A political consensus was created on a broad solution to the crisis.
- The authorities encouraged the greatest possible openness about the problems and the financial situation of the individual banks.
- Bad loans and property values were entered in the accounts in an open and transparent way, and the banks and finance companies

that were not likely to recover from the credit losses were allowed to go into liquidation.

- Bad loans were transferred to special asset management companies, but at realistic market values.

We will return to this list below, in the discussion of the cures for the Asian crisis. Before turning our attention to developments in Asia, however, it should be noted that not all dimensions of the crisis had been solved by 1995. Apart from the recovery in the financial sector, Jonung and Hagberg in Chapter 5 argue that real income growth and industrial production growth were also back to their trend rates by 1995. However, the crisis in public finances remained serious. Automatic stabilizers in the government budgets had created serious deficits in both Finland and Sweden – in 1994, Sweden recorded a budget deficit of over 10 per cent of GDP – and the high unemployment rates in both countries continued to trouble public finances. Considering the history of both Finland and Sweden as developed welfare states with strong interest groups protecting their relative positions, it is remarkable that both countries were able to contain public expenditure and return to balanced budgets within only two or three more years. We will return in the next section to a discussion of the special conditions that facilitated the rapid and broad recovery after the crisis in the Nordic countries, contrasting it with the slower and perhaps more 'normal' processes in most of Asia.

9.2 THE ASIAN CRISIS

The four related problems emphasized above – stock market and property bubbles, a financial crisis, a currency crisis, and a downturn in production and employment – recur in several of the crisis-hit Asian countries. This section starts by summarizing some common features of the crises in different Asian countries, and highlights some of the similarities with the Swedish financial crisis. Thereafter, we point to some of the special characteristics of the Asian crisis that made the problems in the region more severe than in Sweden and contributed to slowing down the Asian recovery process.

9.2.1 Four Crises

Just as in Finland and Sweden, the crisis in Asia was preceded by speculative bubbles in the stock and property markets. In the greater part of the region, economic growth rose sharply in the early or mid-1980s, and the stock markets began to rise rapidly a few years later. In the most developed economies – South Korea and Taiwan – the peak in the stock market was reached even before the end of the 1980s (in the aftermath of the Plaza Accord, which led to an appreciation of the currencies in Northeast Asia) but in other countries share prices continued to rise. At the same time, property prices shot up. The number of property and finance companies grew rapidly. Transactions were financed with borrowed money, and, as in Sweden, borrowing on property and share portfolios often exceeded their market value. This seemed rational, since the economies were growing by almost 10 per cent per year and there were no clear signs of any slowdown.

But the expectations of high economic growth and continuous increases in asset prices proved to be over-optimistic. Real estate prices began to drop as early as 1993–94. The main reason was declining profitability – the yield on property fell as the supply increased. In Bangkok, one square meter of office space cost almost US$ 3000 in 1991. Five years later, before the real collapse in the property market, the price had fallen to US$ 2200. The square meter price in Jakarta fell from US$ 2200 in 1991 to US$ 1600 five years later (Dollar, 1998). The stock market indices in both Bangkok and Kuala Lumpur also peaked in 1993–94, and fell by half by 1996. When prices began to drop, both borrowers and lenders found themselves in trouble. Many borrowers had insufficient cash flow to pay interest. Lenders found that their security and collateral were worth considerably less than they had thought. The financial sector became vulnerable.

The high level of demand and the increase in asset values also led to higher production costs and wage increases. The productivity growth in the export industries could not keep up with the increase in costs, and competitiveness was eroded. The trends in exchange rates made the situation worse. Several of the countries in the region had tied their currencies to the dollar, which began to appreciate in the mid-1990s. In countries that had floating exchange rates, large inflows of foreign capital – both loans and direct investment – contributed to maintaining the strength of the currency.

However, the inflow of foreign currency was based on expectations of high growth and high yields. When foreign investors began to realize that these expectations could not be fulfilled, the problems became acute. Thailand was the first country to be affected. Foreign financiers began to withdraw from the beginning of 1997, and short-term loans were not rolled over as they fell due. When the inflow of capital dried up, the currency weakened. There were several waves of speculation on devaluation in early summer 1997. The repeated defense of the *baht* drained the foreign exchange reserves, until it was no longer possible to resist the pressure.

This happened by the beginning of July 1997, and the fixed rate was abandoned.

The depreciation of the *baht* worsened the financial crisis that had begun with the fall in the stock and property markets, since debts in foreign currency immediately became considerably heavier to service. The turbulence and uncertainty in the market was also too great for new capital to come into the market in the short term. The reduction in import capacity, and the financial market's problems with capital adequacy requirements and liquidity, led to a fall in production and employment – a real crisis. In its major features, the process was the same as in Sweden and Finland half a dozen years earlier.

Given the increased risk of credit losses, lenders also began to review their interests in the rest of the region. It was soon clear that other countries in Southeast Asia had much in common with Thailand regarding the state of the financial sector. The critical assessments also revealed various risks and weaknesses that had been overlooked earlier, when investors were still blinded by high growth rates. In Indonesia, the uncertainty applied both to political stability – mainly concerning Suharto's successor – and industrial structure, where nepotism, corruption and excessive investment in capital-intensive and high-technology sectors caused concern. In Malaysia, attention was directed at several gigantic investment projects under government auspices and at Prime Minister Mahathir's attacks on the market – could the market trust someone who so obviously distrusted the market? For South Korea, a long list of potential problems was discussed, each more serious than the next. These included question marks on the stability and efficiency of the financial markets, the massive indebtedness and weak profitability of industry, which had forced six of the country's 30 largest industrial conglomerates, the *chaebols*, into liquidation within a short period of time; and the links between the large industrial companies and the political leadership. The market reaction was harsh. Capital flows dried up, the currencies weakened, and the financial markets were shaken.

Even nations like Singapore and Taiwan, with relatively sound economies, suffered from stock market falls and depreciation. In these cases, it was an adjustment to a new market situation rather than the result of domestic weaknesses: as a result of the substantial exchange rate changes, the competitiveness of neighboring countries had been strengthened, at the same time as their ability to import had fallen. The two nations that chose to retain their fixed exchange rates against the dollar were also affected. In Hong Kong, an attack on the currency was fought off, which meant that the adjustment to the changes in the regional economy had to come through changes in nominal asset prices and salaries.

China declared that no devaluation should be expected, although the turbulence had some impact on GDP and export growth rates in the short term. The Chinese currency did not come under serious attack, both because the country's foreign exchange reserves were thought to be sufficient to ward off any attack and because remaining restrictions on current and capital account transactions left only limited room for the market to exploit. This notwithstanding, the problems of ineffective financial markets and bad loans, often to government-owned companies, were at least as great in China as in any of the crisis-struck Asian countries before 1997. It is likely that some kind of adjustment will eventually occur in China as well, but the mix of political control and a free-market economy makes it difficult to predict exactly when and how. In Vietnam, the crisis contributed to slower GDP and export growth rates, but the acute problems plaguing some of the neighboring countries were avoided. The Vietnamese currency was not convertible, and it had neither a real estate market nor a stock market where substantial asset bubbles could have developed.

9.2.2 The Supply of and Demand for Capital

A closer look at how the bubbles in the East and Southeast Asian markets were inflated strengthens the impression that the problems developed very much like those in the Nordic countries. The rapid increase in asset prices was caused by simultaneous increases in the supply of and demand for capital.

As in Finland and Sweden, financial deregulation was an important factor in increasing the supply of credit, but in a more comprehensive way than in the Nordic countries. Up until the first half of the 1980s, most of the economies in the region had been relatively inward-oriented, and the growth strategies were largely based on import substitution.[6] Even Korea, which had implemented a strong export-promoting policy between the early 1960s and the mid-1970s, had opted for a strategy involving more import substitution and support to heavy and chemical industries. The results, however, were disappointing. The regulations and trade barriers that were erected to shield domestic producers from foreign competition gave rise to inefficiency, and many of the industries that should have grown strong with the aid of protective tariffs and subsidized credit never became competitive. Consequently, the inward-looking policies were revised throughout the region, from around 1980 in South Korea and 1985 in Thailand, Malaysia and Indonesia.

The new approach emphasized export orientation and greater openness. Most of the countries devalued their currencies and the inflow of foreign investment was encouraged. Credit markets were gradually liberalized, as the need to direct investment capital to selected strategic industries diminished. The result was a large increase in domestic credit to the private sector. The deregulation and liberalization of financial markets continued into the 1990s, but now with reference to the so-called Washington Consensus. This development paradigm, strongly promoted by the IMF and the World Bank, prescribed fiscal discipline, privatization, deregulation and financial liberalization as a recipe for economic development (Williamson, 1994). However, much of East Asia was weakly prepared for the shift to a liberalized financial system, and the expansion in the supply of credits took place without the prudential regulation and supervision that would have been needed to safeguard the stability of the system. For instance, Lee (2003, p. 19) argues that 'financial deregulation in Asia created an institutional hiatus, as it removed government regulation without putting in place institutions necessary for a market-based financial system'.

Parallel with the gradual deregulation of the domestic financial markets, the supply of capital was boosted through large inflows of foreign investment. The US already had substantial investments in Taiwan, Singapore and Malaysia, and Japanese investment started flowing in on a large scale from the mid-1980s. At this time, Japanese export industries had already grown so strong that the trade surplus with the US had become a serious problem. The Plaza Accord in 1985 was intended to help even out the imbalance and involved a gradual appreciation of the Japanese yen, from JPY 239 per dollar in 1985 to about JPY 135 per dollar two years later. The strong yen drove up production costs in Japan, and forced Japanese export companies to move a substantial part of their labor-intensive production to countries such as Thailand, Indonesia and Malaysia, and later also to China.

The inflow of foreign capital – this time with greater emphasis on portfolio investment – increased once again at the beginning of the 1990s. In Japan, the years after 1985 were noteworthy not only for the continuous strengthening of the yen but also for expansive fiscal and monetary policies. The aim was to ward off the downturn in domestic demand that was expected to follow from the appreciation of the yen. The expansionary policies were also encouraged by the US as a way of stimulating Japanese import demand. The chief result was not, however, a reduction in the trade imbalances. Instead, the Japanese exporters succeeded in adjusting their costs, partly thanks to their foreign investments in the region and in the US. The combination of a strong currency and high demand created a substantial asset bubble in Japan. Many economists may recall the anecdotes about Tokyo's high land prices: it was said that the value of the Imperial Palace and the palace grounds matched that of all the land in California.

The Japanese bubble did not last very long. The Japanese stock market and property market began to contract from the beginning of 1990, after worries about increasing inflation had prompted the Japanese Central Bank to raise interest rates. The prices of many assets had soon halved. However, the collapse of asset prices did not result in any acute crisis although many investors, finance companies and banks were badly hurt. Unlike Sweden and most of Southeast Asia, Japan was a large exporter of capital, and the bursting of the bubble did not cause any currency crisis nor did it affect the liquidity of the Japanese financial sector in the short run. Hence, Japan could choose not to address the problems in the financial sector at that time. Instead, bankers and politicians put a lid on the situation, and began to wait patiently for the problems to disappear of their own accord. Meanwhile, to ensure the survival of companies that were burdened with debt, it was essential that interest rates fell significantly.

At the same time as many finance and property companies were burdened with problem credits, the Japanese continued to save, and export companies continued to generate large profits. Rather than invest their savings at a low interest rate in Japan, many banks chose to invest in other Asian countries, where growth and yields were higher – in particular in Thailand, South Korea and Indonesia.[7] The supply of cheap Japanese capital with few restrictions was so great that some observers see this as an important cause of the Asian crisis. Martin Feldstein (1997), for example, believes that Japan's expansive monetary policy and the lax handling of credit by the Japanese banks contributed to many of the countries in the region taking on an unsustainable level of foreign debt.

It was not only the Japanese who were enticed to offer loans to the region. From the beginning of the 1990s, European investors also began to see opportunities in Asia, and, just before the crisis broke, EU banks were, in fact, the largest lenders to the region. Of the total loan stock, the EU was responsible for about 41 per cent and Japan for 32 per cent, while the US share was only 8 per cent (Ostrom, 1998, p. 6). Table 9.1 summarizes the available information on the foreign borrowing by selected countries in East and Southeast Asia at the end of June 1997. Japan, Hong Kong and Singapore are not included in the table, since none of these countries had any significant net foreign debt.

In addition to the high level of indebtedness in the countries hardest hit by the crisis, it is also noteworthy that a very large proportion of the loans were short-term. In South Korea, Thailand and Indonesia, short-term debt alone amounted to more than 50 per cent of the previous year's exports. In all three countries, short-term foreign debt was also far larger

Table 9.1 International bank loans to Asian economies, June 1997

Borrower	Total loans (US$ million)	... as share of GDP (%)	Lender (% of total loans)			Short-term loans (US$ million)	... as share of exports 1996 (%)
			Japan	EU	USA		
South Korea	103432	21.3	23	35	10	70182	54.1
Thailand	69382	38.1	54	28	6	45567	81.8
Indonesia	58726	26.5	39	38	8	34661	69.6
China	57922	7.1	32	48	5	30137	19.9
Malaysia	28820	29.3	36	44	8	16268	20.9
Taiwan	25163	9.2	12	57	10	21966	19.0
Philippines	14115	16.2	15	48	20	8293	40.4

Source: Komine (1998, Tables 6–7).

than the foreign exchange reserves – in South Korea almost three and a half times as large (*The Economist*, 7 March 1998, p. 6). When confidence in the regional market began to fall, it was the problems with refinancing of the foreign short-term debt that triggered the crisis.

Another indication of the significance of capital flows, and the vulnerability of the region's economies, is the growth of trade deficits. Figure 9.1 shows how the current accounts of the countries that were worst hit by the crisis (Indonesia, Malaysia, the Philippines, South Korea and Thailand) turned to deficits in the late 1980s or early 1990s, even though export growth was accelerating. A deficit in the current account does not only mean that imports exceed exports, which requires a net inflow of foreign capital in the form of loans or investment. It also reflects the gap between domestic saving and domestic investment. This financing gap was largely covered by foreign resources. After the crisis, all of these countries have been forced to generate current account surpluses, in order to pay back their foreign loans. The countries that managed the crisis best – Singapore and Taiwan – had avoided building up current account deficits and foreign debt stocks before the crisis. Instead, their domestic savings were sufficiently high to finance domestic investments and to accumulate large currency reserves that facilitated the management of the crisis.

The increase in the supply of capital – both from domestic and foreign sources – makes up half of the explanation for the growth of the bubble. The other half, the increase in the demand for capital, is largely explained

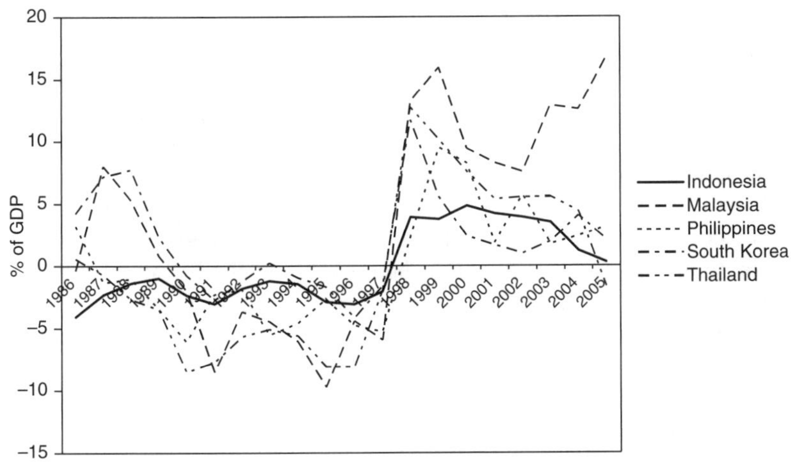

Source: *East Asian Economic Perspectives* (2006), **17** (1).

Figure 9.1 Current account balance as a percentage of GDP 1986–2005

by the shift to a more export-oriented and outward-looking development strategy from about 1985.

When import substitution was abandoned and resources were permitted to flow to industries in which countries had comparative advantages – many countries also carried out substantial devaluations to support the profitability of their export industries – economic growth accelerated. The average annual growth rate nearly doubled in several countries, from 4–5 per cent in the first half of the 1980s to over 8 per cent in 1987–92. The Philippines were an outlier, with only 3–4 per cent growth in the latter period: however, even this was a marked improvement on the first half of the 1980s, when the economy had been in a recession. As the yield on land, capital and other resources increased, so did the demand for and prices of assets.

Until the beginning of the 1990s, the bulk of investment went into the export sector, but as costs began to rise and the real exchange rate began to appreciate, the pattern changed. The growing domestic market became increasingly important, both for manufacturing industry and for a rapidly expanding service sector. The high rate of growth did not only create great individual wealth; it also created a significant middle class demanding consumer durables, cars and homes. The demand for capital for investment in infrastructure and real estate increased strongly.

The large interest differential between domestic and foreign loans was one reason for the high demand for foreign capital in particular. As a result of higher inflation and various limitations on competition, domestic interest rates in several Southeast Asian economies were several percentage points higher than international rates. In 1993, for example, short-term interest rates in Thailand were about 10 per cent per annum, while foreign financiers could offer dollar loans at below 5 per cent interest (Kobayashi, 1997, p. 16). As long as exchange rates were fixed, it was highly attractive to borrow in dollars rather than in the local currency. In Thailand, a special financial market was established to channel international capital to local investors – the Bangkok International Banking Facility. With both a massive supply of and massive demand for capital, all the conditions were present to create bubbles.

9.2.3 The Bubble Bursts

As we noted earlier, the peak in several of the region's stock markets was reached as early as 1993–94 (and even a few years before that in South Korea and Taiwan). The property markets showed signs of excess supply at about the same time, even though the collapses in Thailand, Malaysia and Indonesia did not occur until 1996. The falling asset prices contributed to the vulnerability of banks and financial institutions, but there was a longer time-lapse than in Finland and Sweden before the collapse of the bubble led to serious instability and a financial and currency crisis.

One reason was that the accounting procedures in most Asian companies were (and continue to be) less transparent than they are in Europe. There was, quite simply, insufficient public control of industrial companies, banks and financial institutions for the financiers – in particular the foreign lenders – to realize at an early stage that they had something to worry about (Lim, 1999). In particular, it was not apparent how highly indebted many companies were, and how large their short-term loans were. As an example, South Korea's short-term foreign debt in late 1997 was estimated at US$ 65–70 billion (Table 9.1). It is now believed that the real figure was over US$ 100 billion. To a very great extent, these short-term credits financed long-term investments. It was only after the crisis had broken that it was noted that the average debt–equity ratio among South Korea's 30 largest *chaebols* was over 400 per cent at the end of 1996. The corresponding figure for the USA was 70 per cent (*The Economist*, 7 March 1998, pp. 6–7). This lack of transparency has also been noticed in Thailand, Malaysia, Indonesia and the Philippines, where debt–equity ratios exceeding those of Korean *chaebols* have been revealed after the crisis (ADB, 2001, p. 124).

Many investors seem to have underrated the investment risks in the region. In addition, the strong links between political office-holders and business interests that are common in the region seem to have been interpreted as an implicit credit guarantee. On the one hand, the state directed capital to sectors that were, for some reason, considered particularly important, such as heavy industry in South Korea and Indonesia and infrastructure investment in Malaysia. On the other hand, selected individuals and companies – Suharto's relatives and friends in Indonesia, *chaebols* in South Korea, politically influential businessmen in Thailand – were granted special advantages, such as lucrative government contracts, licenses and subsidized credit. Some investors and many lenders probably concluded that banks and companies with such strong political backing would hardly be allowed to go to the wall. This explains why the initial price falls on the asset markets were not seen as a sign of major risk, and why capital continued to flow in.

The combination of implicit loan guarantees, insufficient transparency and weak supervisory authorities has been interpreted by several observers as the principal reason for the Asia crisis. Paul Krugman (1998a, 1998b), for example, argues that the crisis was primarily a financial crisis rather than a currency crisis. The problems caused by the weaknesses in the financial market are known as moral hazard. The lack of supervision and the dilution of individual responsibility meant that banks and other intermediaries took excessively great risks and pushed up asset prices. In the best cases, the projects were successful, and the investors made large profits; in the worst cases, they expected the government to step in and compensate their losses. This worked for a while, but when the bad investments and losses finally became so large that the state could no longer cover them, the crisis broke out. Capital flows dried up and currencies collapsed. The fall in liquidity led, in turn, to a further decline in asset prices.

Figures 9.2 and 9.3 illustrate some of these consequences. The development of the US dollar exchange rates for Indonesia, Malaysia, the Philippines, South Korea and Thailand are shown in Figure 9.2 (with an index value of 100 for 25 June 1997). The Thai *baht* was floated on 2 July, and the currencies of neighboring countries began to slide a few days later. The largest depreciation took place in Indonesia, where the currency lost 80 per cent of its value by early 1998. The currencies of the other countries included in Figure 9.2 fell by some 40 per cent during the first half-year after the outbreak of the crisis.

It appears that several of the currencies initially fell more than what was justified by the underlying economic problems. One reason for this is, presumably, that there was a certain amount of panic among foreign investors when they began to realize the full extent of the region's problems. Another reason may have been that the effect of the depreciation of the

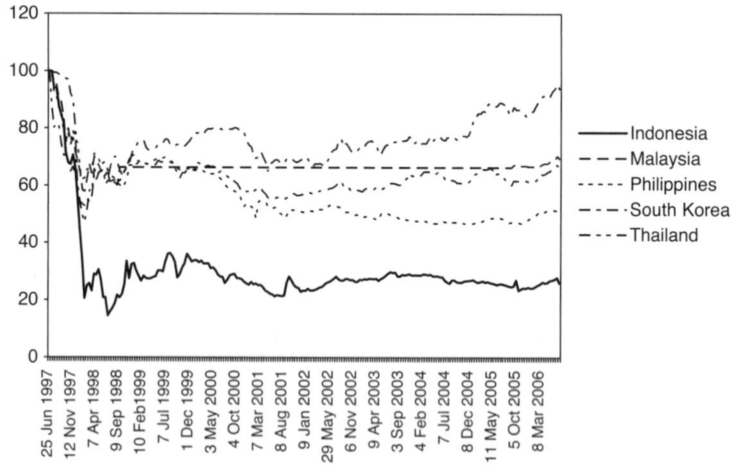

Source: *The Economist*, various issues.

Figure 9.2 Exchange rate changes June 1997–May 2006 (June 1997 = 100)

Thai currency on competition in export markets was overestimated. At the same time as Thailand's competitiveness was improved by a cheaper currency, the opportunities for increasing exports were limited by the instability of the financial markets. The export sector, therefore, was not able to expand as rapidly as Thailand's competitors in the region feared.

All of the currencies saw some strengthening from the end of 1998, but only the South Korean *won* has slowly moved towards its pre-crisis parity since that time. The exchange rate of the Malaysian *ringgit* was fixed in 1998, at two-thirds of its old value (3.8 *Ringgit* per US$, compared with 2.5 MR/US$ before the crisis). The Thai *baht* has been fairly stable at a similar level, whereas the Philippine *peso* weakened further after 2000. The Indonesian currency has not strengthened appreciably since 1999, and remains at about 30 per cent of its value before the crisis. Both Singapore and Taiwan saw depreciations of around 15 per cent, while China and Hong Kong have maintained their fixed rates to the US$.

Figure 9.3 shows the response of the stock markets over the same period. The turbulence meant that all the major stock exchanges in the region lost heavily in dollar terms. A temporary recovery during 1999 turned into a new slump in 2000, as a result of a global downturn in the IT sector. A more sustainable recovery occurred between 2003 and 2007, but the overall performance of the five countries included in Figure 9.3 varies substantially.

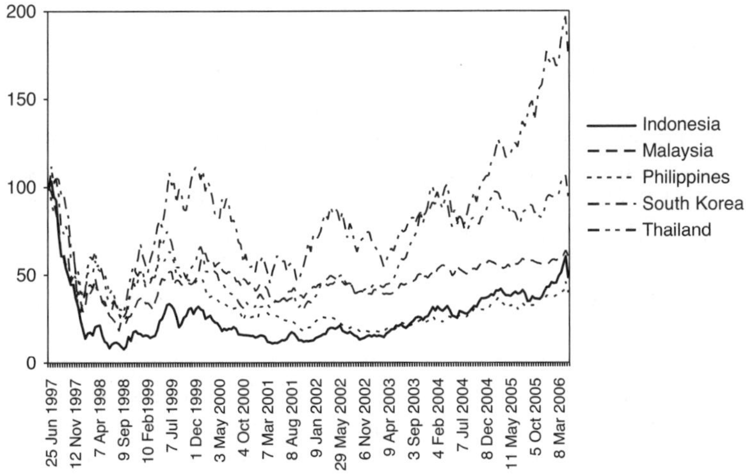

Source: *The Economist*, various issues.

Figure 9.3. Stock market index in US$, June 1997–May 2006 (June 1997 = 100)

While the South Korean stock market has been able to nearly double its pre-crisis level, the other countries are struggling. Thailand managed a recovery in late 2003, but has not been able to progress since that time. The stock markets in Malaysia, Indonesia and the Philippines are all at about 60 per cent of their dollar index values recorded just before the crisis. The development in Indonesia has been particularly dramatic. The dollar value of the Jakarta Stock Exchange fell by 90 per cent during the first year after the crisis, and remained at roughly that level for more than five years. Even Singapore and Taiwan (not shown in Figure 9.3) lost half of their stock market value during the first year after the crisis, but both had recovered by late 1999 or early 2000. However, the slump in the IT and electronics industries in 2000 turned out to be more severe than the financial crisis for these two countries, with further setbacks in connection with the September 11 attacks in the US the following year. The Taiwanese stock market has remained stagnant since that time.

The reduced import capacity and the contraction of the financial sector also led to considerable real effects. Several countries recorded significant GDP falls in 1998, with declines of over 13 per cent in Indonesia, 10 per cent in Thailand, and 5–8 per cent in Hong Kong, Malaysia and South Korea. Several million jobs were lost throughout the region. Hence, the real crisis was much more serious than in the case of Sweden. It was also more severely felt by the population, since the social security networks in Asia were not well developed. The automatic stabilizers in the Swedish public budget generated overall deficits of about 10 per cent of GDP each year between 1992 and 1994. In most East Asian economies, it was difficult to channel funds to the most severely affected population groups, and the budget deficits were generally quite low, rarely exceeding 3 per cent of GDP (EAEP, 2006, p. 8). The main exception was Japan, where the public budget recorded substantial deficits every year from 1992.

9.2.4 Why was the Asian Crisis More Serious than the Nordic Crisis?

Although the roots of the Asian crisis are similar to those of the Finnish and Swedish financial crisis of the early 1990s, there are also some important differences that explain why the Asian crisis was more severe and required more extensive reforms than the Nordic crisis. We have already touched upon three such issues. The first difference is the weak development of supervisory institutions and the unclear accounting rules, accompanied by a lack of transparency in the operations of banks and finance companies. One result of the weakness of the institutions meant to handle a free-market economy was that much of East Asia's deregulation and liberalization turned out to be premature (Lee, 2003). The second difference refers to the link between political and economic interests throughout Asia, which made managers, investors and lenders act as if the state guaranteed some of the business risks. In combination, these two factors contributed to making the bubbles larger than would otherwise have been the case. The third difference is the lack of automatic stabilizers in the government budget, which meant that the drop in economic activity following the crisis was not balanced by any rapid increases in public spending.

A number of other factors made the Asian economies more vulnerable and contributed both to the rapid spread of the crisis and the substantial fall in growth rates following the crisis. These include over-ambitious industrial policies, more intense competition on the world markets for the region's export products as a result of China's rapidly increasing exports, and a shortage of skilled workers. The following sections include a brief discussion of these issues. Of course, there are significant differences across the individual Asian economies that cannot be discussed in detail. For instance, the economic crisis led to political tensions throughout the region, in some cases – primarily Indonesia – with dramatic consequences.

Industrial policy ambitions

The development strategy in many of the East Asian economies was based on Japan's successful industrial policy of the 1950s and 1960s.

Characteristic of the Japanese model was a coalition between the government bureaucracy and the major private industries, which coordinated economic development, channeled investment funds to selected projects, and protected new industries. The country that most obviously attempted to apply a similar model is South Korea. Even though the coalition between the South Korean government and the country's *chaebols*, the great industrial conglomerates, has been remarkably successful over recent decades, it is also clear that the industrial policy aggravated the problems that created the Korean currency crisis in November 1997.

As we noted earlier, in the second half of the 1970s South Korea experimented with a development strategy of import substitution, which emphasized shipbuilding, steelworks, oil refineries and other chemical and heavy industries. The experiment was largely a failure. The bias against other industries created bottlenecks, and many of the investments never became profitable (Kokko, 2006). At the beginning of the 1980s, the program was therefore terminated. A new development strategy was adopted, with a more neutral trade orientation and less systematic intervention in favor of heavy industries. Yet, the state retained a significant influence over development. Growth continued to be markedly capital-intensive. 'Strategically' important industries were promoted in various ways by industrial policy, primarily through investment support. Motor vehicles, steel, consumer electronics, chemical products and computer components were among the products regarded as having the greatest potential.

During a long period, total investment in the economy amounted to 30–35 per cent of GDP. Even though domestic savings were high, they were not sufficiently high to finance all this investment. Thus, it was necessary to mobilize foreign resources. The preferred source of funds was foreign borrowing, since inward direct investment was not encouraged. The current account deficit grew, and with it the vulnerability of the economy. Many of the *chaebols* that dominated the South Korean economy also became heavily indebted. The average level of debt in the large companies was four times higher than equity in 1996, as mentioned earlier. Even relatively limited setbacks could easily become critical with this kind of exposure. Six of the 30 largest conglomerates were bankrupt or on the brink of bankruptcy already before the depreciation of the Korean *won* aggravated the problems.

It is probable that the large debts, and the risks associated with them, were rational from the companies' point of view. Many of the investment projects were encouraged and supported in a variety of ways by the state; the companies, therefore, also expected that the state would guarantee the investments. The projects constituted part of a long-term strategy, and it was not reasonable to expect that all investments would return a profit in the short run. The banks were also in a tight position. During the 1960s, the banking system had to all intents and purposes been nationalized, but the gradual liberalization of later years reduced the level of state control. Yet, the banks were still expected to channel subsidized funds to strategic industries. The concentration on heavy import substituting industries in the late 1970s had been very costly for the banking system, since the stock of bad debts grew rapidly. In the mid-1980s, almost 10 per cent of the lending of South Korean banks was bad debt – the borrowers were unable to service their loans (World Bank, 1993, p. 309).

It is interesting to contrast South Korea and Taiwan. The two countries recorded almost equally high economic growth from the beginning of the 1980s to the mid-1990s, but, while South Korea took on considerable foreign debt as a result of its focus on strategic capital-intensive investments, Taiwan implemented more market-oriented policies with less emphasis on heavy industry. In that way, Taiwan managed to match the performance of Korea with an investment ratio of somewhat above 20 per cent of GDP. Since the Taiwanese saved almost a third of their incomes, Taiwan became a significant exporter of capital, at the same time as it was able to build up very large foreign exchange reserves. These reserves shielded the economy from the worst effects of the crisis.

South Korea was not alone in having adopted an industrial policy involving strong state control. Similar ambitions have, to varying extents, appeared in the other Asian economies as well, with the possible exception of Hong Kong. In both Malaysia and Indonesia, the state had a major influence on the industrial structure, and both nations invested heavily in capital-intensive projects from the late 1980s. In Indonesia, the investment ratio reached close to 30 per cent, while Malaysia's investment ratio exceeded 40 per cent between 1994 and 1997. Massive investments in infrastructure, a domestic automotive industry and high-technology ambitions were found on both sides of the Malacca Straits. Many analysts lay part of the responsibility for Indonesia's massive problems on the former President, B.J. Habibie, who used his earlier position as Minister for Technology to push through a large number of expensive, high-technology projects. A large proportion of them did not become profitable, but added to the country's foreign debt. This grew to almost two-thirds of GDP before the crisis, despite the fact that the domestic savings ratio was remarkably high for a poor country, thanks to the incomes from the petroleum sector. In 1998, after the outbreak of the crisis, Indonesia's foreign debt amounted to nearly 150 per cent of GDP (EAEP, 2006, p. 86).

Governments have had high ambitions for industrial policy in Thailand and the Philippines as well, but weaker state control has made it more difficult to realize these plans. Only a few individual strategic projects

– particularly in steel and petrochemicals – have been implemented in Thailand. In the majority of cases, lobbying and pressure from different interest groups have made it difficult to favor some industries or investors over others. In retrospect, it is therefore possible that the weak political systems in these two nations may have been a blessing in disguise. As the economies have gradually begun to recover, Thailand and the Philippines have been spared a problem that continues to handicap growth in South Korea and Indonesia: massive investment in import-dependent projects that do not benefit very much from a cheaper currency.

Excess supply of strategic products

The concentration on strategic industries has had an additional effect on the crisis. Even if an individual government succeeds in identifying the 'right' sector for its strategic investments, it is not possible to repeat the plan in several countries simultaneously. When production starts in many places at the same time, the increased supply will inevitably lead to price falls. What seemed to be a sensible strategy ex ante, when there were few producers, becomes less attractive ex post, when it emerges that everyone else has done the same. There is good reason to believe that this type of failure in coordination contributed to the crisis in Asia. During 1996 and 1997, there were clear signs of an oversupply of several of the region's export products. The prices of oil products, steel, semiconductors and other computer components fell substantially, contributing to a fall in the export growth of the region. Thailand's exports of computer components, for example, increased in volume by 30 per cent during 1996, while the value of the exports was unchanged.

The appreciation of the US dollar, which began in 1995, should also be noted. Many of the region's currencies were tied to the dollar, and were dragged along with the appreciation. Although changes in exchange rates within the region were relatively limited, the dollar-pegged currencies had risen by about 35 per cent against the Japanese yen by 1997. The region's exports to Japan stagnated from 1995. In the preceding years, they had grown at an annual rate of over 20 per cent. The growth rate fell to 6 per cent in 1996, with China accounting for over half of this. In addition, competition from Japan increased in technologically more advanced industries, which affected the region's exports to the rest of the world.

China's entry into the world market

Another factor which altered the market picture in the region, and which led to many investments giving a poorer return than had been expected, was China's large-scale entry into the international market at the beginning of the 1990s. The Chinese export market had begun to grow as early as the beginning of the 1980s, when a number of coastal regions were designated as special economic zones and permitted to experiment with the market economy. To start with, only eight cities were involved, but the reforms were soon extended to the greater part of the Shenzen, Guangdong and Hainan provinces along the southern and southeastern coasts. The experiment was very successful and generated exceptionally rapid economic growth, which led to a gradual diffusion of the reforms to the rest of the country. Deng Xiao Ping's famous inspection tour of the coastal provinces in 1991 – when he was reported to have stated that it did not matter what color a cat was, as long as it caught mice – was interpreted as a clear indication of a more general transition to a mixed economy.

As openness and market orientation in the rest of China increased, so did Chinese exports. At the beginning of 1994, a further step towards the world market was taken when the currency was devalued by almost 40 per cent. Over the following years, this had a very tangible effect on the supply of exports from the region. Total Chinese exports increased by over 60 per cent in only three years, between 1993 and 1996. At that point China and Hong Kong together were responsible for about half of the total exports from the region. China's entry into the market had a similar restraining effect on the prices for labor-intensive products – textiles, shoes, home electronics and other light industries – as the contemporaneous strategically-motivated investments had on more advanced industries, such as chemicals, steel and computer components. Prices fell, and this had a negative impact on the profitability of investments throughout the region.

Lack of educational investment

In certain parts of the region, serious deficiencies in education and infrastructure have contributed to the difficulties. While the more developed economies, such as Hong Kong, South Korea, Singapore and Taiwan, have been investing in education for years and have built up a well-educated and efficient workforce, there are major problems in other places. In Thailand, only 39 per cent of children in the 12–16 age group attended school in 1994. In Indonesia, the figure was 44 per cent and in Malaysia 56 per cent (*The Economist*, 7 March 1998, p. 14). All these figures are significantly lower than the equivalent measures for South Korea and Taiwan 20–25 years earlier, when these countries were at about the same income level as Thailand was at the time. The result of inadequate investment in education is a serious shortage of skilled workers, which has meant that increases in productivity have not been able to keep pace with increases in wages.

The best illustrations of this problem are found in Thailand. The acceleration of growth at the end of the 1980s was based on large numbers of uneducated workers streaming into Bangkok from the rural areas to manufacture clothes, shoes and toys, and to assemble electronic products. For a number of years, it was possible to expand production without costs becoming a problem. But from about 1992, when growth in the domestic market also took off, the supply of cheap labor began to dry up and competition drove up real wages. By 1996, real wages for unskilled labor had risen by 60 per cent. Because of the low average level of education, it was not possible to increase the degree of value added in export production, with the result that competitiveness declined (Warr, 1997). The depreciation of the Thai currency cut real wages and restored competitiveness, but the shortage of skilled labor still limits Thailand's capability to upgrade its production structure. Extensive investments at all levels of education are essential to support sustainable increases in wages and living standards in Thailand as well as in other Southeast Asian economies.

9.3 REFORM AND RECOVERY

The short-term responses to the Asian crisis were in many ways similar to those in the Nordic region. Most countries allowed their currencies to depreciate in order to strengthen the competitiveness of exports and to reduce current account deficits. Banks and financial institutions were recapitalized or restructured: those whose owners were unwilling or unable to provide more capital were closed or nationalized. Most countries opened up their financial sector (as well as other formerly protected sectors) to foreign direct investment. Various institutional reforms were undertaken to clear out problem credits and to restore public confidence in the financial system. Asset management corporations and financial supervisory agencies were set up across the region. Reforms also sought to increase transparency and to improve corporate governance with stricter accounting rules and revised bankruptcy laws. Negotiations with foreign creditors aimed to establish realistic schedules for debt repayments and to maintain the international credit lines needed to keep the economies operating. In many cases, the IMF was instrumental in closing these financing deals. Most countries also went through a brief period of fiscal and monetary restraint – mandated by the IMF and heavily criticized by many observers – in order to avoid inflation in a situation where the public was withdrawing large amounts of cash from the ailing banking system. The exception was Malaysia, where the government opted not to seek IMF assistance or advice and chose to handle the crisis with more expansionary fiscal and monetary policies. Unlike the other countries in the region, Malaysia also chose to introduce various controls on international capital flows to stop the outflow of capital.

The effects of the reforms in Asia were not as strong as in Finland and Sweden, where most of the impact of the crisis had dissipated by 1995, only three years after the crisis erupted. Figure 9.3 shows that the stock markets in most of the crisis-hit countries remained well below their pre-crisis levels until 2006: South Korea was the only economy where the stock market index had exceeded its pre-crisis level. Investment rates have also remained well below the levels of the mid-1990s. The most substantial contraction has occurred in Malaysia, where the ratio of fixed investment to GDP fell from over 40 per cent in 1995–97 to just over 20 per cent in 2004–05. In the other severely affected countries, the ratio has shrunk by one-third (*Asian Economic Perspectives*, 2006). The same picture holds for overall growth. Although most countries recorded one or two years with growth rates above 7 per cent, none of the severely affected countries have been able to return to pre-crisis growth rates.

The recovery at the micro level was also relatively sluggish. In particular, the asset management corporations in the region were slow to dispose of their NPLs, at the same time as corporate restructuring was slower than expected (Hanna and Huang, 2002). ADB (2001) reports that more than half of the loans in Indonesia were still classified as non-performing in 2001, the share of NPLs in Thailand was over one-fourth, and Korea, Malaysia and the Philippines recorded NPL ratios of over 15 per cent. In Korea and Malaysia, the asset management corporations had managed to sell or restructure about a third of the NPLs in the economy, but little had happened in the three other countries by that time. Four years later, in 2005, the Malaysian and Korean AMCs had largely completed their operations, but corporate debt still remained a problem in Indonesia, the Philippines and Thailand.

One consequence of the slow corporate restructuring process was that the export response to the crisis was delayed. In the case of Sweden, exports started growing rapidly once the currency was allowed to depreciate in late 1992, and the export volume increased by nearly 40 per cent during the following three years. In most of the worst-hit East Asian countries, exports did not begin to grow substantially until after 2002. South Korea and Malaysia exhibited the most rapid increases in exports, which may have been related to their successful short-term performance in terms of corporate debt restructuring: without a debt overhang, the financial system was able to provide fresh credits to the growing export sector. However, their early export success was interrupted by the turbulence in the IT market in 2001, which led to negative export growth throughout East Asia that year. With more favorable external conditions, it is possible that some of these economies (notably South Korea) would have been able to achieve an even faster recovery.

Yet, there are more important reasons than external conditions why the Asian recovery has been relatively slow. A first point, noted already in the previous section, is that the causes of the Asian crisis were deeply embedded in the Asian model of development. Government intervention (in the form of ambitious industrial policy programs) reduced the role of market-determined prices and profits, and the government guarantees that were implied by the active interest of the state led entrepreneurs to accept unusually high levels of risk. It has taken a long time to change the relationship between the government and the corporate sector. Both debtors and creditors delayed realizing their losses as long as possible, hoping that the government would eventually step in to bail them out. However, this also meant that they were not able to invest wholeheartedly in areas with growth opportunities, such as the export sectors.

The links between business and government have also influenced the Asian governments' willingness and ability to implement difficult decisions. Various interests groups have been able to influence politicians, delaying necessary reforms, such as forcing ailing firms to go bankrupt or preventing banks from rolling over debt to insolvent companies. The best example may be Japan, where the intimate links between political leaders, banks and enterprises (particularly in real estate and construction) contributed to a policy environment where even very weak firms managed to survive. Expansionary monetary policies pushed interest rates to zero, and several costly fiscal support programs generated the world's largest public sector debt. Yet, the economy remained stagnant for more than a decade after the crisis in 1990, and it is only recently (in 2006) that the Central Bank of Japan has raised the prime rate above zero again. Similar problems have been encountered in most other countries as well, although the slow speed of corporate restructuring is also related to the weaker institutional structure in many of the Asian economies.

Recalling the four points emphasized by Ingves and Lind (1998) as explanations for the rapid Swedish recovery – a political consensus on the solutions to the crisis, transparency regarding the financial situation of banks, a willingness to liquidate insolvent firms, and the efficient operation of asset management companies – it appears that few Asian countries have been able to follow the Swedish example. In particular, it seems that the political consensus that facilitated the Finnish and Swedish recovery from the crisis has been missing in Asia.

At the same time, it is important to note some crucial caveats regarding the comparison between Asia and Northern Europe. First, it is essential to define what constitutes 'recovery'. If the arguments regarding excessive investments and asset price bubbles are taken seriously, it is obvious that recovery does not necessitate a return to pre-crisis levels of investment,

GDP growth rates and stock market valuations, since these were too high to be sustainable. Second, the recovery should involve structural change to the extent that a crisis is related to structural problems (or weak fundamentals). This necessarily takes time. Third, structural changes are often painful, and defensive reactions from vested interests should be expected. Capital owners that risk losing their investments typically lobby for support from the government, workers whose jobs are in danger are likely to protest, and citizens who see little improvement in economic conditions in spite of painful contraction are likely to suffer 'reform fatigue' and vote for more popular alternatives.

Taking these characteristics into account, it may be normal that the recovery from a deep crisis takes time. In fact, the Asian crisis is not the only one where recovery has been slower than in Finland and Sweden. For instance, the Latin American debt crisis of the early 1980s was not resolved until the early 1990s (Kokko and Zejan, 2000). This suggests that the appropriate question might be 'How could Finland and Sweden manage such a rapid recovery?' rather than 'Why are others not able to recover equally fast?'

9.3.1 Why was Nordic Recovery so Fast?

Looking for special features in the Nordic economies during the 1990s, it is impossible to disregard two major events: the Finnish and Swedish accession to the EU in 1995 and the emergence of the 'new economy', characterized not only by telecom giants like *Ericsson* and *Nokia*, but rather by the emergence of a dynamic IT sector. Both these events had a profound impact on the recovery after the financial crisis.

It is hard to overestimate the role of EU membership. On the one hand, it is clear that participation in the European Union provided some economic benefits to the Nordic countries. In particular, the combination of a sharply depreciated currency and EU membership stimulated significant inflows of FDI to Sweden, providing capital, technology and links to important export markets. Between 1990 and 2000, the share of foreign-owned firms in Swedish manufacturing industry grew from 18 per cent to 32 per cent. At the same time, exports grew faster than ever before. The Swedish export-to-GDP ratio increased from 29 per cent to 48 per cent during the 1990s. Although the main explanation for the export boom was probably the depreciation of the currency in 1992, it is likely that the improved market access in the EU was also important.

The growth of telecommunications and information technologies provided further stimulus. The expansion of companies like *Ericsson* and *Nokia* and the clusters surrounding these firms absorbed much labor and contributed to investment, production and exports. Hence, the deeper integration with the rest of Europe and the emergence of the new economy together facilitated the necessary structural change towards industries with strong comparative advantages. In addition, the stock market boom of the second half of the 1990s was based on the new economy and this accounted for most of the recovery in the stock market indices. Without the IT boom, it would have taken much longer for the Nordic stock markets to exceed the levels attained before the financial crisis.

On the other hand, EU membership imposed a great degree of discipline on macroeconomic management and public finance. As EU members, Finland and Sweden were obliged to meet the Maastrict criteria for participation in the European Monetary Union. These criteria – and the convergence programs required to meet the criteria – aimed to reduce the variation in inflation and interest rates among the EU countries. To do that, caps on national government budget deficits and the level of public debt were also necessary. The restrictions from the convergence program were relevant mainly for the medium-term reforms. The immediate after-care of the crisis was not much affected by the preparations for EU membership, but the need to balance public budgets made it possible to resist calls for compensation from various interest groups.

Similarly, the contraction of the public sector that was necessary to turn the large deficits of the government budget during the first half of the 1990s into surpluses towards the end of the decade would hardly have been possible without external pressure. Considering the Swedish history of strong interest groups and coalitions between labor, capital and government – at times, even characterized as democratic corporatism (Katzenstein, 1985) – it is remarkable that government managed to distribute the costs of the crisis management across most groups of society. It is equally remarkable that government finances, investments, exports, stock markets and growth rates were back on pre-crisis level within five years of the crisis.

While the EU accession and the IT boom are largely exogenous events that can hardly be counted on to solve the next crisis, it has also been suggested that there are systematic differences between Nordic and Asian political structures that may explain the faster recovery in the North. In particular, Suzuki (2006) argues that Finland and Sweden have a higher degree of 'organizational learning capacity' in policy-making, and that this facilitated the design and implementation of effective reforms. By 'organizational learning capacity' he means the ability of an organization – in this case, the policy-making system – to collect and interpret internal and external information and to find efficient solutions for the policy challenges faced by the organization.

Suzuki (2006) asserts that the Swedish policy-making system is stronger in the generation, dissemination and interpretation of information, as well as in the implementation of agreed policy responses. The advantages regarding collection, dissemination and interpretation of information are mainly related to the more transparent and less hierarchical character of the Swedish policy systems. Government collects the opinions of various interest groups in an extensive consultation process with civil society, information is exchanged relatively freely between various actors in the policy-making system, and relatively horizontal decision structures contribute to exchanges of views between policy-makers and experts in the government bureaucracy. As a result, rules are typically relatively transparent, and decisions are implemented with little interference from interest groups. Asian (particularly Japanese) policy-making systems, in contrast, are hierarchical and compartmentalized, with fewer sources of information, fewer challenges to established interpretations of information, and more discretionary decision-making and interference from interest groups in the implementation phase.

Although the structural features of the Nordic policy learning processes probably exhibit systematic advantages compared with those of most Asian countries, there is reason to acknowledge the importance of favorable external circumstances (and perhaps some degree of luck) in explaining the rapid recovery after the Nordic crisis. The next crisis – which may well contain some of the features discussed above – may take longer to resolve even in Finland and Sweden. At the same time, there is reason to highlight those features of the Nordic policy-making system that may be replicated elsewhere. Consensus regarding the necessary reforms and transparency in legislation and implementation of policies appears to be particularly important. Governments and bureaucrats in countries like Japan, where strong domestic interest groups have for a long time obstructed painful but necessary restructuring, may also appreciate the practicality of suitable external pressure. In those Asian countries where these elements were lacking, the recovery process was significantly slower than in the Nordic countries.

NOTES

1. See the account of the Nordic crisis in Chapters 2 and 3 in this volume.
2. See Chapters 2 and 3 in this volume. See also Jonung et al. (1996), who make a more explicit comparison between the Finnish and the Swedish record; Drees and Pazarbasioglu (1998), who look specifically at the banking crises in Sweden, Norway and Finland, and Bordo and Schwartz (1996), who discuss currency crises in a historical perspective.
3. See Chapter 2 in this volume.

4. Chapters 2 and 4 in this volume. *Affärsvärlden* (1992), Lybeck (1994), Jonung et al. (1996) and *Ekonomisk Debatt*'s theme issue on the financial crisis (*Ekonomisk Debatt*, **28** (1), 1998) are examples of detailed analyses of the Swedish crisis. The following paragraphs are partly based on these sources.
5. If the opportunity cost of the bank support – the interest payments which were made or the potential interest income which the government failed to secure – taken into the calculations, Jennergren and Näslund (1998) believe that the bill for the taxpayer amounted to approximately SEK 35 billion.
6. For a more detailed analysis of growth strategies in the region, see Kokko (2006).
7. See Ostrom (1998) for a more detailed analysis. A great deal of Japanese capital was also invested via Hong Kong and Singapore.

REFERENCES

ADB (2001). *Asia Economic Monitor*, Asian Development Bank, Manila, December.

Affärsvärlden (1992), '*När Sverige kraschade' (When Sweden crashed)*, Stockholm: Affärsvärlden.

Bordo, M.D. and A. Schwartz (1996), 'Why clashes between internal and external stability goals end in currency crises, 1797–1994', *Open Economies Review*, **7**, 437–68.

Bäckström, U. (1998), 'Finansiella kriser – svenska erfarenheter' (Financial crises – the Swedish experience), *Ekonomisk Debatt*, **26**, 5–19.

Dollar, D. (1998), 'Has the miracle gone bust?', mimeo, The World Bank, January.

Drees, B. and C. Pazarbasioglu (1998), 'The Nordic banking crises: pitfalls in financial liberalization?', IMF Occasional Paper, no. 161, Washington, DC: IMF, April.

EAEP (2006), *East Asian Economic Perspectives*, **17** (1).

Feldstein, M. (1997), 'Japan's folly drags Asia down', *The Wall Street Journal*, 25 November.

Hanna, D. and Y. Huang (2002), 'Bank restructuring in post-crisis Asia', *Asian Economic Papers*, **1**, 3–42.

Ingves, S. and G. Lind (1998), 'Om att hantera en bankkris' (On the management of a banking crisis), *Ekonomisk Debatt*, **26**, 41–54.

Jennergren, P. and B. Näslund (1998), 'Efter bankkrisen: vad blev notan för skattebetalarna?' (After the banking crisis: what was the cost for taxpayers?), *Ekonomisk Debatt*, **26**, 69–76.

Jonung, L., J. Stymne and H.T. Söderström (1996), 'Depression in the North – boom and bust in Sweden and Finland, 1985–93', *Finnish Economic Papers*, **9**, 55–71.

Katzenstein, P. (1985), *Small States in World Markets: Industrial Policy in Europe*, Ithaca, NY and London: Cornell University Press.

Kobayashi, T. (1997), 'The currency crisis in Thailand', Fuji Research Paper, no. 7, Tokyo: Fuji Research Institute Corporation, October.

Kokko, A. (2006), 'Export-led growth in East Asia: lessons for Europe's transition economies', in S. Söderman (ed.), *Emerging Multiplicity – Integration and Responsiveness in Asian Business Development*, Basingstoke: Palgrave Macmillan, Chapter 2.

Kokko, A. and M. Zejan (2000), 'Asienkrisens effekter i Sydamerika: Chile, Argentina och Brasilien'(The impact of the Asian crisis in South America: Chile, Argentina and Brazil', *Ekonomiska Samfundets Tidsskrift*, no. 1, 61–70.

Komine, T. (1998), 'Currency crisis and financial turmoil in Asia and the potential for future growth', mimeo, Tokyo: Economic Planning Agency, March.

Krugman, P. (1998a), 'What happened to Asia?', mimeo, MIT, January (available at http://web.mit.edu/krugman/www/DISINTER.html).

Krugman, P. (1998b), 'Will Asia bounce back?', mimeo, MIT, March (available at http://web.mit.edu/krugman/www/suisse.html).

Lee, C.H. (ed.), (2003), *Financial Liberalization and the Economic Crisis in Asia*, London and New York: Routledge Curzon.

Lim, L. (1999), 'An overview of the Asian financial crisis', *Journal of Asian Business*, **15**, 79–81.

Lybeck, J.A. (1994), *Facit av finanskrisen* (The key to the financial crisis), Stockholm: SNS Förlag.

Ostrom, D. (1998), 'Japan and the Asian economic crisis: part of the solution or part of the problem?', JEI Report no 8A, Washington, DC: Japan Economic Institute, February.

Suzuki, K. (2006), 'Organizational learning capacity of policy-making system for financial system recovery: the case of Sweden with some suggestions to Japan', in S. Söderman (ed.), *Emerging Multiplicity – Integration and Responsiveness in Asian Business Development*, Basingstoke: Palgrave Macmillan.

Urwitz, G. (1998), 'Erfarenheter från en bankkris'(Experiences of a banking crisis), *Ekonomisk Debatt*, **26**, 55–68.

Warr, P., (1997), 'Why Thai *Baht* had to float', *Australian Financial Review*, 17 July, 6.

Williamson , J. (ed.) (1994), *The Political Economy of Policy Reform*, Washington, DC: Institute for International Economics.

Wohlin, L. (1998), 'Bankkrisens upprinnelse' (The emergence of the banking crisis), *Ekonomisk Debatt*, **26**, 21–30.

World Bank (1993), *The East Asian Miracle: Economic Growth and Public Policy*, Washington, DC and New York: The World Bank and Oxford University Press.

PART III

Lessons from the Nordic crises

10. Twelve lessons from the Nordic experience of financial liberalization

Lars Jonung

INTRODUCTION[1]

The boom–bust cycle in Finland and Sweden from the mid-1980s till the turn of the century has been examined in the previous chapters. The financial crises of these two countries were compared with the experience of other countries and with major crises of the past. In this final chapter, 12 policy lessons from the Nordic experience of financial liberalization and financial crises are distilled. These lessons may be useful for any country subject to financial tensions in the future. As history demonstrates, financial crises are recurring phenomena; there will be new crises. In addition, the long-run effects of financial integration on the Nordic economies are considered briefly. Now, more than a decade after the end of the depression of the 1990s, the lasting impact of financial liberalization on the Nordic countries may be evaluated.

10.1 THE STYLIZED PATTERN OF THE NORDIC CRISES

For a long time, high growth and full employment characterized the macroeconomic record of Denmark, Finland, Norway and Sweden – the Nordic or Scandinavian countries – during the post-World War II period.[2] Prior to the 1990s, the Nordic countries were able to avoid the persistent mass unemployment common to many European countries already in the 1970s. Denmark was the only Nordic country experiencing high unemployment in the 1980s. However, the image of the Nordic economies as successful was crushed at the beginning of the 1990s when Finland and Sweden faced a severe crisis and Norway a milder one.

The Nordic crises had their roots in the process of financial liberalization that was carried out in a monetary regime based on pegged but adjustable exchange rates. In the 1980s, the financial systems of Finland, Norway and Sweden underwent major deregulation. Financial liberalization set off a sustained lending boom, capital inflows, rising asset prices, rapidly increasing consumption and investment and an overheated non-tradables sector, while the exchange rates of the Nordic countries remained pegged. The boom turned into a bust around 1990, with capital outflows, widespread bankruptcies, falling employment, declining investments, negative GDP growth, systemic banking crises, currency crises and depression. Eventually, the central banks of Finland, Norway and Sweden were forced to move to flexible rates in the fall of 1992 in order to avert the depression.

As seen from the earlier chapters, the crisis in Finland, Norway and Sweden was a financial crisis occurring as part of a boom–bust cycle. It displayed the characteristics of a twin crisis, defined as the simultaneous occurrence of a banking and a currency crisis. In fact, in Finland and Sweden the twin crisis turned into a 'triplet' crisis when huge public budget deficits emerged as a consequence of the sharp decline in economic activity.

The previous chapters of this volume traced in depth economic performance and policy responses during the boom–bust cycles that emerged in the 1980s and 1990s. The account in these chapters is condensed below in a stylized manner in order to distil some policy lessons from the Nordic record.[3]

10.1.1 Financial Liberalization and Credit-fuelled Boom

As stressed in several chapters, the financial liberalization of the 1980s affected the incentives of lenders and borrowers in a fundamental way. After decades of non-price-credit rationing, banks were suddenly able to expand their lending without being hampered by regulatory restrictions. Banks entered into fierce competition for market shares by offering loans to households and firms. A lending boom started, channelling credit to asset markets – primarily to housing, to commercial real estate and to the stock market – causing asset prices to rise. Rising asset prices formed the basis for rising collateral values and increasing net wealth of households, further fuelling the credit expansion. Within a couple of years, the aggregate credit volumes were increasing at an unprecedented rate.

These financial developments impacted on the real economy. The macroeconomic outcome was a strong boom, first in the Norwegian economy, and later in the Finnish and Swedish economies in 1988–89, as Norway started its financial deregulation roughly two years earlier than Finland and Sweden. The boom was characterized by overfull employment, rising consumption and falling savings ratios, which eventually turned negative. The current accounts worsened as export performance weakened and imports increased.

Due to the pegged exchange rate, monetary policy was prevented from mitigating the boom through interest rate increases. Fiscal policies were not tightened enough to choke off the boom although national budgets displayed large surpluses due to rising tax revenues from higher consumption, wages, property values and capital gains.

Financial deregulation, the key reason for the birth of the boom in all three countries, was pushed through without any serious parliamentary or public debate. It was not presented as part of a larger policy program, but rather as a series of technical changes, usually too minor to require political decisions and parliamentary attention. Policy-makers argued that financial controls had become ineffective and were anyway largely evaded. For this reason, deregulation was not expected to have any major impact.

At this stage, policy-makers were not able to discern the risks inherent in the process of financial liberalization. Experts in the central banks and finance ministries were not much better informed. The economics profession focused on the beneficial long-run effects of deregulation, not on the possibility of short-run imbalances and crisis. This state of affairs was due to the lack of knowledge and experience of the consequences of financial integration, although a few voices warned of looming danger.

10.1.2 Rising Real Rates and Bust

The boom in the real economy was eventually halted and turned into a bust by a combination of events, exogenous as well as endogenous. Real interest rates rose internationally as a result of the contractionary design of German monetary policy following German reunification. Rising German interest rates exerted strong upward pressure on the interest rates of the Nordic currencies, which were more or less formally tied to the German Mark when the Finnish, Norwegian and Swedish currencies were officially pegged to the *ecu*, the virtual European currency unit, in 1990–91. Previously, their exchange rates had been linked to baskets of currencies. An additional real interest rate shock occurred when the Finnish and Swedish central banks raised their nominal interest rates in attempts to defend their fixed exchange rates against recurring speculative attacks in 1989–92.

Other policy measures increased the real after-tax interest rate. In Finland, stepwise limitations on the tax deductibility of mortgage rates in the early 1990s increased the after-tax cost of servicing debt. The far-reaching Swedish 1990–91 tax reform, which lowered marginal taxes significantly and reduced tax deductibility of mortgage rates, raised real after-tax interest rates. In this way, borrowing turned less attractive while private savings became more attractive. A rapid and less than fully expected decline in the rate of consumer price inflation in 1990–92 contributed to the sharp rise in real interest rates in Finland and Sweden. Within a couple of years, the real after-tax interest rates rose to levels much higher than borrowers had expected a few years earlier.

The sharp increase in the real rate had a profound impact on financial markets. Asset price deflation kicked in when the value of real assets was reduced by rising real interest rates. Balance sheets turned fragile when asset values, primarily property prices, fell below collateral values. At the same time, the nominal values of debts remained unchanged. Wealth losses came to the fore, forcing an adjustment of portfolios, leading to falling private consumption, falling investments and rising private savings.

During the depression of the 1930s in the United States, Fisher (1933) described how such a chain of events gives rise to a process known as debt deflation. In the early 1990s a similar process took place in the Nordic countries. The harder households and firms tried to improve their wealth position by selling assets and increasing savings, the deeper the crisis became. The property sell-off forced down property prices, which, in turn, triggered new sales. The number of bankruptcies increased dramatically. Stock market prices tumbled, in particular for firms engaged in the financial sector, in real estate and in construction.

Investment fell, in particular within the construction sector. With declining prices for existing houses, demand for new construction evaporated. Unemployment soared. As the Finnish and Swedish currencies were overvalued due to high wage and price inflation during the preceding boom, the export sector encountered major problems in 1990–91. In Finland, the collapse of bilateral trade with the Soviet Union contributed to the domestic imbalances.[4] Tax revenues declined and public expenditures rose due to the workings of automatic stabilizers. In Finland and Sweden, the government budget deficit and thus the ratio of government debt to GDP increased dramatically. Norway, however, did not experience any rise in government debt due to strong public finances stemming from revenues from the energy sector.

In 1992, the financial systems of all three countries were rocked when the Finnish *markka,* the Norwegian *krone* and the Swedish *krona* were exposed to major speculative attacks. A European currency crisis erupted in September 1992. The Finnish *markka* was floated in September 1992.[5] The Swedish *krona* followed suit two months later, in November 1992, despite fierce resistance by the *Riksbank*. Finally, the Norwegian currency was floated in December 1992.

10.1.3 Recovery

The floating of the currencies in the fall of 1992, with the ensuing depreciation and receding domestic interest rates, checked the downturn in the Finnish, Norwegian and Swedish economies. The recovery commenced in all three countries in the following year and lasted for more than a decade, although unemployment remained high for a long time. It did not start to decline until the mid-1990s, from which point it fell steadily.[6] The main engine of the recovery was an impressive growth in exports. Export shares rose significantly in all three countries, most markedly in Finland and Sweden (Figure 10.1). This rise continued for more than a decade. The current accounts, previously in chronic deficit, turned to seemingly permanent large surpluses.

The Nordic rate of inflation stayed at a low level, around 2 per cent per annum, throughout the period 1995–2007. Wages and prices remained surprisingly stable given the currency depreciation. Contrary to predictions made during the recession, the large exchange rate depreciations did not have any apparent impact on domestic price and wage levels. The high rate of unemployment contributed to wage moderation.

Post-crisis fiscal policies in Finland and Sweden were directed first towards reducing budget deficits, and later towards lowering national debt. The fiscal consolidation efforts were large and successful. Within five

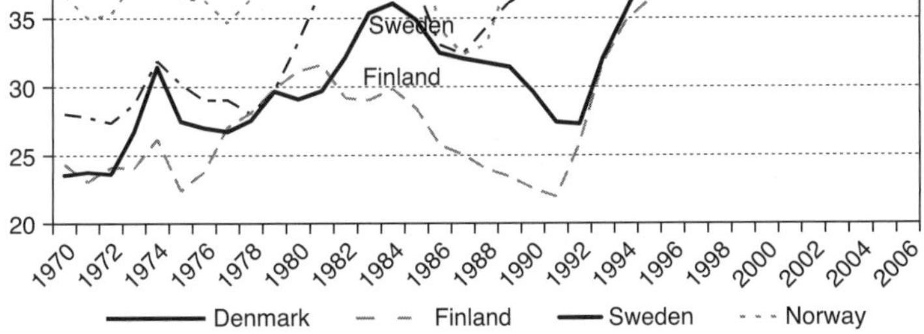

Source: AMECO.

Figure 10.1 Ratio of exports to GDP in the Nordic countries, 1970–2006 (per cent)

ears, Finland and Sweden were able to move from deep deficits to some of the biggest surpluses in Europe. Norway is a special case due to the returns from the oil and gas sector.

The recovery after the boom–bust cycle turned out to be long-lasting – at least until the downturn in worldwide economic activity around 2001. After a short break, rapid growth continued until 2008. The Finnish, Norwegian and Swedish growth rates have remained consistently above the EU average since the depression of the early 1990s.

10.1.4 After the Recovery

Financial integration profoundly changed the economic landscape in the Nordic countries, in particular in Finland and Sweden, the two countries worst hit by the financial crisis. These long-run effects have been overshadowed by the short-run impact of the financial opening, in other words by the dramatic events during the boom–bust cycle, and the post-crisis recovery. But once financial markets were opened up, this impacted on a large number of sectors both inside and outside the financial system.

The stock markets of Finland and Sweden expanded as part of the process of financial opening and integration. Foreign holdings of domestic stocks increased rapidly. Cross-border holdings of financial assets and liabilities grew as well, reflecting financial integration (Figure 10.2). Corporate governance changed once foreign ownership was admitted.[7]

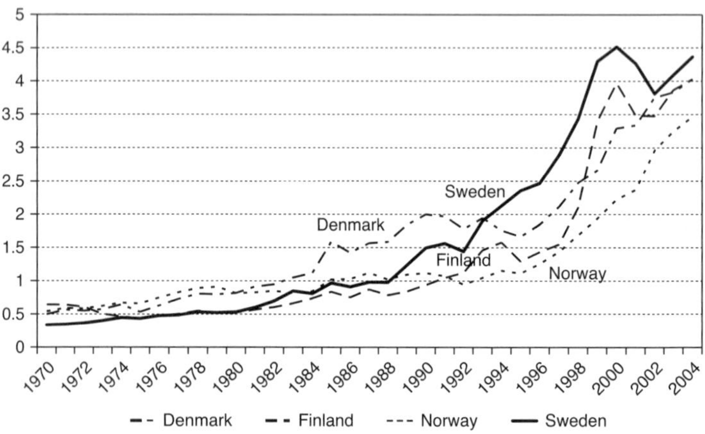

Source: Data kindly provided by Philip Lane.

Figure 10.2 Financial openness in the Nordic countries 1970–2004: total foreign assets plus total foreign liabilities to GDP (per cent)

axation was adjusted to international tax competition. The rules for monetary and fiscal policy-making were reformed and adjusted. Inflation targeting was introduced. Eventually, Finland entered the euro area in 1999 as part of the process of European monetary unification. Norway and Sweden remained outside the euro area. In short, the financial integration that followed the crisis of the early 1990s pushed the process of globalization in the Nordic economies far ahead.

The strong post-crisis performance of the Scandinavian countries has created an international interest in the Nordic or Scandinavian model.[8] It has been hailed as a paradigm for other countries to copy. As argued below, this recent focus on the Nordic record has probably not paid due attention to the impact of the financial crises and financial integration on Nordic developments.

10.2 TWELVE LESSONS FROM THE NORDIC FINANCIAL CRISES

By now there is a substantial literature drawing lessons from financial liberalization and financial crises in emerging-market economies.[9] Most of it deals with the experience of East Asia and Latin America in the late 1990s. A summary of the lessons from financial liberalization, from the ensuing boom–bust, and from the crises and the recovery in Scandinavia is lacking.[10] Still, the Nordic record offers a number of lessons for policy-making that are at least as relevant as those from the emerging-market crises which took place after the Nordic crises.

Lesson-drawing is not an exact science. It is, to a large degree, subjective. Bearing this caveat in mind, the preceding chapters in this volume suggest, in my opinion, 12 lessons. They are categorized below under three headings: first, lessons on how to liberalize without creating a financial crisis, second, lessons on how to deal with a financial crisis once it has surfaced, and third, lessons concerning the long-run effects of financial integration on the design of stabilization policies, on growth and efficiency, and on the distribution of income and wealth.

Many of the lessons presented below are closely related. In addition, some of them are more important than others. Most of them stem from one source: the lack of knowledge of the dynamics created by financial liberalization. Ignorance among policy-makers, forecasters, bankers, economists and the public about the powerful macroeconomic effects of the financial imbalances initiated by financial liberalization explains much of the disastrous record of Finland, Norway and Sweden. Most of the remaining lessons are corollaries to this foremost conclusion.

10.2.1 How to Liberalize without Creating a Financial Crisis

First, we consider the lessons on how a financial meltdown may be avoided. In hindsight, these lessons may seem obvious but Nordic policy-makers were not aware of them prior to the outbreak of the crises.

Lesson no. 1: the dangers of financial ignorance

If knowledge about the processes unleashed by financial liberalization is lacking, the policy response before, during and after financial liberalization is unlikely to be the most appropriate. This was the case in the Nordic countries. When financial deregulation started in Finland, Norway and Sweden in the 1980s, financially driven booms, busts and crises were unknown phenomena to policy-makers in the central banks and the ministries of finance, as well as to forecasters, to financial regulators, to the economics profession, to bankers and other actors in the financial system, and to the public at large.[11] The thinking and thus the behaviour established by many decades of financial controls and regulations continued unchanged, without an understanding that financial liberalization was rapidly creating a new and financially more risky world that replaced the old risk-free environment.

Policy-makers viewed the steps towards financial deregulation in the mid-1980s as technical adjustments of no major consequence for economic performance. In addition, the first impact of the move towards liberalization was a lending boom with rising consumption and wealth. This upturn was initially appreciated by the parties in political power. Thus, no effective counteracting stabilization policy measures were taken to dampen the rapid growth in the volume of credit.

Official forecasts made within the Nordic countries, as well as by international organizations, failed to identify the boom–bust cycle. Significant forecast errors emerged during both the boom and the bust phases of the cycle. The systematic collective bias in forecast performance contributed to the policy mistakes.

Economists at universities in Scandinavia were caught in a Keynesian world of flow variables, unfamiliar with the wealth, portfolio and balance sheet effects created by financial liberalization and by huge swings in the real rate of interest. As a rule, economists were in favour of financial liberalization as part of a policy of structural reforms aimed at improving growth performance, yet lacked an understanding of the dangerous imbalances that financial deregulation could bring about if not combined with proper counter-measures. Thus, hardly any warnings emerged from the economics profession when such advice would have been most appropriate.

Bankers and other actors in financial markets were ignorant about the consequences of financial deregulation. They had only experienced a financially closed and strongly regulated economy where financial risks were exceptionally limited. Thus, they did not understand the dangers of a rapid extension of credit. The same held for private individuals and firms. As soon as credit became freely available due to the deregulation, borrowers quickly entered deeper into debt. Thus, the credit boom was fuelled by lenders and borrowers with little understanding of the risks inherent in the deregulation process.

The policy lesson is straightforward. A thorough analytical and factual understanding of the workings of unfettered financial markets is crucial to make financial liberalization and subsequent financial integration successful. Financial knowledge should be as widely dispersed as possible, among policy-makers, regulators, official and private forecasters, economists, financial sector participants and, most importantly, the public at large. In the future, new risks are likely to build up through the emergence of new financial instruments, techniques, regulations and so on. Of course, these cannot be predicted today, but financial literacy, including the proper learning from other countries and from history, helps in the successful planning and management of financial liberalization.

Lesson no. 2: the dangers of backward-looking policy learning

In the crisis-ridden Nordic countries, policy-makers defended the pegged exchange rate against speculative attacks at high costs to society. They, as well as most economists, supported the pegged exchange rate regime until the bitter end. In hindsight, it seems as if central bankers and ministers of finance were not concerned about the costs to society of the hard currency policy although their economies were driven into deep crisis and soaring unemployment due to the defence of the pegged rate.[12]

This response pattern was due to the backward-looking learning process of policy-makers and economists alike.[13] They had become convinced that the devaluations of the 1970s and early 1980s had not solved any problems in the long run, only masked them in the short run. Consequently, a strict adherence to a pegged exchange rate policy (a hard currency policy) was viewed as a better strategy – as a method of breaking away from the devaluation cycles of the past. The argument was that a credible pegged exchange rate would act as a nominal anchor for a monetary policy intended to achieve low inflation and thus create a proper climate for growth and employment.

When confronted with the emerging crisis in the late 1980s and early 1990s, policy-makers looked back at the most recent crisis experience for lessons to guide their actions. As they had just learnt from the crises of the 1970s and early 1980s that devaluations (a soft currency policy) and subsequent high price and wage rate inflation could and should be avoided by sticking to a hard currency policy, they stubbornly defended the pegged rate. However, relying on the lesson from the most immediate past crisis turned out to be a recipe for disaster when moving from a financially closed world into a financially integrated one.

The lesson is that policy-makers should not become prisoners of backward-looking learning by regarding the present crisis as identical to the most recent one. If they do, they run the risk of basing their policy actions on a faulty interpretation of the historical record. Instead, they should examine the evidence from crises further back in time, and from other countries, before determining the proper policy response.[14]

Lesson no. 3: the dangers of rapid changes in the real rate of interest

The boom–bust episode 1985–93 in Finland, Norway and Sweden demonstrates the central role that rapid, large and unexpected changes in the real rate of interest, or more accurately in the after-tax real rate, may play in driving macroeconomic developments during the opening of financially closed economies with pegged but adjustable exchange rates.

Prior to financial liberalization, the real rate of interest in the three Nordic countries was low or negative, often in the range of minus 2 to plus 4 per cent, as a consequence of prevailing internal and external financial regulations, the system of tax-deductible interest payments on mortgage loans, and high inflation and well-entrenched inflation expectations. Negative real rates created extremely strong incentives for individuals and firms to accept more debt in the mid-1980s when financial controls were loosened or abolished, thus driving the demand for credit. Banks and other financial intermediaries responded by increasing the supply of credit.

Eventually, after major changes in the tax system, rising nominal interest rates and falling inflation, real after-tax rates turned positive. During the bust phase, real rates reached uniquely high levels. The huge and to a large extent unexpected rise in the real rate of interest created massive negative balance sheet or wealth effects, sharply reducing investments and consumption and raising savings as the private sector tried to rebalance the composition of its portfolio. These contractionary balance sheet effects undermined the entire financial system, the wealth position of the private sector and the budget of the public sector.[15]

The policy lesson is straightforward. The monetary and fiscal authorities should avoid starting financial liberalization with the after-tax real rate substantially below the equilibrium rate, thus preventing pronounced and unexpected swings in the real rate when it moves towards the international level. A more gradual and cautious approach aimed at ensuring smooth movements in the real rate may restrain or even prevent boom–bust episodes from occurring during financial deregulation.

Lesson no. 4: the dangers of procyclical stabilization policies
Monetary and fiscal policies were procyclical during the Nordic boom–bust cycle. They reinforced each other in a way that destabilized the economy.

Monetary policy The Nordic episodes illustrate the crucial role played by the exchange rate regime during a process of financial liberalization. By maintaining and defending the pegged exchange rate of their currencies, policy-makers in Finland, Norway and Sweden created a procyclical monetary policy during and after financial liberalization.

During the boom phase, interest rates could not be raised sufficiently to counter the upturn in the domestic economy because higher interest rates would have induced additional capital inflows and thus added more fuel to the credit boom. Once the cycle started to turn downwards, the pegged exchange rate was defended by raising domestic rates, contributing to the recession. Eventually, the defence of the currency made the domestic crisis so deep that the peg was abandoned in all three countries.

The policy lesson is straightforward: keeping a pegged exchange rate during a process of financial liberalization runs the risk of making monetary policy procyclical, creating a conflict between internal and external stability.[16,17] A more flexible exchange rate policy would probably have dampened the amplitude of the Nordic boom–bust cycle.

Fiscal policy Fiscal policy, that is, the design of taxes and government expenditure, played a key role during the Nordic process of financial liberalization. During the boom, it was as a rule procyclical. Fiscal authorities were commonly of the opinion that fiscal policy was countercyclical as the budget was in surplus. However, these surpluses were too small to effectively put an end to the boom. In hindsight, it is easy to conclude that fiscal policy should have been tighter during the boom stage of the business cycle. During the bust phase, due primarily to the workings of automatic stabilizers, budget deficits expanded extremely rapidly. The rise in public deficits induced far-reaching measures to reduce government expenditures and raise taxes in Finland and Sweden. Fiscal policies were thus procyclical during the bust as well.

Two conflicting interpretations exist regarding to what extent the contractionary fiscal policies in Finland and Sweden in the wake of the financial crises impeded or contributed to the recovery. One school of thought advocating fiscal restraint, argues that the rise in the budget deficit during the crisis was so large that it threatened to become unsustainable, creating expectations of an explosion of public debt with sharply rising interest rates, eventually leading to the monetization of public debt and to extreme inflation. To reduce these expectations and keep interest rates in check, policy-makers were compelled to tighten fiscal policy in order to stop a menacing growth of the deficit.[18]

An alternative and opposing view suggests that the rise in budget deficits during the crisis reflected mainly the workings of automatic stabilizers. According to this school, the huge budget deficits were primarily of a cyclical, not of a structural, character. As a consequence, attempts to drastically reduce the deficits during the crisis by raising taxes and cutting government expenditures were counterproductive and probably pushed the economy deeper into depression.

Economists who take this view commonly adhere to a balance sheet approach implying that fiscal policy during a financial crisis should prevent aggregate demand from shrinking further. In this case, the policy lesson is that in the event of a boom–bust cycle, fiscal policy should be based on a tax-smoothing strategy. It should be countercyclical, at least in the sense of letting automatic stabilizers work freely, restraining demand during the upturn and supporting it in the downturn. During the bust phase, budget deficits should be allowed to expand. In short, fiscal policy as well as other types of policies should aim at strengthening the balance sheets of the private sector during the bust.[19]

Lesson no. 5: the dangers of procyclical sequencing of financial reforms

The Nordic record demonstrates that the sequencing of financial reforms, internally and externally, is of the utmost importance for the success or failure of financial liberalization. Financial markets were first deregulated internally in the mid-1980s, which set off a sharp lending boom fuelled by an inflow of capital, while outflows were prevented by capital controls. Later financial markets were externally deregulated, allowing for an outflow of capital, roughly at the same time as the central banks were forced to defend the pegged exchange rate with higher interest rates. The pegged exchange rate was eventually abandoned when the crisis reached its peak. An earlier floating or an earlier adjustment of the peg would have dampened the boom–bust pattern – or even eliminated it if financial liberalization had been combined simultaneously with a more flexible exchange rate policy or a fully floating rate.

The sequencing of deregulatory measures also includes how interest payments on loans are treated by taxation. In the three Nordic countries, real after-tax interest rates were initially kept at low levels through favourable tax treatment of interest payments on loans. At a later stage, taxation was changed, significantly raising real after-tax interest rates. Thus, tax rules made a procyclical contribution, first fuelling the boom and later exacerbating the bust. A better sequencing would have implied tax reforms at a very early stage of the financial liberalization process.

The policy lesson from this aspect is that policy-makers should closely monitor the short-run consequences on the economy of structural changes in regulations and taxes. Such steps may be highly recommendable in themselves as part of a policy for improved growth and efficiency but they may have decidedly undesirable cyclical effects when interacting with other developments. Thus, policy-makers should pay careful attention to initial conditions when changing prevailing financial regulations and schemes of taxation.

Lesson no. 6: the limits of micro-prudential financial supervision

Prior to the financial deregulation in the mid-1980s, the system of financial supervision was well developed in Finland, Norway and Sweden to handle the challenges arising within a financially restricted and closed system. However, it was not prepared to deal with the new risks and dangers arising in an internationally open banking sector. This competence was simply lacking. Still, there were no weak banks, no crony banking, no dubious links between banks and industrial companies, political parties or private families reflecting nepotism and corruption. In addition, no banks were dependent on state subsidies or state support prior to the financial opening. In spite of the existing financial supervision, the financial crises of the early 1990s brought the entire banking system close to collapse, forcing several banks into bankruptcy or into obtaining support through government actions.

The policy lesson is that conventional micro-prudential financial supervision, adopted to monitor tightly regulated financial institutions, was not up to the task of preventing a strong boom followed by a deep crisis from developing once the financial system was opened up for competition and international exposure. The forces of boom and bust unleashed among the Nordics were simply too strong to be neutralized by financial supervision.[20] Thus, it is imperative to reform the supervisory system prior to or simultaneously with financial liberalization.

Lesson no. 7: the need to avoid financial repression

The roots of the Nordic financial crises were in the extensive financial repression that was put in place after World War II. These regulations created huge imbalances as well as behaviour by banks and by the public that contributed to the boom–bust cycle once financial repression was eliminated by the process of deregulation. The transition from a heavily regulated financial system to an open one proved highly risky for Finland, Norway and Sweden in the late 1980s and early 1990s, eventually leading to a deep crisis.

If financial repression is avoided, there will be no call for financial liberalization. In this way, the risk of a financial calamity is reduced. Of course, financially deregulated systems may also undergo crises but for reasons other than deregulation.

The lesson is straightforward: stay away from financial repression. This, however, is a hard lesson to follow. It is difficult today to understand what type of regulations are needed to keep the financial system 'sound', 'stable' and market-based, moving it along an equilibrium path. Some measures may seem appropriate at any given moment in order to make the financial system work better, but in hindsight they may turn out to have contributed to the next financial disaster.

Lesson no. 8: financial liberalization can be crisis-free

To conclude this section on what lessons can be drawn from the Nordic experience on how to prevent the emergence of a financial crisis, the Danish case demonstrates that financial liberalization may be carried out without contributing to a financial calamity, contrary to the experience of Finland, Norway and Sweden. This requires a well-balanced policy approach. Monetary and fiscal policy should be geared towards macroeconomic and financial stability, the process of deregulation should follow a proper sequencing, and the banking system should be well-capitalized.[21] In short, Denmark managed to steer clear of the mistakes that the other Nordics made when they opened their financial systems to the rest of the world.

The policy lesson is a basic one. Financial liberalization can be designed in such a way that it does not trigger a financial crisis. Thus, the benefits of a financially open system can be obtained while avoiding the costs that so many countries have paid in the form of a financial meltdown.

10.2.2 How to Deal with a Financial Crisis

Once the financial crises broke out in Finland, Norway and Sweden, policy-makers were faced with complex decisions concerning the appropriate measures to take to alleviate the impact of the financial turmoil. As the crisis was unexpected – no financial crisis had occurred among the Nordics since the 1930s – they were forced to improvise and experiment. Eventually, a number of lessons concerning resolution policies emerged from this experience.

Lesson no. 9: the benefits of rapid crisis management

The process of financial liberalization set off a chain of events that threatened to wipe out the entire equity of many banks. At this stage, far-reaching steps were taken in Finland to support the banking system; the savings bank group was taken over by the government. In Norway, the three biggest banks were nationalized, eliminating private ownership completely. The government of Sweden offered blanket insurance for claims on Swedish commercial banks, nationalized the two clearly insolvent banks, and set up asset management corporations to take over bad assets of the remaining commercial banks.

The Swedish approach is commonly praised for being swift and resolute.[22] It prevented bank runs; it maintained the solvent commercial banks in private ownership and allowed banks to continue financial intermediation; it prevented any credit crunch to emerge; it kept moral hazard for shareholders at bay; and it was transparent. Eventually, the bad assets taken over by the asset management corporations turned out to be something of a financial success once the economy had recovered – or at least the losses turned out to be much smaller than initially expected.

The policy lesson is clear. Rapid, transparent and determined government actions to maintain public confidence in the strength of the banking system reduce the impact of a financial crisis, dampen any credit crunch and allow for a rapid recovery of the financial system and thus of the real economy.

Lesson no. 10: the insufficiency of the lender-of-last-resort function

Traditionally, in the case of a liquidity crisis, the proper task of a central bank is to serve as the lender of last resort to the banking system by injecting liquidity into individual institutions or into the whole financial system. However, the financial crisis in Scandinavia turned out to be a solvency crisis for the banking system and thus much more severe than a liquidity crisis. The Nordic experience illustrates the standard view that, during a systemic financial crisis, the lender-of-last-resort function of the central bank is inadequate to support ailing banks.

The Nordic central banks were squeezed from two sides during the bust phase: by a currency crisis and by a banking crisis. Their financial resources were simply insufficient in the midst of the financial turmoil when their foreign reserves were falling at the same time as the banking system wanted to borrow from the central banks. Instead, the ministries of finance stepped in to support insolvent banks in all three countries while the central banks stood on the sideline.

The policy lesson is that in the face of a deep systemic financial crisis, a solvency crisis, the government – not the central bank – must serve as the supporter of last resort of failing financial institutions. Only the government can offer the blanket guarantees and capital injections deemed necessary to stabilize the financial system. The rescue of the banking system must be financed by fiscal measures, in other words by the taxpayer.

Lesson no. 11: the insufficiency of the IMF's advice

Finland, Norway and Sweden were members of the IMF almost from its inception. One of its tasks is to give policy guidance to its member states. Judging from the Article IV consultations and other types of recommendations given by IMF representatives, the performance of the IMF was far from successful prior to and during the Nordic crises.[23] The boom–bust cycle came as a surprise to the IMF; it gave no early warnings of an impending crisis. Once the crisis broke out, the focus of the IMF's advice was on defending the pegged exchange rate by making fiscal policy more contractionary, even as the economy was sliding into recession.[24]

The IMF's policy recommendations during the Nordic financial crises have yet to be thoroughly analysed by researchers. At this stage, available documents and interviews with policy-makers in Finland and Sweden suggest that the IMF held the view that the Nordic crises had their main roots in lax fiscal policies which gave rise to large structural deficits. The IMF did not adequately observe the process of financial deregulation that started in the mid-1980s and eventually ended in the banking and currency crises, driving up public budget deficits as part of the depression and forcing the private sector to reconsolidate its balance sheet. The IMF's poor policy advice to the Nordics may have been due to it drawing lessons from the Latin American debt crisis of the 1980s, which it then projected on to the Nordic financial crises.[25]

The policy lesson for a member country of the IMF finding itself in a crisis is to take advice and guidance from many sources. Of course, the IMF has learnt from the global crisis experience of the 1990s but there is no guarantee that the lessons learnt will turn out to be the right ones in the future.

10.2.3 The Long-run Effects of Financial Integration

The Nordic experience of financial deregulation demonstrates that it has far-reaching long-run or structural effects on the design of stabilization policies, the growth potential of the economy, and the distribution of income and wealth in society. These systemic consequences of cross-border financial integration are briefly considered below.

Lesson no. 12: the long-run effects of financial integration

Stabilization policies Financial integration had a major impact on the stabilization policy regime in Finland, Norway and Sweden. The framework for monetary policy as well as for fiscal policy was changed fundamentally.

First of all, concerning monetary policy, the pegged exchange rate regime of the three countries was abolished as it proved to be inadequate as a nominal anchor during the process of financial liberalization. After the crisis, the pegged rate regime was replaced by inflation targeting in Sweden, announced in January 1993 to start in January 1995. This monetary policy strategy, based on openness, accountability and communication through changes in the short-term interest rate set by the central bank, requires the existence of well-functioning financial markets. The financial liberalization of the 1980s and the subsequent financial integration created the prerequisites for a new type of monetary policy regime or policy framework that could not have existed when the Swedish economy was financially closed and heavily regulated with strong administrative controls of short- and long-term interest rates in place.

Finland and Norway also moved away from the pegged exchange rate regime. Finland followed Sweden's approach by adopting inflation targeting in February 1993, as an emergency strategy, with the aim of achieving a 2 per cent inflation rate by 1995. Later, in 1999, Finland joined the euro area, thus adopting a permanently fixed exchange rate. After moving towards greater exchange rate flexibility in the 1990s, Norway eventually adopted inflation targeting in early 2001.

Second, concerning fiscal policy, as a consequence of the experience of large budget deficits during the crisis, the institutional framework for fiscal policy-making was reformed in Finland and Sweden towards a rule-based approach. The aim was to reduce the scope for short-term discretionary fiscal policies by tying the hands of policy-makers through various restrictions. Finland's and Sweden's accession to the European Union in 1995 made their fiscal policy subject to the budget rules set out in the EU institutional framework. Norway, on the other hand, due to its huge revenues from oil and gas, faced the challenge of managing extremely large budget surpluses.

The policy lesson here is a fundamental one. Once the domestic economy is financially integrated with the rest of the world, a market-based monetary policy like inflation targeting can be put in place. With increasing financial integration, the efficiency of fiscal policy is reduced, facilitating a move to diminish the scope for fiscal measures by various means.

Growth and efficiency Financial liberalization is associated with boom–bust patterns in numerous countries, ending in financial crises and deep recessions with negative growth rates. Given this record, many economists are sceptical of financial opening, instead proposing restrictions on capital flows. Others stress the positive relationship between financial development and growth, implying that financial liberalization enhances efficiency and growth by making the financial system more sophisticated. They claim that financial liberalization and subsequent crises have taken place in some of the most rapidly growing countries in the world. No consensus has yet emerged regarding the growth effects of financial liberalization and crises.[26]

The evidence from Scandinavia, not commonly referred to in the international debate, may throw additional light on the relationship between financial liberalization and growth. In short, the Nordic record suggests that financial crises, triggered by a process of financial liberalization, are extremely costly in the short run in many dimensions – to society, to taxpayers, to owners of stocks and equities, and to politicians in power – but contribute to high growth for a long period following the recovery.

In a comparative perspective, the loss in terms of output, industrial production and employment due to the depression of the 1990s was remarkable. In Finland and Sweden, this was by far the deepest depression in the post-World War II period.[27] The fiscal cost of the crisis was enormous as budget deficits and public debt soared when tax revenues declined and government expenditures increased, largely due to the workings of automatic stabilizers. Government support for the financial system ballooned in the short run. The private sector, in particular holders of stocks in banks and other financial institutions, was hit by huge wealth losses. The political costs were significant as well. Governments in power at the start of the crisis lost popularity and were replaced in subsequent elections. Whether or not the policy-makers in power had designed the policies that led to the crisis, they were held responsible by the voters.

Turning from the short-run costs and looking at the long-run consequences of the financial crises of the early 1990s, a more positive picture emerges. The post-crisis growth rates of Finland and Sweden since 1993 have been high compared with the EU average. Much suggests that this growth pattern is associated with financial integration and the financial crises. These contributed to the transformation of the Nordic economies, by making them more dynamic, releasing Schumpeterian processes and raising their growth potential. Rapid developments in the financial systems of Finland and Sweden impacted positively on the growth prospects of the two economies as well.[28] The crises served as a window of opportunity for policy-makers to carry out growth-enhancing structural reforms. However, it remains a task for future research to determine the exact channels through which the crises and financial integration influenced post-crisis growth.[29] Still, there is a policy lesson concerning growth: the process of financial liberalization has long-run benefits for growth and efficiency that should be compared with its short-run costs.

Distribution of income and wealth Most of the discussion of the immediate impact of financial liberalization and financial integration is focused on the banking system and the financial sector. However, once the cross-border barriers of financial flows were eliminated in Finland and Sweden, pressure for policy changes emerged in areas other than the financial system, such as the rules concerning foreign ownership of domestic real and financial assets, the taxation of income and wealth in a financially open economy, and the design of corporate governance laws.

In Sweden, primarily as a consequence of financial liberalization, gift taxes, inheritance taxes and wealth taxes were abolished in 2005–08. These are radical changes for a country with a strong egalitarian tradition. Financial integration is thus likely to impact on the distribution of income and wealth. Recent empirical research suggests that periods of financial integration and freely working financial systems in Sweden are associated with growing differences in income and wealth.[30]

The policy lesson here is simple. Once financial markets are integrated across borders, a pressure to adjust domestic regulations and institutions to international patterns emerges. These developments may not be as dramatic in the short run as the boom–bust cycle that emerged immediately following financial deregulation, but they are still dramatic in their own right seen in a long-run perspective.

To sum up this final lesson, the process of financial integration has changed the Nordic economies and thus also the Scandinavian or Nordic model in fundamental ways. These systemic effects have so far not been given the attention they deserve by researchers.

10.3 CONCLUSIONS

The Nordic case of financial liberalization demonstrates that even rich market economies in Europe with a prior successful economic record, well-developed legal systems and strong democratic traditions may end up in deep financial crises. Here I have presented 12 policy lessons from the Nordic experience. The question arises: are these Nordic lessons the same as the lessons from financial deregulation and crises in emerging-market economies and medium-income countries? Judging from the vast literature on lesson-drawing from financial crises, the answer is a clear yes. The reason is that the Nordic pattern is similar to that of non-Nordic countries experiencing financial crises in the 1990s, in spite of differences in per capita income levels, in political institutions and traditions, in legal structures, in the size of the economy and in historical circumstances.[31]

In short, given a framework of a pegged exchange rate, financial liberalization and credit expansion have proved to be major driving forces behind boom–bust cycles across the globe. The abolition of controls on cross-border capital flows and the sequencing of policy measures have crucially influenced subsequent developments. Once the crisis has developed, the introduction of a floating rate and the ensuing depreciation has marked the end of the depression and signalled recovery. As such a pattern exists across most crisis-hit countries, it is tempting to conclude that the 12 lessons drawn here from the Nordic experience are valid for non-Nordic countries as well.

Still, there are differences. Due to a framework characterized by strong institutions regarding law enforcement, bankruptcy rules and policy transparency, the Nordic financial crises were probably easier to rein in and manage than those in other parts of the world with weaker legal and political structures.[32] Nepotism, corruption and deep political tensions are likely to make crisis resolution more difficult. On this account, the Nordic experience was different as crony capitalism was not a concern in Scandinavia. In addition, the Nordic crises did not emerge as a subject of major political dispute and controversies between the government and the political opposition, which facilitated and speeded up the resolution of the crises.

A report from the World Bank (2001, p. 152) – in a box entitled 'The Swedish experience: a Saab in every garage?' – argues that the lessons from the Swedish financial crisis may be difficult to export to developing countries due to country-specific features. The Swedish crisis was related to real estate, and not so much to corporations, making crisis resolution easier. The legal framework of Sweden was well developed to manage bankruptcy procedures. Emerging countries may aim to acquire these characteristics but it would be like aspiring to have 'a Saab in every garage'. Still, the World Bank report recommends some lessons from Sweden such as the fact that the Swedish government refrained from intervening in the management of private banks and financial institutions.

Financial crises in emerging-market economies in the 1990s inspired requests for changes in the international financial architecture, in particular in the policies of the IMF. As the Scandinavian countries did not receive any financial assistance from the IMF, global financial arrangements did not surface in the Scandinavian debate. The IMF did not come in for criticism either during or after the crises in the Nordic countries. This is another difference, albeit a minor one, between the Nordics and most crisis-hit countries in Asia and Latin America.

To sum up: the Nordic experience of financial integration and of financial crises in the 1980s and 1990s adds to the understanding of the causes and consequences of financial crises. There should be no doubt that the financial opening-up of Finland, Norway and Sweden was the main impulse that initiated a sequence of events that brought these economies into deep depression. The evidence from the Nordic crises generates a number of policy recommendations of a general nature, in this chapter summarized in 12 lessons. One important lesson concerns the long-run effects of the crises. They contributed to major changes and restructuring, which transformed the Nordics into some of the fastest-growing economies in Europe. These long-run effects of financial liberalization and integration are not as dramatic as the short-run effects, but they may prove to be of greater importance over time. The future will tell whether these long-run benefits will balance or even outweigh the enormous short-run costs of the crises.

NOTES

1. This chapter has benefited from the views of many of the collaborators of this volume as well as from comments by Sigbjörn Berg, Michael Bordo, Gerard Caprio, Hongyi Chen, Emil Ems, Thomas Hagberg, Göran Lind, Jarmo Kontulainen, David Mayes, Olaf Unteroberdoerster, Daniel Waldenström and Clara Zverina. A longer version of this chapter is published in *Comparative Economic Studies*, 2008, as 'Lessons from Financial Liberalisation in Scandinavia'.
2. Here Scandinavia is used as a synonym for the Nordic countries although strictly speaking it encompasses only Denmark, Norway and Sweden. The record of Iceland, a Nordic country as well, is not covered here.
3. The following stylized summary of the financial crises in Finland, Norway and Sweden is based on Chapters 2, 3, 4 and 7 of this volume.
4. A detailed analysis of the effects of Soviet trade on the economy of Finland is given by Kiander and Vartia (1998).
5. In addition, Finland devalued the *markka* in the fall of 1991.
6. See Chapter 4 in this volume for an analysis of the unemployment record of Finland and Sweden.
7. The impact of financial integration on corporate governance in Finland is examined by Ylä-Anttila et al. (2005) and in Sweden by Henrekson and Jakobsson (2005).
8. The Scandinavian or Nordic model is evaluated by Kiander (2005a, 2005b), by Andersen et al. (2007) and by Calmfors (2007), among others.
9. For lesson-learning from the crises of the 1990s, see for example Caprio et al. (2001), Eichengreen (1999, 2002, 2003) and Isard (2005, Chapters 4–5). The IMF and the World Bank have produced a set of studies drawing lessons from the crises of the 1990s.
10. There are studies concerning the lessons from individual Nordic countries and from

particular aspects of the financial crisis of the 1990s, but to my knowledge there is no report concerning the general lessons from all the four Nordic countries. See also the individual chapters of this volume.

11. To my knowledge, no thorough study or forecast accurately projecting the macroeconomic consequences of financial deregulation was published in any of the Nordic countries prior to the financial crises of the early 1990s.
12. Economists with a political economy background tend to argue that politicians are inclined to adopt expansionary policies in the short run that turn out to be inflationary in the long run – a phenomenon described as 'inflation bias'. However, in Finland and Sweden the opposite pattern held in the early 1990s. Policy-makers were determined to carry out a contractionary policy in the short run – while bringing about a deep crisis – in order to avoid inflation in the long run. The long-run result of this 'deflation bias' turned out to be a successful one in the sense that Finland and Sweden managed to keep a low rate of inflation for many years after the crisis of the 1990s.
13. See Jonung (2000) for a detailed analysis of the backward-looking learning process of policy-makers and of economists in Sweden during the 1970s, 1980s and 1990s.
14. That policy-makers as well as economists producing policy advice should be forward- rather than backward-looking is easy to advocate but harder to implement in practice as the public perception of the present crisis and of the appropriate policy action to be taken is strongly influenced by prevailing views concerning the most recent past crisis, regardless of its relevance for current circumstances.
15. The Nordic experience of financial liberalization suggests that changes in the after-tax real rate of interest in driving the boom–bust cycle played a stronger role than is suggested in the standard literature on financial crises. See Chapter 6 in this volume for international comparisons concerning the behaviour of the real rate of interest during boom–bust cycles.
16. This is an illustration of the 'Walters critique'. See Walters (1998).
17. This policy lesson is amply illustrated by the crisis experience of other countries as well.
18. This is the view of Henriksson (2007) when describing the Swedish budgetary consolidation program 1995–97 by the Social Democratic government that came into power in the fall of 1994 – well into the recovery phase of the crisis.
19. As consensus is lacking concerning the role of fiscal policy during the Nordic crises, this topic remains a promising subject for future research.
20. The same lesson holds for deposit insurance. Finland and Norway had such a system. Sweden set one up as a result of the crisis. The crisis proved that deposit insurance was an insufficient arrangement. Instead, the government served as the ultimate guarantor of the stability of the banking system.
21. See the analysis in Chapter 8 in this volume on how Denmark avoided a financial crisis.
22. See Chapter 3 on the resolution policies adopted in Finland and Sweden and Chapter 7 on the case of Norway as well as Englund (1999) and Ingves and Lind (1996) on the Swedish model of bank resolution.
23. The policy advice by the IMF during the East Asian crises and the Latin American crises has been the subject of harsh criticism, see Eichengreen (1999, Chapter 7) and in particular Stiglitz (2002). See also various publications by the Office of Independent Analysis associated with the IMF. This office was set up as a response to the criticism of the recommendations by the IMF during the crises of the 1990s.
24. The recommendations for Sweden given by the IMF are revealed in the memoirs of Bengt Dennis, Governor of the Swedish *Riksbank* 1982–94. In September 1992, in the midst of the financial turmoil in Europe, a delegation from the IMF examined the state of the Swedish economy. According to Dennis (1998, p. 64), its recommendations could be summarized in three words: 'consolidate the budget'. The IMF delegation viewed the rising budget deficit as the main cause for alarm and thus recommended a tight fiscal policy. The *Riksbank* held the same view. For this reason, it used the IMF report to successfully press the government and the opposition to tighten fiscal policy in a joint fiscal and monetary

austerity program announced in September 1992. The program succeeded in the sense that it postponed the floating of the *krona* until November the same year.

25. According to Eichengreen (1999, p. 109), the recommendations of fiscal tightening by the IMF in the Asian crisis in the late 1990s were the consequence of 'blindly taking a page from its Latin American debt crisis cookbook' without paying proper attention to the differences between Latin American and Asian economic conditions. I conjecture that the IMF did the same when advising Sweden in the early fall of 1992. Eichengreen (1999, p. 110) summarizes the criticism of the role of the IMF in the Asian crisis in the following way: 'The problem was that the Fund failed to adjust for the cycle. It failed to anticipate the severity of the Asian downturn or see that the restrictive fiscal policies it recommended would themselves make that downturn worse. Once this realization dawned, it modified its advice.' The IMF gave the same type of advice concerning contractionary fiscal policy in Sweden as it did initially during the Asian crisis.
26. See Henry (2007) and Tornell and Westermann (2005) for recent surveys of the issues involved.
27. For Norway, see Chapter 5 in this volume.
28. To my knowledge, there has been no attempt to estimate and compare the short-run welfare costs and the long-run welfare benefits of financial liberalization in any of the Nordic countries.
29. This argument is made by among others Demirgüc-Kunt and Detragiache (2001) and Tornell and Westermann (2005). Of course, the lesson is *not* that financial crises should be created in order to reap long-run growth benefits, but rather that the cost of crises should be compared with any long-run benefits from improved growth and efficiency.
30. See Roine et al. (2008).
31. See for example Allen (2001), Eichengreen (1999, 2002, 2003) and Wyplosz (2001) on crisis lessons from outside the Nordics.
32. This is a major message of Chapter 9 in this volume, which stresses the existence of stronger political institutions in Finland and Sweden than in countries in Asia hit by financial crisis.

REFERENCES

Allen, F. (2001), 'Financial structure and financial crisis', *International Review of Finance*, **2**, 1–19.

Andersen, T., B. Holmström, S. Honkapohja, S. Korkman, H.T. Söderström and J. Vartiainen (2007), *The Nordic Model. Embracing Globalization and Sharing Risks*, ETLA Series B 232, Helsinki.

Calmfors, L. (2007), 'Scandinavia today: an economic miracle?', in *The EEAG Report on the European Economy 2007*, CESifo Group, Munich, Chapter 4.

Caprio, G., P. Honohan and J. Stiglitz (eds) (2001), *Financial Liberalization. How Far, How Fast?,* Cambridge: Cambridge University Press.

Demirgüc-Kunt, A. and E. Detragiache (2001), 'Financial liberalization and financial fragility', in G. Caprio, P. Honohan and J. Stiglitz (eds), *Financial Liberalization. How Far, How Fast*, Cambridge: Cambridge University Press. Chapter 4.

Dennis, B. (1998), *500 %*, Falun: Bokförlaget DN.

Eichengreen, B. (1999), *Toward a New International Financial Architecture: A Practical Post-Asia Agenda*, Washington, DC: Institute for International Economics.

Eichengreen, B. (2002), *Financial Crises and What to Do About Them*, Oxford: Oxford University Press.

Eichengreen, B. (2003), *Capital Flows and Crises*, Cambridge, MA and London: MIT Press.

Englund, P. (1999), 'The Swedish banking crisis: roots and consequences', *Oxford Review of Economic Policy*, **15**, 80–97.

Fisher, I. (1933), 'The debt-deflation theory of great depressions', *Econometrica*, **1**, 337–57.

Henrekson, M. and U. Jakobsson (2005), 'The Swedish model of corporate ownership and control in transition', in H. Huizinga and L. Jonung (eds), *The Internationalisation of Asset Ownership in Europe*, Cambridge: Cambridge University Press.

Henriksson, J. (2007), 'Ten lessons about budget consolidation', Bruegel Essay and Lecture Series, Brussels: Bruegel.

Henry, P.B. (2007), 'Capital account liberalization: theory, evidence, and speculation', *Journal of Economic Literature*, **45**, 887–935.

Ingves, S. and G. Lind (1996), 'The management of the bank crisis – in retrospect', *Sveriges Riksbank, Quarterly Review*, **7**, 5–18.

Isard, P. (2005), *Globalization and the International Financial System*, Cambridge: Cambridge University Press.

Jonung, L. (2000), *Looking Ahead through the Rear-view Mirror. Swedish Stabilization Policy as a Learning Process 1975–1995. A Summary*, Ministry of Finance, Stockholm.

Kiander, J. (2005a), 'Growth and employment in Nordic welfare states in the 1990s: a tale of crisis and revival', in O. Kangas and J. Palme (eds), *Social Policy and Economic Development in the Nordic Countries*, London: Palgrave Macmillan and UNRISD.

Kiander, J. (2005b), 'The evolution of the Finnish model in the 1990s: from depression to high-tech boom', in U. Becker and H. Schwartz (eds), *Employment 'Miracles'*, Amsterdam: University of Amsterdam Press.

Kiander, J. and P. Vartia (1998), 'The depression of the 1990s in Finland: a Nordic financial crisis or a result of the collapse of the Soviet Union', in T. Myllyntaus (ed.), *Economic Crises and Restructuring in History: Experiences of Small Countries*, St. Katharinen: Scripta Mercaturae Verlag.

Roine, J., J. Vlachos and D. Waldenström (2008), 'The long-run determinants of inequality: what can we learn from top income data?', IFN Working paper no. 721, Stockholm.

Stiglitz, J. (2002), *Globalization and its Discontents*, London: Penguin.

Tornell, A. and F. Westermann (2005), *Boom–bust Cycles and Financial Liberalization*, Cambridge, MA and London: MIT Press.

Walters, A. (1998), 'Walters Critique', in K. Matthews (ed.), *The Economics and Politics of Money: The Selected Essays of Alan Walters*, Cheltenham, UK and Northampton, MA, USA: Edward Elgar Publishing.

World Bank (2001), *Finance for Growth: Policy Choices in a Volatile World*, World Bank Policy Research Report, Washington, DC.

Wyplosz, C. (2001), 'Financial restraints and liberalization in postwar Europe', in G. Caprio, P. Honohan and J. Stiglitz (eds) (2001), Chapter 5.

Ylä-Anttila, P., J. Ali-Yrkkö and M. Nyberg (2005), 'Foreign ownership in Finland – boosting firm performance and changing corporate governance', in H. Huizinga and L. Jonung (eds), *The Internationalisation of Asset Ownership in Europe*, Cambridge: Cambridge University Press.

Index